ISSN-1058-1316

CONTEMPORARY

Black

Biography

Profiles from the International Black Community

Volume 43

Ralph G. Zerbonia, Project Editor

GALE®

THOMSON

™

GALE

Detroit • New York • San Diego • San Francisco • Cleveland • New Haven, Conn. • Waterville, Maine • London • Munich

Contemporary Black Biography, Volume 43

Project Editor
Ralph G. Zerbonia

Permissions
Ken Breen, William Sampson

Manufacturing
Dorothy Maki, Stacy Melson

Composition and Prepress
Mary Beth Trimper, Gary Leach

Imaging and Multimedia Content
Robyn V. Young, Leitha Etheridge-Sims, David G. Oblender, Lezlie Light, Randy Bassett, Robert Duncan, Dan Newell

ISBN 0-7876-6731-5
ISSN 1058-1316

Printed in the United States of America
10 9 8 7 6 5 4 3 2 1

Contemporary Black Biography
Advisory Board

Contents

Introduction

Contemporary Black Biography provides informative biographical profiles of the important and influential persons of African heritage who form the international black community: men and women who have changed today's world and are shaping tomorrow's. *Contemporary Black Biography* covers persons of various nationalities in a wide variety of fields, including architecture, art, business, dance, education, fashion, film, industry, journalism, law, literature, medicine, music, politics and government, publishing, religion, science and technology, social issues, sports, television, theater, and others. In addition to in-depth coverage of names found in today's headlines, *Contemporary Black Biography* provides coverage of selected individuals from earlier in this century whose influence continues to impact on contemporary life. *Contemporary Black Biography* also provides coverage of important and influential persons who are not yet household names and are therefore likely to be ignored by other biographical reference series. Each volume also includes listee updates on names previously appearing in *CBB*.

Designed for Quick Research and Interesting Reading

- *Attractive page design* incorporates textual subheads, making it easy to find the information you're looking for.

- *Easy-to-locate data sections* provide quick access to vital personal statistics, career information, major awards, and mailing addresses, when available.

- *Informative biographical essays* trace the subject's personal and professional life with the kind of in-depth analysis you need.

- *To further enhance your appreciation* of the subject, most entries include photographic portraits.

- *Sources for additional information* direct the user to selected books, magazines, and newspapers where more information on the individuals can be obtained.

Helpful Indexes Make It Easy to Find the Information You Need

Contemporary Black Biography includes cumulative Nationality, Occupation, Subject, and Name indexes that make it easy to locate entries in a variety of useful ways.

Available in Electronic Formats

Diskette/Magnetic Tape. *Contemporary Black Biography* is available for licensing on magnetic tape or diskette in a fielded format. Either the complete database or a custom selection of entries may be ordered. The database is available for internal data processing and nonpublishing purposes only. For more information, call (800) 877-GALE. **On-line.** *Contemporary Black Biography* is available online through Mead Data Central's NEXIS Service in the NEXIS, PEOPLE and SPORTS Libraries in the GALBIO file and Gale Group's Biography Resource Center.

Disclaimer

Contemporary Black Biography uses and lists websites as sources and these websites may become obsolete.

We Welcome Your Suggestions

The editors welcome your comments and suggestions for enhancing and improving *Contemporary Black Biography*. If you would like to suggest persons for inclusion in the series, please submit these names to the editors. Mail comments or suggestions to:

The Editor
Contemporary Black Biography
Gale Group
27500 Drake Rd.
Farmington Hills, MI 48331-3535
Phone: (800) 347-4253

Photo Credits

PHOTOGRAPHS AND ILLUSTRATIONS APPEARING IN *CONTEMPORARY BLACK BIOGRAPHY,* VOLUME 43, WERE RECEIVED FROM THE FOLLOWING SOURCES:

All Reproduced by Permission: **Alexander, Khandi,** photograph. CORBIS. **Baker, Dusty,** photograph. AP/Wide World Photos. **Blake, James,** photograph. AP/Wide World Photos. **Blanchard, Terence,** photograph by Jack Vartoogian. Courtesy of Jack Vartoogian. **Bonds, Bobby,** photograph. AP/Wide World Photos. **Brooks, Derrick,** photograph by Chris O'Meara. AP/Wide World Photos. **Brown, Janice Rogers,** photograph by Rich Pedroncelli. AP/Wide World Photos. **Catchings, Tamika,** photograph by John Harrell. AP/Wide World Photos. **Cheney-Coker, Sly,** photograph by Laura Rauch. AP/Wide World Photos. **Combs, Sean,** photograph. AP/Wide World Photos. **Davis, Benjamin O., Jr.,** photograph. Public Domain. **dos Santos, José Eduardo,** photograph. AP/Wide World Photos. **Draper, Sharon Mills,** photograph. AP/Wide World Photos. **Edwards, Esther Gordy,** photograph. AP/Wide World Photos. **Farmer-Paellmann, Deadria,** photograph by Stephen Chernin. AP/Wide World Photos. **Gbagbo, Laurent,** photograph. AP/Wide World Photos. **Gibson, Althea,** photograph. AP/Wide World Photos. **Grier, Mike,** photograph by Associated Press NHL. AP/Wide World Photos. **Hunter, Torii,** photograph by Eric Miller. AP/Wide World Photos. **Kee, John P.,** photograph. Courtesy of Verity Records. **Kobia, Samuel,** photograph by Peter Williams. Courtesy of the World Council of Churches. **Liggins, Alfred III,** photograph by Martin Simon. CORBIS. **Maathai, Wangari,** photograph. CORBIS. **Mayfield, Curtis,** photograph by Jack Vartoogian. Courtesy of Jack Vartoogian. **Nunn, Annetta,** photograph. Courtesy of the Birmingham Police Department. **Parish, Robert,** photograph by Michael Dwyer. AP/Wide World Photos. **Peters, Margaret, and Matilda Roumania Peters,** photograph by Tuskegee University Office of Marketing & Communications. AP/Wide World Photos. **Player, Willa B.,** photograph. Courtesy of Willa B. Player. **Walker, Alice,** photograph. AP/Wide World Photos. **Wilkins, J. Ernest, Jr.,** photograph. AP/Wide World Photos. **Willingham, Tyrone,** photograph by Joe Raymond. AP/Wide World Photos. **Winans, CeCe,** photograph. AP/Wide World Photos. **Wolfe, George C.,** photograph. AP/Wide World Photos. **Wright, Lewin** photography by Chitose Suzuki. AP/Wide World Photos.

Khandi Alexander

1957—

Actress, dancer, choreographer

Though she had never considered a career in show business before enrolling in college, Khandi Alexander has made her mark as a respected and versatile actress. Her work on television dramatic series, sitcoms, and specials, as well as her roles in a range of films, has earned her both a wide audience and critical acclaim.

Fell in Love with Dance

Alexander, who was born on September 4, 1957, to a middle-class family in New York City, did not demonstrate particular interest in the performing arts until she registered for a dance class to fulfill the physical education requirement at Queensborough Community College. There she discovered a passion for dance that her teacher strongly encouraged. As Alexander noted in a *People Weekly* article, the teacher "made me believe I could be a dancer even though everyone else said I was too old." Despite the fact that most aspiring dancers begin physical training in early childhood, Alexander continued studying the demanding art form and, by the early 1980s, had begun appearing in Broadway shows.

Alexander appeared as Susie in *Period of Adjustment* in 1980 and 1981, and then landed the part of

Charlene in the original Broadway run of the hit show *Dreamgirls.* Choreographed by Michael Bennet, who had made his name with *A Chorus Line,* the show—based on the aspirations of three black women singers reminiscent of The Supremes—featured jazz, R&B, soul, and disco style dance numbers. *Dreamgirls* ran for 1,522 performances and won six Tony Awards.

The phenomenal success of *Dreamgirls* led to greater opportunities for Alexander. In 1989, after meeting Whitney Houston backstage at an American Music Awards ceremony, Alexander became the pop star's choreographer, working with her on her world tour. The young dancer had seemingly reached the peak of her career.

Turned to Acting After Rehab

The limelight, however, brought stress as well as acclaim. To deal with this stress, Alexander began to take drugs in the mid-1980s. By the late-1980s, her drug problem began to interfere with her dancing and choreographing. Eventually Alexander had a breakdown and realized that she needed help. In 1990, with Houston's support, Alexander checked herself into a

At a Glance . . .

Born on September 4, 1957, in New York, NY; daughter of Henry and Alverina Alexander. *Education:* Queensborough Community College, BA, late-1970s.

Career: Broadway actress, 1980-1989; choreographer, 1989-1992; film and television actress, 1992–.

Addresses: *Agent*—Innovative Artists, 1505 10th St., Santa Monica, CA 90401.

drug rehabilitation facility in California. After 30 days of treatment, she went back to work for Houston for another two years. But by then Alexander was feeling the need to branch out in new directions. She decided to focus her creative energies on acting.

Success, however, was not immediate. Alexander endured some financially lean times while she struggled to gain acceptance as an actress. She took small roles before finally landing a recurring role on the hit NBC series *ER* in 1995. That same year, she was cast as news anchorwoman Catherine Duke on NBC's *News-Radio,* the role for which she became famous. "She showed such strength in her reading [for the part]," explained the show's executive producer in comments quoted in *People Weekly,* "we knew she could match [co-star Phil Hartman] word for word."

NewsRadio received highly favorable reviews, and critics particularly admired Alexander's portrayal of the feisty news anchor. *Boston Globe* writer Michael Blowen enjoyed the "splendid ensemble" of characters in the series and noted that the part of Catherine Duke, "whose disposition is as sweet as her tongue is tart," was "stylishly played" by Alexander. The actress "brought *NewsRadio* a lot of dignity and grace," observed her friend and colleague Dave Foley in a *Los Angeles Times* article. "She's highly underrated and underused. She should be doing everything."

Indeed, Alexander was juggling roles on two major series at the same time—proof of her ability to switch characters easily. Her part on *ER* as Jackie, the sister of Dr. Peter Benton, was both physically and emotionally different from her *NewsRadio* role. As *Los Angeles Times* writer Greg Braxton put it, Alexander "can disappear into a role, making her virtually unrecognizable from one part to the next."

Took on More Serious Roles

After three years on *NewsRadio,* however, Alexander needed a change. "It was hard being the only black person on a show that was all white," she told the *Los Angeles Times.* "It was OK for three years, and it was a loving atmosphere. I had the best time. But I wanted to act." She left the show in 1997 and began looking for new projects. In 2000 she costarred in the HBO dramatic miniseries *The Corner,* described in *Entertainment Weekly* as a "brilliant look at the inner-city struggle with drugs, tough times, and everyday life." Alexander played the part of Fran, a middle-class housewife, mother, and grandmother who has just kicked a serious drug habit. Describing Alexander's original audition for the part, the show's director, Charles Dutton, told the *Los Angeles Times* that the actress "just took over the room." She refused to make small talk with the producers, glared at the camera crew, and, after finishing her lines, lunged at the camera. Stunned, the production team realized that she was perfect for the part.

From the moment she read the first sentence of the script, Alexander told Greg Braxton of the *Los Angeles Times,* "I knew I had to have [the role]. I just understood it." To research the part, she got to know the woman who was the model for Fran. Respecting the woman's strength and desire to survive, Alexander imbued her character with similar passion. As Braxton noted, "Alexander portrays [Fran] as a bowed but far-from-broken street warrior, bouncing between bouts of uncontrolled rage, dead-eyed drugginess and unrestrained joy.... Alexander's [Fran] defies viewers to admire or sympathize with her, then breaks their hearts." Other critics also expressed enormous praise. Ken Tucker in *Entertainment Weekly* wrote that Alexander portrayed her character "with fierce humor and fiercer cynicism," and another reviewer from the *Los Angeles Times* described her performance as "extraordinary." In the *New York Times,* Caryn James commented that Alexander's "unglamorous performance as Fran gives the series much of its power." Describing the third episode as the best, James wrote: "With a ravaged look, Ms. Alexander ... gets inside the mind of a woman who admits she is a junkie, but defiantly says she is also a good mother who never missed a school meeting or a juvenile hearing. She accepts with chilling matter-of-factness that her son's life will be plagued by drugs and tussles with the law. Her attempt to get herself into a detox program fast is heartbreaking."

After the success of *The Corner,* Alexander continued to take challenging roles. In 2002 she joined the cast of the CBS dramatic series *CSI: Miami,* a spin-off from *CSI: Crime Scene Investigation.* In the new series, wrote *Boston Globe* critic Matthew Gilbert, Alexander "is perfectly tough as the coroner."

Alexander has also appeared in several films, including *Sugar Hill* and *There's Something about Mary.* In her first film lead, in *No Easy Way,* she portrayed an inner-city mother who befriends an HIV-positive white man. More recently she has appeared in *Fool Proof, Emmett's Mark,* and *Dark Blue.*

Passionate about her craft, Alexander told Braxton that for her, acting "all starts from within. It has to be deeper than a gimmick. I want me to go away, to the point that everything I am and have is gone." With several critically-acclaimed roles to her credit, Alexander is looking forward to further creative projects that will continue to enhance her stature.

Selected works

Films

CB4, 1993.
Menace II Society, 1993.
Poetic Justice, 1993.
Sugar Hill, 1994.
House Party 3, 1994.
No Easy Way, 1996.
There's Something about Mary, 1998.
Thick as Thieves, 1998.
Fool Proof, 2002.
Emmett's Mark, 2002.
Dark Blue, 2003.

Television

(choreographer) *Whitney Houston: This Is My Life,* ABC, 1992.
News Radio, NBC, 1995-1997.
ER, NBC, 1995-2001.
The Corner, HBO, 2000.
CSI Miami, CBS, 2002—.

Sources

Books

Contemporary Theater, Film, and Television, Volume 46, Gale, 2003.

Periodicals

Boston Globe, March 21, 1995, p. 32; September 23, 2002, p. B7.
Entertainment Weekly, October 10, 1997, p. 75; April 14, 2000, p. 58.
Los Angeles Times, May 16, 2000, p. 1; September 15, 2002, p. F13; September 23, 2002, p. F14.
New York Times, April 14, 2000, p. E34.
People Weekly, July 1, 1996, p. 196; May 26, 1997, p. 134.
Time, April 17, 2000, p. 84.

On-line

"Dreamgirls," *The Guide to Musical Theater,* www.nodanw.com/shows_d/dreamgirls (November 26, 2003).
"New York City Landmark Guide-Imperial Theater," *Jim's Deli,* www.jimsdeli.com/landmarks/ (November 26, 2003).

—E. M. Shostak

Dusty Baker

1949—

Professional baseball manager

Dusty Baker, who directed the San Francisco Giants to 103 victories in his first season as manager, was named Manager of the Year by the Baseball Writers Association of America in 1993, 1997, and 2001. The prestigious awards were bestowed in recognition of Baker's accomplishments in rebuilding and restoring a floundering Giants franchise, no mean feat for a first-time manager. Baker, who himself played in the major leagues from 1972 until 1986, has usually been perceived as a disciplinarian with an extensive knowledge of baseball and the ability to communicate his knowledge to both players and coaches. In 2003 Baker was also perceived by many as gutsy when he made a move to manage the Chicago Cubs the year after he took the Giants to the World Series.

Life, however, has not always run smoothly for Baker. A top player for the Los Angeles Dodgers franchise that made three trips to the World Series, he was stigmatized by unproven drug abuse allegations that shortened his playing career. After more than a decade in the major leagues, he "retired" from baseball in 1986, embittered and disappointed by the treatment he had received. When, in 1988, he was offered an opportunity to coach the Giants, he decided to lay the

bitterness behind him and begin anew, quietly planning to become a major league manager at some point. Baker told the *Los Angeles Times* that his experience with the Dodgers marked a real turning point in his personal development. "It can either eat you up, or you can get on with your life," he said. "It hurt then. It doesn't hurt anymore."

Conflicted With Disciplinarian Father

Baker was born Johnnie B. Baker, Jr., on June 15, 1949, in Riverside, California. The nickname "Dusty" was earned in infancy, when he showed a penchant for eating dirt from the family's backyard. The oldest of five children in a household where both parents worked, Baker was often called upon to manage his unruly siblings. When things went wrong—as they often did—Baker would be punished. His father, a veteran of World War II, believed in rigid punishment, including whippings with a switch. For his part, Johnnie B. Baker, Sr., felt that by being strict he might save his son from bad influences in the neighborhood. "They say I was quite hard on [Dusty]," the elder Baker told the *San*

At a Glance . . .

Born Johnnie B. Baker, Jr., on June 15, 1949, in Riverside, CA; son of Johnnie B. (a defense industry worker) and Christine (a professor) Baker; married Harriet (divorced 1987); married Melissa; children: (from first marriage) Natosha, (from second marriage) Darren. *Education:* Attended American River College, Sacramento, CA.

Career: Atlanta Braves, outfielder, 1972-75; Los Angeles Dodgers, outfielder, 1976-84; San Francisco Giants, outfielder, 1984-85, first-base coach, 1988-89, hitting coach, 1989-93, manager, 1993-2002; Oakland A's, outfielder and designated hitter, 1985-86; Investment broker, Conli, Michaels, Inc., 1987; Chicago Cubs, manager, 2002–.

Selected awards: Named to National League All-Star team, 1981, 1982; named to Silver Slugger team, 1980, 1981; Gold Glove winner, 1981; inducted to Sacramento Sports Hall of Fame; voted a member of the Los Angeles Dodgers all-time team by fans, 1990; manager of the year, Baseball Writers Association of America, 1993; National League Manager of the Year, 1993, 1997, 2001.

Addresses: *Office*—Manager, Chicago Cubs, Wrigley Field, 1060 West Addison, Chicago, IL 60613.

Jose Mercury News. "But a lot of these [neighborhood] kids, if they're not dead, they're in jail. Dusty had discipline in his life."

Baker's father encouraged the children to participate in sports and was the neighborhood's Little League coach. Their Little League team featured the two highly-motivated Baker sons and another talented local youngster, Bobby Bonds. In comparison to Bonds, Bakers's talents did not seem particularly outstanding. He had to work harder, but with his father's prodding, Baker mastered the skills of baseball.

When Baker was a high school junior, his father took a job at McClellan Air Force Base in Sacramento. The family moved into an all-white neighborhood in Carmichael, where the residents actually "voted" on whether or not to admit them. Baker and his siblings became the only black students at Del Campo High School. There Baker immediately excelled at football, baseball, and track, but he still faced racism at *every* turn.

"Being the only black dudes in high school the last two years, me and my little brother, my temper came out," he told the *Knight Ridder/Tribune Wire Service.* "We'd play black schools and they'd be on me because I was playing with white guys. Playing the white schools, they'd get on me for being a black dude. I was fighting at the drop of a dime." Baker's sports prowess brought him some popularity at Del Campo High, but he still had few close friends and was painfully aware that some of the white children in his new neighborhood were forbidden to play with him and his siblings.

Baker's parents divorced when he was a senior in high school. He stayed with his mother and planned to attend college on an athletic scholarship. Then, in June of 1967, he was drafted by the Atlanta Braves as their 26th pick and offered a contract and a signing bonus. The prospect of ready money, as opposed to a scholarship, was too tempting. Baker signed with the Braves and reported to a minor league team in Austin, Texas—without telling his father what he had done. When the elder Baker discovered what had happened, he took the Braves to court and tried to have the contract voided. He did not win, but he was able to secure Baker's signing bonus and placed it in a trust fund until Baker turned 21. Father and son did not speak for three years.

They have since reconciled, and Johnnie Baker, Sr., told the *San Jose Mercury News* that his son has come to see the wisdom of his decision. "I saw kids come out [of the minor leagues] just like they went in—broke," he said. "They'd borrow on next year's salary. I wanted to make sure he was taken care of. I don't regret it. I guess everything worked out pretty well."

Garnered Baseball Advice From Aaron

Baker began his professional playing career on minor league teams in the deep South. He soon learned that his hair-trigger temper would not serve him well in situations of blatant discrimination. Although legally sanctioned racism, or "Jim Crow" laws had long ago been repealed, he discovered that he was not able to rent apartments where the rest of his white teammates stayed. Nor was he always able to frequent the bars and restaurants where they ate and drank. Having grown up in the relatively tolerant environment of California, he was stunned by the racism he faced in the South.

Help came in the form of advice from the Braves' biggest star, Henry Aaron. Aaron, who faced more than his share of racism as he broke Babe Ruth's record for home runs, saw to it that Baker kept his head without sacrificing his pride. At a time when Baker's relationship with his father was strained, Aaron became a valued parental figure. "He talked to me all the time about everything," Baker told the *San Jose Mercury News.* "He told me about the Negro League.

About how to be a man. About how to play in pain. About how to play the game in your head."

Baker advanced quickly through the minor leagues and was called to Atlanta for two prolonged visits before finally making the club permanently in 1972. He performed well with the Braves, batting .321 in 1972 and .288 with 99 runs batted in during 1973, but he still was not happy in the South. Therefore, Baker was overjoyed when he was traded to the Los Angeles Dodgers in the Fall of 1975. Playing for a California team meant going home to his family and friends. It would mean even more as he found himself situated on a championship squad.

Found Fame Before Being Edged Out

Baker's years with the Dodgers neatly coincided with that team's surge into multiple playoff and World Series appearances. He appeared in four league championship series—1977, 1978, 1981, and 1983—and was named National League championship series Most Valuable Player in 1977, after hitting .357 with two home runs and eight RBI, including a grand slam. He went on that same year to hit .292 in the World Series with four runs on seven hits and one home run.

In Los Angeles, Baker came to be known as "Dr. Scald" for his ability to burn pitchers with clean hits in clutch situations. He was also admired for his defensive play, earning a Gold Glove in 1981. Perhaps most important, in the wake of nagging injuries that never completely sidelined him, Baker began transforming himself from a physical to a mental player. Taking Aaron's advice, he played the game in his head and learned tactical skills that would serve him well in his secondary career as coach and manager.

Twice Baker was named to the National League All-Star team, in 1981 and 1982. He batted .316 in the 1981 National League championship series and appeared in all six games as the Dodgers won the World Series that same year. In 1982 he batted .300 for the season and compiled 88 RBI. The next year, however, his stay in Los Angeles began to turn sour.

His batting average dropped 40 points and by the end of the season, rumors of his drug use began circulating. Baker hotly denied the allegations: "L.A. is the rumor capital of the world," he told the *San Jose Mercury News.* "All I know is the rumors didn't come out until I refused a trade." Baker has said that he thinks the rumors of drug abuse, which were never proven, substantially shortened his playing career. "It affected me," he added. "It affected my family, it probably cost me a couple of million dollars. I learned who my friends were." Baker also explained in the *Los Angeles Times* that he felt he was being "edged out" of baseball before he was ready to go.

Before the 1984 season commenced, Los Angeles freed Baker from his contract, and he signed with the San Francisco Giants as a free agent. He spent one season there and finished his career by playing with the Oakland Athletics for two seasons. Baker retired in 1986. Upon retirement Baker admitted, "I was a little disgruntled. I didn't really know if I wanted to stay in baseball. I wasn't sure what I wanted to do." He worked for one year with his brother in an investment brokerage, and he spent time indulging his passions for hunting and fishing. Eventually baseball beckoned again, and Baker put his bitterness aside to return.

Returned to Baseball as Coach and Manager

The first offer came to Baker in 1987, from Al Rosen, the president of the Giants. However, the offer was made at a time when Baker was undergoing a divorce, and he did not follow up on it. Soon thereafter, Baker ran into the owner of the Giants at a lodge in Lake Arrowhead, who urged him to come aboard with San Francisco. This time Baker accepted. He began his second career in 1988, as the first base coach with the Giants. At the time he quietly resolved to become a manager somewhere in the big leagues within five years. Time passed, and he became the hitting coach for the Giants, but the team was thriving under manager Roger Craig.

At the start of the 1990s, turmoil enveloped the Giants franchise. A group of investors tried to purchase the team and move it to St. Petersburg, Florida. Simultaneously, concerned citizens in San Francisco mounted a campaign to keep the team in town under new ownership. The uncertainty affected everyone in the organization, from the front office personnel down to the players. The Giants, who had appeared in the 1989 World Series, finished their 1992 campaign with more losses than wins. Local entrepreneurs bought the franchise and kept it in San Francisco, but manager Craig was fired. Baker was chosen to replace him in December of 1992. Baker's five-year plan to become a manager had been fulfilled.

At the time, the selection of Baker was somewhat controversial. His hands-on experience as a manager consisted of one short season with a newly founded autumn league in Arizona, where his team finished 25-28 for fifth place in a six-team division. When asked by a *San Francisco Chronicle* reporter if he felt he had enough preparation to be a big-league manager, Baker responded: "Is there an aptitude test to be a manager? Are there defined qualities you have to have? Or do people have to trust in your ability to lead, direct, and fight for a common cause—which is to win? No man's perfect. No man knows what to do until he gets there. I'm not afraid of the unknown. I welcome it."

The 1993 Giants, employing the services of superstar Barry Bonds as a player and his father Bobby Bonds as a coach, won 103 games during the regular season.

Ordinarily this would be more than enough for a team to advance to the league championship series. Unfortunately for the Giants, they shared a division with the surging Atlanta Braves, who edged them out of playoff hopes on the last day of the season. It was one of the closest pennant races in recent history.

Baker's disappointment was only mildly soothed by his being chosen as 1993 Manager of the Year, just days after the World Series ended. Although his team failed to make the playoffs, it had undergone a significant transformation, one that was not lost on the voters for Manager of the Year. In effect, Baker had taken the nucleus of a sub-.500 team, with the important addition of Barry Bonds, and had enticed the team to win more victories than any Giants franchise since 1905. The San Francisco front office expressed supreme confidence in the rookie manager, who signed a two-year contract in 1993. As for Baker himself, the Manager of the Year revealed his new plan for the future in the *San Jose Mercury News*. "I'm changing my goals," he said. "I would like to get into the Hall of Fame as a player [and] manager. This is the first step."

Between 1993 and 2001 Baker was signed on as Giants manager four more times. He also won Manager of the Year twice more. Baker became the first person to be named National League Manager of the Year three times—1993, 1997, and 2001—made especially impressive because all three times were with the same team, the Giants. Barry Bonds of the Giants told *Ebony* magazine of Baker, "Hey, man, he's the best. When you win Manager of the Year three times there's something special about you. He demands respect and gives it in return. For me, a manager who can get the best out of a bad team is a great manager. I've seen Dusty do that."

In early 2001 Baker came to the attention of video game makers at EA Sports. They were watching him talking to an umpire, flailing his arms, scowling, bobbing his head, and other things. They thought it would be perfect for their new game "Triple Play Baseball." So Baker got into a special suit equipped with light sensors and acted out the part of manager for the game. His fame as Giants manager was growing.

Later in 2001 Baker had a bit of a down turn—just two days before Thanksgiving, Baker was diagnosed with prostate cancer. Luckily the disease was caught early and Baker went through surgery at Stanford Hospital on December 17, 2001, successfully. After the surgery Baker told *Knight Ridder/Tribune Wire Service*, "You see life differently, definitely. You're appreciative of things. You don't worry so much, and you realize things aren't in your control so much. They're in the hands of God. Life's beautiful. It was beautiful before, but it's even more beautiful now. I think you don't begin living sometimes until you see death."

When it came time in 2002 for Baker to sign new contracts there were a few issues. Some blamed the problem on Baker's relationship with principal owner Peter Magowan. In the end, though, contract negotiations were dropped and finally it came to the time when other teams could make offers for Baker. Both the Seattle Mariners and the Chicago Cubs were known to want to hire him and Baker made it known that he was willing to listen to offers. Kirk Rueter of the Giants said of the loss of Baker, "It's kind of a double loss. Last week we dealt with losing the World Series and this week we're dealing with losing our manager."

In 2003 Baker made a controversial move to become manager of the Chicago Cubs. *Ebony* magazine quoted Baker as having said, "[When the Cubs job came available], I prayed on it, and the answer I got was to go to Chicago. I always loved the town, and this is where the Lord wanted me to go. I realize the challenge, but this is the best move of my career. I can't give you a concrete reason; I just feel it. I'm supposed to be here." And it would seem that in his first year with the Cubs he was already starting to work his magic. The Cubs made it to the playoffs. Unfortunately they lost to the Marlins before the final game. Baker was extremely disappointed, but his spirits were lifted a bit when he was invited to New York to accept the "Manager Move of the Year" award, an award that was co-sponsored by Major League Baseball and the National Prostate Cancer Coalition. The award celebrated the brave and successful move that Baker made to manage the Chicago Cubs. And as of 2003 the future for Baker managing the Cubs looked bright. Sammy Sosa of the Cubs said of Baker, "So many managers have been through Chicago since I've been here and nobody has done what he's done. He's the greatest. All the credit he deserves. You've got to give it to him. He's awesome. He's a guy that makes you believe and makes you do the right thing."

Sources

Christian Science Monitor, July 15, 2003, p. 09.
Ebony, July, 1998, p. 84; July, 2001, p. 148; September, 2003, p. 116.
Jet, November, 27, 2000, p. 50; March 12, 2001, p. 50.
Knight-Ridder/Tribune Wire Service, March 11, 1993; September 2, 1993; August 5, 2000; October 11, 2000; November 9, 2000; February 26, 2001; July 26, 2001; December 17, 2001; January 5, 2002; February 19, 2002; March 28, 2002; June 7, 2002; June 10, 2002; October 1, 2002; October 9, 2002; October 25, 2002; October 27, 2002; November 6, 2002; November 7, 2002; December 12, 2002; April 29, 2003; July 5, 2003; July 6, 2003; July 11, 2003; July 12, 2003; July 19, 2003; October 6, 2003; October 19, 2003.
Los Angeles Times, March 9, 1993, p. C-2.
San Francisco Chronicle, March 1, 1993, p. D-1; December 17, 1992, p. B-1.
San Jose Mercury News, December 16, 1992, p. E-1; April 4, 1993, p. D-1; October 27, 1993, p. E-1.

Sporting News, October 27, 1997, p. 32; May 10, 1999, p. 18; October 30, 2000, p. 8; May 19, 2003, p. 18.
Sports Illustrated, August 23, 1999, p. 76.

—Mark Kram and Catherine V. Donaldson

Lindsay Barrett

1941—

Journalist, poet, novelist, playwright

Born and raised in Jamaica, Lindsay Barrett worked as a journalist in Europe and Africa, eventually settling in Nigeria. During the 1960s and 1970s Barrett was well-known as an experimental and progressive essayist, poet, novelist, and playwright. His work revolved around issues of black identity and dispossession, the African Diaspora, and the survival of descendants of black Africans, now dispersed around the world. As a political analyst and commentator on Nigerian current events, Barrett is looked to as a reliable source of information on this troubled and divided nation, the most populous country in Africa and the continent's largest oil producer.

Worked as Journalist

Lindsay Barrett was born on September 15, 1941, in Lucea, Jamaica, the capital of the western Jamaican parish of Hanover. After graduating from high school, Barrett went to work as an apprentice journalist at the *Daily Gleaner,* Jamaica's major newspaper, and for its sister afternoon tabloid, the *Star.* Early in 1961 he became a news editor for the Jamaica Broadcasting Corporation. However, less than a year later Barrett moved to England. There he worked as a freelancer for the British Broadcasting Corporation's overseas department and for the Transcription Centre, an organization that encouraged African writers by recording and then broadcasting their works in Europe and Africa. After a year, Barrett left England for France. For the next four years he traveled throughout Europe and

North Africa as a journalist and feature writer based in Paris.

After traveling to the Dakar Arts Festival in Senegal in 1966, Barrett decided to remain in West Africa. He lectured at Fourah Bay College in Sierra Leone and taught in Ghana. He eventually settled in Nigeria, where he married Beti Okotie, a prominent Nigerian actress. At the University of Ibadan in Nigeria, Barrett lectured on the roots of African and Afro-American literature. He also worked in Nigerian radio and television. In the 1970s Barrett was a founding member of the progressive Nigerian Association of Patriotic Writers and Artistes.

As colonialism ended in much of Africa, a spirit of optimism prevailed. Many black American and Caribbean intellectuals moved to the newly-independent African nations. Nigeria gained its independence from Great Britain in 1960. But by 1967, civil war had broken out, and the Eastern Region's military governor declared the independent state of Biafra as a homeland for the Igbo people. The civil war lasted for 30 months, and during that time between one and three million Biafrans died from violence, disease, and starvation. During the conflict, Barrett headed the Information Service of the East Central State, the heartland of the Igbo.

Joined the Black Arts Movement

Barrett's first book, *The State of Black Desire,* was published privately in Paris in 1966. It included three poems and three essays focusing on black alienation,

At a Glance . . .

Born Lindsay Barrett on September 15, 1941, in Lucea, Jamaica; married Beti Okotie.

Career: Jamaica *Daily Gleaner, Star,* apprentice journalist, c. 1959-61; Jamaica Broadcasting Corporation, news editor, 1961; British Broadcasting Corporation, overseas department and transcription center freelancer, 1962-63; freelance journalist and political analyst, 1963–; author, poet, playwright, novelist, 1966–; Fourah Bay College, Sierra Leone, lecturer, c. 1967; Information Service of the East Central State, Nigeria, c. 1967-70; Nigerian television and radio, producer, c. 1970–.

Memberships: Nigerian Association of Patriotic Writers and Artistes, founding member, 1970s.

Awards: Illinois Arts Council, Conrad Kent Rivers Memorial Award, c. 1971.

Addresses: *Office*—c/o Publicity Director, Fourth Dimension Publishing Co. Ltd., House 16, Fifth Ave., City Layout, New Haven, Enugu, Nigeria PMB 01164.

exile, and black art. The essays were characteristic of the black aesthetic movement of the 1960s, which argued that black art, particularly jazz and other black music, contained the basis for building a black movement in the western world. However, it was Barrett's lyrical and exciting prose that drew critical acclaim.

In 1968 an essay from *The State of Black Desire,* titled "The Tide Inside, It Rages!," was reprinted in *Black Fire: An Anthology of Afro-American Writing,* edited by LeRoi Jones (Imamu Amiri Baraka) and Larry Neal. The first and last sections of this essay were reproduced in *Black Arts: An Anthology of Black Creations* in 1969. The essay's opening statement read: "The situation of the black man in the western world today, is that of a man in the midst of an open war without the benefit of a complete knowledge of the weapons he holds." Barrett went on to discuss black jazz as a metaphor for blacks in a white world: "If a black man could grasp a [John] Coltrane [saxophone] solo in its entirety as a club, and wield it with the force that first created it centuries before the white man moved Coltrane and his ancestors from the cave of history out into the bright flats of their enslavement, the battle would be near ending and in his favour." In 1970 Barrett's writing received the fifth Conrad Kent Rivers Memorial Award from the Illinois Arts Council.

In 1973 Barrett published a collection of poems, *The Conflicting Eye,* in London, under the pseudonym "Eseoghene." Barrett's other volumes of poetry, published in Nigeria, include *Lipskybound* in 1977 and *A Quality of Pain and Other Poems* in 1986. Barrett's militant poems deal with racial and emotional conflict and exile. His poem "In My Eye and Heart" concerns Birmingham, Alabama, police chief "Bull" Connor, who unleashed police dogs against peaceful civil rights demonstrators in Birmingham, Alabama, in 1963.

Mumu Received With Mixed Reaction

Barrett's first novel, *Song for Mumu,* while popular in some academic communities, was not widely reviewed, even in the Caribbean, and most of the reviews were ambivalent. Some critics questioned the novel's plotting and readability. Martin Levin of the *New York Times Book Review,* however, said that it is not the plot that makes *Song for Mumu,* worth reading, but instead, "What shines … is its language." Barrett had written the novel in Frankfurt, Germany, Paris, and Accra, Ghana, between April of 1962 and October of 1966. It was published in Great Britain in 1967 and in the United States in 1974.

Song for Mumu is an allegorical novel of desire, love, and loss. Mumu's loves and losses reflect the uprooting of the peoples of the black Diaspora and their children's search for identity. Although *Song for Mumu* has a relatively simple plot, the story is intense, passionate, erotic, and violent. Set on an unnamed Caribbean island, the beauty of the lush countryside contrasts with the stark, cold city. A country boy named Scully is drawn to the language and nightlife of the city. However, after contracting a venereal disease from a prostitute, he returns to the country, where he is adopted by a farmer, Papa Peda. Scully and Peda's daughter Meela fall passionately in love and run away to start their own farm. But the farmers in the area are unable to compete with the white plantation owner— the Rich Man—and Scully is forced to work for him as a stable boy. When he is kicked in the head by the Rich Man's horse, he goes mad. Meela gives birth to twins and Scully blinds Papa Peda with his whip and kills the younger twin, a boy, because of the pain he has caused Meela during childbirth. Scully later kills himself in an insane asylum. The surviving twin, Mumu, and her mother take as lovers a father and son, who both drown in the "evil river," that is, the sea.

The Old River Woman reveals the past to Mumu in poetry: "Yes yes Mumu the king cast camp upon the ocean shores and massed/his men to attack the roaring thing on the following day,/but in the night the white men sailed up to the shores and found the camp.// Over the years they stole humanity from that world to fulfil hungers of this world, dragging us across the evil river./The evil river claims its toll./The king leapt from that first boat and all his people followed/him but one. … But without their king our ancestors deeper in the/green were lost. It was not difficult to drag them here./And so we came./Yes yes Mumu we are the descendants of the Evil River's victims./Only the rivers in the land have we mastered./The ocean is not our friend." Mumu then asks the Old River Woman about his father: "Mother River, who was he?" Old River Woman answers, "He was the king's brother's child five generations gone, my child, but he did not know he was a prince."

Mumu and Meela move to the city to escape their grief. They experience more loves and losses as Mumu searches for her origins in the identity of her father. Eventually Mumu becomes the willing victim of a ritualized murder committed by Meela's lover, the Preacher. The novel opens with the final scene: Meela throws herself into Mumu's grave, where she is killed by Papa Peda. It is a novel in which suffering and loss are resolved by death.

The prose story of *Song for Mumu* is accompanied by the choruses of the River Women, who carry out their gruesome revenge on the Rich Man and return the land to the farmers. Barrett's prose, as well as the poetry of the River Women, are grounded in black music, including hymns, work songs, chants, religious ritual and dance.

Wrote in Many Genres

Jump Kookoo Makka, one of Barrett's many plays, was performed at the Leicester University Commonwealth Arts Festival in 1967, under the direction of Cosmo Pieterse. *Home Again* was performed in 1967 by Wole Soyinka's company. Barrett's theatrical collage of drama, dance, and music, *Sighs of a Slave Dream,* was performed in London and at the Keskidee Center of Islington in the early 1970s, by a Nigerian troupe under the direction of Pat Amadu Maddy. It portrays the capture and enslavement of Africans, their transport across the Atlantic, and their suffering on American plantations. Barrett's play *Blackblast* was performed in London in 1973 and *After This We Heard of Fire* was produced by the Ibadan Arts Theatre in Nigeria. Various plays by Barrett have been performed at the Mbari Theatre of the University of Ibadan and on Nigerian National Radio. In addition, Barrett has written critically acclaimed radio and television programs on jazz, the arts, and Caribbean-African cultural issues.

Barrett's work has appeared in anthologies, and he has been a contributing editor to the British magazines *Frontline* and *West Indian World.* He has also contributed short stories, poems, essays, and articles to numerous journals including *Negro Digest/Black World, Revolution, Two Cities,* the *New African, Magnet, Daylight,* the *Black Scholar,* and *Black Lines.* Barrett's second published novel, *Veils of Vengeance Falling,* appeared in 1985.

Fourth Dimension in Enugu, Nigeria, has published many of Barrett's political writings. *Danjuma, the Making of a General,* published in 1979, profiled the military leader who oversaw the massacre of Biafrans during the Nigerian civil war and who later became the Nigerian defense minister. *Agbada to Khaki: Reporting a Change of Government in Nigeria* was published in 1985 as an account of the political changes in Nigeria between 1979 and the 1983 coup d'état. Barrett also has written on conflicts in Liberia.

Barrett wrote the foreword to a new edition of Amiri Baraka's *Four Revolutionary Plays: Experimental Death Unit 1, A Black Mass, Great Goodness of Life, Madheart,* published in 1997. Widely recognized as an expert on the politics of Nigeria, Barrett has also written about oil production and its effects on the economy and the environment of Nigeria. In an article titled "Blaming the Blameless," Barrett discussed Nigeria's role in the Organization of Petroleum-Exporting Countries (OPEC).

Outspoken on Political Issues

In November of 2002 Barrett was quoted by the *Reuters News Service* in stories about the rioting among Muslims, Christians, and security forces that took place before the Miss World Pageant was about to be held in Nigeria. "It is unfortunate for Obasanjo [president of Nigeria] that the protests against the pageant were spearheaded by Muslim fundamentalists," Barrett told *Reuters.* "People will conclude the president is not as much in charge as he thinks." The pageant was subsequently moved to London.

Barrett was widely quoted in news reports following the re-election of Nigeria's president, Olusegun Obasanjo, in April of 2003, amid widespread reports of blatant election fraud. Barrett told Daniel Balint-Kurti of *Reuters,* in an article that appeared on the *Biafra Nigeria World* website, "I am sitting in a state where Obasanjo was credited with 100 percent victories, and there is no celebration." Barrett predicted that there would be more civil unrest in the oil-producing Niger delta, where many people have died in outbreaks of ethnic violence and protests over environmental degradation.

Barrett has also contributed online political analyses to the Niger Delta Congress, including an essay on Chief Festus Okotie-Eboh, the Nigerian finance minister who was assassinated in 1966. Barrett wrote, "There is no greater tribute anyone could give to his memory than to acknowledge the fact that much of what needs to be done to bring Nigeria back to economic life can be found in the legacies of economic policy which he left behind." Jerry Gana, the Nigerian Minister of Information and Orientation, has also been the subject of a report written by Barrett.

Selected Writings

Nonfiction

The State of Black Desire, Corbiére et Jugain, 1966; Ethiope, 1974.

"The Tide Inside, It Rages!," in *Black Fire: An Anthology of Afro-American Writing,* Jones, LeRoi and Larry Neal, eds., William Morrow & Co., 1968; excerpted in *Black Arts: An Anthology of Black Creations,* Alhamisi, Ahmed and Harun Kofi Wangara, eds., Black Arts Publications, 1969.

Danjuma, the Making of a General, Fourth Dimension Publishers, 1979.

Agbada to Khaki: Reporting a Change of Government in Nigeria, Fourth Dimension Publishers, 1985.

Liberian Notes: A Study of Conflict and Resistance: A PACs Report, Yandia Printing Press, 1993.

Report on Liberia, Yandia Printing Press, 1993.

(Foreward) Imamu Amiri Baraka, *Four Black Revolutionary Plays: Experimental Death Unit 1, A Black Mass, Great Goodness of Life, Madheart,* Marion Boyars, 1997.

Novels

Song for Mumu, Longmans, Green and Co., 1967; Howard University Press, 1974.

Veils of Vengeance Falling, Fourth Dimension Publishers, 1985.

Poetry

(As Eseoghene) *The Conflicting Eye,* Paul Bremen, 1973.

The Quality of Pain and Other Poems, Gaskiya, 1976.

Lipskybound, Bladi House, 1977.

On-line

"Blaming the Blameless," *Niger Delta Congress,* www.nigerdeltacongress.com/barticles/blaming%20 the%20blameless.htm (December 8, 2003).

"Jerry Gana and the Revelations That Matter," *Niger Delta Congress,* www.nigerdeltacongress.com/jarticles/jerry_gana_and_the_revelations_t.htm (November 18, 2003).

"Okotie-Eboh and Yesterday's Vision," *Niger Delta Congress,* www.nigerdeltacongress.com/oarticles/ okotie.htm (December 11, 2003).

"Revolution or Uprising?" *Niger Delta Congress,* www.nigerdeltacongress.com/rarticles/revolution_ or_uprising.htm (December 11, 2003).

Other

Barrett is the author of numerous plays and radio and television programs.

Sources

Books

Edwards, Norval, "Nadi," in *Fifty Caribbean Writers: A Bio-Bibliographical Critical Sourcebook,* Dance, Daryl Cumber, ed., Greenwood Press, 1986, pp. 26-34.

Herdeck, Donald E., ed., *Caribbean Writers: A Bio-Bibliographical-Critical Encyclopedia,* Three Continents Press, 1979, pp. 25-26.

Periodicals

New York Times Book Review, September 29, 1974, p. 40.

Obsidian II: Black Literature in Review, Summer 1987, pp. 3-22.

On-line

"(Eseoghene) Lindsay Barrett," *Contemporary Authors Online,* reproduced in *Biography Resource Center,* www.galenet.com/servlet/BioRC (November 25, 2003).

"Jubilant Obasanjo Ignores Fury Over 'Vote-Rigging,'" *Biafra Nigeria World,* http://news.biafranigeriaworld.com/archive/2003/apr/23/001.html (November 25, 2003).

"Riots Persist in Nigeria, Beauty Queens Fly to U.K.," *Reuters Wire (Charlotte Observer),* www.charlotte.com/mld/charlotte/4591073.htm (December 11, 2003).

—Margaret Alic

James Blake

1979—

Tennis player

James Blake is a rising international tennis star. He turned professional in 1999 and won his first ATP singles title in 2002. He became only the fourth African-American male to win an ATP title. He was also the first African-American man to break into the top 50 tennis rankings since 1997. Blake's tennis talent, quiet demeanor, and graciousness on and off the court have led many to compare him to his hero, the great American tennis star and the first great African-American player, Arthur Ashe. Blake is working hard to live up to the expectations that the tennis public has for him.

Born into a Tennis Family

James Blake was born on December 28, 1979, in Yonkers, New York, into a tennis family. His father, Thomas, and his mother, Betty, met on the public tennis courts of New York. Thomas Blake learned to play tennis during his tenure in the United States Air Force, while Betty Blake picked up the game as a grade school student in Banbury, England. The Blakes played tennis regularly at the 369th Armory in Harlem and they took their young children with them. By the age of

five James began playing tennis with his older brother Thomas, Jr.

When Blake was six years old, his family moved to Fairfield, Connecticut. His father worked as a salesperson for 3M Worldwide, a technology company, while his mother worked as a secretary at the local tennis club. Both Thomas and James took lessons at the Trumbull Tennis Club in Connecticut. It was at this club that Blake met Brian Barker, who began coaching Blake at age 12.

Yet the Blakes ties to Harlem remained strong. They continued to play tennis in Harlem on a regular basis and volunteered at the Harlem Junior Tennis League, a program aimed at introducing tennis to inner-city children. As a result of their parents' involvement in the Harlem program, Blake and his brother participated in the League's tennis clinics. As a biracial child, Blake moved comfortably between the very different worlds of middle-class Fairfield and inner-city Harlem with tennis as a bridge between them. It was at one of the tennis clinics in Harlem that James first heard the famous African-American tennis player Arthur Ashe speak. Ashe was the first black man to reach the number one rankings in international tennis. He was a

At a Glance . . .

Born on December 28, 1979, in Yonkers, NY; son of Thomas and Betty Blake. *Education:* Harvard University, economics major, 1997-1999.

Career: Professional tennis player, 1999–.

Memberships: Association of Tennis Professionals, 1999–; Harlem Junior Tennis League, guest coach; Starlight Children's Foundation; Arthur Ashe Kids' Day.

Awards: All-American, Harvard University, 1998; Number one ranked collegiate tennis player, Harvard University, 1999; Rookie of the Year, World Team Tennis, 2000; ATP singles title, Washington, DC, 2002; ATP double title, Cincinnati, 2002; ATP doubles title, Scottsdale, 2003.

Addresses: *Office:*—c/o Carlos Fleming, IMG, 1360 E. 9th Street, Suite 100, Cleveland, OH 44114.

pioneer for African Americans in a sport that has been dominated by whites. Ashe's passionate speech and his reputation as both a great tennis player and a well-respected person inspired Blake to consider a career in tennis.

Blake's parents encouraged both of their sons to pursue their tennis interests, but they did not pressure them into choosing tennis as a career. On the contrary, the Blakes tried to provide a normal, healthy family life for their children. "I believe our family enjoyed a wealth greater than material goods can supply," Betty Blake wrote in *Deuce Magazine* in 2003. "Harmony pervaded our home, a feeling of mutual respect, love, and that essential ingredient, humor. Importantly, we spent time together." Blake's father insisted that the boys spend at least two days a week without television and they were creative in how they spent their time. Aside from playing tennis, Blake had several small jobs to earn spending money, such as delivering newspapers, taking care of pets, raking leaves, and shoveling snow.

Slowly Developed Tennis Career

Much of Blake's early tennis career was spent playing "catch up." His brother Thomas, who was three years older, developed his tennis game more quickly, in part because he was physically stronger and the taller of the two boys. At age 13 Blake was diagnosed with scoliosis, a curvature of the spine. His treatment options were to have surgery or to wear a back brace. Surgery

would have meant that Blake could no longer play tennis, so he chose to wear the brace. He only took it off for a few hours each day to play tennis. Aside from his back problem, Blake was also small as a child. "I was resigned to being the short one in the family. Being unable to use my serve as a weapon, I learned to play small, scrapping out points, getting the ball back," Blake explained to Peter Bodo of *TENNIS Magazine* in April of 2002. "And that helped me later on, because I feel like I can still create points and win matches without having to rely on a weapon."

Despite his physical setbacks, Blake was able to succeed as a junior tennis player. In 1996 he won the United States Tennis Association Boys 18s Indoors Championship and a year later he won the clay court title. In 1997 he was ranked the number one U.S. junior in 18s. During this time his brother Thomas was attending college at Harvard University. He became captain of the tennis team and was an All-American tennis player. Blake was determined to keep up with his brother. He was hesitant to follow Thomas to Harvard because of the academic demands of the prestigious college, but he decided to accept the challenge. Like his brother, Blake studied economics at Harvard and joined the tennis team. During his first year of college Blake became the first Harvard freshman to be named All-American. In 1999 he was the number one collegiate tennis player in the country. He and his brother were also successful doubles partners.

After spending two years at Harvard, Blake made the difficult decision to leave college and become a professional tennis player. "It wasn't a popular move within the family for me to drop out of school," Blake told Justin Brown of the *Christian Science Monitor* in May of 2002. "But I had gotten to the point where I needed better opponents to improve as a player." Blake moved from Boston to Tampa, Florida, where he lives and trains with his brother Thomas. When Blake joined the professional ranks he quickly realized just how much better his opponents were than him. He struggled during his first year as a professional and was very frustrated by his performance. "James was the best college player, but when you come to the pros, no one gives a darn," explained U.S. Davis Cup captain Patrick McEnroe to the *Washington Times* in August of 2002.

Blake spent most of the 2000 tennis year on the Challenger circuit, trying to quickly bring his game up to the level of his professional peers. He won his first career Challenger title in Houston and another in Rancho Mirage. He was named the 2000 Rookie of the Year for World Team Tennis. In 2001 he had continued success in the Challenger circuit and began to progress in the Association of Tennis Professionals (ATP) matches. He reached his first career ATP semifinal round in Newport and he reached the second round of the U.S. Open. In 2001 Blake also made his debut as a Davis Cup team player.

By the beginning of the 2002 season Blake had broken into the top 100 of the men's tennis rankings. That year he also won his first career ATP singles title in Washington, D.C. He was the first African-American man to win that tournament since his hero, Arthur Ashe. He became only the fourth African-American man to win an ATP title in the Open Era. Blake also won his first ATP doubles title in Cincinnati playing with fellow American Todd Martin. His rankings steadily improved and Blake became the first African-American man to break into the top 50 rankings since MaliVai Washington had accomplished this in 1997. In 2003 Blake was not able to secure another singles title, but he did win a second ATP doubles title in Scottsdale. His singles record for the 2003 season was 32 wins and 26 losses and he was ranked 37th in the world.

Role Model and Fashion Model

Blake's steady improvement in the rankings, his commanding forehand, and his ability to think quickly on his feet have made him one of the rising American male tennis stars. He has also gained the respect of his peers and the tennis community through his professional attitude, affable demeanor, and graciousness on and off the court. Because of these qualities, Blake is often compared to the great Arthur Ashe. "With so few African American men on the tour, comparisons to Ashe are inevitable. In Blake's case, though, the similarity goes beyond skin color and quiet competitiveness to the heart of his character. Like Ashe, Blake seems to be decent, dignified, and quietly determined," wrote Thomas Hackett of *TENNIS Magazine* in April of 2003.

Blake is well aware of the added pressure that is put on him by the media and the public because of his status as the only top-ranked African-American male player. The expectations of him as a role model quickly became obvious during a 2001 U.S. Open match against the men's best player at that time, Australia's Lleyton Hewitt. Hewitt was frustrated by two foot faults called by a black linesman and allegedly made an inappropriate comment. While the media was expecting Blake to make a scene about the incident, Blake very graciously returned his attention back to the game. He later spoke with Hewitt privately in the locker room, but he did not turn the incident into a media spectacle. Blake is not naive about racism in professional sports, but he appreciates the opportunities he has been given because of earlier pioneers. "For me to say there is still a ton of racism on the tour would be disrespectful to Arthur Ashe and MaliVai Washington, and all the things they've gone through," Blake explained to Chip Brown of the *Dallas Star* in April of 2002. "I haven't seen the things they saw. I feel progress is being made."

Blake is flattered by the comparisons that are often made between him and Ashe, although he realizes those are big shoes to fill. Blake is eager to step up to the expectations the public has of him to be a role model for other African Americans as a tennis star and more generally as an athlete. "[Being a role model] just comes with the territory. That's our job. I take it very seriously," Blake told Patrick Hruby of the *Washington Times* in August of 2002. During his time off Blake is involved in several charities. He and his brother both volunteer to teach lessons at the Harlem Junior Tennis League. Blake has also worked for the Starlight Children's Foundation in New York and participates in the annual Arthur Ashe Kids' Day at the U.S. Open.

In addition to his talent and personality, Blake's good looks and fashion sense have fueled his popularity. In 2002 he began a modeling career, appearing in *GQ* and *Vogue* magazines. He was also named the "Sexiest Male Athlete" by *People* magazine. In December of 2003 Blake made a bold fashion move and cut off his trademark dreadlocks in exchange for a clean-shaven look. While Blake is pleased with the media and fan attention due to his looks, he wants the focus to remain on the game of tennis. As he told *People Weekly*, "I never really thought of myself as a good-looking guy. But I hope if fans are coming out just to look at me, they'll end up noticing there's tennis going on."

Sources

Periodicals

Baltimore Sun, December 4, 2003; December 5, 2003.
Black Enterprise, September 1, 2003.
Christian Science Monitor, May 3, 2002.
Dallas Star, April 3, 2002.
Deuce Magazine, 2003.
ESPN Magazine, June 23, 2003.
Jet, May 24, 1999.
Harvard University Gazette, May 7, 1998.
Independent, June 2002.
Ivy League Sports, 1998.
Los Angeles Times, March 11, 2002.
Mirror, June 24, 2002.
Observer, May 4, 2003.
People Weekly, July 29, 2002, p. 65.
Sports Illustrated, April 15, 2002, p. R8.
TENNIS Magazine, September 1999, p. 26; April 2002; May 2003.
USTA Magazine, 2002.
Washington Times, August 12, 2002.

On-line

"Blake, Roddick Are Hits in Climb Up ATP Charts," *ESPN,* www.espn.com (January 3, 2004).
"James Blake," *ATP Tennis,* www.atptennis.com/en/ players/playerbios/ (January 3, 2004).
"James Blake," *U.S. Open 2003,* www.usopen.org/ en_US/nios/profile/ms/atpb676.html (January 3, 2004).

"James Blake Athlete Bio," *Olympics USA,* www. olympic-usa.org/cfdocs/athlete_bios/ (January 3, 2004).

James Blake Tennis, www.jamesblaketennis.com (January 3, 2004).

—Janet P. Stamatel

Terence Blanchard

1962—

Jazz musician

Terence Blanchard is a musician of many talents. His skill as a trumpeter made him one of the leading jazz voices of the last 20 years, but he has also developed as a writer, composing scores for Spike Lee's *Bamboozled* and *Malcolm X*. Although Blanchard would be "one of the first 'Young Lions,'" noted Scott Yanow in *All Music Guide,* "to develop his own sound …," some critics have opined that writing scores has distracted him from his commitment to jazz. Blanchard, however, inherited a strong work ethic from his father, allowing him to devote ample time to each of his talents. "I could easily make more money just writing films, but I'm still out on the road," he told Ted Panken in *Down Beat.* "I love playing music, I love playing jazz and it will never be my choice to give that up."

Blanchard was born on March 13, 1962, in New Orleans, Louisiana. His father, Joseph Oliver Blanchard, was an insurance salesman who loved opera, and sang part-time in the 1930s and 1940s. Joseph Blanchard idolized early jazz greats like Louis Armstrong and Earl Hines, and encouraged his son to become a musician. Terence Blanchard began playing piano at five. He enjoyed clowning around, and learned to play television theme songs like *Batman,* but his father pushed him to take the music seriously. "'If you're going to do this music thing,'" Blanchard later recalled his father saying in *Essence,* "'you're going to do it right and take some lessons.'" Blanchard decided to change instruments, however, after a jazz band visited his grade school: he loved the sound of the trumpet.

In the early 1970s Blanchard attended St. Augustine, a black Catholic school, and played in the marching band. He grew disappointed in the music program, however, and quit to enroll in public school. Although the abrupt change put his future music career at risk, he signed up at a public school that allowed him to attend the New Orleans Center of Creative Arts (NOCCA). Blanchard studied with Ellis Marsalis, the father of Wynton and Branford Marsalis, at NOCCA. He immersed himself in the music of Miles Davis, Clifford Brown, and John Coltrane, and met a number of future musical partners including Donald Harrison. In addition to his studies at NOCCA, Blanchard expanded his musical palette playing Dixieland on Sunday after-

At a Glance . . .

Born on March 13, 1962, in New Orleans, LA; son of Joseph Oliver Blanchard. *Education:* Rutgers, classical music major, 1980-82.

Career: New Orleans Civic Orchestra, trumpet player, late 1970s; Blue Room night club, trumpet player, late 1970s; Lionel Hampton's Band, trumpet player, 1980-82; Art Blakey's Jazz Messengers, trumpet player, 1982-86; Quintet featuring Donald Harrison, co-leader and trumpeter, 1986-90; Terence Blanchard Quintet, founder, leader, and trumpeter, 1990–; Movie soundtrack scorer, 1991–; Thelonious Monk Institute of Jazz Performance, artistic director, 2000–.

Selected awards: Artist of the Year, Jazz Album of the Year, Jazz Trumpeter of the Year, *Downbeat* Magazine, 2000; Nominee, Best Original Score for *25th Hour,* Golden Globes, 2002; numerous Grammy nominations.

Addresses: *Record company*—Blue Note, 304 Park Avenue South, 3rd Floor, New York, New York 10010.

noons, and playing with the New Orleans Civic Orchestra.

In 1980 Blanchard enrolled in Rutgers and studied classical and jazz trumpet with William Fielder and band instruction with Paul Jeffrey. Thanks to Jeffrey, the young trumpeter began performing with veteran vibes player Lionel Hampton, a gig that extended a year and a half. In February of 1982, Wynton Marsalis recommended Blanchard to take his place with Art Blakey and the Jazz Messengers, leading the young trumpeter to drop out of Rutgers to go on the road. His new education, however, was just beginning. Blakey encouraged the young trumpeter to abandon his imitative style and search for a distinctive approach. "I grew so much in just the first month...," he told Panken. "Art made me understand that as long as I set my goals and worked toward them, I could do anything I wanted."

Blanchard's first foray into film came in 1988 when he was hired as a session musician on Spike Lee's *School Daze.* Despite his skill as both a composer and a player, he had no immediate plans to start a career in scoring films. "I thought I'd be in my sixties by the time that happened to me," Blanchard told *Jazz Improv Magazine,* "after I had two hundred recordings, and was on my death bed." He returned to the set of Lee's next film, *Mo' Better Blues,* and impressed the director by composing and scoring a piece for the movie. This led Lee to choose the trumpeter to score *Jungle Fever* in 1991, but Blanchard worried that he lacked the experience necessary to write the soundtrack by himself. "I was scared to death," he told Lisa Leigh Parney in the *Christian Science Monitor.* Not knowing where to turn, he called a mentor for advice. "Trust your ears," his friend told him. "You know how to write. Do your job." Blanchard relaxed, and soon found himself in great demand. He collaborated with Lee on eight other films including *Malcolm X* and *25th Hour,* and also scored a number of other films including *Sugar Hill, Eve's Bayou,* and *Barber Shop.*

Following Blanchard's work with Art Blakey and the Jazz Messengers, he reached a crisis in his growth as an artist. Although he believed that his interpretive skills were growing emotionally and musically, he discovered that his method of playing was preventing him from growing technically. "I kept hearing ideas in my head that I wanted to play but couldn't execute, and that was very frustrating" he told Panken. "My bottom lip was rolled over my teeth and I was cutting my lip." Determined to improve his embouchure, Blanchard took a two-year hiatus from playing, allowing time for his lip to heal and re-learning his technique. "Terence was willing to undergo two years of absolute misery for long-term gain," Branford Marsalis told Panken. "For a professional working musician to decide to take a hit like that shows an enormous level of personal honesty."

Blanchard remains one of the most creative musicians currently working on the contemporary jazz and film scenes, and has frequently been nominated for Golden Globe and Grammy awards. "Over the last five years," wrote *Jazz Improv Magazine,* "Blanchard has matured from a vigorous young lion into an established artist..." In 2000 *Downbeat* readers chose him as the Jazz Artist and Trumpeter of the Year, while also choosing *Wandering Moon* as the Jazz Album of the Year. Similar praise greeted *Bounce* in 2003. "...Blanchard proves that he is the trumpet player, composer, and bandleader who is moving jazz...," wrote Thom Jurek in *All Music Guide,* "in new directions that encompass both a new look at Western musical systems and never leave the human heart out of the equation." Besides his film and studio work, Blanchard is the artistic director of the Thelonious Monk Institute's Master's program and tours regularly. "Nothing," he told *Jazz Improv Magazine,* "can beat being a jazz musician, playing a club, playing a concert."

Selected works

Discography

New York Second Line, Concord, 1983.
Black Pearl, Columbia, 1988.

Malcolm X Jazz Suite, Columbia, 1992.
The Billie Holiday Songbook, Sony, 1993.
Wandering Moon, Columbia, 2000.
Bounce, Blue Note, 2003.

Film Scores

Jungle Fever, 1991.
Malcolm X, 1992.
Housesitter, 1992.
Sugar Hill, 1994.
Trial By Jury, 1994.
The Inkwell, 1994.
Backbeat, 1994.
Eve's Bayou, 1997.
Barber Shop, 2002.
25th Hour, 2002.

Sources

Periodicals

Christian Science Monitor, June 15, 2001, p. 20.
Down Beat, December 3, 2000.
Essence, April 1, 2001, p. 76.

On-line

"Terence Blanchard," *All Music Guide,* www.allmusic. com (December 15, 2003).
"Terence Blanchard," *Biography Resource Center,* www.galenet.com/servlet/BioRC (December 15, 2003).
"The Heart Speaks," *Jazz Improv,* www.jazzimprov. com (December 15, 2003).

—Ronnie D. Lankford, Jr.

Bobby Bonds

1946-2003

Baseball outfielder

Former San Francisco Giants outfielder Bobby Bonds attracted new attention in the early 2000s as his son, modern-day slugger Barry Bonds, marched toward and then surpassed one hitting record after another. To old-er baseball fans, however, the elder Bonds was already well known as a key member of the powerhouse Giants squads of the 1960s, the crowd-pleasing teams that included stars such as Bonds's childhood idol, Willie Mays. If some felt that Bobby Bonds did not fully live up to his tremendous potential as a natural athlete, he neverthe-less notched several all-time records over a major league career that was a success by any standard.

Bonds was born on March 15, 1946, in Riverside, California, and grew up in that suburban Los Angeles community. Schoolmates remembered him as a one-of-a-kind talent right from the start. "He's probably the best athlete I've ever known," future major league manager and Bonds's childhood friend Dusty Baker told *Baseball Digest*. "He could have been anything he wanted to be, a football or basketball star, an Olympian." Indeed, Bonds was a multi-sport star at Riverside Poly High School, taking state long-jump championship honors in his senior year, leading his school's football league in both rushing and passing as a tailback, and attracting the attention on the basketball court of Jerry Tarkanian, then the coach at Long Beach City College.

Like many other California youngsters, Bonds admired San Francisco Giants outfielder Willie Mays, one of the first wave of African Americans to play in the major leagues and perhaps the first to become a true fan favorite. Bonds was so thrilled by the idea of playing on the same field as Mays that he spurned financially more lucrative offers from the Los Angeles Dodgers and Minnesota Twins, to sign with the Giants in 1964. After several years in the Giants' farm system, Bonds was clearly ready for the majors in 1968. An indication of things to come was the grand slam home run he hit during his major league debut on June 25 of that year—the first time a player had hit a debut grand slam since 1898.

Bonds's all-around athletic ability showed itself in his combination of power and speed. In 1969, his first full season in the majors, Bonds notched 32 home runs and 45 stolen bases, becoming only the fourth player in major league history to record a so-called "30-30" season. It was the first of five such seasons for Bonds (the others were in 1973, 1975, 1977, and 1978), an all-time record he shares only with his son Barry; no other player has had more than three. Some billed Bonds as Mays's successor as Mays entered the final stages of his career.

Bonds demurred at such comparisons. "A guy like that you can't follow," he was quoted as saying by *Sports Illustrated*. And, it was true, his high strikeout totals—he set what was then a National League record in 1970 with 189—partly counterbalanced his impressive hitting statistics. But Bonds played some of the best baseball of his career after Mays left San Francisco for the New York Mets. Batting leadoff, Bonds hit 33 home runs with 102 runs batted in (RBIs) for the Giants in 1971, pacing the team to the division title and the postseason playoffs.

In 1973 Bonds did even better; with 39 home runs and 43 stolen bases, almost notching an unprecedented "40-40" combination. Bonds shone in the 1973 All-Star Game, hitting a two-run home run and winning the Most Valuable Player designation. At the end of the following year, however, Bonds was traded to the New York Yankees, as the powerful Giants roster was broken up for financial reasons. Quaint as it may seem in an era of multimillion-dollar payrolls, the trade of Bonds for the Yankees' Bobby Murcer was the first in the major leagues that involved players paid over $100,000 a year.

Bonds bounced from team to team after that, recording several strong years but suffering at times from injuries and slumps. Traded to the California Angels for the 1976 season, he was sidelined for much of the season with a hand injury. The following year, however, he notched 115 RBIs, a career best. Bonds then did stints with the Chicago White Sox, Texas Rangers, Cleveland Indians, St. Louis Cardinals, and Chicago Cubs before retiring at the end of the 1981 season. He was signed by the Yankees in 1982 but did not play. Bonds retired with an impressive 332 career home runs, 461 stolen bases, and 1,024 RBIs.

Bonds then moved easily into coaching. He signed on with the Cleveland Indians in 1984 and later moved back to San Francisco. It wasn't long before he crossed professional paths with his son Barry, who had been born when the elder Bonds was 18 years old. The relationship between the two was centered mostly on baseball. "I was a momma's boy," Barry Bonds told *People*. "I didn't get anything from Dad, except my body and baseball knowledge. The only time I spent with him was at the ballpark."

Nevertheless, when Barry Bonds attained stardom and began to annoy some fans with his private, reclusive nature, Bobby Bonds and Barry's Swedish-American wife Sun (whom he married in the late 1980s) became two of his strongest defenders. Bobby Bonds contributed to his son's skill on the field as well. "I think I'm harder on Barry than on other players," he told *People* in reference to his stint as Giants hitting coach from 1993-96. As batting records fell before Barry Bonds's bat in the early 2000s, his father was often watching from the stands of San Francisco's Pacific Bell Park. The last game Bonds watched took place three days before his death on August 23, 2003, from the triple onslaught of lung cancer, a brain tumor, and heart disease.

Sources

Periodicals

Baseball Digest, November 2003, p. 78.
Jet, September 8, 2003, p. 51.
People, October 4, 1993, p. 101.
Sporting News, September 1, 2003, p. 61.
Sports Illustrated, September 1, 2003, p. 58.

On-line

"Bobby Bonds," *Baseball Library*, www.baseballlibrary.com/baseballlibrary/ballplayers/B/Bonds_Bobby.stm (December 17, 2003).
"Bobby Bonds," *Baseball-Reference*, www.baseball-reference.com/b/bondsbo01.shtml (December 17, 2003).

—James M. Manheim

Derrick Brooks

1973—

Professional football player

Derrick Brooks is best known as the powerful and fast linebacker that helped the Tampa Bay Buccaneers win their first Super Bowl in 2002. He has won awards for his play on the field including defensive MVP awards and numerous Pro-Bowl appearances. Yet Brooks is also known off the field for his work in the Tampa Bay community. With his Brooks Bunch, a group of inner-city children with whom he works with through the Ybor City Boys and Girls club, Brooks is teaching children the value of education as well as showing them the opportunities and wonders that the world has to offer. Brooks and the Brooks Bunch have traveled everywhere from the Grand Canyon to South Africa, and Brooks' focus is always on teaching the children about history and the different cultures that they encounter. Many people wonder how Brooks can show so much energy and commitment on the football field and still give his all to helping people off the field. But as Brooks told the *ESPN* website, "That's who I am. I come here to do a job and be a winner. When I'm away from here, I think the Lord has put me in a position to help others."

Learned the Importance of Education

Derrick Dewan Brooks was born on April 18, 1973, in Pensacola, Florida, to Gerri Brooks. Brooks, who never met his biological father until he was 16 years old, was raised by his mother, grandmother, and his stepfather A.J. Mitchell—who married Brooks' mother when Derrick was six years old. Brooks' lessons started early in life, starting first with the idea of charity. His grandmother, Martha, ran a make-shift soup kitchen for strangers out of her own house.

Brooks also soon learned the importance of education. His parents knew that he was a bright child and would accept nothing less than excellence in the classroom. Once, when Brooks was ten years old, his stepfather Mitchell came into the school unannounced to check on his stepson. What Mitchell saw did not please him. Brooks was not paying attention, making jokes, and shooting staples at other students in the class. Mitchell burst into the room and gave Brooks a spanking in front of the room full of students. Though he did not appreciate being humiliated before all of his peers, Brooks told Joel Poiley of *Boys' Life* "That's the most embarrassing moment of my life. But I obviously never forgot it, and it set me straight on what my priorities should be and what my parents expected of me." The

At a Glance . . .

Born Derrick Dewan Brooks on April 18, 1973, in Pensacola, FL; son of Gerri Brooks; married Carol; children: Brianna, Derrick Jr., Dewan. *Education:* Florida State University, BA, 1994, MA, 2001.

Career: Tampa Bay Buccaneers, linebacker, 1995–.

Awards: *USA Today* High School Defensive Player of the Year, 1990; *Parade* All American, 1990; First team All-ACC, 1992-94; Consensus All-American, finalist for the Lombardi Award, 1993-94; GTE Academic All-America, 1994; First Team All-Rookie honors, 1995; Pro Bowl selection, 1997-02; *Associated Press* first team All-Pro, 1999-00; *Associated Press* second team All-Pro, 2001; Walter Payton/NFL Man of the Year Award, 2000; Tampa Bay's Most Valuable Player, 1998-00; Silver Medallion Humanitarian Award, 2001; winner of EDDIE Award, winner of Giant Steps Award, *Associated Press* Defensive Player of the Year, 2002, named to the Florida State University Board of Trustees, 2003.

Addresses: *Office*—c/o Tampa Bay Buccaneers, One Buccaneer Place, Tampa, FL 33607.

message about the importance of education led him to achieve stellar grades throughout school, to earn an advanced degree, and in March of 2003 to be named to the Florida State University (FSU) Board of Trustees.

At Booker T. Washington High School in Pensacola, Brooks excelled in both the classroom and on the gridiron. At the end of his time in high school Brooks was named the *USA Today* High School Defensive Player of the Year, a *Parade* All-American, and was rated the best defensive player in the country by *Super Prep* magazine. Perhaps even more impressive for a football player of this stature, Brooks destroyed the stereotype of the dumb jock by graduating from high school with a 3.94 grade-point average. Brooks had the choice of any university in the country, but decided to stay close to home and attend FSU.

Brooks started his career at FSU as a safety and became one of two true freshman to earn a varsity letter. Before the following season Brooks was shifted over to outside linebacker during spring practice and was able to make an immediate impact in his sophomore year tallying 98 tackles and earning First Team All-ACC. The honors and awards kept piling up throughout a college career which saw Brooks finish as a two-time consensus All-American, a two-time finalist for the Vince Lombardi Award given to the nation's top lineman or linebacker, and a GTE Academic All-America who graduated five months early. Typically superstar football players leave school five months early to prepare for the NFL draft, but Brooks had accumulated enough credits to graduate one semester ahead of his class. Brooks would eventually return to FSU and earn a masters degree in business communications.

Though Brooks enjoyed a level of success that few athletes can even dream of, one of his most influential college experiences occurred off the field. In his junior year at FSU Brooks went to visit his cousin, who was serving time in a work camp in Tallahassee. After putting off the visit several times, he finally decided to go to the prison, but he brought two of his teammates with him. The group drove to Tallahassee, three confident young college football players without a care in the world, but the drive back was different. Where there had been laughing and joking on the way there, on the drive back there was silence. Brooks told David Fleming of *ESPN The Magazine* about his comments to his teammates: "What's happened to us? We are dying off in the streets and the jails, and the people we believe in to fix this—politicians, pastors our fathers—are not doing anything." Brooks pulled off the freeway and the three players vowed to make a difference in the lives of people who had been left behind by society.

Drafted by Buccaneers

Brooks became the second first-round draft choice of the Tampa Bay Buccaneers in 1995 after Miami's Warren Sapp, and many observers around the NFL thought the six foot, 235 pound linebacker would be too small to be an effective professional player. When it came time to play, Brooks proved all of his doubters wrong. In his first professional season Brooks started 13 games and played in all 16 contests. He did not start every game because Tampa Bay started another defensive back instead of the bigger, less mobile linebacker against teams that primarily used the pass as a way to attack the defense. By the second year of his career, he had remedied that one weakness and started in all 16 games for Tampa Bay. He even turned the element of his game which kept him out of the lineup into a strength for the team. Brooks is so fast and can cover so much ground that the Buccaneers can keep two linebackers in the game at all times unlike most NFL teams which have special packages to defend the pass but are then vulnerable against the run.

In his second NFL season Brooks led the team with 133 tackles, but was next to last in recognition from the outside world. Then Tampa Bay coach Tony Dungy told John Oehser of *The Florida Times Union* about Brooks' value to the team: "He had a very good year for us. Unfortunately, if you're not an outside linebacker who's a blitzer, or who gets a lot of sacks, the recognition can be slow to come. Derrick played well for us, and I think he'll play at a real high caliber for a long time."

Brooks continued his quiet excellence in 1997 starting all 16 regular season games and tallying 182 tackles. He was starting to get some recognition around the league as one of the NFL's premier linebackers and was selected to play in the first of his many Pro Bowls. The following season continued in the same way except that Brooks was now starting in the Pro Bowl and was named an All Pro by nearly every sports publication in America. He recorded the third highest tackle total in team history with 189 including double-digit stops in nine games.

Started the Brooks Bunch

The accolades continued for Brooks during the 1999 and 2000 seasons after making 180 and 179 tackles. Brooks would make the Pro Bowl both years and be named the Buccaneers' Most Valuable Player in 2000, but there was one award that stood out above all the honors he received for being an outstanding football player. After the 2000 NFL season Brooks received the Walter Payton/NFL Man of the Year Award for his efforts for the children of the Tampa Bay area.

When Brooks first came into the NFL he began to look at ways he could help the community. Remembering all the hours he spent at the Boys and Girls Club when he was growing up, he made arrangements to send a group of kids from the Tampa Bay area Boys and Girls Clubs to each Buccaneers game. In 1996 he started to make appearances at the clubs to encourage the kids to do well in school, but then he decided that he had to do more. Brooks started to put together educational trips for the kids as a means of rewarding them for good grades. First the excursions were small, such as a cross-state bus trip to Fort Lauderdale, but the next year he took the Brooks Bunch to Atlanta to visit the Martin Luther King Center. The year after that he took the kids to Washington, D.C., to study the government. And unlike many athletes, who have foundations or give money for charitable enterprises, Brooks is very hands-on when he decides he is going to get involved with a project. He not only pays for the trips and gives the kids spending money, he leads the expeditions. Bertha Gary, director of Tampa's Ybor City Boys and Girls Club told Paul Attner of *The Sporting News,* "That's what really impresses me about Derrick. He is incredibly hands-on. He's not one of these athletes who gives money and has cameras take his picture, and then you never see him again. He is in the middle of everything. He doesn't dominate; he blends in. But he knows exactly what is happening."

After the 2000 season Brooks took a group of 40, including then Buccaneers head coach Dungy and his wife, to South Africa and Swaziland. The group toured Soweto, went on a safari, and saw the prison where Nelson Mandela was held. In his work with the clubs around the Tampa area he usually just shows up and begins to talk with the kids there. After years of dropping by unannounced to the Boys and Girls Club, the kids are used to his presence and feel they can relate to him. Brooks has taken his bunch to visit Oprah Winfrey's studio in Chicago, to New York, and after the 2002 season, he took them on a trip out west to see the Grand Canyon and the Golden Gate bridge. Brooks told Thomas George of the *New York Times* that for him, the Brooks Bunch is about expanding the kids' horizons: "I will not allow my group or anyone else to use the words 'underprivileged kids' when talking about them. Sure, we've got students who come from homes with single parents, both parents, some being raised by their grandparents, and others, frankly, who are raising themselves. This group is about breaking down stereotypes. It's about educating themselves with these trips and then passing it on to their friends about the possibilities. It's a dynamic situation and I have earned their respect. Now my job is to live up to it."

Won Defensive MVP

On the field Brooks continued with his usual excellence. Once again after the 2001 season he led the team in tackles with 165, as he had done every year since 1998 for the leagues best defense. Not only was he an excellent all-around player who was named to his fifth straight Pro Bowl, but Brooks was durable, playing in all of his teams 16 games for the sixth straight season.

While the 2001 season was another measure of Brooks' excellence, the 2002 campaign was truly exceptional for the linebacker and his team. For the last five seasons Brooks had consistently been the best player on the NFL's best defense winning the Team's Defensive MVP from the 1998 through the 2000 seasons, but after the 2003 regular season Brooks was named the *Associated Press* Defensive Player of the Year. He again led his team in tackles with 170 and scored four touchdowns on turnovers including one in the Super Bowl as the Buccaneers destroyed the Oakland Raiders. He became the only linebacker in NFL history to return three interceptions for a touchdown in a single season. Brooks achieved career highs in interceptions with five and passes defended with 15. The 2002 season ended with Brooks' selection to the Pro Bowl for the sixth straight time and with his games-started streak having reached 128 after having started every Tampa Bay game for seven straight seasons.

It was finally time for the pass rushers to take a back seat to the smaller, quicker linebacker who could cover any receiver and blow up any play better than anyone else in the league whether it was a run or a pass. Now the whole league and all the fans of the NFL saw what the players and people surrounding the Buccaneers had seen since 1995—the best linebacker in football.

Teammate John Lynch told Greg Garber on the *ESPN* website, "He's just a tremendous man of character. He does his best in every aspect of life, and I don't care if (he's) playing board games, he's going to want to win. He wants to be the best whether it's playing or helping the community or helping kids. A lot of people put their money out there, Derrick puts his time and money in, and I think that's what separates him."

Sources

Periodicals

Boys' Life, September 2000.
ESPN The Magazine, September 15, 2003.
Florida Times Union, July 27, 1997.
New York Times, June 23, 2003.
Sporting News, July 31, 2000.

On-line

"Brooks' Big Heart Leaves Teammates in Awe," *ESPN,* http://espn.go.com/nfl/playoffs02/columnist/2003/0123/1497846.html (January 20, 2004).
"Derrick Brooks," *NFL website,* www.nfl.com/players/playerpage/3160/bios (January 20, 2004).

—Michael J. Watkins

Janice Rogers Brown

1949—

Judge

Of the various jurists nominated by President George W. Bush to fill court vacancies, several have stirred controversy and inspired Democrats in the United States Senate to dig in their heels in resistance. Perhaps none was more controversial, however, than that of Janice Rogers Brown, a justice of the California Supreme Court whose strong opinions and outspoken mode of expression polarized observers of the judicial scene and American politics in general. To some, Brown was a brilliant and independent-minded jurist who probed deeply in questioning the assumptions behind previous judicial decisions. Others considered her a right-wing extremist who played a part in an effort on the President's part to change the orientation of the nation's judicial system.

The daughter of a sharecropper, Brown was born in Greenville, Alabama, on May 11, 1949. She grew up during the segregation era, and attended all-black schools. Two grandmothers taught her to prize dignity and hard work, and one of them told her about Fred Gray, the pioneering African-American attorney in Alabama who defended Rosa Parks and Martin Luther King, Jr., in court, and who played an important role early in the civil rights revolution. If her family had had a motto, Brown was quoted as saying by the *Montgomery Advertiser,* it would have been "Don't snivel." The result of this upbringing was a young woman who thought for herself. She was also determined to become a lawyer.

The family moved to Sacramento, California, when Brown was a teenager, and she attended California State University at Sacramento, graduating in 1974. During her college years Brown espoused many of the liberal ideas of the time. "I'm sure you've heard the saying, 'If you aren't a liberal before you're 30 you have no heart, and if you are not a conservative before you're 40 you have no brain,'" Brown told the *San Francisco Chronicle.* "That saying applies to me." Her change of heart came at the University of California at Los Angeles Law School, where Brown earned a law degree in 1977. She came to believe that the court system was an inappropriate mechanism for effecting broad social change.

Brown married twice and had one son. Her first husband, Allen, died in 1988, and three years later, she married Dewey Parker, a jazz musician. A reclusive person, she tended to avoid the public spotlight. This

At a Glance . . .

Born on May 11, 1949, in Greenville, AL; married Allen (died 1988); married Dewey Parker (a jazz musician), 1991; children: one son. *Education:* California State University at Sacramento, BA, 1974; University of California at Los Angeles, JD, 1977.

Career: California Department of Justice, deputy attorney general, 1979-87; California Business, Transportation, and Housing Agency, deputy secretary and general counsel, 1987-91; office of California Governor Pete Wilson, legal affairs secretary, 1991-94; California Court of Appeals, associate justice, 1994-96; California Supreme Court, justice, 1996–.

Addresses: *Office*—California Supreme Court, 302 SE St., South Tower, 9th Floor, San Francisco, CA 94107.

was easy enough to do during the long stretch of her life when she worked as an attorney in the middle levels of a vast state bureaucracy. Admitted to the California Bar at the end of 1977, she served as deputy legislative counsel from 1979, deputy attorney general from 1979-87, and deputy secretary and general counsel for the California Business, Transportation, and Housing Agency from 1987-89. From 1989-91 she worked in private practice.

Brown's rise to prominence began when she joined the administration of California's Republican governor Pete Wilson in 1991. Working with Wilson on such issues as death-penalty cases, she gained the ear of the crusading governor, who was identified with several high-profile conservative causes. Wilson appointed Brown to the Third District California Court of Appeals in 1994 and nominated her for a State Supreme Court vacancy two years later.

By that time, Brown had already begun to generate controversy. A 27-member California Bar panel gave her a rare "not qualified" rating, pointing not only to Brown's scant two years as a judge, but also to the subjective nature of her opinions, which the panel said tended to disregard legal precedent when it conflicted with Brown's personal views. But Wilson refused to abandon the nomination. And Brown claimed a number of defenders within California's judicial community, including some who disagreed with her conservative philosophy. In May of 1996 Brown was confirmed by the state legislature and elevated to the California Supreme Court.

Although Brown rarely granted interviews, and lived in semi-seclusion with her husband in a gated community in suburban Sacramento, she was never far from the center of the political whirlwind. Brown generally aligned herself with the court's most conservative wing, voting in favor of drug testing for job applicants to public agencies and for allowing cities to restrict the movements of gang members. In 1997 Brown dissented from the court's ruling allowing minors to obtain abortions without the consent of a parent or judge. Particularly galling to many African-American activists was Brown's 2000 decision upholding Proposition 209, a voter-approved initiative banning preferential treatment for minorities and women by California's educational institutions and public agencies.

Yet Brown sometimes took positions generally affiliated with a liberal judicial philosophy, strongly dissenting, for example, from a court decision that upheld a police search of a man stopped for riding his bicycle on the wrong side of the street. Sometimes it was the language rather than the content of Brown's opinions that antagonized lawmakers and fellow jurists, and the sweeping nature of her decisions left her open to criticism. Her decision to uphold Proposition 209 contained a lengthy repudiation of the entire history of affirmative action, which Chief Justice Ronald George, according to the *San Francisco Chronicle,* condemned as "unnecessary and inappropriate."

In 2003 President Bush nominated Brown to fill a vacancy on the U.S Court of Appeals for the District of Columbia Circuit, a key post that historically had often served as a stepping stone to the U.S. Supreme Court. The battle lines were drawn in the U.S. Senate, where liberal members had already mounted filibusters against several Bush judicial nominees. Arguing that Brown held views well out of the judicial mainstream, Democratic senators pointed especially to a 2000 speech that Brown gave before the conservative Federalist Society, in which, according to the *Houston Chronicle,* she referred to the enactment of the New Deal reforms of the 1930s as "the triumph of our own socialist revolution."

Brown responded that the speech was meant to stir up new intellectual currents, and that she, having worked for most of her life in the public sector, would readily agree that government had an appropriate role in delivering services. Once again some liberals, including presidential candidate the Rev. Al Sharpton, rose to Brown's defense. In November of 2003, Brown's nomination was approved on a party-line vote by the Senate Judiciary Committee. The nomination seemed likely to encounter a filibuster on the Senate floor. But whatever its ultimate fate, Janice Rogers Brown had clearly established herself as a major force in American jurisprudence, a bare-knuckled advocate for her interpretations of American legal principles.

Sources

Periodicals

Atlanta Journal-Constitution, October 23, 2003, p. A3; November 6, 2003, p. A3.

Austin American-Statesman, October 23, 2003, p. A6.

Houston Chronicle, November 7, 2003, p. 4.

Montgomery Advertiser, October 23, 2003, p. A1.

St. Petersburg Times, November 23, 2003, p. P7.

San Francisco Chronicle, May 3, 1996, p. A1; August 16, 1996, p. A21; April 29, 2001, p. A6; July 26, 2003, p. A1l; October 21, 2003, p. A1; October 26, 2003, p. D1.

Washington Times, November 6, 2003, p. A4.

—James M. Manheim

Octavia Butler

1947—

Science fiction writer

"I didn't decide to become a science fiction writer," Octavia Butler claimed in an interview with Frances M. Beal in the *Black Scholar.* "It just happened." Butler— the only recognized black woman writer in the genre— has become one of sci-fi's leading lights, having published the *Patternmaster* series, the *Xenogenesis Trilogy,* the celebrated historical fantasy *Kindred,* and 1993's highly praised dystopian saga *The Parable of the Sower,* among other works. Along with "cyberpunk" novelist William Gibson, Terri Sutton of the *LA Weekly* listed Butler among "science fiction's most thoughtful writers." *Vibe* magazine's Carol Cooper declared that what Gibson "does for young, disaffected white fans of high tech and low life, Octavia Estelle Butler does for people of color. She gives us a future."

Butler's work has helped put race and gender into the foreground of speculative fiction, exploring these and other social and political issues with a developed sense of ambiguity and difficulty. Such explorations, Cooper noted in *Vibe,* were previously absent from science fiction: "In the '70s, Butler's work exploded into this ideological vacuum like an incipient solar system." As the award-winning author told *Black Scholar,* "A science fiction writer has the freedom to do absolutely anything. The limits are the imagination of the writer."

Inpsired Early By Science Fiction

Butler was born on June 22, 1947, in Pasadena, California. Her father died during her infancy and her mother's occupation provided Butler with early lessons in racism and economic inequity: "My mother was a maid and sometimes she took me to work with her when I was very small and she had no one to stay with me," Butler recalled to *Black Scholar.* "I used to see her going to back doors, being talked about while she was standing right there, and basically being treated like a non-person." Butler recognized these kinds of working conditions as a tradition in her own ancestry, and that legacy helped alienate her from her peers, who in the 1960s blamed their parents' generation for contemporary problems. The realizations sparked by these issues helped inspire Butler's novel *Kindred,* in which a modern black woman travels back in time to the antebellum South and confronts slavery first-hand.

Butler discovered her vocation at an early age. "I was writing when I was 10 years old," she told *Black Scholar.* "I was writing my own little stories and when I was 12, I was watching a bad science fiction movie [*Devil Girl From Mars*] and decided that I could write a better story than that. And I turned off the TV and proceeded to try, and I've been writing science fiction ever since." The story upon which Butler embarked would form the basis for her first published novel and the rest of the *Patternmaster* series.

Butler later attended Pasadena City College, winning a short-story contest during her first semester. After receiving her Associate's degree in 1968, she moved on to California State University at Los Angeles, taking "everything but nursing classes," as she recollected to Lisa See of *Publishers Weekly.* "I'm a little bit dyslexic and worried about killing people." Thanks to the Open Door Program at the Screen Writers' Guild, Butler was

At a Glance . . .

Born Octavia Estelle Butler on June 22, 1947, in Pasadena, CA; daughter of Laurice and Octavia M. (Guy) Butler. *Education:* Pasadena City College, AA, 1968; attended California State University at Los Angeles, 1969; attended University of California at Los Angeles, 1970; attended Clarion Science Fiction Writers' Workshop, 1970.

Career: Freelance writer, 1970-76; author, 1976–.

Selected awards: Hugo Award for "Speech Sounds," 1984; Nebula, Hugo, and Locus awards for *Bloodchild,* 1985; Nebula Award nomination for *The Evening and the Morning and the Night,* 1987; MacArthur Foundation Fellowship Award recipient, 1995.

Addresses: *Office*—P.O. Box 25400, Seattle, WA, 98125.

able to attend a class taught by esteemed science fiction writer Harlan Ellison. The venerated Ellison was supportive of her work, offering to publish one of her stories in an anthology and encouraging her to attend the Clarion Science Fiction Writers' Workshop in Pennsylvania, described as a "boot camp" for would-be practitioners of the genre.

Butler spent six weeks at Clarion. "We were all social retards," she quipped to *Publishers Weekly* about her class there, "but we seemed to get along with each other." She elaborated on this sense of isolation among her peers, believing that "to write science fiction you do have to be kind of a loner, live in your head, and, at the same time, have a love for talking. Clarion was a good place for that." The workshop published an anthology in 1970 that included one of her stories. Ellison's collection, meanwhile, didn't get published.

Found First Success With Patternmaster

After leaving Clarion, Butler hit something of a wall professionally, and ended up taking a series of low-paying jobs. She supported herself and woke during the wee hours to write. She originally only wrote short stories but finally deciding to undertake a novel near the end of 1974. The result was *Patternmaster,* which she executed rather quickly after getting over her fear of novelistic length. She sent the manuscript to Doubleday where an editor saw promise in the story. It was only after Butler made some of the major revisions sug-

gested by the editor that Doubleday agreed to publish the book, and by 1976 *Patternmaster* was on bookstore shelves.

Patternmaster addressed issues of class division with a plot revolving around telepathic people known as "Patternists" and their domination over the mute, nontelepathic masses and mutant beings called "Clayarks." *Vibe's* Carol Cooper praised Butler's characterizations, stating that "her lead characters—whether telepaths or human/alien half-breeds—remained assertive black homegirls with attitude."

Butler wrote her next novel, a sequel to *Patternmaster,* while Doubleday was reviewing her first. Published in 1977, *Mind of My Mind* followed the saga into the next generation, as did the third book in the series, *Survivor* in 1978. The series sold well, but the people at Doubleday were still leery of publishing science fiction that attempted to bring in both African-American and female audiences, groups that had notoriously stayed away from the genre. Hence, Butler interrupted her work on the series to write a very different story.

Deleved Into History With Kindred

Motivated by considerations of what previous generations of black people—especially women—had experienced, Butler wrote *Kindred,* a novel in which a present-day black woman, Dana, travels back in time to Maryland during the time of slavery. There she confronts a white ancestor whom she must rescue repeatedly in order to preserve her own future. Writing *Kindred* helped Butler exorcise some of her feelings about generational distrust. "If my mother hadn't put up with those humiliations, I wouldn't have eaten very well or lived very comfortably," she reflected to *Publishers Weekly.* "So I wanted to write a novel that would make others feel the history: the pain and fear that black people had to live through in order to survive."

In the March/April 1986 issue of *Black Scholar,* Butler discussed the trouble she had placing *Kindred* because it didn't fit into any preconceived literary category. "I sent it off to a number of different publishers because it obviously was not science fiction. There's absolutely no science in it. It was the kind of fantasy that nobody had really thought of as fantasy because after all, it doesn't fall into the sword and sorcery or pseudo-medieval fantasy that *everyone* expects with lots of magic being practiced." Eventually Doubleday published the novel in 1979, but as fiction rather than science fiction.

Kindred met considerable praise upon its arrival, and has continued to generate discussion. "Probably no contemporary African-American novelist has so successfully exercised the imagination of her readers with acute representations of familial and historical relations as has Octavia Butler," surmised Ashraf H. A. Rushdy in *College English,* "and nowhere more so than in ... *Kindred.*"

Won Hugo Award

Coming off the success of *Kindred,* Doubleday published *Wild Seed* in 1980, the fourth book in the *Patternmaster* series. St. Martin's Press took over the series in 1984 and published the fifth book, *Clay's Ark.* By that time, Butler's work had begun to receive more serious recognition from her peers. She won a Hugo Award from the World Science Fiction Society in 1984, for the short story "Speech Sounds"; her short novel *Bloodchild,* which explored issues of power surrounding childbirth, won the Nebula, Hugo, and Locus awards the following year. Her novella *The Evening and the Morning and the Night* was nominated for a 1987 Nebula award as well.

In the late 1980s Butler embarked on a new series of novels, the *Xenogenesis Trilogy,* which began in 1987 with *Dawn: Xenogenesis.* The series depicts the plight of human beings who must choose between certain death or hybridization with a race of rational, compassionate space-faring creatures. Both the characters and the reader are forced to question what it means to be human, and to what lengths human beings might go to preserve their species.

As Eric White wrote in his analysis of the series for *Science-Fiction Studies,* despite the initial horror induced in the human survivors by the alien beings— known as Oankali—who want to mate with them, "the loss of human specificity entailed in hybridization with the irreducibly other is, in the last analysis, depicted affirmatively." The next two books in the *Xenogenesis Trilogy, Adulthood Rites* and *Imago,* were published in 1988 and 1989, respectively. "The *Xenogenesis* books," wrote Sutton in the *LA Weekly,* "are weighted with the horror and rebellion of what are in effect an enslaved people: change is no cheap date."

Found New Direction

As Butler attempted to leave behind the *Xenogenesis* books and move in a new direction, she experienced what she alternately described to Lisa See of *Publishers Weekly,* as a "literary metamorphosis" and "literary menopause." Taking a new direction wasn't as easy as she expected: "I knew that I wanted my next book to be about a woman who starts a religion, but everything I wrote seemed like garbage.... I also had this deep-seated feeling that wanting power, seeking power, was evil." She finally resorted to expressing her ideas in poetry, which became the expressive medium of her next novel's protagonist. "I'm the kind of person who looks for a complex way to say something," she told See. "Poetry simplifies it." This simplification helped her to conceive *Parable of the Sower.*

In *Parable of the Sower,* half-black, half-Latina protagonist Lauren Oya Olamina escapes the walled city of the middle class to venture into the unknown "outside," where she ends up leading an attempt to build a new human community. Sprinkled throughout the text are quotations from Lauren's poems, called "Earthseed: The Books of the Living." *L.A. Weekly*'s Terri Sutton called the novel "the plainer sister to Butler's elaborate, luminous Xenogenesis series," a tale in which change becomes, simply, God. As Butler herself put it to See, "One of the first poems I wrote sounded like a nursery rhyme. It begins: 'God is power,'and goes on to: 'God is malleable.' This concept gave me what I needed."

Shortly after publishing *Parable of the Sower* Butler received perhaps one of the most lucrative honors of her career when she was named a recipient of a Catherine T. MacArthur Foundation Fellowship Award. The award, given to the brightest and most promising African Americans in their field, allows the recipient to pursue new and ground-breaking activities without worry of financial backing. When Butler received the fellowship in 1995, she was presented with a prize of $295,000 which would be paid out over five years. When asked what she would do with the money by *Jet* magazine, Butler said that she would continue to write new and genre breaking science fiction in order to reach a wider variety of readers interested in the genre, especially those readers of the African-American community.

True to her word, Butler continued to write significant science fiction which commented on social issues. In a follow-up to *Parable of the Sower,* Butler produced the critically acclaimed *Parable of the Talents* in 1998, which traced the path of Lauren Olamina as she attempted to reconcile her world by starting a community called Acorn. Much like *Parable of the Sower, Parable of the Talents* is more a study of the character of human beings instead of an action or sci-fi genre novel. Butler said to *Poets & Writers Magazine* that she felt the need to continue to write about the future world she had created in *Parable of the Sower* because "I examined a lot of the problems in *Parable of the Sower,* and now I'd like to consider some of the solutions. Not *propose* solutions, you understand— what I want to do is look at some of the solutions that human beings can come up with when they're feeling uncertain and frightened."

Collected Works Published

In 1995 Butler's early work was compiled for the first time in a book called *Bloodchild: And Other Stories.* The collected work included her Hugo and Nebula award winning story "Bloodchild," as well as "The Evening of Morning Sounds," "Near of Kin," "Speech Sounds," and "Crossover." Also included were insights from Butler herself, including an afterword to each short story and two essays, "Positive Obsessions" and "Furor Scribendi," which talk about the habit of writing and overcoming personal challenges, including racism and poverty, to achieve a goal. According to *Publishers Weekly,* this book was one of the first instances where the reading public was able to "clarify what excites and motivates this exceptionally talented writer."

However, Butler has always been very open about what types of themes and issues her writing deals with. "I don't write utopian science fiction because I don't believe that imperfect humans can form a perfect society," Butler confessed in *Black Scholar.* "Nobody is perfect," she insisted to *Vibe.* "One of the things I've discovered even with teachers using my books is that people tend to look for 'good guys' and 'bad guys,' which always annoys the hell out of me. I'd be bored to death writing that way. But because that's the only pattern they have, they try to fit my work into it."

Most importantly, she tried, in her later writings, including the *Parable* tales, to explore issues of nation building and community building without some of the fantastic ingredients she and other science fiction writers had relied upon in the past. She asserted to *Vibe,* "Part of what I wanted to do in the new book was to begin a new society that might actually get somewhere, even though nobody has any special abilities, no aliens intervene, and no supernatural beings intervene. The people just have to do it themselves." Sutton seconded this in *LA Weekly:* "In Butler's bible, the meek don't inherit the earth: they refuse both the earth and the idea of meekness."

Though much of Butler's work confronts the sort of bedrock difficulties of co-existence that many of her fellow science fiction authors tend to avoid, Butler has repeatedly emphasized that she finds the genre intensely liberating. When asked by *Black Scholar* what drew her to the form, she replied "The freedom of it; it's potentially the freest genre in existence."

Selected writings

Patternmaster, Doubleday, 1976.
Mind of My Mind, Doubleday, 1977.
Survivor, Doubleday, 1978.
Kindred, Doubleday, 1979.
Wild Seed, Doubleday, 1980.
Clay's Ark, St. Martin's, 1984.

Dawn: Xenogenesis, Warner Books, 1987.
Adulthood Rites, Warner Books, 1988.
Imago, Warner Books, 1989.
Lilith's Brood, SFBC, 1989.
Parable of the Sower, Four Walls Eight Windows, 1993.
Bloodchild: And Other Stories, Four Walls Eight Windows, 1995.
Parable of the Talents, Seven Stories Press, 1998.

Also contributed to anthologies *Clarion,* edited by Robin Scott Wilson, New American Library, 1970; *The Last Dangerous Visions,* edited by Harlan Ellison, Harper, 1978; and *Chrysalis 4,* 1979. Contributor to periodicals, including *Isaac Asimov's Science Fiction Magazine, Omni, American Visions, Essence, Future Life, Transmission,* and *Writers of the Future.*

Sources

Books

Black Writers, Gale, 1993.
The Complete Marquis Who's Who, Marquis Who's Who, 2003.

Periodicals

Black Scholar, March/April 1986, pp. 14-18.
College English, February 1993, pp. 135-57.
Emerge, June 1994, pp. 65-6.
Jet, July 3, 1995, pp. 34-5.
L.A. Weekly, March 4, 1994, pp. 37-8.
Library Journal, November 1, 1998, p. 123.
Publishers Weekly, December 13, 1993, pp. 50-1; August 21, 1995, pp. 50-1; October 19, 1998, p. 60.
Science-Fiction Studies, 20 (1993), pp. 394-408.
Vibe, February 1994.

On-line

"Octavia E(stelle) Butler," *Contemporary Authors On-line,* reproduced in *Biography Resource Center,* www.galegroup.com/servlet/BioRC (September 24, 2003).

—Simon Glickman and Ralph G. Zerbonia

Mary Schmidt Campbell

1947—

Educator, administrator, curator, art historian

Dean of the Tisch School of the Arts at New York University (NYU), Mary Schmidt Campbell has been an effective advocate for the role of the arts in public life and a vital participant in New York City's cultural scene. *Crain's New York Business* selected her as one of the city's 100 most influential women in 1999, and she is a reliable presence on advisory committees and boards of directors serving many of the city's top cultural institutions. Campbell came to her high-visibility educational post after a long and varied career that has included work in the field of visual arts and a position as a public arts administrator.

Campbell was born in Philadelphia on October 21, 1947, the daughter of Harvey N. Schmidt and Elaine Harris Schmidt. As a young girl she was enthralled by the world of film, and would often spend the entire day at her neighborhood movie theater. "A friend of our family's took me and her children to see *The King and I*," Campbell recalled in an interview on the *Kodak* website. "When the movie was over, she said, 'Mary, it's time to go.' I absolutely would not move. So we sat through the whole film a second time."

Campbell attended prestigious Swarthmore University in suburban Philadelphia, and married George Campbell, a physicist in training, in 1968 while she was still in school. The family took up residence in the Greenwich Village neighborhood of New York City, and the couple had three children over a period of 20 years.

Campbell graduated from Swarthmore in 1969 with a degree in English literature, and took a job for two years teaching English to refugees in the African nation of Zambia. She described on the *Kodak* website that she still became "completely and psychologically engaged" when the weekly film delivery arrived from the United States. But after she returned home to the United States, Campbell began to pursue another interest, that of art history. She enrolled in graduate school, earning a master's degree from the University of Syracuse in 1973. She was awarded a Ford Fellowship that year to pursue further art-related historical research. During this period, Campell also wrote about art for the *Syracuse New Times* and curated several museum exhibitions.

In 1977 Campbell was hired as executive director of the Studio Museum in Harlem, building it over the ten years she spent there into one of New York's premier cultural institutions. By the time she left the Studio Museum in 1987, Campbell had completed a Ph.D. at Syracuse University. She submitted as her dissertation a study of the African-American artist Romare Bearden, a work that would later become part of a book of essays co-written with another author.

Campbell has also written numerous articles on the arts. Some of those articles were focused on the subject that occupied Campbell during the next phase of her career: that of public arts policy. In 1987, at the invitation of Mayor Edward Koch, Campbell accepted the post of commissioner of cultural affairs for the City of New York. In that capacity, Campbell oversaw budgeting and capital improvement outlays for some of the largest and most important cultural institutions in the world—the Metropolitan Museum of Art and Carnegie Hall, among others. She also supervised the

At a Glance . . .

Born on October 21, 1947, in Philadelphia, PA; daughter of Harvey N. and Elaine Harris Schmidt; married George Campbell (a physicist), 1968; children: Garikai, Sekou, Britt. *Education:* Swarthmore College, BA, 1969; Syracuse University, MA, 1973; PhD, 1982. *Politics:* Democrat.

Career: *Syracuse New Times,* art editor, 1973-77; Everson Museum, Syracuse, NY, curator and guest curator, 1974-76; Studio Museum in Harlem, New York, NY, executive director, 1977-87; City of New York, commissioner of cultural affairs, 1987-91; Tisch School of the Arts, New York University, dean, 1991-.

Selected memberships: Tony Award nominating committee, member, 1996-98, 2000-02; Brooklyn Museum of Art, member, board of trustees, 1999-2002.

Selected awards: Ford Fellowship, 1973-77; Rockefeller Fellowship in the Humanities, 1985.

Addresses: *Office*—721 Broadway, 12th floor, New York, NY 10003.

awarding of block grants to more than 500 arts groups in the city, ranging from the famous to the fledgling, in an effort to help the department serve a wider range of New York's population.

Campbell, however, was presiding over the division of a shrinking pie, as federal and municipal arts budgets shrank during the recessionary years of the late 1980s and early 1990s. The cultural community, Campbell lamented in a *Back Stage* interview, had not been successful in convincing the public and power brokers that "culture is an essential part of the civic infrastructure. We know that fire and sanitation and police are, but we're always questioned when it comes to culture."

After she left city government for academia once again, Campbell continued to hammer away at this theme during her numerous public speaking engagements. Imagination, she told a Hawaii audience in 2002, is a muscle. She was quoted by the *Honolulu Advertiser* as saying, "If you don't exercise it, it gets saggy and atrophies. When we take the arts out, we remove the opportunity for students to use their imagination. That, over time, will have an adverse effect on the way we conduct business and finding new ways of doing things."

When she took the job of Dean of the Tisch School of the Arts at New York University (NYU) in 1991, Campbell was in some ways returning to her first love, that of film. The school comprised three separate institutes, two of them concerned with film and one with the performing arts in general. The school's alumni included such prestigious industry figures as Spike Lee, Martin Scorcese, and Billy Crystal. Campbell boosted the school's enrollment and funding, and drew on her expertise in the public arena to establish a new Department of Art and Public Policy, and subsequently served as the department's chair.

Campbell's general educational philosophy in her work at NYU grew out of her ideas about the relationship between the arts and the wider society, but that philosophy was also shaped by contemporary events. She was quoted on the *Kodak* website as saying, "We're training [students] to be citizens, to go out and have some responsibility towards the world, to understand that they have a role in the world, and to make sure that they have the intellectual capacity, along with their creative and imaginative capacity, to be able to speak to that world, and speak about that world."

Campbell found that the events of September 11, 2001, lent a new urgency to her efforts to forge links between creative artists and the public. "September 11 brought home the idea that we can't cloister ourselves," Campbell told *Kodak*. "That event has made our students incredibly intense and focused and serious." It seemed sure bet that another generation of America's creative students would be influenced by the contributions and work of Mary Schmidt Campbell.

Sources

Periodicals

Back Stage, August 2, 1991, p. 1.
Honolulu Advertiser, October 13, 2002, p. D11.

On-line

"Interview with Dean Mary Schmidt Campbell," *Kodak,* www.kodak.com/US/en/motion/students/deans/campbell.shtml (December 30, 2003).
"Mary Schmidt Campbell," *Center for Arts and Culture,* www.culturalpolicy.org/archive/networks/listing.cfm?ID=2749 (December 30, 2003).
"Mary Schmidt Campbell," *History Makers,* www.thehistorymakers.com/historymakers/biography/biography.asp?bioindex=152 (December 30, 2003).
"Mary Schmidt Campbell," *New York University Office of Public Affairs,* www.nyu.edu/publicaffairs/leadership/academic/campbell/campbell.html (December 30, 2003).

—James M. Manheim

Victoria A. Cargill

19(?)(?)—

Physician, AIDS researcher

In 1998 Dr. Victoria A. Cargill was appointed as director of minority research and director of clinical studies at the Office of AIDS Research (OAR) in the National Institutes of Health, Bethesda, Maryland. She has spent much of her career as a physician and a researcher on the disease, and has made it her personal charge to educate at-risk groups about prevention and treatment methods.

Cargill's introduction to medicine began at a young age. Her father was a licensed practical nurse and paramedic in New York City, and she was intrigued by his many stories about his work. When her family moved to an 84-acre farm, she became interested in the health and care of the farm animals. A profile of Cargill on the *National Institutes of Health, Office of Scientific Education* website described Cargill's first patient, a rooster with a broken leg. Cargill set the rooster's leg with tongue depressors in an effort to heal the break. As her animal patients on the farm increased in number, so did her fondness for science and medicine. After a high school biology class introduced her to the subject of genetics, Cargill became focused on the subject, and it seemed inevitable that she would become a physician.

After graduating from high school, Cargill attended Mt. Holyoke College in South Hadley, Massachusetts, earning a bachelor's degree in biological science with the honor of magna cum laude. She earned her M.D. degree from Boston University School of Medicine, and while in medical school she became involved in community outreach programs for sickle cell patients and homeless alcoholic men. During her medical school tenure she received both the Bertha Curtis Award for clinical excellence and the Solomon Carter Fuller Award for compassion in medicine.

Cargill completed her medical residency at Brigham and Women's Hospital in Boston, and did two years of community service at the Brookside Park Family Life Center in Jamaica Plain, Massachusetts. She then returned to academia, where she entered the Andrew Mellon Fellowship in Clinical Epidemiology program at the University of Pennsylvania, earning a master of science degree in clinical epidemiology. At the conclusion of the program she was hired by Case Western Reserve University in Cleveland, Ohio, as an assistant professor of Medicine, and later was promoted to the rank of full professor, the first African-American woman at Case Western to obtain that rank.

Despite the many demands on her time, Cargill became involved in other ventures. She founded a program in the Greater Cleveland area called Stopping AIDS Is My Mission (SAMM), and served as the organization's executive director. SAMM's message about AIDS prevention and treatment was aimed at young people, particularly those at the middle and high school levels, and Cargill's project was able to reach more than 80,000 teens in the Cleveland area. While working with the SAMM program, Cargill traveled to schools to speak, educating young people about the dangers of AIDS. Today SAMM continues to thrive and has become part of the AIDS Training and Education Center network.

In 1998 Cargill accepted a position with the Office of AIDS Research (OAR), a division of the National

At a Glance . . .

Born Victoria A. Cargill; daughter of a paramedic and licensed practical nurse; married; two children. *Education:* Mt. Holyoke College, BA; Boston University School of Medicine, MD; University of Pennsylvania, certificate in epidemiology; MS, clinical epidemiology.

Career: Case Western Reserve University, Cleveland, Ohio, assistant professor of Medicine, 1980s, professor of Medicine, 1990s, adjunct professor of Medicine, 1990s–; Stopping AIDS Is My Mission (SAMM), founder and executive director, 1980s–; Office of AIDS Research (OAR), director of minority research, director of clinical research, 1998–; Dept. Health and Human Services, Washington, DC, acting director, office of HIV/AIDS, 1990s–.

Selected memberships: American Public Health Association; International AIDS Society—USA; National Institutes of Health, AIDS Research Prevention Sciences, past member, advisory panel.

Selected awards: Bertha Curtis Award; Solomon Carter Fuller Award; Cleveland Chapter, Council of Negro Business and Professional Women, Women of the Year award; African-American Women's Community Award, Cleveland, Ohio; assistant secretary for Health, Department of Heath and Human Services, citation for Outstanding Team Performance.

Addresses: *Office*—c/o National Institutes of Health (NIH), 9000 Rockville Pike, Bethesda, MD 20892.

Institutes of Health (NIH) in Bethesda, Maryland, becoming the agency's director of minority research and director of clinical studies. According to the *Office of AIDS Research (NIH)* website, OAR "is responsible for the scientific, budgetary, legislative, and policy elements of the NIH AIDS research program." In this capacity, Cargill has focused on the impact of HIV and AIDS on minorities. Her position has allowed her to form professional liaisons with other federal agencies, as well as with community organizations that have similar interests.

Cargill has authored and co-written numerous research reports, studies, and abstracts. Her research has included such topics as those of condom use among poor inner-city women, and the path that the HIV virus follows in order to infect a single cell. She has also been committed to educating the medical community and the public about AIDS therapy, including antiretroviral therapy, or HAART—a drug cocktail that can suppress the replication of HIV-infected cells in the body.

While the fight against AIDS is an ongoing battle, it appears that Cargill's efforts have not been in vain. An article published in the *American Journal of Public Health* reported that Cargill and her colleagues studied HIV prevention in low-income housing developments. They found that with intervention, the percentage of women who had unprotected sex decreased nearly 13 percent over the course of two months and the percentage of women who used condoms increased by 17 percent. Though the research targeted only one community, it proved that intervention was in fact effective, a small but significant victory in an area of great need.

In an interview reported on the website for *The Body: An AIDS and HIV Information Resource*, Cargill reported that for women, there is a great need for prevention education and dialogue about the increased risk of cancers, like cervical cancer, in HIV-infected women: "A broader societal view dictates that we consider the economic futures of the women who are becoming infected. Until we offer greater incentives and opportunities for economic growth, the complex forces of racism, poverty and social alienation will continue to affect women and serve as fuel for the HIV epidemic, robbing these women of their very lives."

Cargill continues to conduct research and participate in educational forums. Her efforts with the NIH continue, with her appointment as acting director of the Office of HIV/AIDS Policy for the Department of Health and Human Services in Washington, D.C. Although her work through the NIH constitutes her most recognized efforts, Cargill continues to treat HIV-infected patients in the Washington, D.C., area, where the numbers of HIV and AIDS cases are as high as those in some African countries. Cargill has maintained her teaching position with Case Western as an adjunct professor of Medicine, and is the mother of two children.

Sources

Periodicals

American Journal of Public Health, January 2000.
Ebony, October 2003.

On-line

"About OAR," *Office of AIDS Research, National Institutes of Health,* www.nih/gov/od/oar/about/about_oar.htm#nathst (December 28, 2003).
"Doctor's Opinion, Dr. Victoria Cargill," *The Body: An AIDS and HIV Information Resource,* www.thebody.com/features/women/doc3.html (December 20, 2003).

"Haart 101: What you Need to Know; Why It's Important!" *National Minority AIDS Council,* www. nmac.org/publications/transcripts/cargillNov18chat .htm (December 28, 2003).

"Victoria Cargill," *National Institutes of Health, Office of Science Education,* www.science.education. nih.gov/spkbureau.nsf/speakersmenu?openform (December 20, 2003).

—Shellie M. Saunders

Tamika Catchings

1979—

Professional basketball player

The daughter of a professional basketball player, Tamika Catchings grew up immersed in the game. "Whatever I wanted to work on, [my father] was there," she told the Westchester, N.Y., *Journal News.* "We were always going to the gym. He was helping me out, helping me with my post moves, making sure that I took my jump shot and developed my 3-point shot, too." Catchings was an excellent study, possessing a fearlessness that stunned her father. "She's much more aggressive and creative on offense than I ever was," he told *Sports Illustrated.* Her skill on the court earned her honors in high school, college, and in the Women's National Basketball Association (WNBA). It has also earned her extensive praise. "Catchings is the now and the future of the game," Basketball Hall-of-Famer Nancy Lieberman told the *New York Times.* "I've played and coached against the best players in the world, and no one has played like she does."

Found Haven in Basketball

Catchings was born on July 21, 1979, in Stratford, New Jersey, to Harvey and Wanda Catchings. Her father, an 11-season NBA player, taught all three of his children the game. "They all enjoyed playing," he told the *New York Times,* "but Mika is like an addict." After retiring from the NBA, Harvey Catchings settled his family in Deerfield, Illinois, a suburb of Chicago, where Catchings became even more focused on basketball. Born with a severe hearing loss in both ears, Catchings had to wear boxy hearing aids as a child. Almost instinctively she turned to basketball as a way to deal with this adversity. "Basketball was everything to me," she told *Sports Illustrated.* "Whenever I got mad, I would play basketball; whenever I was happy, I would play basketball. Anything I was feeling, I'd play basketball." In the same article her father explained, "I think the fact that people considered it a disability really pushed her. Where others might use a disability as an excuse, she used it as a driving force."

The more time she spent playing ball, the more competitive Catchings became. "She goes out to win at all costs, whatever it takes," her father told *Knight Ridder/Tribune News Service.* One of her coaches at the University of Tennessee would later tell *Sports Illustrated,* "She cannot stand to lose." Fortunately for her disposition, Catchings didn't lose much during high

coach who would push me," she told *Sports Illustrated.* The two were a good match and, according to the *New York Times,* "Catchings bloomed under Summitt's exacting system."

Earned Numerous Honors

Catchings proved herself worthy as a team member, scoring an average of 18.2 points per game that season, a Tennessee freshman record. She also set high standards in rebounds and assists. Her skill helped drive Tennessee to the NCAA 1998 tournament, where she scored a team-high 27 points, and felt the thrill of a national championship when Tennessee beat Louisiana Tech 93 to 75. Many thought that Catchings should have won the Most Valuable Player (MVP) award for that game, but the honor went to another teammate. In her typically humble fashion, Catchings shrugged it off, telling *Sporting News,* "In my eyes, it doesn't really matter. We won the championship. Who cares who got what honors?" Catchings did end up with several honors, including the Naismith National Freshman of the Year award and the U.S. Basketball Writers Association Freshman of the Year award. She was also named a Kodak All-American team member. The Kodak team, made up of the top ten NCAA women's basketball players, is one of the oldest and most prestigious honors in college basketball, and Catchings was only the fourth freshman to be appointed to their ranks.

Catchings continued to rack up awards over her next three years at Tennessee. She became only the second Lady Volunteer in the school's history to score 2,000 points. During her junior year she was once again singled out for a Naismith trophy, this time for National Player of the Year. Also in 2000 she received an ESPY award—the sports world's answer to the Oscars—for College Player of the Year. She landed three more nominations to the Kodak All-American team, becoming only the fourth female athlete to make the team four times in a row. Other all-star teams that nominated her to their rosters included the Associated Press, *Sports Illustrated, Sporting Journal,* and the *Women's Basketball Journal.* In 2000 she demonstrated her mettle by rejoining the Lady Volunteers during the NCCA Mideast Regional playoffs after suffering a pain-searing ankle sprain in the first half of the game. Her steely dedication earned her the Most Outstanding Player honors for the game.

Catchings did not confine her best performances to the basketball court. She excelled in the classroom, making the honor roll during her senior year with a 4.0 GPA. In December of 2000 she graduated a semester early, with a degree in sports management. However, the joy she felt in finishing school was soon dampened by injury. The following month her right anterior cruciate ligament (ACL) snapped during a game against Mississippi State. At the time she was being touted as the number one draft choice for the WNBA, but a torn

school. In 1995 she and her sister Tauja led their school to the Illinois state high school championships. The game earned Catchings the title of Miss Basketball in Illinois. It was the last time the sisters would play together. The following year Catchings's parents divorced and her family split apart. She moved to Duncanville, Texas, with her mother, while her sister and brother remained behind in Illinois. Catchings found refuge from the trauma of the separation on the court. Soon she was leading Duncanville High to the 1997 Texas championship title. For her efforts she earned a Naismith Award as the national schoolgirl player of the year.

The Naismith Award, the most prestigious honor in high school basketball, brought Catchings national recognition, as well as scholarship offers to more than 200 universities and colleges. In an act of modesty that has become characteristic of her off-court personality, Catchings wrote thank-you notes to each of those schools. "For me not to say anything would have been selfish," she told the *New York Times.* The school decision was made after Catchings watched the University of Tennessee's Lady Volunteers on television, being coached by Pat Summitt. With five NCAA championships under her belt, Summitt was known throughout the world of college basketball as an extremely intense, hard-driving coach—just what the extremely intense, hard-playing Catchings needed. "I wanted a

ACL severely injures the knee and can require up to a year of recovery. Her college basketball career was over. However, prior to the injury she had led Tennessee in scoring and rebounding, helping to push the Lady Volunteers into the number two slot in the national rankings, and the WNBA did not overlook her track record or her skill. She was the third overall pick by the Indiana Fever during the first round of the WNBA 2001 Draft. Though she tried to speed up her recovery with the hopes of going professional during her first season, it wasn't to be. She remained sidelined—and frustrated—as she watched the Fever limp to a dismal 10 to 22 record.

Proved Herself a Champion

Catchings roared onto the court as a forward with the Fever in 2002, quickly making up for lost time. She was named WNBA Player of the Week for averaging 25 points per game in her very first week as a professional. She kept up the pace all season, leading the Fever to their first-ever appearance in the playoffs. Along the way she made her mark in several league statistical categories—first in steals, second in scoring, and fourth in rebounds. "When you talk about do-it-all players, you should just put 'equals Tamika Catchings,'" a New York Liberty player told *Sports Illustrated.* "She can shoot it, rebound it and push it. Man, she is everywhere." The league was impressed, too, and voted her WNBA Rookie of the Year. She also came in second in votes for Defensive Player of the Year, and third for MVP. Catchings's performance also landed her a starter position on the East Conference team for the WNBA's All-Star game.

Catchings continued tearing up the courts in 2003, leading the Fever to the number six spot in the league. Again she posted some impressive numbers, including second in overall points, second in steals, and third in points per game. However, as her coach Nell Fortner pointed out, statistics are one thing, but "you have to see her in person to truly appreciate the kind of player she is. She is absolutely relentless." After playing with Catchings during the 2002 All-Star game, WNBA superstar Sheryl Swoopes was quoted by the University of Tennessee's *Daily Beacon* website as saying, "Tamika Catchings is just absolutely fabulous. She plays all-out, all the time." The end of 2003 found Catchings back on the All-Star team and in second place in voting for the league's MVP.

When not with the Fever, Catchings made impressive debuts with several other teams. She led the start-up National Women's Basketball League in nearly every statistical category while playing for the Chicago Blaze. Overseas she was a star player in the Women's Korea Basketball League, leading her Woori Bank Hansae team to the title championships. Catchings was also the only rookie to be named to the 2002 U.S. National team. According to the *New York Times,* Catchings saved the day at the final game of the World Championships. "Superstars Swoopes and Lisa Leslie struggled with poor shooting, and the Chinese crowd, sensing a possible upset, began to chant 'Rus-si-ya! Rus-si-ya!' Catchings took control, dumping in 16 points and grabbing 11 rebounds." Her efforts paid off with a gold medal for the United States.

Dedicated to Community Causes

On the court, Catchings is everywhere. The same applies off-court. From an appearance on a Multigrain Cheerios cereal box, to the covers of dozens of magazines, to television features across the dial, Catchings seems to be everywhere. "[The WNBA] want her to be the public persona for the league," her lawyer told the *Indianapolis Star.* Entering its eighth season in 2004, the WNBA remained a burgeoning entity, still looking for a fan base and wider recognition. Players like Catchings are proving crucial in the efforts to achieve those goals. "She's so passionate as a person. I think that shows on the court," an executive at the WNBA declared in the *Indianapolis Star,* adding, "That same passion applies to her off-the-court life as well, in terms of marketing and the community." In addition to marketing the WNBA, Catchings has reached out to hearing-impaired children, speaking at schools and other events. "As a kid I always pictured pro athletes as perfect," she told *Sports Illustrated.* "Talking to these kids lets them know they're not alone."

As she prepared to enter her third season as a professional basketball player with the WNBA, Catchings looked forward to her next goal. "I'm very hungry [for a championship], that's what you play for," she told *Sports Illustrated for Kids.* "I've won a championship on just about every level. I want to win one on the WNBA level." Whether that happens or not, one thing is certain—women's basketball will remain forever changed by the appearance of Catchings and her colleagues. "For me, I was always looking at [my father] and watching him and his teammates play," she told the Appleton, Wisconsin, *Post-Crescent* website. "But it's cool now to look around and go to our games and see girls wearing our jerseys and talking about their role models being a female athlete. It's really important for me to set a good example and be out there and be visible."

Sources

Periodicals

Indianapolis Star, July 12, 2003; July 26, 2003; August 16, 2002.
Journal News (Westchester, NY), April 2, 2000, p. 13C.
Knight Ridder/Tribune News Service, March 30, 2000.
New York Times, May 25, 2003, p. 26.
Sporting News, November 30, 1998, p. 90.

Sports Illustrated, November 23, 1998, p. 144; July 8, 2002, p. R2.
Sports Illustrated for Kids, July 1, 2003, p. 49.

On-line

"Catchings Embraces Status as Role Model," *WisInfo (Appleton Post-Crescent),* www.wisinfo.com/post-crescent/sports/archive/sports_13706102.shtml (December 23, 2003).
"Tamika Catchings," *WNBA,* www.wnba.com/player-file/tamika_catchings/bio.html (December 23, 2003).
Tamika Catchings Official Website, www.catchin24.com (December 23, 2003).
"WNBA Trying to 'Catch' Former UT Star," *University of Tennessee (Daily Beacon),* www.dailybeacon.utk.edu/article.php/6599 (December 23, 2003).

—Candace LaBalle

Syl Cheney-Coker

1945—

Writer

Sierra Leonean writer Syl Cheney-Coker, whose name is sometimes spelled "Cheyney-Coker," is the author of a novel that won the 1991 Commonwealth Writers Prize for outstanding English-language fiction. He had also published numerous volumes of verse for some two decades before that. Much of his work paints a brutal portrait of life in Sierra Leone, an African country whose newfound independence was shattered by civil strife during his early adult years. The country's problems have endured almost as long as Cheney-Coker's career as a writer, and he has spent much of his life in exile. "Cheyney-Coker's poems are cries of bitter agony and bright illumination at one and the same time," a *Contemporary Poets* essayist asserted of his work. "They present the picture of a nation and a poet tortured by a culture and a religion imposed upon them, but a nation and a poet who may find salvation through defiance."

Cheney-Coker was born on June 28, 1945, in Freetown, Sierra Leone's capital. He was of "Krios" or Creole heritage, as is much of the population in this West African nation of 27 million. It was originally the land of the Temne and Mande, who were subdued first by the Portuguese—who called the land "Serra Lyoa,"

or lion mountains—and then by the British. An Atlantic seaboard country, it emerged as a vital trading port for West Africa, and in the 1800s became a colony for freed slaves from America and the Caribbean. Their descendants, as well as the Krios, or mixed-European Sierra Leoneans, eventually made up the country's middle class. Tensions simmered between this group and the predominantly Muslim Temne for generations, and there were also tensions between the Temne and the once-powerful Mande kingdom, which had been suppressed early in the twentieth century.

In the first years of Cheney-Coker's life, Sierra Leone's nationalist movement gained momentum. A Mande, Milton Margai, was elected president in 1951, and the country gained full independence in 1961. But tensions lingered, and a series of military coups ensued after 1967 that ousted a legitimately elected Temne prime minister and instigated years of unrest. Cheney-Coker left the country that year, heading to the University of Oregon, where he studied literature and worked as a journalist for a local paper. He also spent time at the University of California at Los Angeles and at the University of Wisconsin's Madison campus in the early 1970s, before returning to Freetown, where he found

At a Glance . . .

Born on June 28, 1945, in Freetown, Sierra Leone; son of Samuel B. and Lizzie (a trader; maiden name, Dundas) Coker. *Education:* Attended University of Oregon, 1967-70; attended University of California—Los Angeles, 1970; attended University of Wisconsin—Madison, 1971-72.

Career: *Eugene Register Guard,* Eugene, OR, journalist, 1968-69; Radio Sierra Leone, Freetown, Sierra Leone, head of cultural affairs, 1972-73; freelance writer and poet, 1973–; University of the Philippines, Quezon City, visiting professor of English, 1975-77; University of Maiduguri, Nigeria, lecturer, 1977-79, senior lecturer, 1979–.

Awards: Ford Foundation grant, 1970; Commonwealth Writers Prize, Africa Region, for *The Last Harmattan of Alusine Dunbar,* 1991.

Addresses: *Office*—c/o Heinemann, P. O. Box 6926, Portsmouth, NH 03802-6926.

a post as head of cultural affairs for Radio Sierra Leone. Since 1973 he has worked primarily as a freelance writer.

Cheney-Coker's first book of poetry, *Concerto for an Exile: Poems,* appeared in 1973, and was a historic first for Sierra Leone: it made Cheney-Coker the first writer from that country to publish a volume of poetry. He had no grand ambitions when he began, as he once told *Contemporary Authors.* "My being a poet was largely dictated by a nagging desire to understand the contradictions of the elements of my people," he explained. Much of his early work was influenced by the Négritude literary movement, which flourished among French-speaking African exiles in Paris in the 1930s and 1940s, among them Léopold Sédar Senghor and Aimé Césaire. The movement's literary style was characterized by a disdain for oppressive European attitudes toward African culture.

The verses in *Concerto for an Exile* contain imagery that is often violent, and its verses express anger and dismay at the actions of his fellow Sierra Leoneans. Yet Cheney-Coker is also highly critical of his own background as well, as part of the privileged minority descended from the freed slave community. "The poetry is passionate, almost masochistic, as [Cheney-Coker] poetically figures himself as a Christ-like figure, to be martyred for his community," according to an essay by Mark L. Lilleleht in *Encyclopedia of World Literature in the 20th Century.* A second volume of Cheney-Coker's verse, *The Graveyard Also Has Teeth,* quickly followed in 1974, with a revised edition published five years later. In this second collection, Cheney-Coker's anger seems to give way to a yearning for his homeland, and a desire to contribute to its future. "I want only to plough your fields / to be the breakfast of the peasants who read," one poem asserts. Lilleleht found "a much deeper sense of mission in these new poems together with a recognition of his needs and limitations as a poet."

In the late 1970s Cheney-Coker accepted a teaching position at the University of Maiduguri in Nigeria. New poems were published in his 1990 volume *The Blood in the Desert's Eyes,* and he also wrote his first novel that same year. *The Last Harmattan of Alusine Dunbar* took the prestigious Commonwealth Writers Prize for the Africa Region a year later. The story is a fictionalized history of a fictional Atlantic port city-state called Malagueta. Two hundred years of its traumas are chronicled, concluding with a coup. The "harmattan" of the title refers to a fierce, dust-carrying seasonal wind from the Sahara Desert that plagues this part of Africa. A prophet, Sulaiman the Nubian, appears and forecasts doom for Malagueta because of human folly, and he returns generations later as Alusine Dunbar. Cheney-Coker's literary style uses elements of the surreal, including distorted physical features and outlandishly outré events. *Publishers Weekly* reviewer Penny Kaganoff wrote that "in the tradition of magical realism, a sense of history and psychological drama make the story believable."

In the 1990s tensions continued in Sierra Leone, and even escalated in the spring of 1997 when a military junta took power. Cheney-Coker was living back in the Freetown area by then, but was once again forced to flee when rebel forces tried to break into his home. For a time he taught in New York, but then settled in Las Vegas, Nevada, where he was offered asylum as part of a new program that provided a home for writers who were fleeing political strife around the world. The program was funded in part by a casino and resort owner, Wole Soyinka, himself a writer. Grace Bradberry of the London *Times* reported that "the idea of bringing a writer to a place notorious for its shallow values and fake sphinxes was hatched over dinner by Wole Soyinka," the esteemed Nigerian novelist and 1985 Nobel Prize laureate in literature, and a professor at the University of Las Vegas. Cheney-Coker arrived in the fall of 2000, and was given an apartment, the use of a car, and an annual stipend of some $30,000 for his living expenses. He began working on *Stone Child,* a novel about the illicit diamond trade in Sierra Leone, which had served to finance the insurgency for years. "I expect Las Vegas to be a place where imagination is allowed to run wild," he said in a *Los Angeles Times* interview with Tom Gorman. "I hope this will be a very fruitful experience."

Selected writings

Concerto for an Exile: Poems, Africana Publishing, 1973.

The Graveyard Also Has Teeth (poems), New Beacon Press, 1974; revised edition, Heinemann, 1979.

The Blood in the Desert's Eyes (poems), Heinemann, 1990.

The Last Harmattan of Alusine Dunbar (novel), Heinemann, 1990.

Sources

Books

Contemporary Poets, 7th edition, St. James, 1991.

Serafin, Steven R., ed., *Encyclopedia of World Lit-* erature in the 20th Century, Volume 1: A-D, St. James, 1999, pp. 479-480.

Periodicals

Los Angeles Times, October 12, 2000, p. A1.

Publishers Weekly, December 21, 1990, p. 49; September 27, 1999, p. 100.

Times (London, England), October 23, 2000, p. 13.

On-line

"Syl Cheney-Coker," *Contemporary Authors Online,* reproduced in *Biography Resource Center,* www. galenet.com/servlet/BioRC (December 16, 2003).

—Carol Brennan

Johnnetta B. Cole

1936—

Educator, anthropologist, writer

Johnnetta Cole has been many things in her long career: an anthropologist, a teacher, a college administrator, and even an author. But to most people, she will be remembered for her groundbreaking work at Spelman College, one of the oldest and most respected institutions of higher learning for black women in the United States. She became Spelman's first female black president in 1987 and during her ten-year administration she proved to be a dynamic administrator, an energetic fundraiser, and a source of inspiration to both faculty and the student body. At a time when historically black colleges were deemed obsolete by some commentators, Cole emerged as one of their most passionate advocates. She has since gone on to teach anthropology and African American studies at Emory University and once again took the reigns as the president of a traditionally women's black college when she became the president of Bennett College in 2002. Discussing women's black colleges with an interviewer from *Dollars & Sense,* Cole stated that students are often attracted to these institutions "by the ambiance, by the affirming environment, by our insistence that African American women can do anything that they set out to do."

Johnnetta Betsch Cole was born on October 19, 1936, in Jacksonville, Florida. Higher education and high standards of achievement are traditions in Cole's family. In 1901 her great-grandfather, Abraham Lincoln Lewis, cofounded the Afro-American Life Insurance Company of Jacksonville, Florida. That business grew and thrived, eventually employing both of Cole's parents, each of whom had graduated from a black college. Her mother had worked as an English teacher and registrar at Edward Waters College prior to becoming a vice-president of Afro-American Life Insurance, and it was assumed that Johnnetta would also join the family business after completing her education.

Discovered Anthropology By Accident

Johnnetta was precocious, finishing high school by the age of 15. She earned outstanding scores on an entrance examination for Fisk University's early admissions program and began studying there in the summer of 1952. Her stay at Fisk was brief, yet pivotal. While there, a world of intellectual endeavor far beyond anything she'd experienced in Jacksonville's segregated schools was revealed to her. She had frequent contact with Arna Bontemps, the noted writer who also held a job as Fisk's librarian. Seeing this respected author in a work setting was important to her because, as she later wrote in a *McCall's* column, "When our ... heroes are portrayed as bigger than life, living, working, accomplishing beyond the realm of the normal, when they are depicted as perfect human beings, ... they are placed so far from us that it seems impossible that we could ever touch them or mirror who they are in our own lives."

After just one year at Fisk, Cole was eager to move on to new horizons. In 1953 she transferred to Oberlin College, where her sister was majoring in music. Seventeen-year-old Johnnetta was by then tightly focused on a career in medicine, but an anthropology course (taken to fulfill a liberal arts requirement) and its

At a Glance . . .

Born Johnnetta Betsch Cole on October 19, 1936, in Jacksonville, FL; daughter of John, Sr. (an insurance company employee) and Mary Frances (an educator, registrar, and insurance company vice-president) Betsch; married Robert Cole (an economist), 1960 (divorced, 1982); married Arthur Robinson, Jr. (a public health administrator), December 1988; children: (first marriage) David, Aaron, Che. *Education:* Oberlin College, BA, 1957; Northwestern University, MA, 1959, PhD, 1967.

Career: Washington State University, assistant professor of anthropology and director of Black Studies, 1967-70; University of Massachusetts—Amherst, professor of anthropology and Afro-American Studies, 1970-83, provost of undergraduate education, 1981-83; Hunter College of the City University of New York, Russell Sage Visiting Professor of Anthropology, 1983, professor of anthropology, 1983-87, director of Latin American and Caribbean Studies, 1984-87; Spelman College, Atlanta, GA, president, 1987-97; writer, 1988–; Emory University, Presidential Distinguished professor, 1999-02; Bennett College, president, 2002–.

Selected memberships: National Council of Negro Women; American Anthropological Association, fellow; board of directors, Global Fund for Women; board of directors, Points of Light Initiative Foundation.

Selected awards: Elizabeth Boyer Award, 1988; *Essence* Award in Education, 1989; inducted into Working Woman Hall of Fame; Jessie Bernard Wise Woman Award and American Woman Award, 1990; Sara Lee's Frontrunner Award, 1992; numerous honorary degrees.

Addresses: *Office*—Office of the President, Bennett College, 900 E. Washington Street, Greensboro, NC 27401.

enthusiastic instructor changed her direction permanently. "On my own little track, I would have simply taken my science courses, and never would have taken a class with George E. Simpson. This white American professor played Jamaican cult music in the classroom, jumping up and down, beginning to hyperventilate,

talking about African retentions in the New World! 'This is what anthropologists try to understand,' said he. 'Good-bye, premed and hello, anthropology!' said I," Cole was quoted as saying in a *Ms.* magazine article.

After earning her bachelor's degree in anthropology at Oberlin in 1957, Cole went on to graduate study at Northwestern University. There she worked under noted anthropologists Paul J. Bohannan and Melville J. Herskovits. To her surprise, she also fell in love with a white graduate student in the economics program. "It was not my plan to fall in love with Robert Cole," she remarked in *Ms.* "And I doubt seriously that this man coming from an Iowa dairy farming family … intended to fall in love with a black woman from Jacksonville, Florida." Nevertheless, the two were married. Robert Cole shared his wife's fascination with Africa, and after their wedding day, they traveled to Liberia to work cooperatively on research that would form the basis of both their dissertations.

Conducted Anthropological Studies Abroad

Cole did anthropological field studies in villages while her husband conducted economic surveys of the area. She has stated that the experience of living in Africa imparted a unique perspective to her and her husband that helped their interracial marriage endure for more than twenty years, despite the fact that they returned to the United States at the beginning of the black power movement. It was "a time when for many *black* folk interracial marriage was a problem," she was quoted as saying in *Ms.* "But perhaps because I was working largely in an academic setting, with students, it was not just manageable, it was all right."

By 1967 Cole had completed her dissertation, "Traditional and Wage Earning Labor in Liberia," received her Ph.D. from Northwestern, and joined her husband as a faculty member at Washington State University. Beginning as an assistant professor of anthropology, she went on to become a key player in the creation of the school's Black Studies program, also serving as director of the program. In 1970 Cole and her husband moved to New England, where she had been offered a tenured position at the University of Massachusetts at Amherst. She spent 13 productive years there, developing the existing Afro-American Studies program, increasing the interaction between her school and the others in the Connecticut River valley, teaching courses in anthropology and Afro-American studies, and serving as provost of undergraduate education.

Cole's marriage ended in 1982, and the following year she moved on to Hunter College of the City University of New York. She remained on the staff of the anthropology department until 1987 and was director of the Latin American and Caribbean Studies program. She continued her field work, which since her days in

Liberia had encompassed studies of households headed by women, the lives of Caribbean women, Cape Verdean culture in the United States, and racial and gender inequality in Cuba.

Cole's focus on cultural anthropology, Afro-American studies, and women's issues all came together in a groundbreaking book published in 1986. *All-American Women: Lines That Divide, Ties That Bind* was cited by numerous reviewers for its perceptive synthesis of issues concerning race, class, gender, and ethnicity. Cole remarked in *Ms.* that her fieldwork has definitely influenced the administrative side of her career: "I tend to look at problems in ways that I think are very, very much in the anthropological tradition. Which means, first of all, one appreciates the tradition, but second, one also at least raises the possibility that there are different ways of doing the same thing. And it's in that discourse where interesting things can happen."

Became President of Spelman College

When Spelman College began looking for a new president in 1986, finding a black woman for the job was a top priority. When the school was founded in 1880 by white abolitionists from New England, it was conceived as a missionary school where emancipated slave women could learn literacy, practical skills, and Christian virtues. Its first four presidents were white women; the first black to fill the office, Albert Manley, was not hired until the 1950s. When he left in the mid-1970s, a small but very vocal group of students demanded a black woman president for this black woman's school. The search committee had three excellent candidates that fit the criteria, but two of them withdrew from the selection process before it was completed. The third was offered the job, but had already accepted another. Donald Stewart, former associate dean at University of Pennsylvania, was hired. A group of Spelman students reacted angrily to the announcement, locking the trustees in their boardroom for 26 hours.

When Stewart left office ten years later, Cole was clearly the standout choice of all the applicants for the vacancy, not just because of her race and sex but because of her strong background as a scholar, a feminist, and a student of black heritage. "Her credentials were not only impeccable, but her incredible energy and enthusiasm came through during the personal interview. She showed certain brilliance in every sense of the word," Veronica Biggins, co-vice-chair of Spelman's board of trustees, was quoted as saying in *Working Woman.* "Cole's charismatic personality, cooperative leadership style, and firm 'black womanist' attitude … raise[d] expectations for an exciting new era at Spelman," according to a *Ms.* article published shortly after Cole took office. "While [she] is a highly qualified, purposeful, serious-minded individual, she is also a thoroughly warm and unpretentious sister—in both the black and feminist senses of the term."

Cole's presidency had an exciting kickoff—during her inauguration, Bill and Camille Cosby announced a gift of $20 million to Spelman. Delighted with the donation, Cole was nevertheless quick to point out that there is never enough money. She estimated that fund-raising took up 50 percent of her time. The other half was divided between teaching (one class per term), building up academics, and starting new traditions such as her Mentorship Program, in which CEOs of six major Atlanta corporations were paired with promising students from Spelman. She was committed to building and maintaining a powerful liberal arts program at the school, for it was her belief that a good liberal arts education was the proper foundation for any career. "I tell my students to write, to learn to think, and the rest will fall in place," she told *Working Woman.*

Moved on From Spelman

Even while she was at Spelman, Cole was working on numerous projects. One of them, her 1993 book *Conversations: Straight Talk with America's Sister President,* attempted to broaden her call for a new order, targeting "a multiplicity of audiences" with her message of equality. Mixing enthusiastic discourse on race, gender, and learning with ruminations on her own experiences as a black woman, she argues for the eradication of racist and sexist views through education, tolerance, and expanded social awareness. While reaching readers of both sexes and all races, Cole marshals the forces of young black women in the United States to act for change, stating, "We African American women must cure whatever ails us."

In 1997 Cole decided that it was time for her to move on from Spelman in an effort to make other colleges more culturally diverse and educationally sound. As she said in a speech at Spelman that was reprinted in *Ebony,* "While I would love to remain at Spelman, it is not necessary." She went on to reveal that she would be going back to teaching full time at Atlanta's Emory University. Her reasons, according to *Ebony,* were simple: "The president [of Emory University] has invited me to be of assistance to him to more solidly connect the university to Africa-American and women communities. So I will be continuing to do the same work, I'll just be doing it from the other side."

Before starting her career at Emory, Cole took a year off to write and produced *Dream the Boldest Dreams: And Other Lessons of Life.* The book is filled with sayings and short passages that explore the different ways in which people make their way through life and how that way can be made easier by learning certain lessons sooner. The book also focuses on ways in which a person can make their lives more full, including getting involved in community service, getting to know the people in the community starting with the person that lives next door, and being willing to work for those things that really mean something.

Returned To Administration At Bennett

Cole spent three years at Emory as a Presidential Distinguished Professor of Anthropology, Women's Studies, and African-American Studies. Then, in early 2002, Cole was made aware of the state of affairs at Bennett College for Women, a university that had been known for its education of minority women since 1926. Even though Bennett had a prestigious history, years of mismanagement had caused the college to face lower enrollments, dropping accreditation levels, and a $2 million deficit on top of infrastructure woes that were causing the campus to become unsafe. Unwilling to let a black women's college suffer this fate, Cole decided to come out of retirement from administration and take on the job of president of Bennett.

In her first year at Bennett, Cole was aggressive in her efforts to get the college back on track. She has appealed to local business, churches, and organizations in order to secure financial backing for the college and its programs. She has also looked within the college itself for support, turning to alumni, trustees, and national organizations that were already associated with the college. Going into June of 2003 Cole had already raised in excess of $9.1 million in grants, pledges, and gifts which more then took care of the $2 million deficit that Bennett was facing and continued to look for ways to make sure that Bennett will have a long standing surplus of funds to support itself.

Even though Cole was rigorously campaigning for funds for Bennett in 2002, she also found the time to do anthropologic research with fellow educator Beverly Guy-Sheftall. The results of this research was the book *Gender Talk: The Struggle for Women's Equality in African American Communities*. The book, according to the *United Press International*, "presents a credible rationale for the tangled web of black gender issues, going back to the institution of slavery." The book has been praised not only for its well-researched premise but has also been noted to be easy to read and intriguing by critics. Cole agreed with this assessment of her book in *Current Anthropology* calling the book "grounded in what we know about race and racism but something that is very accessible to the public, so we see it, again, as a work for a general audience."

Cole firmly believed that black colleges are vital to black success. She has frequently quoted statistics showing that although only 17 percent of black students enter black colleges, 37 percent of those who make it to graduation were attending black colleges, and a full 75 percent of black professional women are graduates of black colleges. She remained convinced that these schools give black students more opportunities to ex-cel, to discover their heritage, and to see role models in their own image. When asked by *Dollars & Sense* what lies ahead for black colleges, she responded: "A good deal of continuity and some intriguing changes.... Tradition is important however ... not just for its own sake, but because it works."

Selected writings

All-American Women: Lines That Divide, Ties That Bind, 1986.
Conversations: Straight Talk with America's Sister President, Doubleday, 1993.
Dream the Boldest Dreams: And Other Lessons of Life, Longstreet Press, 1997.
(with Beverly Guy-Sheftall) *Gender Talk: The Struggle for Women's Equality in African American Communities,* Ballantine Books, 2003.

Editor of *Anthropology for the Eighties* and *Anthropology for the Nineties.* Contributor to numerous magazines and journals, including a regular column for *McCall's.* Member of editorial board of *Anthropology and Humanism Quarterly, Black Scholar, Emerge,* and *SAGE: A Scholarly Journal on Black Women.*

Sources

Books

Bateson, Catherine, *Composing a Life,* Atlantic Monthly Press, 1989.
Cole, Johnnetta, *Conversations: Straight Talk with America's Sister President,* Doubleday, 1993.

Periodicals

Art in America, September 1990.
Black Issues in Higher Education, July 17, 2003, p. 8.
Change, September/October 1987.
Current Anthropology, April 2003, p. 275-88.
Dollars & Sense, March 1992.
Ebony, February 1988; March 1997, p. 73-4.
Essence, November 1987; July 1990.
Jet, June 28, 1999, p. 20; May 13, 2003, p. 14-5.
McCall's, October 1990; February 1991.
Ms., October 1987.
Publishers Weekly, July 13, 1992; November 30, 1992.
SAGE: A Scholarly Journal on Black Women, Fall 1988.
United Press International, June 5, 2003.
Working Woman, June 1989; November 1991.

—Joan Goldsworthy and Ralph G. Zerbonia

Sean "Puffy" Combs

1969—

Rap musician, producer, music executive, fashion designer, entrepreneur

Very few people can follow popular culture today without knowing the name of Sean Combs, whether it is as Puff Daddy, the rapper of the mid-nineties, as P. Diddy, the rapper/actor/entertainer of the new millennium, or as Sean Combs, the mind behind Bad Boy Entertainment, the Sean John clothing line, and the producer with sure-fire hit making instincts. While he has had monstrous successes, Combs has had his share of rough times in the past decade. But, no matter where critics stand on Sean Combs the man, it is true that Combs' name is synonymous with the rise of the hip hop culture in America.

Combs has had a prolific presence in the media. He has grown from producing albums for other artists to being the artist featured on his own albums. He has moved from the music world to acting in movies like the 2001 acclaimed *Monster's Ball*. Lately, his entrepreneurial exploits have allowed him to depart from the entertainment industry to found a successful urban clothing line, Sean John. In 1997, he had a number one single "I'll Be Missing You". This single was replaced as number one on the Billboard Top 100 by a hit single by Notorious B.I.G., featuring Combs, "Mo Money, Mo Problems". This feat was previously only met by Elvis Presley, the Beatles, and Boyz II Men.

Started Early in Music Business

Sean Combs was born in New York City on November 4, 1969, to Janice and Melvin Earl Combs. Combs grew up believing his father was killed in a car accident when Combs was three, but found out at age 14, through research at a public library, that his father had been a small time hustler who was shot in the head on Central Park West. His widowed mother worked three jobs, including work as a teacher and a model, in order to scrape together money to buy a house in suburban Mount Vernon, New York.

"At first I thought nobody would accept me as a rap artist," Combs later told Chuck Phillips of the Minneapolis Star-Tribune. "After all, it's not like I came from the 'hood," he added. But his mother maintained the family's ties to New York's Harlem, and it was there that young Sean Combs obtained a remarkable cultural education, soaking up the creations of the founders of rap music: Grandmaster Flash, Run D.M.C., KRS-One, and more. "I would be 12 years old, and sometimes I'd

At a Glance . . .

Born Sean J. Combs on November 4, 1969, in New York, NY; son of Janice and Melvin Earl Combs; divorced; children: Justin and Christian Combs. *Education:* Attended Howard University, 1988-90.

Career: Uptown Records, New York, intern, 1990-91, director of artists and repertory, 1991, vice president, 1991-93; record producer, 1994–; Bad Boy Entertainment, founder and chief executive officer, 1994–; rap musician, 1997–; Sean John clothing line, founder and chief executive officer, 1998–; actor, 2001–; television producer, 2002–.

Memberships: American Federation of Television & Radio Artists; American Federation of Musicians; Daddy's House Programs; Sean "Puffy" Combs and Janice Combs Endowed Scholarship Fund, founder.

Awards: 3M, Visionary Award for Producing, 1994; Impace, Award of Merit for Creative Excellence, 1994; ASCAP, Rhythm & Soul Award "Juicy", 1995; Gavin, Rap Indie (Dist. by a Major) of the Year, 1995; Grammys, Award for Best Rap Performance By a Duo or Group, with Faith Evans and 112, Best Rap Album, 1998; Howard University, Alumni Award for Distinguished Postgraduate Achievement, 1999.

Addresses: *Office*—Chief Executive Officer, Bad Boy Entertainment, 1540 Broadway, 30th Fl, New York, NY, 10036.

be out until 3, 4 in the morning, seeing the music. I had to sneak out to do it, but I was doing it," he told Rolling Stone's Mikal Gilmore. He obtained the nickname "Puffy" from a childhood friend. "Whenever I got mad as a kid, I used to huff and puff…. That's why my friend started calling me Puffy," he told *Jet.*

Combs enrolled at Howard University in Washington, D.C., in 1988. Although he spent much of his time promoting rap-music events, he managed to remain at Howard for at least two years. Recommended by rapper Heavy D., he parlayed his musical activities into an internship at New York's Uptown Records in 1990. After just three months, Combs attracted the attention of label head and former rap artist Andre Harrell, who named his young protege director of artists and repertoire, a position of extraordinary influence for a twenty-year-old with a keen understanding of the city's flour-

ishing rap scene. Within a year he became vice president. Combs quickly became an accomplished producer, working on such successful Uptown releases as Jodeci's *Forever My Lady* and Mary J. Blige's *What's the 411?.*

Started Bad Boy and Recording Career

Things took a turn for the worse at a disastrous celebrity basketball event that Combs promoted at New York's City College in December of 1991. Nine people were killed in a stampede at the gates. In the aftermath, Combs received some blame for the deaths, but was successfully defended in court by renowned attorney William Kunstler. In 1993 he was fired from Uptown Records. The split with Harrell was difficult for him. "It was like the old sensei (teacher) rejecting the student," Combs told *Rolling Stone.*

A scant two weeks later, however, Combs finalized a deal with the large music conglomerate Arista to distribute the musical output of his new company, Bad Boy Entertainment. Bad Boy succeeded from the start and over the first four years of its existence posted skyrocketing sales; estimates of total sales over the period 1993 to 1997 range from $100 million to $200 million. Arista rewarded Combs with a $6 million cash advance when he renegotiated his relationship with the label in 1997.

Although Combs has produced top-chart-level recordings by Bad Boy artists Mase, Craig Mack, and others, and has worked with outside artists of the magnitude of Aretha Franklin and Sting, his greatest success at the helm of Bad Boy came with the recordings of New York rapper Christopher Wallace, better known as Biggie Smalls, who recorded under the name of the Notorious B.I.G. Smalls was Combs' first major project at Bad Boy. "He saw things so vivid," Combs recalled in a 1997 interview with Rolling Stone. "If you sat and listened to a Biggie Smalls record in the dark, you see a whole movie in front of you." The first Notorious B.I.G. album, *Ready to Die,* attracted widespread attention; the second, the prophetically named *Life After Death,* was one of 1997's top sellers, spawning an unprecedented two Number One singles after Smalls' murder in March of that year. Combs, who had earlier moved in the direction of mainstream R&B and was credited by some with founding a hybrid named hip-hop soul, proved himself, as executive producer of the Notorious B.I.G. recordings, master of the hardcore gangsta rap style during its period of maximum sales.

He was to achieve even greater success on his own, recording with various other Bad Boy artists under the name Puff Daddy & the Family. The *No Way Out* album, released in July of 1997, included "I'll Be Missing You"; the album took the theme of a tribute or a requiem for the murdered Smalls. Musically, the album was marked by wholesale adoption of the melodies and rhythm tracks of familiar pieces of R&B and rock from the 1970s and 1980s. Writer Sean Piccoli of the Fort Lauderdale *Sun Sentinel* dubbed the practice "stapling," as opposed to the "sampling" present on earlier rap recordings, where only short snippets of music would be borrowed from earlier sources. "I'll Be Missing You" was directly based on the 1983 Police hit, "Every Breath You Take."

Combs has taken criticism for this practice, both from other hip-hop artists and from fans of the artists whose work he borrows. Yet Combs was not the inventor of such wholesale borrowing; as he was putting the finishing touches on the *No Way Out* disc, movie star/rapper Will Smith recycled Patrice Rushen's 1982 hit "Forget Me Nots" on the soundtrack of the film Men in Black. The style dated back at least to MC Hammer's 1990 "U Can't Touch This" (based on Rick James's "Super Freak" of a decade earlier). Furthermore, those who claimed that Combs in "I'll Be Missing You" was coasting along on the strength of the Police recording mostly failed to notice the other quotation contained in the song: the early twentieth-century Protestant hymn "I'll Fly Away," and, on the album, the classical orchestral work Adagio for Strings, composed in 1915 by Samuel Barber. Clearly, for millions of listeners, the works blended into a convincing expression of Combs' grief over his friend's death.

Success Hampered by Court Cases

The end of the 1990s saw a rise in Combs' presence in various courtrooms throughout the country as well as a rise in Combs' presence in the business and philanthropic world. Daddy's House Social Programs began in 1995. This charity organization, guided by both Combs and Executive Director Sister Souljah, seeks to promote the positive influence of parents, teachers and mentors for urban youth. Daddy's House has spearheaded programs in academic tutoring, promoting higher education, and international travel for students. The charity even runs summer camping programs in upstate New York.

In 1997 Combs opened up Justin's, a fine dining restaurant in New York and another in Atlanta in 1999. He has plans to build restaurants in various locations like Washington, D.C., Chicago, Miami, and Detroit. In 1998 Combs made his run at a clothing line, Sean John. Designed with urban male youth in mind, the clothing line became an almost immediate success and has been nominated for a CFDA fashion award *every* year since its inception. In 2000 Combs appeared on his own reality show on ABC called *Making The Band*. The series ran for two seasons on ABC, but moved to MTV under the name *Making The Band 2* for its third season. Recently, Combs has been slated to make his Broadway debut in the revival of *Raisin In The Sun*.

In 1999 Combs was brought up on charges of assaulting record executive Steve Stoute. Stoute was one of the executives who allowed the airing of a video on MTV that pictured Combs nailed to a cross. Combs was upset at the disrespect he believed the video showed to God. After a public apology to Stoute, the charges were dropped. In 2000 Combs was charged with criminal possession of a weapon stemming from an incident at a New York nightclub on December 27, 1999. Combs was at the club with then girlfriend singer-actress Jennifer Lopez. A jury, in March of 2001, found Combs not guilty of all charges. On May 24, 2000, Combs settled the lawsuit that was a result of the 1991 New York City College tragedy.

All of Combs' legal and personal problems culminated in a public persona name change. In 2001, Sean "Puff Daddy" Combs made an announcement that the entertainment world would now know him by the name "P. Diddy." The name change stemmed from the legal issues, but that was not the only reason. Combs believed that he was not given the respect and admiration he deserved for his entertainment work. He looked at himself as a person who, for the most part, stayed out of the east coast/west coast rap wars, looked to better the quality of hip hop entertainment, and tried to become a role model and leader for people of his race. A name change would allow him to wipe the slate clean and start anew. However, Combs found that even as P. Diddy, his past still haunted him and his respectability was still in question. On New Year's Eve of 2003, according to *Villa*, Combs announced at a party, "First they called me Puff Daddy, then they called me P. Diddy. But now I'm just Sean Combs." It is clear that with the success Combs has had since his first name change, the next few years will prove to be both exciting and profitable for Sean Combs.

Selected works

Discography

No Way Out, Bad Boy, 1997.
Forever, Bad Boy, 1999.
The Sage Continues, Bad Boy, 2001.

Film

Made, 2001.
Monster's Ball, 2001.

Record production

Britney Spears, *In The Zone*, BMG International, 2003.
Faith Evans, *Faith,* Bad Boy, 1995.
L.L. Cool J, *Phenomenon*, Def Jam, 1997.
Lil' Kim, *Notorious K.I.M.*, Atlantic, 2000.
Mary J. Blige, *Love & Life*, Geffen, 2003.
The Notorious B.I.G., *Ready to Die*, Bad Boy, 1994.
The Notorious B.I.G., *Life After Death*, Bad Boy, 1997.
The Notorious B.I.G., *Born Again,* Bad Boy, 1999.

Other

Combs has also produced recordings by Bad Boy artists Total, 112, the Lox, and others; he has produced recordings for artists associated with other labels, including Michael Jackson, Aretha Franklin, Mariah Carey, Keith Sweat, and the Police. He has worked in remixing on a number of albums by artists like Janet Jackson and even the 1999 tribute album to Princess Diana. He also appears in his own reality show called Making the Band.

Sources

Periodicals

Billboard, August 30, 1997.
Black Enterprise, December 1, 1999.
Entertainment Weekly, October 31, 1997.
Fort Lauderdale Sun Sentinel, October 19, 1997.
Hip Hop News, January 13, 2004.
Jet, January 12, 1998; February 21, 2001; April 16, 2001; January 12, 2004.
Minneapolis Star Tribune, May 26, 1997.
New York Times, January 1, 1998.
Rolling Stone, April 20, 1995; August 7, 1997.
Source, May 1997.
USA Today, July 22, 1997.
Vibe, December 1997/January 1998.

On-line

P. Diddy & the Bad Boy Family, www.p-diddy.com (February 2, 2004).

—James M. Manhiem and Adam R. Hazlett

Peggy Cooper Cafritz

1947—

Education activist

Peggy Cooper Cafritz is a prominent community activist in Washington, D.C., who was elected chair of the District of Columbia Board of Education in 2002. Cooper Cafritz's mission was to lead the board in its mandate to improve the poorly performing, problem-plagued school district. She is best known in the Washington area, however, as the founder of the Duke Ellington School of the Arts, a public high school for students wishing to pursue careers in music, theater, dance, the visual arts, or museum studies. "Ellington is an extraordinary ground," she enthused in an *Ebony* interview with Richette L. Haywood in 1996.

Cooper Cafritz was born on April 7, 1947, in Mobile, Alabama, the daughter of Algernon and Gladys Cooper. She arrived in Washington, D.C., to attend George Washington University in 1964, earning a degree in political science four years later. While in law school at the same university, she became involved in arts education in the city, initially in a project with choreographer Mike Malone that held workshops for students interested in pursuing careers in the arts. After completion of the project, Cooper Cafritz decided that the city needed a performing arts high school, a concept based on renowned institutions like New York City's High School for the Performing Arts, later made famous in the film and television series *Fame*.

In the late 1960s, Cooper Cafritz began gathering what would amount to some $6 million in donations, and argued convincingly before the District of Columbia school board, which agreed to provide additional support through tax dollars. The Duke Ellington School of the Arts opened its doors in 1974 to a largely minority student body drawn from some of the city's roughest neighborhoods. As Cooper Cafritz recalled in *Ebony,* "I wanted the school to be a place where kids without other opportunities, who were very talented, could come and learn and develop into intelligent artists." In a hire that was eerily prescient of her role in the movie *Fame,* actress and dancer Debbie Allen, who appeared in both the film and television versions, was Ellington's first dance teacher.

In the early 1970s Cooper Cafritz chaired the executive committee of the DC Arts Commission, and was also a fellow at the Woodrow Wilson International Center for Scholars, a prestigious research organization for social sciences and the humanities run by the Smithsonian Institution. At the time, she was the youngest fellow ever to be admitted to the center. In 1973 she was named to the executive committee for the District of Columbia Board of Higher Education, whose mission was to oversee the merger between the Federal City College and Washington Teachers College. The institution that eventually came about was the University of the District of Columbia.

For a time in the 1970s, Cooper Cafritz worked as special assistant to the president of Post-Newsweek Stations Inc., based in the District of Columbia, and also worked as a programming executive and documentary producer for WTOP-TV in Washington. From 1977-79 she headed the Minority Cultural Project, founded by singer Harry Belafonte and a Pittsburgh public broadcasting station, that provided a forum for new as well as forgotten writers. For a number of years Cooper Cafritz appeared as an arts reviewer in

At a Glance . . .

Born on April 7, 1947, in Mobile, AL; daughter of Algernon Johnson and Gladys (Mouton) Cooper; married Conrad Cafritz, December 21, 1981; children: two; primary custody of six other children. *Education:* George Washington University, BA, 1968, JD, 1971; Woodrow Wilson International Center for Scholars, fellow, 1972. *Politics:* Democrat.

Career: Workshops for Careers in the Arts, Washington, DC, co-founder, 1968; Duke Ellington High School of Fine and Performing Arts, Washington, DC, founder, developer, fundraiser, 1968–; DC Arts Commission, executive committee chair, 1969-74; Post-Newsweek Stations Inc., assistant to the president, 1970s; Minority Cultural Project, exec. dir., 1977-79; WETA-TV (Channel 26), Washington, DC, arts critic, 1986–. District of Columbia Board of Education, president, 2000–.

Selected memberships: DC Commission on the Arts and Humanities, chair, 1979-87; Washington Performing Arts Society, 1983; PEN/Faulkner Foundation, board of directors, 1985-88; National Jazz Service Organization, 1985–; Kennedy Center for the Performing Arts, board of trustees, 1987; Smithsonian Cultural Education Committee, chair, 1989–; President's Committee on the Arts and Humanities, after 1994.

Selected awards: John D. Rockefeller International Youth Award, 1972; President's Medal for Outstanding Community Service, Catholic University, 1974; New York Black Film Festival Award, 1976; George Foster Peabody Award for Excellence in Television, 1976; Mayor's Art Award for Arts Advocacy, 1991.

Addresses: *Home*—3030 Chain Bridge Rd. NW, Washington, DC 20016.

"Around Town," a show on WETA-TV in Washington. Her involvement in numerous other organizations continued at both the federal and local levels, and included the National Assembly of State Art Agencies, the PEN/Faulkner Foundation, the National Jazz Service Organization, and the Washington Performing Arts Society. She was also named to the board of trustees of the Kennedy Center for the Performing Arts in 1987, and after 1989 co-chaired the Smithsonian Institution's Cultural Equity Committee, which sought to bring more diversity to the museum's exhibits and programs, as well as to the ranks of its staff.

Cooper Cafritz ran for the presidency of the District of Columbia board of education in 2000, campaigning on a platform that called for a serious overhaul of the troubled district. "People in this town who have a lot to bring to the table don't run," she said of her decision, in an interview with *Washington Times* writer Marlene T. Johnson. "I just felt I had to do it." Though known for her bluntness, she was considered an ideal leader to help the board reform what had become one of the nation's most poorly performing urban school systems.

Cooper Cafritz won the election, and deployed her formidable skills over the next two years to resolve the budgetary crises and in-fighting that had plagued the District's administration and political overseers. An opinion piece in the *Washington Times* by Deborah Simmons commented on Cooper Cafritz's track record and the challenges she faced. "To be sure, it's easy to criticize the Cafritz school board, but it's difficult to challenge Mrs. Cafritz, who cannot be bought off by unions and other special-interest groups," Simmons declared. "Even Washington powerbrokers, quick to call her controlling and combative, even brusque and ornery—now find themselves having to take a deep breath and deal with her in the fight to reform D.C. schools." With an impressive track record that resonated with parents, Cooper Cafritz ran unopposed in her re-election bid for the school board presidency in 2002, and though she failed to win the mayor's endorsement, she won another two-year term.

Cooper Cafritz married Conrad Cafritz in 1981, and has two children. She also took over primary custody and guardianship of six other children. The Ellington School is still thriving after nearly three decades in operation, and counts among its graduates the soprano Denyce Graves and comedian Dave Chappell. More than 90 percent of its graduates go on to college. The school receives same per-pupil dollar amount as other D.C. high schools, but its wealth of programs necessitate a major ongoing fundraising campaign, and Cooper Cafritz helps raise $1 million annually for the Ellington School's endowment fund. As she told *Ebony,* she considers Ellington a haven, where the teens' "dreams are so big and real that they've propelled these kids out of difficult, poor, often illiterate families and into some of the finest artistic arenas in America."

Sources

Periodicals

Business Week, October 13, 2003.
Ebony, January 1996, p. 37.
Financial Times, February 23, 2001, p. 15.
Jet, October 17, 1994, p. 33.

Washington Times, October 27, 2000, p. 4; November 8, 2000, p. 1; March 7, 2001, p. 2; March 16, 2001, p. 19; July 13, 2001, p. 4; August 24, 2001, p. 1; December 7, 2001, p. 4; November 8, 2002, p. A23.

On-line

"Peggy Cooper Cafritz, statement and biography," *DCWatch,* www.dcwatch.com/archives/election2000/cafritz05.htm (December 17, 2003).

—Carol Brennan

Jayne Cortez

1936—

Poet

Acclaimed as original, versatile, and multifaceted, Jayne Cortez is a poet whose extraordinary career includes literary success and impassioned activism inspired by the ideals of human dignity and social justice. Cortez is considered to be the primary link between the creative sound-based poetics of the Black Arts Movement and what became synonymous with poetry in the last years of the twentieth century: hip hop and performance poetry. Cortez has been writing and performing her poetry for over 40 years at museums, universities, and festivals throughout the United States, South America, Europe, Asia and Africa. Her poetry, which has been translated into twenty-eight languages, fuses politics with surrealism, and blends traditional poetry with the African oral and aural traditions, American black culture, jazz, and blues. Cortez, who has described her work as a mix of art and politics, as well as confrontational, has been included in several anthologies, journals, and magazines. Cortez has published ten volumes of poetry, recorded nine albums, and she has received numerous awards. In addition, she has appeared in the Canadian film, *Poetry In Motion* and in the film *Women in Jazz*. She also participated in the music video *Nelson Mandela is Coming* and her poem, *I Am New York City,* was featured in an episode of *Tribeca,* the Fox television network series.

Her career as a social activist is impressive. Cortez traveled to Mississippi in 1963 to help register black voters. In 1964 Cortez organized writing and drama workshops in the Watts neighborhood in Los Angeles, ultimately co-founding the Watts Repertory Theater Company. Like many other black artists who wanted control over their work, Cortez established her own publishing company, Bola Press, in 1972. She co-founded, and is president of, the Organization of Women Writers of Africa. A tireless organizer, she coordinated the Yari Yari International Conference of Women Writers of African Descent as well as directed the film *Yari Yari.* She also helped to organize the international symposium, *Slave Routes: The Long Memory* and was a participant in a round table discussion at the United Nations Millennium Summit in 2000.

Influenced by Jazz and Politics

Cortez was born on May 10, 1936, in Fort Huachuca, Arizona. She grew up in Los Angeles, where she attended an arts-based high school where she focused on painting and she studied the cello. She also loved to write and was an avid journal keeper. Playing the cello, Cortez became acquainted with classical music but in the Cortez household, she was exposed to Spanish and Native American music as well as blues and jazz. After high school she attended Compton Junior College and also studied drama at Ebony Showcase. Unfortunately, she interrupted her studies due to financial constraints. She did not, however, put down her pen and continued to write.

Many critics define Cortez as a jazz poet. Most of what Cortez has written is best experienced when heard, rather than read from a page. Her voice and choice of words are her instruments. As an artistic young woman living in Los Angeles during the 1950s, Cortez was

At a Glance . . .

Born Jayne Cortez on May 10, 1936, in Fort Huachuca, AZ; married Ornette Coleman, 1954 (divorced 1964); married Melvin Edwards, 1975; children: (first marriage) Denardo Coleman. *Education:* Attended Compton Junior College; studied drama at Ebony Showcase.

Career: Watts Repertory Theater, co-founder, 1964; poet and performance artist, 1969–; Bola Press, founder, 1972–; Livingston College of Rutgers University, writer-in-residence, 1977-83; Dartmouth College, lecturer; Howard University, lecturer; Queens College, lecturer; Wesleyan University, lecturer; Eastern Michigan University, M. Thelma McAndless Distinguished Professor in Humanities, 2003.

Memberships: Organization of Women Writers of Africa, co-founder, president; Poetry Society of America.

Awards: New York State Council on the Arts Poetry Award, 1973, 1981; National Endowment for the Arts, 1979-86; American Book Award, 1980; Before Columbus Foundation Award, 1987; Afrikan Poetry Theater tribute and award, 1994; Fannie Lou Hammer Award, 1994.

Addresses: *Office*—Bola Press , P.O. Box 96, Village Station, New York, NY 10014.

critics consider the Black Arts Movement the most important movement in American literature precisely because it effected a paradigm shift whereby the meaning and function of literature were redefined. Essentially, the artist had a responsibility to his or her community, and this responsibility included the duty to redefine the world on the basis of culture-specific symbols and terms. Writing for *Chicken Bones*, Kalamu ya Salaam explained, "[T]he effort of the black arts movement was to make art based on the speech and music of black people, drawn from the everyday lives of our people and returned to them in an inspiring and potent form...." The Black Arts Movement environment encouraged black artists to join this new frontier, but unfortunately, not many of the initially recognized poets remained active.

Cortez drew inspiration from the Black Arts Movement, but she considerably expanded the movement's intellectual horizons. While the black poets of the 1960s forged a new type of literature—replacing traditional literary forms by modes of discourse informed by artistic creation in reaction to the dominant cultural paradigm—Cortez went a step further. As a black female, Cortez sought to create a literary discourse that was free of both the traditional white poetical aesthetic and the sexism that was evident in all cultures. Writing for *Modern American Poetry*, Karen Ford asserted, "For most women who came of age artistically during the Black Arts movement and who were tutored in the Black Aesthetic, the struggle to create a place for themselves in the literary environment was arduous. Giovanni, Sanchez, Rodgers, ... frequently retreated to some form of conventional femininity that was almost as disabling as the over bearing masculinity they sought to escape. An exception to this pattern and a harbinger of future development in African American poetry is Jayne Cortez."

Developed Own Brand of Poetry

Cortez was of her time. According to Salaam, "[T]he black arts movement proper covers the time period of 1965 to 1976." Yet, Cortez's life choices reflected many of the Black Arts Movement ideologies before the movement formally began. While Cortez may have "come of age" during the height of the Black Arts Movement, she seems to have been able to be both immersed in, and able to circumvent, the movement, continuing to evolve into the twenty-first century. The controversial and unsentimental columnist and critic, Stanley Crouch, claimed that Jayne Cortez was the only female poet that was interesting during the Black Arts Movement—interestingly, this was the same Stanley Crouch who learned to play the drums so that he could accompany Cortez while she performed her poetry in the mid-1960s. In an interview with Robert Boynton (posted on his website), Crouch stated, "I'd never met anyone with that kind of aesthetic commitment, who'd drawn a line in the dirt and said, 'I am an artist.'"

attracted to the exciting jazz scene that was evolving in California during that time. In 1954, when she was eighteen, Cortez married jazz saxophonist, Ornette Coleman; the marriage lasted until 1964. Because Cortez had a musical background and lived in a musical environment, her writing gravitated toward lyrical verse, and at a further point she began to interweave her poetry with music. While fusing jazz and poetry was nothing new, Cortez, who learned from various arts movements and absorbed the experimental spirit exemplified by such writers as Langston Hughes, Jack Kerouac, and Amiri Baraka (Leroi Jones), developed her own style.

Critics have also described Cortez as a political poet. It is important to note that during the 1960s, many black artists, including Cortez, were influenced by the Black Arts Movement. The Black Arts Movement, considered to be the artistic branch of the Black Power Movement, has been criticized by several black scholars, including the esteemed Henry Louis Gates, Jr. However, many

Tony Bolden wrote a critical essay for *African American Review*, where he discussed Cortez's work at length. Bolden declared, "Black Aesthetic poetic theories are best exemplified in the poetry of Jayne Cortez, whose work demonstrates the full potentiality of what I call a blues poetics; that is, the most profound manifestation of the tradition of African American Resistance poetry." Bolden further explained "Black Arts poets, who were attuned to the impact of Malcolm X and James Brown on black audiences, realized that the sermon and song/shout could be utilized to create a popular people's poetry as reading material, poets attempted to incarnate—that is, become—the black performer and thereby blur the distinction between poetry and song by using the voice as an instrument." In the essay, Bolden explained the term, *tonal semantics*, which is an African-American form of paralinguistics, "a term that performance scholars use to describe a mode of communication that cannot be conveyed adequately in print." Comparing Cortez with other poets, including Amiri Baraka, Sonia Sanchez, Kalamu ya Salaam, and Askia Toure, who all employ tonal semantics, asserted that her work is unique largely because she rehearsed "with her own band, which allows her to fine-tune her use of tonal semantics in her interaction with band members. Her band, The Firespitters, has a distinct sound, yet it is clear to listeners that the band has been structured around her voice and the rhythms of her poetry. Cortez often employs vocal techniques that simulate those of blues singers and/or instrumentalists. She also uses what I call terms of rememory: allusions, words, and/or images that recall important aspects of the black cultural experience." Cortez , who maintains that her poetry swings with or without music, emphasized to Luke Woods, writer for the *Eastern Echo*, "The most important part of poetry and art is that you've got to find your own way, otherwise you're not in it."

The early 1960s were extremely challenging for Cortez. Not only had she become a political activist and had established herself as a poet, she traveled to Africa, Asia, and Europe. In 1967 she moved to New York City and began to get more recognition for her work. Since 1969, when she published her first book, *Pisstained Stairs and the Monkey Man's Wares*, Cortez has published a book every few years, most of which have been illustrated by Melvin Edwards, whom she wed in 1975. It is interesting to note that in 1956 Cortez and Ornette Coleman had a son, Denardo who, at a young age became a proficient drummer. Denardo often accompanied his father, and later became a member of The Firespitters and has played on all of his mother's albums. In 2003, at the age of 67, Cortez and the Firespitters released *Borders of Disorderly Time*. Most people think about retiring at that age, but Cortez continues to perform, lecture, and teach. While Cortez was the M. Thelma McAndless Distinguished Professor in Humanities at Eastern Michigan University in 2003, she told Carol Anderson of *Focus EMU*, "I look at my work today, then tomorrow it looks different. I say, 'That' pretty good, but tomorrow I'll write a new masterpiece.'"

Selected works

Books

Pisstained Stairs and the Monkey Man's Wares, Phrase Text, 1969.
Festivals and Funerals, Bola Press, 1971.
Scarifications, Bola Press, 1973.
Mouth on Paper, Bola Press, 1977.
Firespitter, Bola Press, 1982.
Coagulations: New and Selected Poems, Thunder's Mouth Press, 1984.
Poetic Magnetic, Bola Press, 1991.
Somewhere in Advance of Nowhere, Serpent's Tail, 1997.
Jazz Fan Looks Back, Hanging Loose Press, Brooklyn, 2002.

Film

Poetry in Motion, 1982.
Nelson Mandela is Coming (music video), 1991.
Women in Jazz, 2000.

Recordings

Celebrations and Solitudes, Strata East, 1975.
Unsubmissive Blues, Bola Press, 1980.
There It Is, Bola Press, 1982.
Maintain Control, Bola Press, 1986.
Everywhere Drums, Bola Press, 1991.
Mandela is Coming, Globalvision, 1991.
Taking the Blues Back Home, Harmolodic/Verve, 1997.
Borders of Disorderly Time, 2003.

Sources

Periodicals

African American Review, Spring 2001, p. 61.
Billboard, March 2, 1991, p. 62.
Eastern Echo, October 1, 2003.
Focus EMU, October 14, 2003, p. 4.
Publishers Weekly, April 29, 2002, p. 66.

On-line

"Biography," *Jayne Cortez Official Website*, www.jaynecortez.com (October 19, 2003).
"Black Poetry Text & Sound: Two Trains Running Black Poetry 1965-2000 (notes towards a discussion & dialogue)," *Chicken Bones: A Journal for Literary & Artistic African-American Themes*, www.nathanielturner.com/whatisblackpoetry.htm (November 11, 2003).

"Inside the River of Poetry," *In Motion*, www.inmotionmagazine.com/ac/rivera.html (November 11, 2003).

"Jayne Cortez, Poet, Jazz Artist," *Black Voices: Black History Month,* www.blackvoices.com/feature/blk_history_98/women/html/4.htm (November 6, 2003).

"Jayne Cortez & The Firespitters," *Philadelphia City Paper,* http://citypaper.net/articles//021501/cw.pick.jayne.shtml (October 19, 2003).

"On Cortez's Poetry," *Modern American Poetry,* www.english.uiuc.edu/maps/poets/a_f/cortez/poetry.htm (October 27, 2003).

"The Professor of Connection: A Profile of Stanley Crouch," *Robert Boynton Official Website,* www.robertboynton.com (November 30, 2003).

"Voices From the Gaps: Women Writers of Color, Jayne Cortez," *University of Minnesota*, http://voices.cla.umn.edu/authors/CORTEZjayne.html (October 27, 2003).

—Christine Miner Minderovic

Kia Corthron

1961—

Playwright

In today's dramatic world, few playwrights have the force of Kia Corthron. While many have written as many plays as she has, few have written so many under commission. Fourteen of her twenty plays have been commissioned, which means Corthron was directly hired to write a piece for the commission granters' playhouse. This shows the power of her work. Her plays encompass all range of human emotion, like most plays do, but Corthron pushes past the surface to dig deep into the human psyche.

Often called a "political" playwright, Corthron finds her plays in issues, not in characters or stories like other playwrights. Most of her plays deal with African-American issues, yet skirt the realm of all human consciences. According to Weber in *Columbia Magazine,* "Corthron pulls her ideas from movies, newspapers and the Zeitgeist, or the general moral, intellectual and cultural climate of an era. Her works reach out to all ages, genders, races and nationalities."

Kia Corthron was born on May 13, 1961, in Cumberland, Maryland. Cumberland was a factory town located on the small portion of the state between West Virginia and Pennsylvania. Corthron's father worked at a paper mill in the area and died at age 51 of an aneurysm while working at the mill. Growing up in the mostly white, industrial town, Corthron found writing early in life. It became a way for her to process the world around her. She recalled her second grade teacher, Mrs. Proudfoot, as being the person who first encouraged her to write. She continued to create dialogues, more out of a need for entertainment while her older sister was at school rather than some innate artistic drive. She would often use clothespins, pencils and various household items to act out her created dialogues.

Corthron attended the University of Maryland for an undergraduate degree in communications and film. Even though she had begun writing early in life, it was not until the last semester of her senior year that she first turned on to playwriting. During a creative writing class, Corthon was assigned a group project of creating a play. She worked on the play for the entire semester, revising and reworking the text, which culminated in a final performance. The plot dealt with a returning Vietnam soldier and his sister, but the success of the short piece was not the plot, it was the impact the play had on the classroom audience. She told the Theater Development Fund's periodical *Sightlines,* "When it came time to do scenes from our plays, I was embarrassed when mine lasted 30 minutes when everyone else's was only five (they were all supposed to be five), but I was soon gratified when the lights came up and I saw how my writing affected the other students."

That love for affecting audiences was something that excited Corthron. This was also something which drove her to work on her craft as a playwright. After graduating, Corthron was chosen for a one year workshop with George Washington University playwright Lonnie Garter. Under the direction of Garter, Corthron applied to the Master of Fine Arts program at Columbia. Corthron was accepted and attended Columbia where she studied under professors like Howard Stein, Glenn Young, and Lavonne Mueller. Upon graduation in 1992, Corthron began writing plays and was granted a

At a Glance . . .

Born Kia Corthron on May 13, 1961, in Cumberland, MD. *Education:* University of Maryland, BA, 1980s; Columbia University, MFA, 1992.

Career: Playwright 1992–.

Memberships: New Dramatist.

Awards: Daryl Roth Creative Spirit Award, 2001; Kennedy Center Fund for New American Plays, 1996; New Professional Theatre Playwriting Award; Callaway Award; Van Lier Fellowship; Delaware Theatre Company's Connections contest winner; NEA/TCG Theatre Residency Program for Playwrights; Fadiman Award.

Addresses: *Agent*—c/o Sarah Jane Leigh, International Creative Management, 40 West 57th Street, New York, NY 10019.

commission from the Goodman Theater in Chicago to write the play *Seeking the Genesis,* a piece dealing with parents drugging their children with Ritalin and the proposed government drugging of urban youth to prevent violence.

Since her graduation, Corthron has received commissions for workshops, readings, and productions throughout the country. Her work has garnered critical and audience acclaim. Beginning with the commission from Chicago's Goodman Theater, she has gone on to receive many other commissions for plays. Although commissioned works are not the only indication of the skill and power a playwright has, they are good indications that the particular playwright is good. Among Corthron's commissions are commissions from the Royal Court Theatre in London, the Alabama Shakespeare Festival, the Atlantic Theatre Company, the Manhattan Theatre Club, the Mark Taper Forum, the Public Media Foundation, the Children's Theatre Company, and National Public Radio with The Public Theater.

As a playwright, workshops play an important role in honing the pieces of dramatic art that playwrights create. Corthron is no exception to this rule. She has developed her work through numerous reputable workshops including the National Playwrights Conference, the Sundance retreat at Ucross, the Hedgebrook writer's retreat, the Audrey Skirball-Kenis Theatre Project,

the Shenandoah International Playwrights Retreat, Intiman Theatre, A Contemporary Theatre, Crossroads Theatre Company's Genesis Festival, The Public Theater's New Work Now! Festival, Voice and Vision, and the Circle Rep Lab.

Most of Corthron's work revolves around socio-political issues. The themes of her work have encompassed many issues found in newspapers. For instance, her work *Force Continuum* from 2000 dealt with the issue of police brutality. Her shorter piece, *Safe Box,* centered on the industries that dump cancer-causing chemicals into the air and water. Her two-act drama *Glimpse of the Ephemeral Dot* dealt with veteran's issues. In other plays she has examined the land mine issue, girl gangs, prisons, the death penalty, youth violence, and disability, to name a few.

With the commissions, works, and impact of Corthron's work, she has garnered many awards. These include the Daryl Roth Creative Spirit Award, the Mark Taper Forum's Fadiman Award, NEA/TCG Theatre Residency Program for Playwrights, a Kennedy Center Fund for New American Plays, the New Professional Theatre Playwriting Award, the Callaway Award, a Van Lier Fellowship, and was Delaware Theatre Company's first Connections contest winner.

The most provocative thing about Corthron as a playwright has been said to be her language. Sometimes called poetic and sometimes called unusual, her rhythmic style is one thing that has been a constant throughout her work. It is song-like in a sense, but comes from her youthful experience. She stated to Amy Reiter in an *American Theatre* article from October 1994, "I don't know where I get my funny language from ... but it is influenced by where I grew up. Nobody there speaks exactly that way, but it has a lot of rhythms. It's music." It is clear that with a voice so unique and catching the eye of so many critics, audiences and theater company's, that Corthron's will the be name soon brought to the forefront and always remembered in American theatrical history.

Selected plays

Catnap Allegiance, Manhattan Theater Club, 1990s.
Wake Up Lou Riser, Circle Repertory Company Lab, 1992.
Cage Rhythm, Long Wharf Theater, 1993.
Come Down Burning, Long Wharf Theater, 1993.
Life by Asphyxiation, Playwrights Horizons, 1995.
Seeking the Genesis, Goodman Theater, 1996.
Digging Eleven, New York Stage and Film, 1997.
Anchor Aria, Mark Taper Forum Square Project, 1997.
Suckling Chimera, Public Theater, 1998.
Up, Audrey Skirball-Kennis Theater, 2000.
Safe Box, Goodman Theater, 1999.
Breath, Boom, Royal Court Theater, 2000.

Slide Glide the Slippery Slope, Mark Taper Forum, 2000s.

Glimpse the Ephemeral Dot, Alabama Shakespeare Festival, 2000s.

Light Raise the Roof, Manhattan Theater Club, 2000s.

Force Continuum, Atlantic Theater Company, 2001.

Somnia, Cooper Union, 2001.

Sweat, Public Media Foundation, Boston, 2002.

Snapshot Silhouette, Children's Theater Company, 2003-04.

Sources

Periodicals

American Theatre, October 1994, p. 77.

On-line

"A Playwright of Ideas," *Columbia Magazine,* www. columbia.edu/cu/alumni/Magazine/Fall2003./kia-corthron.html (February 2, 2004).

"For These Theatre Professionals-It All Began In School," *TDF Sightlines Online,* www.tdf.org/pub lications/sightlines/sightlines01fall.html (February 2, 2004).

"Kia Corthron," *New Dramatists,* www.newdrama-tists.org/kia_corthron.htm (February 2, 2004).

"Kia Corthron," *Southern Writer's Project, Alabama Shakespeare Festival,* www.asftisckets.com/swp (February 2, 2004).

"Kia Corthron: A Playwright Who's Unafraid to Admit She's Political," *Don Shewey's Online Archive,* www.donshewey.com/theater_articles/kia_ corthron.htm (February 2, 2004).

— Adam R. Hazlett

Benjamin O. Davis, Jr.

1912-2002

Lieutenant general of the U.S. Air Force

Benjamin O. Davis, Jr., fought and won both military and civil rights battles. As a World War II fighter pilot he engaged Axis forces across the European theater. At the same time, he helped defeat segregationist policies in his own country by proving beyond a shadow of a doubt that black soldiers were in every way as competent as their white counterparts, and deserving of equal standing. In 1948 the United States Military became one of the first American institutions to adopt a policy of complete integration—in part because of the stellar performance of Davis and his men.

Davis was born on December 18, 1912, in Washington, D.C. His father, Benjamin O. Davis, Sr., was a career military man who rose from the rank of private to that of brigadier general in charge of an all-black cavalry unit. In *Benjamin O. Davis, Jr., American: An Autobiography,* his son noted that his last promotion, made on the eve of World War II, was "motivated primarily by the hope of winning black votes in the 1940 election ... but my father had richly deserved it for many years." According to *Washington Post Book World* contributor Joseph Glattharr, Davis's parents gave their son a simple set of values by which to live: "Treat others ... as you wish them to treat you. Feel

sorry not for yourself, but for those whose blinding prejudice bars them from getting to know your wonderful qualities. And work hard at everything you do."

Endured Racism Early

Davis was taught to face squarely even the most virulent forms of racism. In the early 1920s, while the elder Davis was stationed at Tuskegee Institute in Alabama, the Ku Klux Klan organized a march in support of a policy requiring an all-white medical staff at a nearby black veterans hospital. Black residents were advised to stay indoors with their lights out during the demonstration, in order to avoid any eruption of violence. But Davis's father had his own notion of how to properly deal with the Klan; donning his white dress uniform, he seated his entire family under a bright porch light and stood defiantly as the Klansmen—hooded and carrying flaming torches—passed within inches of him.

Memories of his father's courage undoubtedly helped Benjamin Davis, Jr., endure the trials he faced upon entering the United States Military Academy at West Point in 1932. His entrance qualifications were impec-

At a Glance . . .

Born Benjamin Oliver Davis, Jr., on December 18, 1912, in Washington, DC; died on July 4, 2002, in Washington, DC; son of Benjamin Oliver (an officer in the U.S. Army) and Sadie (Overton) Davis; married Agatha Scott, June 20, 1936. *Education:* United States Military Academy, West Point, BS, 1936. *Politics:* Democrat. *Religion:* Protestant.

Career: U.S. Air Force, lieutenant, 1936-42, commander of 99th Fighter Squadron, 332nd Fighter Group, 477th Bombardment Group, and 332nd Fighter Wing, 1942-49, Air War College professor, 1949-50, fighter branch chief, U.S. Air Force headquarters, 1950-53, commander, 51st Fighter Interceptor Wing, Suwon, Korea, 1954-54, director of operations and training, Far East Air Forces headquarters, 1954-55, promoted to brigadier general, 1954, commander, Air Task Force 13, Taiwan, 1955-57, deputy chief of staff, operations headquarters, U.S. Air Force, Europe, 1957-61, promoted to major general, 1957, director of manpower and organization, U.S. Air Force headquarters, 1961-65, promoted to lieutenant general, 1965, chief of staff, United Nations Command and United States Forces, Korea, 1965-67, commander, 13th Air Force, Philippines, 1967-68, deputy commander-in-chief, U.S. Strike Command, MacDill Air Force Base, 1969-70; Cleveland city government, director of public safety, 1970; U.S. Department of Transportation, director of civil aviation security, assistant secretary of environment, safety, and consumer affairs, 1971-1975.

Selected awards: Three Distinguished Service Medals with two Oak Leaf Clusters; Croix de Guerre with Palm; Star of Africa; Army and Air Force Silver Star; Distinguished Flying Cross; three Legions of Merit; Air Medal with five Oak Leaf Clusters; made a 4-Star General by President Clinton, 1998; numerous honorary degrees.

cable, but the prestigious academy's tacit racist practices were designed to force his resignation. Davis's fellow cadets—encouraged by their superiors—subjected him to a variety of mental cruelties they called "silencing." For four years, no one roomed with him, ate with him, acknowledged his presence—even if he asked a direct question—or spoke to him, except to issue an order. Davis stood firm against their mute, solid front and graduated 35th in a class of 276, becoming the first black in the twentieth century to complete four years at West Point, and only the fourth black ever to have graduated from the Military Academy.

His high standing in his class entitled Davis to choose which branch of service he would enter. Flying had been a lifelong dream, and accordingly, he selected the Air Force. Officials curtly informed Davis that blacks, no matter what their standing at West Point, were not eligible to become part of the flying elite. Instead, the young lieutenant was assigned to Fort Benning, Georgia. There he and his wife, Agatha, endured another "silencing" ordeal. Davis wrote that his exclusion by the Fort Benning Officers' Club was the most deeply insulting of all the racist behavior that dogged his career. After a transfer to Fort Riley, Kansas, the couple found themselves in slightly better circumstances; but they were still barred from the Officers' Club and had to attend a segregated movie theater on the base.

Commanded First Black Fighter Pilots

Just as they had for his father, election-year politics finally gave Davis the break he deserved. President Franklin Roosevelt's need for the black vote led him in 1941 to approve what was billed as a bold military experiment—giving black men the chance to serve as fighter pilots. Only the best and the brightest were chosen for the 99th Pursuit Squadron; Davis was selected to command them. The Air Force's attitude toward the 99th paralleled West Point's treatment of Davis: officially they were accepted, but off the record, they were encouraged to fail. According to veteran pilot and *Smithsonian* contributor Edward Park, the squadron was given inferior equipment and sketchy training. "Usually, when new units arrived at a World War II base, they got a thorough briefing and a flight or two with an old hand during their initial combat missions. Not the 99th. With the squadron formed and Davis in command, the black Tuskegee pilots arrived at a dirt airstrip in North Africa and simply started flying missions.... [The] attitude was: let 'em sink or swim." Davis told Park, "Fortunately, before our unit was deployed, three old pilots gave us a hand.... They showed us some of the tricks and how to survive." Park concluded: "Ben Davis had two wars to fight—one against Hitler's Luftwaffe, the other against the prejudice of the U.S. Army Air Forces."

During their first months in action, the 99th's performance was comparable to any new squadron's. Still, white air corps officers sent an unfavorable report back to the Pentagon stating that "the Negro type has not the proper reflexes to make a first-class fighter pilot." Herbert Mitgang pointed out in the *New York Times* that "this language matched the theories of racial inferiority espoused by the Klan and by Hitler." As General Davis told *Jet* magazine years later, "All the Blacks in the segregated forces operated like they had to prove they could fly an airplane when everyone believed they were too stupid."

Davis, fearing that the 99th would be assigned to routine coastal patrols, went to Washington to personally defend his squadron's right to remain in combat. When he returned to the war zone, it was to command four black squadrons known as the 332nd Fighter Group. The 332nd saw action throughout Europe; in two days during January of 1944, they shot down 12 German fighters over the Anzio beachhead in Italy. By July of 1944 Davis was a full colonel, and a highly-classified study by the Air Force had acknowledged that the 332nd's record was equal to that of any other unit in the Mediterranean. According to *Jet* the 332nd Fighter Group was said to have never lost any plane that relied on them for support.

Helped Integrate U.S. Armed Forces

In 1948, due at least in part to the wartime accomplishments of Davis and his men, the U.S. Armed Forces became one of the first institutions in America to adopt an official policy of full integration, thus becoming the first workplace in which black Americans could hope for equal opportunity. Davis played a key role in the integration process, and later went on to command the integrated 51st Fighter Wing in Korea and the 13th Air Force in Vietnam. By 1965 he had reached the rank of Lieutenant General.

In 1970 Davis retired from the Armed Forces. The first charge he was given after his military duties were finished was the federal sky marshal program, which he was put in charge of to stop airline hijackings. The following year he was named assistant secretary of the Department of Transportation, where Davis was a leader in the development of airport and aviation security and an advocate of the 55-mile-per-hour speed limit designed to save fuel and lives.

Throughout his career Davis overcame prejudice because he "refused to acknowledge race distinctions," wrote a reporter for *Jet*. He demonstrated the strength of his convictions when in February of 1991 a press conference announcing the publication of his autobiography was billed as the opening event of Black History Month. As recounted by *Jet*, Davis issued a statement saying that his military career was "not a Black History Month feature" and that his accomplishments were "but a footnote in American history to the hundreds of Black airmen who stood shoulder to shoulder with their White counterparts." In Davis's autobiography—which Glattharr called in *Washington Post Book World* "must reading for anyone interested in race relations or American military history"—Davis further detailed his

belief that focusing on color divisions only served to perpetuate them. He wrote: "I do not find it complimentary to me or to the nation to be called the first Black West Point graduate in this century." He also took issue with black leader Jesse Jackson's suggestion that black Americans identify themselves as African Americans, for in his opinion, "We are all simply American."

Davis, who left the military as a Lieutenant General with three stars—the senior black officer in the armed forces at the time—was awarded a fourth star in 1998 by President Clinton. While awarding Davis the star, Clinton stated, according to *Jet*, magazine that "General Davis is here today as living proof that a person can overcome adversity and discrimination, achieve great things, turn skeptics into believers and through example and perseverance, one person can bring truly extraordinary change."

On July 4, 2002, Davis died at the Walter Reed Medical Center in Washington, D.C. He was 89-years-old. Davis left an extraordinary legacy behind him. As President Clinton said, "To all of us General Davis [was] the very embodiment of the principal that with firm diversity we can build stronger unity. If we follow [his] example we will always be a leader for democracy, opportunity, and peace. I am very, very proud of [his] service."

Selected writings

Benjamin O. Davis, Jr., American: An Autobiography, Smithsonian Institution Press, 1991.

Sources

Books

Davis, Benjamin O., Jr., *Benjamin O. Davis, Jr., American: An Autobiography,* Smithsonian Institution Press, 1991.

Periodicals

Air and Space Power Journal, Spring, 2003, p. 16.
American History Illustrated, July/August 1991.
American Visions, April 1991.
Chicago Tribune, January 27, 1991.
Foreign Affairs, Summer 1991.
Insight, March 4, 1991.
Jet, February 11, 1991; September 5, 1994, p. 52; December 28, 1998, p. 24; July 22, 2002, p. 14.
New York Times, February 20, 1991.
Publishers Weekly, January 4, 1991.
Smithsonian, March 1991.
Washington Post, February 4, 1991.
Washington Post Book World, March 17, 1991.

—Joan Goldsworthy and Catherine V. Donaldson

José Eduardo dos Santos

1942—

Politician

José Eduardo dos Santos became president of Angola in 1979 and was one of the African continent's longest serving leaders at the onset of the twenty-first century. Dos Santos heads the Movimento Popular de Libertação de Angola (MPLA), the party that led the country in its prolonged and contentious struggle for independence from Portugal in the 1960s.

The son of a bricklayer, dos Santos was born in Luanda, the capital of what was then Portuguese West Africa, on August 28, 1942. As a teen, he won admittance to the prestigious Liceu Salvador Carreia, where the Portuguese elite sent their offspring and which admitted only a small number of African students. The Angola in which dos Santos grew up was an overseas province of Portugal, but there was widespread dissatisfaction, and several resistance groups emerged in the late 1950s, inspired and aided by other African nations' successful campaigns for independence. In 1961 dos Santos joined one of these groups, the MPLA, as the opposition movement in Angola grew in strength and fervor. For his role in the movement, he was forced to flee the country, and in Kinshasa, Zaire—later the Democratic Republic of the Congo—he became a key player in the formation of the MPLA Youth organization.

The MPLA was a dedicated Marxist organization at the time, and in 1963 dos Santos won a party scholarship for study in the Soviet Union. He trained as a petroleum engineer at the Institute of Oil and Gas in Baku, graduating in 1969, and returned to Angola the following year. He immediately resumed his political activities there, joining a guerrilla unit of the MPLA that was active in the oil-rich area of Cabinda. The war against Portuguese colonial rule finally ended in 1974, when a coup in Lisbon ousted the military dictatorship and the new government declared a truce with the Angolan rebels.

In 1974 dos Santos went from a post as second in command of telecommunications services in Cabinda to the MPLA's coordinator for foreign affairs. That same year he was elevated to the MPLA Central Committee, and became an active participant in the formation of the first Angolan government. The country formally became the People's Republic of Angola on November 11, 1975, and dos Santos became the first minister for foreign affairs in the new government of President António Agostinho Neto. In 1978 he also

At a Glance . . .

Born José Eduardo dos Santos, on August 28, 1942, in Luanda, Angola; son of a bricklayer; married Ana Paula dos Santos; three children. *Education:* Institute of Oil and Gas in Baku, graduated, 1969.

Career: Movimento Popular de Libertação de Angola (MPLA), Youth organization leader, early 1970s, second-in-command of telecommunications services in Cabinda, 1974, coordinator of the Foreign Affairs department, 1974; Angolan government, foreign minister, 1975-78 minister for economic development and planning, 1978, president, 1979–.

Addresses: *Office*—Gabinete do Presidente, Luanda, Angola.

became minister for economic development and planning.

The road to independence had been a long one for Angolans, but the various resistance groups remained at odds after 1975, and the conflict quickly turned into a civil war. The country was a strife-ridden, dangerous place when dos Santos became president after Neto died of cancer in September of 1979. The National Front for the Liberation of Angola (FNLA) and the União Nacional para a Independência Total de Angola (UNITA) took control of various parts of the country, and over the next decade the world's superpowers, specifically the United States and the Soviet Union, provided aid to the warring factions and turned the country into a Cold War battleground. The MPLA received assistance from the Soviets, and a large Cuban military also battled UNITA forces, which were receiving covert aid from the United States as well as from South Africa's apartheid regime. For years, dos Santos and UNITA leader Jonas Savimbi were avowed mortal enemies.

In 1991 dos Santos announced that the MPLA was abandoning its Marxist platform, and elections were held the following year. He was one of 11 candidates for the presidency, but his main opponent was Savimbi, whom he beat in the polls by nine percentage points. In response, Savimbi claimed vote fraud, and refused to take part in a runoff election. The civil war resumed, and by law dos Santos remained as interim president. He and Savimbi continued their mutual enmity, despite the signing of the 1994 Lusaka Protocol between the two and the subsequent government of national unity formed between the MPLA and UNITA

in 1997. Savimbi died on the battlefield in February of 2002, and the following month UNITA and Angolan army commanders announced a cessation of the fighting, which by then had endured for some four decades.

Dos Santos is president of a nation of ten million inhabitants, which exports oil, coffee, and diamonds. Its economy, however, remains in shambles and it must import food to feed it citizens. The offshore oil reserves of Cabinda provide about 85 percent of government revenue, but observers charge that the government skims about $1 billion of the $7 billion it receives annually. The 1992 election remains the only one ever held in Angolan history, but dos Santos has said that when the country stabilizes, he will set a date for new elections. In late 2003 he asserted that elections would take place before 2005. Having dismissed his prime minister some years earlier, dos Santos has served in that role, as well as that of president and head of the MPLA party. That situation could leave a potentially disastrous power vacuum if dos Santos should step down prematurely. "If … I were to nominate someone for the position of prime minister, the current government will consider itself dismissed and this prime minister would propose his own government to the head of state," he was quoted as saying in 2001 in a *BBC News* report by Justin Pearce. "It is evident that not all people that have the confidence of the prime minister are the same ones that have the confidence of the head of state."

Sources

Books

Worldmark Encyclopedia of the Nations: World Leaders, Gale, 2003.

Periodicals

African Business, April 1995, p. 29.
Christian Century, March 22, 2003, p. 8.
Economist, June 8, 1996, p. 45; September 23, 2000, p. 52; November 10, 2001.
Nation, April 29, 2002, p. 7.
Time, September 29, 1986, p. 47; October 17, 1988, p. 43; July 3, 1989, p. 28.
U.S. News & World Report, October 5, 1992, p. 56.

On-line

"Biography of the President the Republic of Angola," *Republic of Angola,* www.angola.org.uk/facts_bio_pres.htm (December 31, 2003).
"Profile: José Eduardo dos Santos," *BBC News,* http://news.bbc.co.uk/1/hi/world/africa/1506759.stm (December 26, 2003).

—Carol Brennan

Sharon Mills Draper

1952—

Educator, writer

As an author, poet, and master educator named 1997 U.S. Teacher of the Year, Sharon Draper has introduced thousands of children and young people to the world of words. Draper said that teaching has been her "calling and vocation," describing herself as a teacher who "teaches because I must. It is in my heart and soul; part of the definition of me. I end up teaching wherever I am." As a teacher who has also become a writer she has testified to the value of story and the power of words to generations of students. Her published work, including two young adult novels, a series of juvenile fiction, and two collections of poetry has been grounded in the conviction that books could and must speak to the lives and dreams of young readers. Choosing African-American male characters has been Draper's way of giving the power of words to African-American young men.

Born to Victor and Catherine Mills in 1952 in Cleveland, Ohio, Draper was the eldest of three children raised in a close-knit neighborhood. Her father worked as a hotel manager and her mother as an administrator at the *Cleveland Plain Dealer*. Theirs was a family where education was a given. The question was not "would you attend college, it was where and to study what," Draper said. In her home, books were part of everyday life. Reading and the learning that naturally flowed from written words surrounded Draper and her siblings. Schools and schooling were always considered an open door through which the three Mills children were expected to walk with success.

Taught Students the Value of Writing

Sharon Draper's vision, in the classroom and as she wrote, has been to challenge young people to embrace learning without limits and without hesitation. She credited her family and early schooling with giving her the gift of an unlimited love of learning. Draper entered Cleveland Public Schools in the 1950s from a home where she had grown up surrounded by books. Her mother read stories, poems, fairytales, and nursery rhymes to Draper and her siblings from the time they were very young. She recalled a teacher who once "gave me O's for outstanding, saying an A wasn't good enough." A fifth grade teacher gave Draper and her fellow students poetry by Langston Hughes and Robert Frost. They read and

At a Glance . . .

Born in 1952 in Cleveland, OH; daughter of Victor Mills (a hotel manager) and Catherine Mills (newspaper administrator); married Larry Draper, 1971. *Education:* Pepperdine University, BA, 1971; Miami University of Ohio, MA, 1974.

Career: Cincinnati Public Schools, teacher, 1970-97; author, 1991–.

Awards: Coretta Scott King Genesis award for Literature, 1995; American Library Association Best Book for Young Adults award, 1995; Ohio State Teacher of the Year, 1997; U.S. National Teacher of the Year, 1997; National Board Certification, National Board for Professional Teaching Standards, 1995; Board of Directors, National Board for Professional Teaching Standards, 1997; National Council of Negro Women's Excellence in Teaching Award, 1997; Delta Kapa Gamma Honor Society for Women Educators.

Addresses: *Office*—c/o Janell Agymeman, Marie Brown Associates, Inc., 990 NE 82 Terrace, Miami, FL, United States 33138.

loved Shakespeare. "We didn't know we weren't supposed to be able to do that in fifth grade. She gave it to us and we loved it," Draper said. "It was part of making me the teacher I am today."

Draper completed secondary school in the Cleveland Public School system, taking advanced and AP coursework. She attended Pepperdine University as a National Merit Scholar, majoring in English. Upon graduation in 1971, Pepperdine offered the then-20-year-old a teaching position and opportunity to pursue a Master's degree. She declined, returning instead to Ohio where she married and assumed a teaching position in the Cincinnati Public Schools where as of 2003 she still spent each day on the educational frontline. Draper knew even then that teaching at the high school, not the university level, was where she belonged.

In the classroom Draper soon became known among students as a challenging and no-nonsense educator likely to recite selections from *The Canterbury Tales* from memory or launch into a discussion of issue-laden contemporary books. Nearly half her senior English students went on to become teachers themselves. As an educator who saw joy and challenge as partners in the learning process, Draper looked for ways to cap-

ture and challenge her senior students, wanting them to stride away from high school with a sense of confidence and accomplishment. She assigned a lengthy, demanding research paper due in the last quarter of her students' senior year. Designed as a test and challenge of skills in writing, analysis, and research, the assignment soon was dubbed "The Draper Paper." Within a few years t-shirts were designed to be doled out only to those hardy survivors of Draper's literary challenge. She once spotted a former student at the airport in London wearing one of these shirts. Who else would dare to sport an "I Survived the Draper Paper" t-shirt? Juniors "start to tremble just hearing about it," Draper said. This master-teacher was as respected as she was in demand among students at Walnut Hills High School in Cincinnati. She would not have it any other way.

Started Writing Career

Draper's first personal venture into writing came when a student handed her a writing contest application and said, "Why don't you write something?" The resulting short story "One Small Torch" was chosen from 20,000 entries as the winner of the 1991 *Ebony* Magazine Short Story Contest. According to an interview she did with *Ebony* magazine, the day after the magazine hit stands Draper started receiving phone calls and letters congratulating her on her story and her win. "Her most treasured letter came from *Roots* author Alex Haley. 'It was on his own letterhead and in his own writing.... To get a letter from Alex Haley, is that powerful or what?'"

That first success was impetus for Draper to combine her love of teaching with her love of words and story as an author and poet. Her first novel, *Tears of a Tiger,* grew out of Draper's recognition that powerful, once-timely works by authors like Dickens were missing the mark with her students. She wanted to create a contemporary book of literary quality to reach the cultural, ethnic, and daily realities of students in today's high school classrooms. Her novel's main character, Andy, was the drunken driver in an accident that killed his best friend. Draper encouraged young writers by telling the story of rejection by 24 of 25 publishers to which *Tears of a Tiger* was sent. Once published, this book was affirmed as "strong, vivid, and ringing true" in *School Library Journal.* It was embraced by young readers and received both the 1995 American Library Association Best Book for Young Adults and Coretta Scott King Genesis Awards.

A 1997 sequel, *Forged by Fire* was her second novel. It was the second novel in what would become the "Hazelwood High" trilogy. *Forged by Fire* was about Gerald, one of Andy's—the main character in *Tears of a Tiger*—basketball teammates. The conclusion to the trilogy was *Darkness before Dawn,* which followed Keisha, Andy's ex-girlfriend through her last year of high school. Her first volume of poetry for children was accepted by Boyd's Mills Press.

As a classroom teacher and mentor to novice educators, Draper knew that even the best contemporary titles often failed to draw young boys into the world of reading. Fewer books still were written with young African-American boys in mind. Her next venture, the *Ziggy and the Black Dinosaurs* series, was written for those young readers. "I know what interests kids," Draper said. "I know what will catch them and make them readers in spite of themselves." In *Lost in the Tunnel of Time,* Ziggy and his fellow clubmates, the Black Dinosaurs, discover a tunnel once used as a station on the Underground Railroad. Always the teacher, Draper filled the book with history, knowing students would absorb the information effortlessly because of the strong, interesting story. "I tell my students that if they learn nothing else in my class, I want them to understand that a powerful connection exists between historical and cultural events and the literary creations of the time," Draper told the Ohio Department of Education upon her selection as Ohio Teacher of the Year in January of 1997.

Her next book was "Double Dutch," a story about a girl, Delia, who can not read, but has somehow managed to make it to her ninth grade tests before she thinks she'll be found out. She's worried about being discovered because it would mean that she could not continue competing in the Double Dutch jump rope contests that she loves. In 2003 Draper published "The Battle of Jericho." In this novel, according to *Publishers Weekly,* Draper "conveys the seductive power of teen clubs and the dangers of hazing rituals."

Became Teacher of the Year

While her writing continued on, Draper was also named both Cincinnati and Ohio Teacher of the Year, and in 1997 Draper was awarded the highest award a teacher can acquire, the coveted U.S. Teacher of the Year Award. She was given the award in 1997 by President Clinton at the White House. Being named U.S. Teacher of the Year brought diverse facets of Sharon Draper's life and personal gifts together. As a master-teacher and mentor of other educators, Draper was an able spokesperson for her profession. As a creator of fiction of interest to hard-to-reach students, Draper was an able model for high standards and innovative teaching. As a teacher "by calling and vocation" she was a spokesperson for the value of teachers and teaching to every child and every community.

As Teacher of the Year, Draper spoke to and on behalf of educators across the country. "I was singled out, but there are thousands of teachers doing a wonderful job who receive no recognition," she said. "Teachers who work all year with a class of 25 or more. At the end, every child is confident, loves school, and is ready to move on to the next grade. Does that teacher get her picture in the paper? Is he invited to speak because of an excellent job done? My privilege and challenge as Teacher of the Year is to speak for and about those

teachers. The ones teaching in every school and every community who are just doing their jobs."

As spokesperson and master-educator, Draper encouraged school systems and communities to re-think the place and contribution of teachers. "Teachers need affirmation and validation," Draper said. "They deserve respect and support. They need space … time to think and reflect … and to learn." Draper called the teacher-student connection a spark where true education happened. "We must find that spark, wherever it occurs and fan it into a flame. We need to ask ourselves where and why true education is happening and try to duplicate those conditions, increasing the probability of its happening again and again."

Teachers and students in every state in the U.S. meet each fall for Ready, Set, Goal conferences. Evaluation of past achievement is discussed. Goals for that and subsequent years are set. What are Sharon Draper's goals? Having long-since completed a Master of Arts degree in English at Miami University in Ohio, Draper engaged in ongoing post-graduate study. Completion of doctoral studies was in her ten-year plan. Personal and professional goals also included making time to write more poetry and add to her *Ziggy and the Black Dinosaurs* series. Draper was interested in further literary experimentation with the goal of reaching African-American students, especially boys.

Touring and meeting with teachers as Teacher of the Year has sparked a dream to find ways to mentor and encourage teachers and quality teaching. "When a students asks, 'Should I teach?' I say, 'Yes. Absolutely,'" Draper said. "Some young people think teachers don't make enough money and don't get enough respect. I tell them I'll never make as much as Michael Jordan, but neither will you. I tell them if you want to make a difference in somebody's life, then go into teaching."

As a member of the National Board for Teaching Standards, Draper worked with colleagues within the educational community, business and community leaders, and government to develop standards by which teachers and teaching may be quantitatively and actively measured. Professional development for teachers was a personal priority that Draper addressed by writing for professional publications and speaking to educators.

"During my tenure as Teacher of the Year I have communicated the importance of creating a nurturing environment for teachers. Teaching is such a difficult, challenging job. I'd like to find ways to develop planning strategies that come not from the administration down, but from teachers up." Spending 1997 touring the country as Teacher of the Year provided Draper with a forum for speaking—and teaching, of course, about the critical need for cooperation and bridge-building between communities and schools. Her work with the National Board for Teaching Standards challenged educators wary of accountability outside the educational community and challenged business and government to join schools as team members rather than outside critics.

Finally, Draper's goal as education foraged ahead in the twenty-first century was to spend decades, day in and day out, in school classrooms teaching students. She would measure her success in the names of students graduating with a deep sense of accomplishment and confidence in their own abilities and skill. Her legacy would be generations of students entering colleges and universities armed with a love of learning—and wearing t-shirts declaring "I Survived the Draper Paper."

Selected writings

Tears of a Tiger, Simon & Schuster, 1994.
Ziggy and the Black Dinosaurs, Just Us Books, 1995.
Forged by Fire, 1996.
Romiette and Julio, Simon & Schuster, 1997.
Jazzimation, Scholastic, 1999.
Teaching from the Heart, Heinemann, 1999.
Not Quite Burned out but Crispy around the Edges, Heinemann, 2001.
Darkness Before Dawn, Simon & Schuster, 2001.
Double Dutch, Simon & Schuster, 2002.
The Battle of Jericho, Simon & Schuster, 2003.

Sources

Books

Major Authors and Illustrators for Children and Young Adults, 2nd Edition, Gale Group, 2002.
Writer's Directory, 19th Edition, St. James Press, 2003.

Periodicals

Ebony, December 1990, p. 18; May, 1998, p. 126.
Jet, May 12, 1997, p. 25.
Publishers Weekly, October 31, 1994, p. 64; June 17, 2002, p. 66; June 9, 2003, p. 53.
School Library Journal, February 1995, p. 112; August 1996, p. 142.

On-line

Chief State School Officers Official Website, www.ccsso.org/ntoy.html (January 1997).

Other

Additional information for this profile was obtained through a news release, from the Ohio Department of Education on January 9, 1997; and the Ohio Teacher of the Year Program publications, Ohio SchoolNet, February 11, 1997.

—Catherine V. Donaldson

Esther Gordy Edwards

1920(?)—

Music executive, museum administrator

The sister of Motown Records founder Berry Gordy, Esther Gordy Edwards held various titles within the Motown organization during her career. In the label's early years, she was fond of saying, she was Berry Gordy's "gal Friday," a versatile multitasker who kept the label running smoothly in many capacities. Later she was the director of the Artists Personal Management Division, helping to develop the careers of such pop music superstars as Diana Ross, Stevie Wonder, and Marvin Gaye. Later still, after she applied her financial expertise to the management of the growing corporation, she assumed the titles of vice president and chief executive officer. No matter what her title, Esther Gordy Edwards remained a vital cog in the machinery of popular music's most reliable hitmaking organization of the 1960s.

Edwards was named after her paternal grandmother, Esther Johnson, a Georgia slave. She was the oldest girl among the eight children born to Berry Gordy Sr. (whose father was also named Berry Gordy) and his wife Bertha, a woman of African-American and Native American descent. Born in Oconee County, Georgia, around 1920, Edwards moved north to Detroit with her family as a child, after the elder Berry Gordy made

a large profit on a lumber deal and feared violence from local whites as a result. After the family landed in Detroit, Esther Gordy's younger brother Berry was born in 1929.

Most of the Gordy children, daughters as well as sons, shared their father's business sense. Education was valued highly in the family, and Esther attended Detroit's Wayne State University as well as Howard University in Washington, D.C. Back in Detroit after World War II, she opened a print shop, the Gordy Printing Company, with two of her brothers. Though Berry Gordy, Jr., seemed at this point to be an exception to the family tendency toward industriousness, a hint of things to come was apparent when a radio commercial jingle he composed for the print shop boosted the business substantially.

Esther Gordy Edwards married twice. She had one son, Robert Berry Bullock, by her first husband, and in 1951 she married politician George H. Edwards, later one of the first African-American members of the Michigan State Legislature. In the 1950s she established a family loan fund called the Ber-Berry Co-Op (named for her parents); the idea was that each family member would

At a Glance . . .

Born ca. 1920 in Oconee, GA; divorced first husband; married George H. Edwards (a politician), April 12, 1951; children: Robert Bullock. *Education:* Attended Howard University, Washington, DC; attended Wayne State University, Detroit. *Politics:* Democrat.

Career: Gordy Printing Company, Detroit, co-owner and general manager, 1947-59; Motown Records, Detroit, secretary, 1959-1960s, director of Artists Personal Management Division, 1960s, senior vice president and chief executive officer, 1960s-88; Motown Industries, senior vice president, 1973-88; Motown Historical Museum, Detroit, founder, chairman, and chief executive officer, 1985–.

Selected memberships: Bank of the Commonwealth, board of directors, 1972-79; Greater Detroit Chamber of Commerce, Metropolitan Detroit Convention and Visitors' Bureau, Economic Club of Detroit; African American Heritage Association (founder).

Addresses: *Office*—Motown Historical Museum, 2648 W. Grand Blvd., Detroit, MI 48208.

contribute ten dollars a month, and the resulting pool would finance new business projects.

One of the first loan applicants was Berry Gordy, Jr., who in 1959 asked for $800 to start what eventually became the Tamla and then the Motown record label. Edwards, who later took such a large role in the company's operations, was Berry Gordy's toughest questioner. "I just wanted to know how he intended to pay it back; he didn't have a job," Edwards later told the *Knight Ridder/Tribune News Service.* She didn't have to wait a long time, for by 1961 the song "Shop Around" by Smokey Robinson and the Miracles had reached gold record status with sales of 500,000 copies.

Soon Esther Gordy Edwards was part of the new family business. One of her first jobs was to assist in booking and managing the national and international tours that did much to put Motown on the map, for they featured polished pop production values that put a new face on African-American music for a range of concert-goers. Edwards often found herself in the role of crisis manager, learning the cutthroat businesses of booking and artist management and coping with new problems as

they arose. It was Edwards, for example, who worked with the Michigan Department of Labor to waive child labor laws so that a 12-year-old prodigy who went by the name of Stevie Wonder could record and perform.

Edwards played a key role in holding Motown's mostly youthful group of artists together. "I think that I was probably more strict than I needed to be," she told the *Detroit Free Press* in response to a question about whether she represented a mother figure for Motown stars. "I just had a burning desire to protect the artist. These were young people who came from less fortunate families or one-parent families. Motown was a family itself. ... I wound up learning a lot about young people." In the hectic atmosphere of Motown during its 1960s glory days, Edwards became an anchor for the aspiring young artists.

As Motown grew to become the largest seller of 45 rpm records in the music business, Edwards became more and more involved with Motown's financial operations. Although she rose to the level of vice president and CEO in the Motown hierarchy, Edwards bowed out when the label moved to Los Angeles in 1972 to be closer to the center of action in the entertainment industry. Never interested in pursuing big money, Edwards decided that the ties she had cultivated over the years in Detroit were most important to her, so she continued to manage Motown's assets and affairs in Detroit, which included several scholarship and foundation operations.

Edwards left her mark on the city of Detroit in other ways that were independent of her activities with Motown. She served on the boards of directors of the Detroit Bank of the Commonwealth and the Greater Detroit Chamber of Commerce in the 1970s, was the prime mover behind many of her husband's political campaigns, and became involved with numerous nonprofit organizations. Edwards was also instrumental in launching the city's annual Sterling Ball fundraiser for inner-city children's organizations, and she chaired a development group that built Trappers Alley (later transformed into Greektown Casino), an innovative set of shops constructed in a loft space in the city's Greektown neighborhood.

Edwards's greatest efforts were reserved for Motown and its position in history. When the label departed for Los Angeles, she established her Detroit offices in the label's former "Hitsville U.S.A." headquarters, a house on West Grand Boulevard. She carefully maintained the Motown studios in their original condition and worked toward turning the site into a museum. The Motown Historical Museum opened in 1980 and soon began to attract visitors from around the country and from all over the world. "Esther is the pillar," Detroit disc jockey Wade Briggs (known as Butterball Jr.) told the *Detroit Free Press.* "She has done more to maintain the legacy of Motown than Berry. ... If it wasn't for her, it's a story that could be lost."

Sources

Books

George, Nelson, *Where Did Our Love Go? The Rise and Fall of the Motown Sound,* St. Martin's, 1985.
Smith, Jessie Carney, ed., *Notable Black American Women,* Book 3, Gale, 2002.

Periodicals

Detroit Free Press, November 2, 1986.
Knight Ridder/Tribune News Service, February 12, 1998, p. 212K0555.

On-line

"Esther Gordy Edwards," *Motown Historical Museum,* www.motownmuseum.com, (January 2, 2004).

—James M. Manheim

Deadria Farmer-Paellmann

1966—

Activist

Deadria Farmer-Paellmann set aside a promising law career to become one of the foremost researchers into the links between the slave trade and American corporate interests of the nineteenth century. In 2002 she gained media attention for launching a lawsuit that demanded reparations for the descendants of American slaves, based on the premise that several U.S. corporations had profited from the practice of slavery in the years before the Civil War of 1861-65. Named in the suit was Aetna, the largest insurer in the United States, along with a financial corporation and a railroad. "They have played a role and they should be held responsible," said Farmer-Paellmann in an interview with Virginia Groark of the *New York Times,* adding, "And later on down the road there will be more companies."

Fascinated by Family History

Born in 1966, Farmer-Paellmann spent her early years in East New York, a suburb of the city of Brooklyn. She grew up in a single-parent household headed by her mother, Wilhelmina Farmer, who sometimes depended on public assistance to feed and clothe Farmer-Paellmann and her five sisters. When Farmer-Paellmann was about seven years old, the family moved to the largely white Brooklyn enclave of Bensonhurst, where they became the only African-American family in their immediate area. They were harassed constantly, Farmer-Paellmann told *New York Times* reporter Robin Finn. "Probably not a day went by when I didn't hear [a racial slur]. It seemed like every time the window was repaired, something would get thrown through it again."

A gifted pianist as a child, Farmer-Paellmann eschewed a career in music and instead earned a degree in political science from Brooklyn College. She had long been fascinated by stories about her ancestors, who had been rice farmers in South Carolina. The grandparents of her grandfather, Willie Capers, were once slaves on a rice plantation on St. Helena Island. Farmer-Paellmann told Christina Cheakalos in a *People* interview that, in telling this family history, her grandfather Capers sometimes remarked, "'They still owe us 40 acres and a mule.'"

At first, noted Farmer-Paellmann in *People,* "I didn't know what he was talking about." Her grandfather's observation stemmed from an 1865 assertion by

At a Glance . . .

Born in 1966, in Brooklyn, NY; daughter of Wilhelmina Farmer; married a German executive; children: one daughter. *Education:* Brooklyn College, BA in political science, 1980s; George Washington University, MA, 1995; New England School of Law, JD, 1999.

Career: Freelance legal researcher and reparations activist, 2000s–; Restitution Study Group, Inc., executive director, 2000s–.

Addresses: *Office*—Restitution Study Group, Inc., P.O. Box 1228, New York, NY 10009.

Union Army General William T. Sherman, who led the forces that routed the Confederates in several Southern states. Sherman declared that every slave freed by U.S. President Abraham Lincoln's 1863 Emancipation Proclamation would receive a parcel of land and the livestock with which to work it. Lincoln's 1865 assassination resulted in a changed political landscape, and the order was rescinded by his White House successor, Andrew Johnson.

Studied Reparations Issue

Under Johnson's plan for the reconstruction of the South in its new, post-slavery economy, the plantation lands were returned to their original owners, who simply hired the freed but now destitute and essentially homeless former slaves for pennies a day. There were some legal attempts to win the promised reparations, but the best challenge, filed in 1910, failed in the courts. "I was shocked," Farmer-Paellmann told *People,* of the time when she learned of this history. "Then I got angry." In 1992 she was serving as the artistic director for a vigil near Manhattan's City Hall. She and the other protesters were trying to prevent the excavation of a seventeenth-century African burial ground in order to create a new parking lot. She was allowed onto the site one day, where some 20,000 black Americans had been laid to rest generations earlier, and realized that they, too, "lived, worked and died in this city, and they never got their reparations," she told Finn in the *New York Times.* "It moved me."

After earning a master's degree in lobbying and political campaign management from George Washington University, Farmer-Paellmann entered the New England School of Law in the mid-1990s. She decided to write a paper for one class on the reparations issue, and began researching the subject. She was particularly intrigued by recent court challenges filed on behalf of

Holocaust victims from World War II. The German government had bowed to pressure and compelled some prominent corporations, which had operated factories during World War II using slave labor culled from the conquests of the Nazi regime, to contribute to a reparations fund.

In one New York archive, Farmer-Paellmann unearthed a crucial document during her five-year quest: an insurance policy from the pre-Civil War years that offered payouts to slaveholders to protect what was then considered their "property." Typical of what she discovered was a brochure from the Charter Oak Life Insurance Company of Hartford, Connecticut, which explained that, for a premium of $2 per year, a slave owner would receive $100 should a ten-year-old slave die. A similar document she found was from a company that later evolved into Aetna Insurance of Hartford.

Intrigued, Farmer-Paellmann wrote Aetna and asked them to send her the archival records dating from this era regarding slave insurance, and she received two documents in response. "I was really moved when I saw the policies," she recalled in the *New York Times* interview with Groark. "It's one thing to read about it and it's another thing to actually see a copy of the policy, and it really caused me to pause. I have to say it was a very emotional experience." Farmer-Paellmann brought the issue to the media, and Aetna publicly apologized. "We express our deep regret over any participation at all in this deplorable practice," a report by Tony Allen-Mills, writing in the *Sunday Times* of London, England, quoted the Aetna statement as saying. Farmer-Paellmann was stunned that the company had been so forthcoming about its past. She told *People* that at first "I thought, 'Wow, this is going to be easier than I thought.'" Not long afterward, the California legislature also passed a law that required all insurance companies doing business there to show present records of any slaveholder insurance policies they may have issued in the nineteenth century.

Took Reparations Issue to Court

The Aetna admission and the new California law soon hit the news headlines, and the reparations issue was formally revived. Some historians noted that if the value of the once-promised 40 acres and a mule were adjusted, it could mean that every African-American family descended from slaves would be owed $40,000. The debate that Farmer-Paellmann's actions ignited sometimes turned unpleasant, with one Canadian newspaper describing her as "a moral extortionist," according to Finn in the *New York Times.* Farmer-Paellmann responded to such criticism by pointing out in the article that "no one calls the Jewish Holocaust survivors and their descendants moral extortionists. I know this is justice. People say we waited too long, but these guys were on it a hundred years ago, the ex-slaves themselves."

In March of 2002, Farmer-Paellmann stepped up her efforts and became the coordinator for nine lawsuits filed in several states, including one in United States District Court in Brooklyn, against Aetna, FleetBoston Financial, and the CSX Railroad, in which she was listed as a plaintiff. FleetBoston, one of New England's largest banks, had a corporate history dating back to John Brown, whose family fortune helped found Brown University in Rhode Island. Brown was a slave trader who, with a group of other investors, chartered the Providence Bank of Rhode Island in 1791. CSX of Richmond, Virginia, used slaves to build its first railroad lines. Nearly all of the existing railroad lines east of the Mississippi River and south of the Mason-Dixon line that date back to the pre-Civil War era were built by slaves. "The court strategy invokes a concept known as unjust enrichment, in which not only was someone injured, but also that another party was enriched as a result," explained *Seattle Times* writers Tony Pugh, Maureen Fan, and Ken Moritsugu. Farmer-Paellmann clarified this position when she spoke with *CNN* correspondent Peter Viles about the court cases. "These are corporations that benefited from stealing people, from stealing labor, from forced breeding, from torture, from committing numerous horrendous acts," she told *CNN*, "and there's no reason why they should be able to hold onto assets they acquired through such horrendous acts."

Instead of cash payouts, Farmer-Paellmann and other groups involved in seeking reparations are looking to the German model, hoping that reparations could be placed in a trust fund to be used for jobs, housing, and education. Interestingly, Farmer-Paellmann is married to a German executive, with whom she has a daughter. She lives in the New York area, and continues to research the murkier side of American corporate history. Her efforts have linked some 60 U.S. companies to the slave trade. Though her grandfather died in 1999, he already knew of her work on the reparations cause. "I called him when I was in law school to tell him I was developing the case," she told *People*. "He was proud."

Sources

Periodicals

Knight-Ridder/Tribune News Service, March 26, 2002.
New York Times, August 8, 2000; May 5, 2002.
People, October 28, 2002, p. 95.
Post-Standard (Syracuse, NY), May 20, 2002.
Seattle Times, March 27, 2002, p. A1.
Sunday Times (London, England), June 10, 2001, p. 26.

On-line

"Suit seeks billions in slave reparations," *CNN,* www.cnn.com/2002/LAW/03/26/slavery.reparations/ (December 29, 2003).

—Carol Brennan

A. Oveta Fuller

1955—

Virologist

A. Oveta Fuller has spent her scientific career studying how viruses infect host cells. The long-term goals of her research include developing methods for controlling viral diseases and using viruses for genetic engineering. Specifically, Fuller studies the means by which viruses attach themselves to host cells and penetrate the host cell membrane or outer protective layer. Fuller is an associate professor in the department of Microbiology and Immunology at the University of Michigan Medical School in Ann Arbor. She also teaches in the medical, dental, and graduate schools at the University of Michigan.

Grew Up on a Farm

Almyra Oveta Fuller was born on August 31, 1955, in Mebane, North Carolina. Her father, Herbert R. Fuller, managed their family farm near Yanceyville, North Carolina. Oveta Fuller's mother, Deborah Evelyn Woods Fuller, taught junior high school. Her paternal grandmother, Lillie Willis Fuller Graves, along with Oveta's father and his two siblings, had inherited the 100-acre farm from Oveta's great-grandmother. After her husband's death Lillie Fuller had remarried, and her four sons from the new marriage were part of the household while Oveta was growing up. In addition to these uncles, she also had two brothers.

When Fuller was four years old, she moved with her immediate family from her grandmother's farmhouse into a nearby home that her father and uncles had built. However, Fuller continued to spend a great deal of time with her grandmother while her parents worked. The farm supplied most of the family's needs, including fruit, vegetables, and grains, as well as cows, pigs, and chickens. Their cash crops were cattle and tobacco.

Fuller's interest in biology began early. She noticed that her grandmother's diabetes could be treated, but that there were few treatments for her mild arthritis. Oveta was particularly impressed after her grandmother was bitten by a water moccasin, but recovered immediately after treatment with an antivenin, an antidote to the snake venom.

Studied Biology at UNC

Although Fuller was encouraged by her high school biology teachers, she was not yet thinking about a career in science. Following her junior year in high school, Fuller's guidance counselor nominated her for the North Carolina Governor's School, a prestigious summer program at Salem College in Winston-Salem, North Carolina. There Fuller studied mathematics but found herself stimulated by other subjects as well, including literature and music.

After high school Fuller was awarded an Aubry Lee Brooks Scholarship for a full four years at the University of North Carolina (UNC) at Chapel Hill, just an hour from her home. There she majored in biology, but also studied English literature, composition, and journalism, and worked on one of the college newspapers.

During the summer between her junior and senior years of college, Fuller worked as an apprentice at a

At a Glance . . .

Born Almyra Oveta Fuller on August 31, 1955; daughter of Herbert R. and Deborah Evelyn (Woods) Fuller; married Jerry Caldwell, June 18, 1984; children: Brian Randolph Caldwell. *Education:* University of North Carolina, Chapel Hill, BA, 1977, PhD, 1983; University of Chicago, postdoctoral study, 1983-87.

Career: University of North Carolina, Chapel Hill, graduate research assistant, 1977-83, assistant director of the Summer Apprentice Research Program, 1981-82; University of Chicago, post-doctoral research fellow, 1983-87, instructor, 1984-86, research associate, 1987-88; DeVeras Inc., consultant, 1987-89; University of Michigan Medical School, Ann Arbor, department of Microbiology and Immunology, research scientist, assistant professor, associate professor, 1988–.

Memberships: National Technical Association, co-founder of the Research Triangle Chapter, 1980; American Association for the Advancement of Science, 1984–; American Society for Microbiology, 1984–; Lineberger Cancer Research Center, advisory committee to fellows programs, 1989–; Howard Hughes Doctoral Fellowship panel, 1991.

Awards: Aubry Lee Brooks Scholarship, 1973-77; National Technical Association Service Award, Research Triangle Chapter, 1983; Anna Fuller Fund Postdoctoral Award, 1983-84; Thornton Professional Achievement Award, National Technical Association, Chicago Chapter, 1984; NIH Post-doctoral Research Award, 1984-86; Ford Foundation, fellow, 1987.

Addresses: *Home*—9398 Hidden Lake Circle, Dexter, MI 48130. *Office*—University of Michigan Medical Center, Microbiology and Immunology, 6736 Medical Science Building II, Ann Arbor, MI, 48109-0620.

local health clinic that served many older, chronically ill patients. In addition to helping the physicians, Fuller worked as a laboratory assistant. She discovered that she enjoyed laboratory work and began to contemplate a career in research. A recent outbreak of Legionnaire's Disease had launched a massive research effort to identify the responsible microorganism, and during

her senior year at UNC, Fuller wrote a major paper describing how biologists, public health practitioners, and physicians had joined forces to discover the path by which the disease-causing microorganism had infected its victims.

After graduating from UNC with a bachelor of arts degree in 1977, Fuller spent the summer in Louisiana, marketing children's reference books for a national publishing company. However, she already had decided to enter a university doctoral program to study biology. After considering the programs at Howard and Georgetown Universities in Washington, D.C., as well as at the University of Illinois, Fuller decided to stay in Chapel Hill and take advantage of UNC's excellent microbiology program. She received a graduate fellowship from UNC that covered her tuition and expenses. During the summer following her first year of doctoral study, Fuller again worked in publishing. During the school year she tutored high school students in math and science. She also worked with undergraduates in UNC's Upward Bound program, which helped prepare disadvantaged students for a college curriculum. During 1981 and 1982, Fuller served as assistant director of the summer apprentice research program.

For her doctoral research Fuller studied the biological effects of two similar and very potent toxic chemicals from plants—abrin, that comes from the seeds of the rosary or jequirity pea, and ricin from castor beans. Although both chemicals have potential medical applications, particularly as cancer treatments, their potential as chemical weapons has also been of special concern to researchers. During this time, Fuller also became a founding member of the local chapter of the National Technical Association, an organization of black American scientists and engineers who were working in the larger academic institutions.

Switched to Virology

By the time Fuller earned her Ph.D. in 1983, she had become very interested in viruses, particularly in the chemistry of the cell surfaces of both the viruses and the host cells they infect. She moved to the University of Chicago to study herpes and other viruses, in the laboratory of Professor Patricia G. Spear. Herpes viruses attack the soft linings of the body, such as the mouth and genitals, causing cold sores, fever blisters, and genital inflammations. These viruses may be sexually transmitted and often cause recurring problems for the patient. Fuller was interested in how the virus attaches to host cell membranes in order to penetrate and infect the cells. Fuller and Spear were able to identify some of the molecules on the host cell surface that appeared to provide at least partial immunity to herpes infection by preventing viral attachment and/or penetration. Since viruses also have the potential of directing useful genes into human cells to treat various medical conditions, Fuller also investigated the genetic engineering of the herpes virus in order to develop a method for introducing new genetic material into cells for gene therapy.

In Spear's laboratory Fuller demonstrated that the interaction between the virus and the host-cell membrane requires specific combinations of viral and host-cell proteins—large molecules that are made up of chains of amino acids. If the host cell lacks a required protein, the virus may be unable to infect the cell. This may explain, in part, why viruses can infect some people and not others, and why humans are often immune to viruses that infect other animals.

During her first three years at Chicago, Fuller was a research fellow. Her post-doctoral funding came from the Anna Fuller Cancer Fund, a relatively small private foundation, and from other sources including the U.S. Public Health Service and the National Institutes of Health (NIH). She also taught introductory genetics at the University of Chicago in 1984 and an advanced course in human genetic disorders in 1986. On June 16, 1984, Fuller married Jerry Caldwell, and the couple had one son.

Joined University of Michigan Faculty

In 1987 Fuller was awarded a Ford Foundation fellowship and became an independent research associate at the University of Chicago. The following year she joined the medical school faculty at the University of Michigan, as a research scientist in the department of Microbiology and Immunology. Fuller was promoted first to assistant professor and then to associate professor. Although her initial research funding came from the university, she was soon awarded research grants from the National Science Foundation and from the NIH, to direct a research team that included both undergraduate and graduate students.

Fuller has used the herpes simplex virus (HSV) and pseudorabies virus (PRV) as model systems for examining the interactions between viruses and the host cells they infect. She has found that a series of specific attachments between the virus and the host cell triggers the fusion of the virus and the host cell membrane, mediating viral entry into the cell. Her research has focused on identifying the individual events of viral entry, the roles of both viral and cellular proteins in entry, and how these events might be circumvented to prevent viral infections. Fuller's research has had important implications for the pathogenesis of HSV and other human and animal viruses.

Viruses use proteins called receptors, located on the host-cell surface, to enter cells. Fuller's research group has been attempting to identify, clone, and characterize certain receptors for HSV-1 and HSV-2 on the surface of human cells. HSV and PRV use some of the same receptors to enter susceptible cells. Fuller has found that swine (pig) cells are resistant to HSV infection because they lack an important receptor. In addition, Fuller's laboratory is identifying and characterizing host cell factors that enable PRV to replicate or reproduce within swine cells but not within human cells. They have also examined host cell factors that appear to influence the expression or activity of PRV genes early in the virus's reproductive cycle, since PRV has fewer such genes than HSV.

Gained Professional Recognition

In 1992 Fuller co-chaired a session at the International Herpes Conference in Edinburgh, Scotland, and she has given numerous lectures in the United States and abroad. In 1999 Fuller and her collaborators were awarded a patent titled "Compositions and Methods for Identifying and Testing Therapeutics Against HSV Infection." In 2002 Fuller published a review with P. Perez-Romero in Frontiers in Bioscience that summarized what was known about the human cell surface viral receptors and the entry of some common DNA viruses into human cells, as well as the early events that occur once the virus has entered the cell.

At the University of Michigan, Fuller teaches microbiology and immunology within the Molecular Mechanisms in Microbial Pathogenesis Training Program. This is an interdepartmental program for graduate students and postdoctoral fellows that integrates studies of the molecular and cellular biology of pathogenic microorganisms and the host responses to infection by these organisms. In 2003 Fuller was the course director for Microbiology 532, in which she taught introduction to micro-pathogens and the virology lecture series. She also teaches dental microbiology and molecular and cellular determinants of viral pathogenesis. In addition, Fuller is a faculty member in the gene therapy curriculum of the program in Biomedical Sciences.

Fuller has collaborated with other University of Michigan researchers on the development of HSVs as vectors for introducing foreign genes into cells, for genetic engineering and gene therapy applications. In 1997 she co-authored a paper demonstrating that a common retroviral vector used to introduce genes into human cells may not survive in the cell long enough for the gene to be transferred into the host DNA.

Selected writings

(With L. M. Stannard and P. G. Spear) "Herpes Simplex Virus Glycoproteins Associated with Different Morphological Entities Projecting from the Virion Envelope," *Journal of General Virology,* 1987.

(With R. E. Santos and P. G. Spear) "Neutralizing Antibodies Specific for Protein H of Herpes Simplex Virus Permit Viral Attachment to Cells but Prevent Penetration," *Journal of Virology,* 1989.

(With W. C. Lee) "Herpes Simplex Virus Type 1 Entry through a Cascade of Virus-Cell Interactions Requires

Different Roles of gD and gH in Penetration," *Journal of Virology,* 1992.

(With W. C. Lee) "Herpes Simplex Virus Type 1 and Pseudorabies Virus Bind to a Common Saturable Receptor on Vero Cells that is not Heparin Sulfate," *Journal of Virology,* 1993.

"Microbes and the Proteoglycan Connection," *Journal of Clinical Investigation,* 1994.

(With Deborah S. McClain) "Cell Specific Kinetics and Efficiency of Herpes Simplex Virus Type 1 Entry are Determined by Two Distinct Steps of Attachment," *Virology,* 1994.

(With G. Subramanian, D. S. McClain, and A. Pérez) "Swine Testis Cells Contain Functional Heparan Sulfate But Are Defective in Entry of Herpes Simplex Virus," *Journal of Virology,* 1994.

(With G. Subramanian, R. A. LeBlanc, and R. C. Wardley) "Defective Entry of Herpes Simplex Virus Types 1 and 2 into Porcine Cells and Lack of Infection in Infant Pigs Indicate Species Tropism," *Journal of General Virology,* 1995.

(With S. T. Andreadis, D. Brott, and B. O. Palsson) "Moloney Murine Leukemia Virus-Derived Retroviral Vectors Decay Intracellularly with a Half-Life in the Range of 5.4 to 7.5 Hours," *Journal of Virology,* 1997.

(With S. Andreadis and B. O. Palsson) "Cell Cycle Dependence of Retroviral Transduction: An Issue of Overlapping Time Scales," *Biotechnology and Bioengineering,* 1998.

(With Aleida Pérez) " Stable Attachment for Herpes Simplex Virus Penetration into Human Cells Requires Glycoprotein D in the Virion and Cell Receptors that are Missing for Entry-Defective Porcine Cells," *Virus Research,* 1998.

(With P. Perez-Romero) "Mechanisms of DNA Virus Infection: Entry and Early Events," *Frontiers in Bioscience,* 2002.

Sources

Books

Kessler, James H., J. S. Kidd, Renée A. Kidd, and Katherine A. Morin, *Distinguished African American Scientists of the 20th Century,* Oryx Press, 1996, pp. 112-116.

Notable Black American Scientists, Gale, 1998.

Notable Women Scientists, Gale, 1999.

On-line

"A. Oveta Fuller," *University of Michigan, Dept. of Microbiology and Immunology,* www.med.umich.edu/microbio/faculty/fuller.html (November 18, 2003).

—Margaret Alic

Laurent Gbagbo

1945—

President of Côte d'Ivoire

Since being granted its independence from France in 1960, Côte d'Ivoire, or the Ivory Coast, was led by President Fé Houphouët-Boigny, who ruled under an essentially one-party political system. Once envied by other African nations for its prosperous economy, as the economy turned downward during the latter decades of the twentieth century, a growing group of dissidents became increasingly vocal. During the 1970s, Laurent Gbagbo, a young, charismatic teacher, emerged as a leading voice of resistance.

When Houphouët-Boigny died in 1993 with no real plan for the democratic transfer of power, the country quickly fell into political disarray, leaving room for Gbagbo to eventually rise to power. He was inaugurated as the country's president in 2000, but his tenure has been marred by accusations of improper elections, which led to widespread political unrest. A revolt in 2002 turned into a stagnated revolution in 2003 that divided the country between the mainly Christian south, where Gbagbo still holds power, and the mainly Muslim north, which is controlled by rebel forces. Under international pressure to form a representative government, Gbagbo has been thus far unwilling or unable to come to terms with opposition leaders. This dissenter-turned-president has yet to pull his country from the grasp of widening ethnic, religious, and political division.

Began Political Organizing

Gbagbo was born on May 31, 1945, in Gagnoa, a major city in west-central Ivory Coast. His parents, Zepe Paul Koudou and Gado Marguerite Koudou Paul, belonged to the Bété tribe. Reared in the Roman Catholic faith, Gbagbo is aligned with the Christian south. Gbagbo attended primary school in Agboville and Gagnoa, graduating in June of 1958. He attended intermediate school at St. Dominique Savio in Gagnoa, graduating in June of 1962. In June of 1965 he earned his high school diploma from the Traditional College of Abidjan. After completing his freshman year at the University of Abidjan, Gbagbo enrolled at the University of Lyon in France to study Latin, Greek, and French. His nickname during his school days was "Cicero" because of his love of Latin. He did not finish his degree, however, and returned to the Ivory Coast to complete his undergraduate studies at the University of Abidjan, earning a bachelor's degree in history in 1969.

At a Glance . . .

Born on May 31, 1945, in Gagnoa, Ivory Coast; son of Zepe Paul Koudou and Gado Marguerite Koudou Paul; married Jaqueline Chanoos, July 20, 1967 (divorced, June of 1982); married Simone Ehivet, January 19, 1989; children: (from first marriage) Koudou Michel, Gado Lea, (from second marriage) Gado Marie-Patrice, Popo Marie-Laurence, three step-children. *Education:* University of Abidjan, BA, 1969; University of Paris, Sorbonne, MA, 1970; University of Paris VII, PhD, 1979. *Politics:* Ivorian Popular Front (FPI). *Religion:* Roman Catholic.

Career: Classical College (Lycée Classique), professor of history and geography, 1970-73, education department, 1973-74; Institute of History, Art, and African Archaeology (IHAAA), researcher, 1974-1977, director, 1980-82; Ivorian Popular Front, abroad organization representative, 1983-1988, secretary general, 1988-90; Ivory Coast presidential candidate, 1990; Ivory Coast National Assembly, elected member, 1990-99; president of Ivory Coast, 2000–.

Addresses: *Office*—Présidence de la République, 01 BP 1354, Abidjan 01, Côte d'Ivoire.

Gbagbo was first arrested for his political organizing activities in the Ivory Coast in 1969. After spending two weeks in jail, he returned to France and completed a Master of Arts degree in history at the University of Paris at the Sorbonne in 1970. In the same year he returned to the Ivory Coast to teach history and geography at the University of Abidjan. Within a year Gbagbo found himself in trouble once again for unauthorized teaching, participating in teacher unionism, and publishing materials the government deemed subversive. He was arrested on March 31, 1971, and imprisoned without a trial at the Seguela military camp. After his release in January of 1974, he briefly worked for the department of education.

In 1974 Gbagbo became a researcher for the Institute of History, Art, and African Archaeology (IHAAA) at the University of Abidjan. In 1977 he took a break from his responsibilities at the IHAAA to complete his doctoral studies at the University of Paris VII at Sorbonne. After successfully defending his doctoral thesis, he received his Doctorate of Philosophy in June of 1979. On returning to his duties at the IHAAA, Gbagbo was named the institute's director in 1980, a position he held for two years.

Organized the Ivorian Popular Front

During his tenure at the IHAAA, Gbagbo's reputation as a dissident continued to grow. He was highly critical of the Ivory Coast's essentially one-party system that had concentrated political power in the hands of Houphouët-Boigny. In 1982 Gbagbo began his clandestine organization of the unauthorized Ivorian Popular Front (FPI). He also secretly published and distributed a speech critical of the government that called for a multi-party system. These activities enraged Houphouët-Boigny, who also blamed Gbagbo for organizing a wide-spread teachers' strike. Coming under increasing government scrutiny, Gbagbo went into voluntary exile in France in 1982.

Gbagbo continued to organize the FPI from abroad and, in 1983, published his political reform plan for the Ivory Coast as *Côte d'Ivoire: pour une Alternative Démocratique.* Although he was officially granted political asylum by France in 1985, the following year France's new prime minister, Jacques Chirac, who was unhappy with Gbagbo's socialist activities in France, pressured Gbagbo to leave. Accordingly, Gbagbo returned to his homeland on September 13, 1988.

Within a week of Gbagbo's return to the Ivory Coast, the FPI held its inaugural congress and elected Gbagbo as the party's secretary general. Despite suffering intimidation by members of Houphouët-Boigny's Democratic Party of Ivory Coast (PDCI), the FPI held another congress in 1989. Finally, in April of 1990, Houphouët-Boigny succumbed to external pressure from the World Bank and the International Monetary Fund, both of whom threatened to withhold funding, by announcing that multi-party elections would be held for the first time in the country's history. Gbagbo was Houphouët-Boigny's only opponent on the ballot and was sounded defeated, earning only 18.3 percent of the vote, compared to Houphouët-Boigny's 81.7 percent. Although Gbagbo and the FPI declared the election was rigged, the Supreme Court refused to consider their demand for a new election. Gbagbo and eight other FPI members did manage to win seats in the National Assembly, but the PDCI continued to dominate the body by holding the remaining 163 seats.

Arrested for Leading Demonstrations

In 1991 large-scale protests erupted in the academic community over planned decreases in teacher's salaries. The protesters were treated brutally by security forces, and later Houphouët-Boigny's army chief of staff, General Robert Guei, came under investigation for his part in allowing the brutality. When Houphouët-Boigny publicly supported Guei, declaring that the brutal force employed against the demonstrators was necessary, over 20,000 protesters took to the streets, led by Gbagbo. Three days later Gbagbo was arrested under a law that provided that leaders of public disturbances could be held personally responsible. He was sentenced to two years in prison, but after four months Houphouët-Boigny declared amnesty for all those involved in the protests. Gbagbo was freed on July 31, 1992.

On December 7, 1993, Houphouët-Boigny died of prostate cancer, and control of the country was turned over to the Minister of Finance, Henri Konan Bédié. With little hope of challenging Bédié's claim to the presidency, Prime Minister Alassane Ouattara, a Muslim from the northern area and Bédié's strongest opponent, left the Ivory Coast to take a post with the International Monetary Fund in Washington, D.C. Bédié moved quickly to neutralize Ouattara by introducing legislation that required that all presidential candidates be of pure Ivory Coast descent and have lived in the country for the last five years. Ouattara, currently living in the United States and whose father was from neighboring Burkina Faso, failed to qualify on both counts.

Due to numerous election irregularities attributed to Bédié, both the FPI and the Rally of Republicans (RDR), a new Muslim party organized in the days following Houphouët-Boigny's death, boycotted the presidential election held in October 1995, leaving the way free for Bédié to easily retain the presidency. Nonetheless, Bédié's hold on power was becoming increasing perilous. The country's economy, once a model for all of Africa, had dissolved into disarray. Dissatisfaction remained high in the academic community and was growing rapidly among the overworked and underpay military ranks.

Elected President

On December 24, 1999, a group of military officers staged a coup and occupied the streets of Abidjan. When they convinced Guei to take up their cause as their leader, Bédié recognized his situation as hopeless and fled. On December 27, 1999, the country came under the military's control with Guei at the helm. Although Guei promised multi-party elections, he upheld Ouattara's disqualification and placed himself on the ballot for the presidency. As a result of Ouattara's exclusion, Gbagbo was once again the only opposition candidate on the ballot.

When early election returns pointed toward Gbagbo as the potential winner, Guei quickly dissolved the Electoral Commission and ordered an official from the Interior Ministry to declare him the winner. The announcement rocked the country and tens of thousands of protesters immediately filled the streets of Abidjan. Military forces loyal to Guei fired on the crowds with little warning and 60 people were killed. As the violence continued over the next several days, the parliamentary police defected to join the protesters, followed by parts of the military forces. Ultimately, Guei was forced to flee, and Gbagbo declared himself president. He was inaugurated on October 26, 2000.

In response to Gbagbo's claim to the presidency, the RDR immediately called for new elections so that Muslim-supported Ouattara could be placed on the ballot. Most RDR supporters had boycotted the election due to Ouattara's absence on the ballot, thus they claimed Gbagbo's election was not, in fact, a result of a fair democratic process. Most of the international community agreed, including the United Nations, South Africa, and most Western countries. Nonetheless, Gbagbo claimed that he was properly elected under the constitution that had been approved by the people of the Ivory Coast. As a result, angry Muslims once again took to the streets, this time clashing with FPI mobs. Over 300 people were killed in the four days following the election.

Faced Opposition

In January of 2001 opposition forces staged a coup, but government forces responded quickly and the attempt to overthrow the government was thwarted. Gbagbo blamed Muslim northerners and foreigners for instigating the attack, thus further deepening the chasm between the Christian south and Muslim north. Muslims and foreign-born people came under increasing harassment by Gbagbo's security forces. During 2001, with the European Union refusing to resume financial aid to the country until all sides were represented in negotiations regarding the country's future, Gbagbo staged several half-hearted attempts to work with oppositional leaders that proved fruitless.

On September 19, 2002, while Gbagbo was in France, mutinous troops took to the streets of three cities. At least 270 people died in the initial conflict, including Guei. Although loyalist forces were able to regain control of Abidjan by September 25, 2002, rebel forces quickly secured control of the northern area of the country. In the ensuing months rebel forces were gaining ground to the south when France stepped in, sending in peace-keeping forces to stand between opposition forces in the north and government forces in the south, bringing the conflict to a virtual stalemate.

During 2003 Gbagbo agreed to meet with facilitators in Paris to open negotiations with opposition forces. However, Gbagbo balked at allowing elections before 2005 as well as rebels' demands that they be given control of the defense and interior ministries. At the same time, violence continued to erupt within the Ivory Coast, and Gbagbo was tied to the actions of government death squads whose offenses included the massacre of 200 Muslim civilians. The bodies were found in a mass grave by French troops on March 9, 2003. Despite a United Nations report implicating him, Gbagbo hotly denied his involvement in the massacre or other human rights violations.

Signed the Marcoussis Accord

In April of 2003, Gbagbo signed the Marcoussis Accord, which conceded nine cabinet positions to rebel leaders and a restructuring of citizenship laws to include more Muslim northerners. In exchange, opposition forces would disarm. However, Gbagbo allotted no budgets for the rebel-held cabinet positions and continued to promote the need for strict enforcement of citizenship laws. By October of 2003 tensions were so high that rebel forces gave up all pretense of disarming and opposition leaders pulled out of the government, saying they had been denied any real power.

At the beginning of 2004, Gbagbo continued to retain his slippery grip on the presidency, but he is still faced with the ongoing problems that have plagued the once-stable country for a decade, namely, a decrepit economy that is overburdened by debt, an ongoing political, religious, and ethnic crisis, a stagnated civil war, and pressure from the international community to find a way to integrate all interests into the political process. How Gbagbo responds to these challenges will determine his place in the history of his country.

Selected writings

Réflexions sur la Conférence de Brazzaville, Éditions CLE, 1978.
Soundjata: le Lion du Manding, Éditions CEDA, 1979.
(with Robert Bourgi) *Débat sur la Conférence de Brazzaville et la Décolonisation de l'Afrique Noire,* Institut d'Histoire, d'Art et d'Archéologie Africains, 1981.
Le Côte d'Ivoire: économie et Société á la Veille de l'Indipendence, 1940-1960, L'Hartmann, 1982.
Côte d'Ivoire: pour une Alterative Démocratique, L'Hartmann, 1983.
Côte d'Ivoire: Histoire d'un Retour, L'Hartmann, 1989.

Côte d'Ivoire: Agir pour les Libertés, L'Hartmann, 1991.

Sources

Books

Newsmakers, Issue 2. Farmington Hills, Mich.: Gale, 2003.
Worldmark Encyclopedia of the Nations: World Leaders. Farmington Hills, Mich.: Gale, 2002.

Periodicals

Africa News, October 7, 2002; November 14, 2003.
Africa Report, November/December 1992.
Agence France Presse, December 3, 2003; November 17, 2003.
Christian Science Monitor, October 30, 2000.
Economist, October 28, 2000; November 24, 2001; September 28, 2002; January 1, 2003; April 12, 2003; October 4, 2003.
New African, December 2000; May 2003.
New Republic, November 24, 2003.
New York Amsterdam News, March 13, 2003.
Newsweek, February 18, 2003.

On-line

"Laurent Gbagbo," *Biography Resource Center,* www.galenet.com/servlet/BioRC (January 21, 2004).
"Laurent Gbagbo: Curriculum-Vitae," *Laurent Gbagbo,* www.gbagbo.com (January 21, 2004).
"Profile: Laurent Gbagbo," *BBC News,* http://news.bbc.co.uk (January 21, 2004).

—Kari Bethel

Althea Gibson

1927-2003

Professional tennis player, golfer, coach, singer

Althea Gibson's accomplishments in tennis rank among the most inspiring in modern professional sports. At a time when the game of tennis was completely dominated by whites, Gibson emerged with enough talent and determination to win multiple championships at Wimbledon and the U.S. Open in the late 1950s. Gibson was not only the first black woman to compete in these prestigious tournaments, she was also the first black person ever to win a tennis title. Having achieved national prominence in a sport long associated with upper-class whites, she became a role model for blacks of both sexes who sought the right to compete in previously segregated sporting events. Doors of opportunity that Gibson opened in both tennis and golf have been pursued by the likes of Arthur Ashe and Zena Garrison in tennis, and Calvin Peete in professional golf.

The titles of Gibson's two memoirs, *I Always Wanted To Be Somebody,* and *So Much To Live For,* serve as testimony to her personality and ambition. Her difficult childhood in a Harlem ghetto offered her little in the way of encouragement, but timely help from tennis coaches and supportive black professionals gave her opportunities never before extended to a black woman.

Gibson forged into the previously all-white field of women's tennis with the conviction that racism could not stop her, and she handled difficult situations with a grace and earthy humor that brought her a firm following among American sports fans.

Chose Tennis Over Education

The oldest of five children, Althea Gibson was born in Silver, South Carolina, on April 25, 1927. At the time of her birth, her father was working as a sharecropper on a cotton farm. The crops failed several years in a row, and the impoverished Gibson family moved to New York City in 1930 where her aunt was said to have made a living by selling bootleg whiskey. There they settled in a small apartment in Harlem, and four more children were born.

In her memoirs Gibson described herself as a restless youngster who longed to "be somebody" but had little idea how to pursue that goal. School was not the answer for her. She often played hooky to go to the movies and had little rapport with her teachers. After finishing middle school, despite her truancy problems, she was promoted to the Yorkville Trade School. Her

At a Glance . . .

Born on August 25, 1927, in Silver, South Carolina; died on September 28, 2003, in East Orange, New Jersey; daughter of Daniel (a mechanic) and Anna (Washington) Gibson; married William A. Darben, October 17, 1965 (divorced); married Sidney Llewellyn, April 11, 1983. *Education:* Florida Agricultural and Mechanical University, BS, 1953.

Career: Tennis player, 1941-58; author, 1958, 1968; singer, musician, spokesperson for products, and actress, 1958-63; Ladies' Professional Golf Tour, golfer, 1963-67; tennis coach, member of athletic commissions, and associate of Essex County (NJ) Park Commission, c. 1970-92.

Awards: Winner of national Negro girls' championships, 1944, 1945, 1948-56; winner of English singles and doubles championships at Wimbledon, 1957 and 1958; winner of U.S. national singles championships at Forest Hills, 1957 and 1958; named Woman Athlete of Yr., AP Poll, 1957-58; named to Lawn Tennis Hall of Fame and Tennis Mus., 1971, Black Athletes Hall of Fame, 1974, S.C. Hall of Fame, 1983, Fla. Sports Hall of Fame, 1984, Sports Hall of Fame of NJ, 1994.

problems continued there and became so severe that she was referred to a series of social workers, some of whom threatened her with the prospect of reform school.

Solace was hard to find for the brash youngster. Movies and stage shows at the Apollo Theater offered a glimpse of another world beyond the crowded Harlem streets, and Gibson longed for that world—and her own independence. Even before she was of legal age to drop out of school she applied for working papers and quit attending her classes. She held a series of jobs but was not able to keep any of them very long. A promise to attend night school lasted through only two weeks of classes. By the time she was 14, Gibson was a ward of the New York City Welfare Department. The social workers helped her to find steady work, and they steered her into the local Police Athletic League sports programs.

Gibson's first contact with tennis was through the game of paddleball. The game is similar to conventional tennis but uses wooden paddles instead of rackets. In paddleball Gibson found a challenge she could answer. She would practice swatting balls against a wall for hours at a time, and before long she was winning local tournaments. Her prowess brought her to the attention of musician Buddy Walker, a part-time city recreation department employee. Walker encouraged her to switch to regular tennis and even bought her a racket—a second-hand model he re-strung himself. Walker also introduced Gibson to the members of the interracial New York Cosmopolitan Club. Some of them were also impressed with Gibson's natural talents, and they sponsored her for junior membership and private lessons with a professional named Fred Johnson.

The well-to-do members of the Cosmopolitan Club— particularly a socialite named Rhoda Smith—helped Gibson to curb her wild behavior and adopt a more reasonable and conservative lifestyle. Just one year after her lessons began in 1941, Gibson won her first important tournament, the New York State Open Championship. In 1943 she won the New York State Negro girls' singles championship, and in 1944 and 1945 captured the National Negro girls' championship.

Faced Racism in Professional Tennis

Even though she lost the 1946 Negro girls' championship, Gibson drew the backing of two quite influential patrons. A pair of surgeons, Dr. Hubert Eaton of Wilmington, North Carolina, and Dr. Robert Johnson of Lynchburg, Virginia, made Gibson an attractive offer. They would provide room and board for her and pay for her tennis lessons if she agreed to finish high school at the same time. Gibson accepted and moved to Wilmington to live with Eaton's family. There she attended the local public school and practiced her tennis moves on Eaton's private court. In the summertime she returned to Harlem for coaching by Fred Johnson. Beginning in 1948, Gibson won nine consecutive Negro national championships, a feat that quickly brought her recognition within the white tennis community as well.

Having finally realized the value of a good education, Gibson graduated tenth in her class at North Carolina's Williston Industrial High School in 1949. She then accepted a tennis scholarship to Florida Agricultural and Mechanical University in Tallahassee. She wanted to study music, as she could play the saxophone and had a fine singing voice. Counselors at the college persuaded her to stay with tennis, and she majored in physical education instead.

The biggest battle of Gibson's college years was securing the right to compete in major tennis tournaments against white opponents. That she had the talent to do so could not be denied, but many of the clubs that hosted major tournaments did not admit blacks. In 1950 Gibson sought an invitation from the United States Lawn Tennis Association to play in the National Grass Court championships at Forest Hills, Long Island. The invitation never came. Other tournaments at private clubs barred her as well. Frustrated but undefeated by the rampant racism, Gibson expressed her disappointment in a dignified and professional manner. Before too long she began to find allies in prominent positions.

One such ally was Alice Marble, an editor of *American Lawn Tennis* magazine. In the July 1950 issue of that periodical, Marble wrote a piece about the "color barrier" keeping Gibson from the top competitions. "The entrance of Negroes into national tennis is as inevitable as it has proven in baseball, in football, or in boxing; there is no denying so much talent," Marble contended. "The committee at Forest Hills has the power to stifle the efforts of one Althea Gibson, who may or may not be succeeded by others of her race who have equal or superior ability. They will knock at the door as she has done. Eventually the tennis world will rise up en masse to protest the injustices perpetrated by our policymakers. Eventually—why not now?"

Became Wimbledon Champion

The reaction to the editorial was almost instantaneous. Within one month of its publication, Gibson was invited to the national tournament at Forest Hills, as well as a number of other important competitions that had once been closed to her. In her first appearance at Forest Hills, Gibson advanced to the second round where she met Wimbledon champion Louise Brough. Gibson was leading in a tie-breaking set, 7-6, when play was interrupted by a severe thunderstorm. When the game resumed the next day, a frazzled Gibson—who had been hounded by the media throughout the delay—lost the match 9-7.

The following three years saw even greater disappointments. In 1952 Gibson was ranked seventh nationally in women's singles; the following year she dropped to 70th. Gibson seriously considered retiring from tennis completely, especially after she earned a Bachelor's degree in 1953, and took a teaching position at Lincoln University in Missouri. A former Harlem coach, Sydney Llewellyn, encouraged her to return to the circuit, and in 1955 she was chosen as one of four American women sent on a "good will" tennis tour of Southeast Asia and Mexico. In the months that followed those trips, Gibson also played in tournaments in Sweden, Germany, France, England, Italy, and Egypt, winning in 16 of 18 appearances. She raised her fortunes even higher in 1956 when she won her first major singles title at the French Open.

Black people seeking equal treatment in all walks of American life pointed proudly to the success of Althea Gibson in 1957 and 1958. The game of tennis has no more prestigious tournament than that held at Wimbledon in England every year. Not only was Gibson the first black ever to appear in that tournament, she was seeded first both years and won the Wimbledon singles

and doubles championships both years. In 1957 Gibson defeated Darlene Hard in the singles competition, 6-3, 6-2, and then teamed with Hard in the victorious doubles match. Gibson returned to a ticker-tape parade in New York City and then proceeded to defeat her old nemesis Louise Brough at the U.S. national championships at Forest Hills. Returning to Wimbledon in 1958, she beat Great Britain's Angela Mortimer 8-6, 6-2 in singles and then paired with Brazilian star Maria Bueno for the doubles win. Yet another U.S. national championship followed that summer.

Sought Other Careers

It seemed that Gibson's future in tennis was quite secure by 1958. Although she had just turned 30, she was at the top of her game and had achieved international acclaim. Then she shocked the world by announcing her retirement from the sport. She admitted that the most pressing reason for her decision was money—she simply did not make enough playing tennis to meet her needs. In the wake of her announcement, Gibson began to earn far more by trading upon her fame. She embarked on a singing career that took her to the *Ed Sullivan Show* and led to the release of several albums; she received product endorsement contracts; she even appeared in a John Ford Western, *The Horse Soldiers,* with John Wayne and William Holden.

The lure of sports was a powerful one, however. By 1963 Gibson had embarked on another quest, just as ground-breaking as the first. She qualified for the Ladies Professional Golf Association and began competing in important golf tournaments—the first black woman to achieve that honor. Gibson never had the success with golf that she had with tennis, however. She never won a tournament and took home little prize money, although she participated in the LPGA tour from 1963 until 1967. As late as 1990, she attempted a comeback with the LPGA but failed to qualify.

In the 1970s and 1980s Gibson also served as a tennis coach and a mentor to athletes, especially young black women. Her views on modern tennis stars were solicited regularly, and she showed a particular admiration for Martina Navratilova. Having married a New Jersey businessman named William A. Darben, Gibson concentrated her efforts in Essex County, New Jersey, where she served for many years on the Park Commission. She also took posts with the New Jersey State Athletic Control Board and the Governor's Council on Physical Fitness. Darben and Gibson were divorced and Gibson later married Sidney Llewellyn. Gibson retired in 1992, save for personal appearances in connection with golf or tennis events.

No other black woman athlete has yet risen to the prominence in tennis that Gibson achieved in the 1950s where Gibson ultimately won 56 tournaments. In 1971 Gibson was elected to the Tennis Hall of

Fame. In 1990 Zena Garrison advanced to the Wimbledon finals but was defeated; she was the only other black woman star to have advanced so far in the game by that time. This does not in any way diminish Althea Gibson's contribution to American sports. Her determination to play in the top tournaments at a time when blacks had little access to the exclusive tennis clubs helped to create a climate of acceptance that persists to this day. Elitism may never be completely eliminated in sports such as golf and tennis, but the contributions of Althea Gibson—and their effect on subsequent generations of black American athletes—are of lasting value to the sporting world.

Receieved Honors Late in Life

Gibson's health later started to fade, and by 1997, according to *Time* magazine, "Gibson [was] suffering in silence from a series of strokes and ailments brought on by a disease she [was] simply said to have described as 'terminal'." She had all but faded from the public's eye and it seemed she would die quiet and alone without anyone noticing. But some female athletes and coaches hearing about how she was living in all but poverty in East Orange, New Jersey, because her medical bills were overwhelming her, staged a benefit and tribute to the great Althea Gibson and raised, eventually, close to $100,000 to help defray the costs of her medical care. When Gibson learned of the effort that went into raising all the money to help her, her spirits were much lifted and her health improved somewhat.

In 1997 the Arthur Ashe Stadium was dedicated in New York to fellow black tennis great Arthur Ashe. The event took place on Gibson's 70th birthday and accolades were raised to her as well. In 1999 East Orange, New Jersey, dedicated the Althea Gibson Early Childhood Education Academy in Gibson's honor. The school's purpose, according to *Tennis* magazine, was to "provide kids ages six and under with a safe, nurturing environment in which to grow." Betty Debnaun, the principal of the new school said, "It's only fitting to name the school after a woman as great as Althea Gibson. She excelled in everything she did. She's a living legend." Also in 1999 a documentary of Gibson's life was published, an obvious indication that Gibson's accomplishments had not been forgotten. In 2000 *The Sports Authority* took upon itself to rank the ten top moments in women's sports. Gibson's becoming the first black woman to win Wimbledon and the U.S. Open was named one of the ten.

On September 28, 2003, Gibson died after a long illness of respiratory failure at East Orange General Hospital in New Jersey. She was 76-years-old. According to the *Sports Network* several hundred mourners showed up to pay their respects to Gibson. David Dinkins, former mayor of New York spoke at the service about her greatness. Among other things Dinkins reminded listeners of a very important fact: "A lot of folks stood on the shoulders of Althea Gibson." And this is something that people should never forget.

Selected writings

I Always Wanted To Be Somebody, Harper, 1958.
So Much To Live For, Putnam, 1968.

Sources

Books

Ashe, Arthur, *A Hard Road to Glory: A History of the African-American Athlete since 1946,* Warner Books, 1988.
Gibson, Althea, *I Always Wanted To Be Somebody,* Harper, 1958.
Gibson, Althea, *So Much To Live For,* Putnam, 1968.
Henderson, Edwin B., and others, *The Black Athlete: Emergence and Arrival,* Publishers Agency, 1976.
Smith, Jessie Carney, ed., *Notable Black American Women,* Gale, 1992.
St. James Encyclopedia of Popular Culture, St. James Press, 2000.

Periodicals

American School & University, November, 1999, p. 28.
Black Enterprise, September, 1997, p. 144.
Ebony, November, 1997, p. 146; March, 2002, p. 74.
Jet, March 30, 1987, p. 49; October 13, 2003, p. 51.
Knight Ridder/Tribune News Service, March 27, 1997.
Library Journal, March 1, 1999, p. 125.
Newsweek, October 13, 2003, p. 12.
Sports Illustrated, September 10, 1990, p. 26; November 29, 1999, p. 114.
Sports Network, October 2, 2003.
Tennis, September, 1999, p. 37.
Time, September, 8, 1997, p. 4.
WWD, November 17, 2000, p. 23.

—Mark Kram and Catherine V. Donaldson

Mike Grier

1975—

Hockey player

Mike Grier's debut on ice with the Edmunton Oilers made him the first African-American player in National Hockey League (NHL) history. There were a few other minority skaters in professional hockey, but they had either grown up or been trained in Canada. "It doesn't seem strange to me, because I've always been a black hockey player," he told Bergen County *Record* writer Mark J. Czerwinski. "But I understand what it means, and it makes me proud that I could be a role model."

Became Standout Player Early

Grier was born on January 5, 1975, in Detroit, Michigan, where his father was serving as an assistant coach for the Detroit Lions. Two years later his father took a job with the New England Patriots, and the Griers lived in the suburban Boston area for the next several years. Grier began skating at the age of four, following his older brother onto the ice. Within a few years he had become such a talented player that he earned a *Sports Illustrated* mention at the age of nine for scoring 227 goals in two seasons with his team, the Holliston Mites. During this era, youth hockey was a largely white, suburban sport, and Grier was almost always the only black player on his team. He had no role models in the professional league to emulate, but that didn't prevent him from dreaming of a future in the sport. "I always knew I wanted to be a hockey player, but I didn't talk about it much," he recalled in a *Seattle Times* interview.

After a brief attempt at playing football, where his size was deemed too large for the youth league, Grier went on to play hockey at St. Sebastian's Country Day School in Needham, Massachusetts. The school boasted a famously winning hockey team, and Grier was one of its standout players. Still, he sometimes encountered difficulties during his youth career because of his race, when a parent from an opposing team would hurl an occasional slur from the stands. "Parents would yell things like, 'Hey, kid, you're in the wrong sport; you should be playing basketball,'" Grier recalled in an interview with *Sports Illustrated* writer Gerry Callahan. "But my mom always told me the best way to shut them up was to score a goal."

During his senior year at St. Sebastian's, Grier was drafted by the St. Louis Blues. He opted to play college hockey at Boston University (BU) instead, but arrived for his freshman year weighing 255 pounds, and the coach judged him too heavy to play. He sat out the season, paying his own tuition because he was not eligible for any scholarship money, and shedding 20 pounds. A walk-on with BU's Terriers the next season, he soon proved to be the team's powerhouse. During that sophomore year, he scored 29 goals in 37 games, and helped take BU to a 1994-95 National Collegiate Athletic Association (NCAA) hockey championship title. The racial issue surfaced again, during a game against cross-town rival Boston College (BC). The year before, Grier had run into a BC player with what Michael Felger of the *Boston Herald* termed "a thunderous body check. The hit drew gasps from the Boston Garden crowd and was replayed on sportscasts across the country." Grier took a penalty for it, but during the next year's match-up, the same player uttered a racial epithet at him that went unheard by officials. Grier failed to bring it to their attention but, according to Felger, he replied to the other player, "You are the highlight of my highlight reel."

Joined NHL with the Oilers

While he played college hockey, Grier still retained his option to play in the NHL at a future date. But by the time he finished his junior year, the St. Louis Blues had traded his future rights to the Edmonton Oilers. He decided to join the team, leaving BU prior to his senior year. Initially Grier was not expected to play his first season in the NHL—whose roster is dominated by players who came up in the minor leagues, not college—but he performed so well at training camp that he made his debut during the 1996-97 season, and scored 15 goals as a rookie. He handled the naysayers with his characteristic grace. "Sure, a lot of people had doubts," he told Felger in the *Boston Herald* interview. "They weren't as optimistic as I was. It's always good to prove people wrong, but I never really listened to that stuff anyway."

During his rookie year, Grier was the NHL's first African-American player. There had been other blacks before him on the ice, beginning with Willie O'Ree in 1958, but they had been born or trained in Canada. At the time, only six out of 600 NHL players were black. Both he and another minority rookie, Calgary Flames' player Jarome Iginla, were soon dubbed the potential "Tiger Woods" of their sport, the standout black athlete who would bring legions of new minority players into youth hockey. Grier gave many interviews that first year due to overwhelming press interest, but tried to downplay his historic first. In an interview, he simply pointed out to *St Louis Post-Dispatch* writer Dave Luecking, "It was bound to happen—an African-American playing in the NHL. I'm just lucky it happened to me."

During his second season with the Oilers, Grier experienced a rare name-calling from another player, this time from Chris Simon, a player of Ojibwa heritage who played with the Washington Capitals. The incident occurred during a heated exchange between players, and the NHL reaction was swift. Simon was suspended for three games, and Grier went on to heed his mother's advice, scoring his first goal in what had until then been a moribund season. Once again, he earned kudos for handling the situation well, and tried to put the incident behind both of them. "(Simon) showed a lot of heart by doing what he did," *Boston Herald* writer Karen Guregian quoted Grier as saying on a local radio show. "He came to see me and talk to me man-to-man. He seemed genuinely sorry and he was honest about everything that happened. I forgave him and hopefully now, we can both move on."

Grier played well for the Oilers, scoring a total of 81 goals in six seasons with the team. He even played under the most trying of conditions, with a shoulder dislocated from its socket during a 2001 game. "Those present said they heard the scream all the way up in the press box," reported *Knight-Ridder/Tribune News Service* sportswriter Dan Noxon, of the incident. Grier then headed off the ice to have it reset, "doubled over by pain, knowing another blinding, white-hot flash would rip through his upper body when the trainers reset the joint," Noxon wrote. "Two minutes later, Grier was back on the ice, taking his regular shift."

In October of 2002, the Oilers traded Grier to the Washington Capitals after budget constraints made his $1.3 million contract a financial drain on dwindling team resources. He went on to score 15 goals and 17 assists in 82 games in his first season with his new teammates. Off the ice, he was active in NHL diversity efforts, including the landmark Ice Hockey in Harlem program. Grier knew that his presence and the NHL's work to increase minority involvement in the sport would have a positive impact. "I know if I hadn't been alone all the time growing up," he told Callahan in *Sports Illustrated,* "it might have been easier for me."

Sources

Boston Herald, July 19, 1997, p. 31; November 2, 1997, p. B15; November 12, 1997, p. 96; November 15, 1997, p. 43.
Buffalo News, November 11, 1997, p. B7.
Daily News (Los Angeles, CA), November 17, 1997, p. S27.
Denver Post, May 1, 1998, p. D10.
Knight-Ridder/Tribune News Service, April 13, 2001.
Record (Bergen County, NJ), February 13, 1997, p. S1.
Rocky Mountain News (Denver, CO), May 2, 1997, p. 16H.
San Francisco Chronicle, November 11, 1997, p. E7; November 18, 1997, p. D2.
Seattle Times, March 9, 1997, p. D7.
Sports Illustrated, February 20, 1995, p. 146.
Sports Illustrated for Kids, January 1, 1999, p. 44.
St. Louis Post-Dispatch, March 9, 1997, p. 1F.
Washington Times, November 29, 1996, p. E3; October 8, 2002, p. C7; December 14, 2002, p. C2; April 15, 2003, p. C1.

—Carol Brennan

Bessie Blout Griffin

1914—

Physical therapist, inventor, forensic scientist

During World War II, many different inventions were innovated as ways to help the war effort. Bessie Blout Griffin, a physical therapist who assisted amputees at various U.S. veterans' hospitals during the war, created new tools that would help those with physical disabilities. Griffin's most famous invention was a device that allowed disabled people in wheelchairs feed themselves without the use of their hands. While many of her inventions were not readily accepted by the United States government, she found much success in foreign countries such as France and Belgium who also were looking for ways to support their soldiers who had come back from the war with disabilities.

Bessie Blout Griffin was born Bessie Blout on November 24, 1914, in Hickory, Virginia. Not much is known about her early years and family life other then the fact that her parents highly valued education and pushed Griffin to succeed in her early studies. It is also known that she was influenced in her early life to study medicine due to relatives she had in this field, but it is not known how close these relatives were to Griffin.

By the 1930s Griffin had graduated from high school and headed north to Panzer College of Physical Education (later Montclair State University) in East Orange, New Jersey, in order to get her degree to work as a physical therapist. Griffin studied and graduated from Panzer in the mid-1930s and then went on to study at Union Junior College in Roselle, New Jersey. During the 1940s, America entered the second World War and there was a great need for medical personal across the country. For a time, Griffin stayed in New Jersey and worked at the veteran's hospital there, but she soon transferred to a veteran's hospital in Chicago.

Much of Griffin's work at the veteran's hospitals focused on physical therapy involving amputees and those soldiers who had otherwise lost the use of their limbs. Griffin broke many boundaries while working with these soldiers, teaching them how to compensate in many ways that were not standard practice at the time, such as using their feet in place of a hand or a limb that was no longer functional. Griffin, however, realized that for certain tasks no amount of physical therapy was going to be completely successful. It was these tasks that Griffin focused on and began inventing around.

One of the first inventions that Griffin developed was an apparatus that assisted in the feeding of people who were not able to use their limbs to reach their mouths. The device consisted of a tube that was attached to a mouthpiece which fed into a larger machine. When the user bit down on the tube, the machine, powered by electricity, delivered a bite-size portion of food to the mouthpiece which could then be eaten with the mouth alone. This allowed the user to eat an entire meal at their own pace without needing assistance. It wasn't long before Griffin began to use this machine in her physical therapy to great success.

While it was clear that Griffin had made an advance in the field of physical therapy, she had a difficult time obtaining a patent for her idea and faced the even more arduous task of convincing medical supply companies to sell the device. Many of the companies said that the machine was too large and bulky and that no hospital

At a Glance . . .

Born Bessie Blout on November 24, 1914, in Hickory, VA; married Griffin, 1951. *Education,* Panzer College of Physical Education, physical therapy degree, 1930s; attended Union Junior College, 1930s.

Career: Physical therapist, 1930s-1969; inventor, 1940s-1960s; Vineland Police Department, forensic scientist, 1969-1970s; Norfolk Police Department, forensic scientist, 1970s; Portsmouth Police Department, chief document examiner, 1970s-1977; Scotland Yard, forensic scientist and agent, 1977-1980s; forensic consultant, 1990s–.

Addresses: *Home*—New Jersey.

would have room to store one for each patient. Hence, in the late 1940s, Griffin redesigned her idea. The new version, called the "Portable Receptacle Support," was a tube that was attached to a bowl or a dish, which was connected to a brace that the person could wear around the neck. While not as useful in providing bite size portions, it did allow the user to eat at their own pace, and again allowed for the user to eat without assistance. In March of 1948 Griffin applied for a patent for her "Portable Receptacle Support" and on April 24, 1951, she received her first U.S. patent, No. 2,550,554.

Even though Griffin was now a recognized inventor, it did not help her to sell either of her original ideas in the United States. She again approached different medical-device makers and even brought her ideas to the U.S. Veterans Administration, but was met with only disinterest. Finally, in 1952, Griffin gave up her endeavors in the United States and turned her sights to foreign countries. It wasn't long before the French government contacted her and purchased her "Portable Receptacle Support," for use in their military hospitals. She is quoted as saying in a New York newspaper, and later reprinted on the *African American Registry* website, that her sale of the device proved "that a black woman can invent something for the benefit of humankind."

Married in 1951 to a man by the last name of Griffin, Griffin moved first to New York and then back to New Jersey. She continued to work in the medical industry, both as a physical therapist and an inventor. In the mid-1950s Griffin became the personal assistant and caretaker of the mother-in-law of Theodore M. Edison, the son of the famous inventor Thomas A. Edison. It wasn't long before Griffin became a close friend with

Edison and began sharing her ideas for inventions with him. By the 1960s Edison's company had already produced two of her inventions. A third invention, disposable cardboard emesis (regurgitation) basins, which she created from a baked combination of newspaper, flour, and water, never took hold in the United States, but was purchased by the Belgian government and many are still used in Belgium hospitals today.

In 1969 Griffin switched gears and began a career in forensic science. She started out in the Vineland, New Jersey, Police Department, but would move on to work in Norfolk and Portsmouth, Virginia. She advanced quickly in her new career and was the chief document examiner in Portsmouth by 1972. Yet Griffin had even bigger aspirations. In 1976 she turned in an application with the United States Federal Bureau of Investigation (FBI). She was turned down by then director J. Edgard Hoover, but this spurred her onto apply to other high ranking law enforcement offices. This resulted in a first for Griffin for in 1977 she became the first black woman to train and work at Scotland Yard, the British equivalent of the FBI

Griffin worked as a forensic scientist into the 1990s when she retired and started her own business. She now does a good deal of freelance forensic work, both in the areas of law enforcement and in historical records. She has authenticated many African-American slave "papers" and Native American treaties for various museums and she is often taken on as a consultant for law enforcement investigations in New Jersey.

Sources

"Bessie Blout," *About Inventors,* http://inventors.about.com/library/inventors/blblout.htm (February 2, 2004).

"Bessie Blout," *Colors of Innovation, Bucknell University,* www.listproc.bucknell.edu/archives/femecon-1/200302/msg00086.html (February 2, 2004).

"Bessie Blout," *Memphis Schools,* www.memphis-schools.k12.tn.us/schools/craigmont.mi/BessieBlountpart2picture.htm (February 2, 2004).

"Besie Blout Griffin," *Cal Poly Poma University,* www.csupomona.edu/~plin/inventors/blout.html (February 2, 2004).

"Savior of the handicapped, Bessie Blout," *African American Registry,* www.aaregistry.com/african_american_history/2143/Savior_of_the_handicapped_Bessie_Blout.html (February 2, 2004).

"Women Inventors," *Holt Rinehart, and Winston-Lemelson Center Invention Features,* www.hrw.com/science/si-science/chemistry/careers/innovative_lives/womeninventors.html (February 2, 2004).

— Joseph DiCostanza

Gar Anthony Haywood

1954—

Author

Gar Anthony Haywood writes successful crime fiction featuring Los Angeles private investigator Aaron Gunner. Often compared to Walter Mosley or Gary Phillips, other black authors in the genre with devoted followings, Haywood has earned praise for his gritty depictions of Los Angeles and its more dangerous quarters. His plain-talking, wryly observant Gunner has lured legions of fans to the series, and critics often remark on Haywood's ability to toss a trenchant remark about relevant social topics of the day—politically incorrect or not—into his dialogue. Still, noted *Booklist* critic Bill Ott, Haywood's "treatment of these issues never gets in the way of crisp, character-centered storytelling."

Debut Won Prestigious Award

A native of Los Angeles, Haywood was born on May 22, 1954. He read avidly as a child, from comic books to science fiction, and as a young adult took a job as a computer-service technician, which he held for nearly twenty years. His first book, 1987's *Fear of the Dark,* served to introduce Gunner and launch Haywood's career. It also won the St. Martins' Press/Private Eye Writers of America Best First Private Eye Novel Award. Writing in the *New York Times,* Stewart Kellerman found some flaws in dialogue and prose in this tale of Gunner's involvement in a bar slaying with links to the Black Panther movement, but asserted that "Haywood's wit overcomes much of the awkwardness." Kellerman also noted that "there's a nice twist at the end, just when readers may be getting smug." Haywood followed his award-winning debut with *Not Long*

for This World three years later, in which a do-gooder Los Angeles minister is gunned down in an apparent drive-by shooting. One suspect is nabbed, but the court-appointed defense attorney hires Gunner to find the missing driver.

In the early 1990s Haywood's career was inadvertently boosted by a chance remark that presidential candidate Bill Clinton made on the campaign trail. Asked what he had been reading lately, Clinton praised Mosley's *Devil in a Blue Dress* and *A Red Death,* and sales for Mosley's subsequently skyrocketed. In the end, noted *Ebony's* Christopher Benson, "Clinton's endorsement ... created new interest in Black mystery, and a demand for new voices that publishers were eager to meet." Haywood wrote his third novel, *You Can Die Trying,* in which a much-loathed white police officer is accused of shooting an unarmed black teen. Excoriated in the media, the officer commits suicide, but then a witness comes to Gunner to claim that he saw the teen fire twice at the cop. Multiple plot turns reveal much about all parties involved. "Gunner is a rarity in recent detective fiction: soured, yet utterly believable, tough and resourceful without being cartoonishly overblown," noted a *Publishers Weekly* contributor of Haywood's third novel.

Haywood took a break from the crime scene for a bit to write a lighter detective series featuring a pair of African-American retirees, Joe and Dottie Loudermilk, who travel the United States in their Airstream trailer. "I wanted to do a second series because I didn't want my

At a Glance . . .

Born on May 22, 1954, in Los Angeles, CA; married; two daughters.

Career: Computer-maintenance technician, 1970s-1990s; detective fiction writer, 1987–; television script writer, 1998–.

Awards: St. Martins' Press/Private Eye Writers of America Best First Private Eye Novel Award, 1987, for *Fear of the Dark.*

Addresses: *Office—* c/o Gar Anthony Haywood, G. P. Putnam's Publicity, 375 Hudson St., New York, NY 10014.

character to get stale," Haywood told *American Visions* writer Carolyn Tillery. In 1994's *Going Nowhere Fast,* Joe, a former police officer and his college-professor wife encounter the youngest and most troubled of their five children, Bad Dog, at the Grand Canyon, who is being tailed by an angry ex-football player. Bad Dog's nickname fulfills its promise when a dead body turns up in Joe and Dottie's bathroom, and the Loudermilks piece together the story. Neither that nor a follow-up, *Bad News Travels Fast,* were as well received by critics as Haywood's Aaron Gunner mysteries, however.

Haywood brought Gunner back in 1996 with *It's Not a Pretty Sight,* in which the Shelby Cobra-driving detective tries to solve the mystery behind his ex-girlfriend's death. A *Booklist* review from Thomas Gaughan likened Haywood to other Los Angeles detective fiction writers, among them such stellar names as Mosley, Ross MacDonald, and even Raymond Chandler. "Each of those writers has given us a different Los Angeles," Gaughan asserted, "and Haywood adds another precinct" with his series. The plot of his next work, *When Last Seen Alive,* concerns two women—one who hires Gunner to find her brother, who never came back from the Million Man March in Washington, D.C., and the other the wife of a local politician who is determined to catch her husband's infidelities on camera. The job draws Gunner into a web that involves the Federal Bureau of Investigation as well as operatives from a black extremist group called Defenders of the Bloodline. "Deaths accumulate and then coalesce into a pattern as Haywood continues to deepen this impressive series," noted a *Publishers Weekly* contributor in its review of the book.

"Someone Realistic, With Human Frailties"

Critics often remarked on what an appealing character Gunner was, and in an interview that appeared on the *MysteryOne* website, Haywood conceded that it was a form of alter-ego writing for him. "Internally, my characters are very much reflections of myself," he reflected. "They tend to be stronger willed, though. And I think it would be more accurate to say that I regularly have them do things I [could] never do." He has also said that his motivation for creating Gunner was to portray "an African-American character—someone realistic, with human frailties, who wasn't a superhero or too good to be true," as he told Tillery in the *American Visions* interview.

For his sixth Gunner mystery, Haywood earned a slew of positive critical reviews. *All the Lucky Ones Are Dead,* which appeared in 2000, opened with the suicide of a major gangsta rap star, C.E. Digga Jones. His father believes it was a murder, and hires Gunner to find his son's killer. But Gunner, his business struggling, must also take a second job as bodyguard to a conservative talk-show host, Sparkle Johnson, whom he loathes. Once again, his job entangles him with the violent Defenders of the Bloodline group. "What is impressive," maintained *Black Issues Book Review* critic Shaun Neblett of this plot, "is that Haywood merges two significant story lines together through one character," with Gunner learning "what strange bonds can unite people." *Publishers Weekly* also commended Haywood's characterization, noting that "Gunner's savvy intelligence makes it a pleasure to follow the PI through a maze of betrayals and greed." A *Houston Chronicle* journalist, Amy Rabinovitz, declared that "most authors couldn't even say 'gangsta rapper' without sounding a little ridiculous. Maybe Haywood can't say it either, but he certainly can deliver in print."

Haywood has also worked in television. He adapted the Dennis Rodman autobiography, *As Bad As I Wanna Be,* for a 1998 television movie, and has written episodes of *New York Undercover* and *The District.* On writing for television versus writing fiction, Haywood asserted "there is absolutely no comparison," he said in a *MysteryOne* interview. "With very few exceptions, what I want goes in a novel, while writing a television episode is work-for-hire, there is absolutely nothing about the work I have any real control over. So your expectations are different before you ever put your first word on the page, and I think those expectation affect what you write, and how you write it."

Began Third Series

For his 2002 thriller *Man Eater,* Haywood took the pen name Ray Shannon to distance himself from his Aaron Gunner series. As he told *Publishers Weekly* interviewer Adam Dunn, he did so in part because "there were some misconceptions about who I am and what I'm capable of in my writing that I wanted to address." The new work featured a likable female protagonist, a Hollywood production-company executive named Ronnie Deal, who finds herself the target of a hit man and must team with an ex-convict with a script he's trying to plug in order to extricate herself. "Ronnie and Ellis become an effective, if unlikely, team as they fight for their lives and careers," noted Craig Shufelt in a *Library Journal* assessment. *Booklist*'s Keir Graff found the plot an intricate one, and claimed that "Shannon sets a lot of flaming balls in motion, but he doesn't drop any."

Not surprisingly, Haywood was characteristically forth-right about *Man Eater*'s cynical take on just what it took to get a script into production in Hollywood. "In all my writing, I generally have one ax or another to grind," he told *WWD*. "Up to this point, I've been fairly subtle in grinding it." That book earned comparisons with the fast-paced, darkly comic crime novels of Elmore Leonard—comparisons that were echoed upon publication of the second Ronnie Deal book, *Firecracker*, in 2004. Deal is now a rising entertainment-industry executive who becomes pregnant by a famous pro football player. Spurning the cash payoff his camp offers her to avoid a paternity suit, she lands in trouble with a Super Bowl betting slip that the Dallas Cowboys tight end gave her in an attempt to woo her one night—a revelation that would end his lucrative pro career forever. "Everything comes to a head in Las Vegas on Super Bowl Sunday, and there's loads of action and double-crossing," noted a *Publishers Weekly* reviewer, who also found "the pace is fast and the plot suitably outrageous."

Haywood doesn't mind the comparisons to Leonard, as he told Dunn in *Publishers Weekly*. "I've read quite a bit of his work, and I feel that he's the inventor, so to speak, at least the modern inventor, of the modern serial comic ensemble crime novel." Haywood is married, and lives with his wife and two daughters in the Silverlake area of Los Angeles. Initially, he said, his daughters were impressed with his career move from the computer industry to authorship. "At first they thought my writing books was pretty exciting," he told Tillery in *American Visions*. "But now it's no big deal."

Selected writings

"Aaron Gunner Mystery" series

Fear of the Dark, St. Martin's Press, 1987.
Not Long for This World, St. Martin's Press, 1990.
You Can Die Trying, St. Martin's Press, 1993.
It's Not a Pretty Sight, Putnam, 1996.
When Last Seen Alive, Putnam, 1997.
All the Lucky Ones Are Dead, Putnam, 2000.

Other

Going Nowhere Fast, Putnam, 1994.
Bad News Travels Fast, Putnam, 1995.
(Under pseudonym Ray Shannon) *Man Eater,* Putnam, 2003.
(Under pseudonym Ray Shannon) *Firecracker,* Putnam, 2004.

Sources

Periodicals

American Visions, April-May 1997, p. 18.
Black Issues Book Review, July 2000, p. 23.
Booklist, September 1, 1996, p. 56; December 15, 1999, p. 759; January 1, 2003, p. 856.
Ebony, September 2003, p. 110.
Entertainment Weekly, November 8, 1996, p. 63.
Houston Chronicle, April 2, 2000, p. 18.
Library Journal, January 1998, p. 148; January 2003, p. 159.
New York Times, October 9, 1988, p. BR39.
People, April 3, 2000, p. 53.
Publishers Weekly, April 27, 1990, p. 55; May 10, 1993, p. 55; June 27, 1994, p. 59; June 12, 1995, p. 51; July 15, 1996, p. 58; December 1, 1997, p. 48; December 6, 1999, p. 56; December 2, 2002, p. 32; December 15, 2003, p.52.
WWD, January 21, 2003, p. 24.

On-line

"Interview with Gar Anthony Haywood a.k.a. Ray Shannon," *MysteryOne,* www.mysteryone.com/GarHaywoodInterview.htm (January 5, 2003).

—Carol Brennan

Torii Hunter

1975—

Baseball outfielder

A three-time Golden Glove award winner, Minnesota Twins centerfielder Torii Hunter ranked as one of the most exciting defensive players in baseball in the first years of the twenty-first century. American League batters looked on helplessly as Hunter made leaping catches to rob them of hits, running headlong into the outfield walls so often that it came to be almost a personal trademark. As he moved toward an age when many professional baseball players reach the peak of their abilities, many observers felt that Hunter had the potential to become one of the greats of the game; he was already one of the most fun to watch.

Torii Kedar Hunter was born in Pine Bluff, Arkansas, on July 18, 1975, the son of a cotton mill engineer father and a schoolteacher mother. He and his three brothers (Taru, Tishque, and Tramar) all played baseball, and he first began to develop his fielder's legs by chasing down baseballs and footballs thrown by his brothers. But it was Torii who was the standout at Pine Bluff High School. He was spotted by Minnesota Twins scouts by the time he was a sophomore, and was named to the 1992 Junior Olympics baseball team and

to the *USA Today* newspaper's national all-star team. Straight out of high school, he was drafted by the Twins (he was picked 20th) and given a $450,000 signing bonus.

The Twins took their time developing their young prospect, and he moved up slowly through the team's farm system, starting out in the Gulf Coast League. During his first season he had a batting average of only .190. He developed an affection for Texas, eventually building a large home in a Houston suburb for his wife Katrina and their four children (three of whom were Hunter's from previous relationships). But soon Hunter was off to the Twins' New Britain, Connecticut, affiliate. Hitting was more of a problem than fielding from the start, and Hunter sometimes despaired of getting the knack of it.

Struggling through the 1997 season in New Britain with a .231 average, Hunter didn't seem to be improving much. "I'd come home after every game and lie on the bed in my apartment and look at the ceiling, replaying my at-bats, trying to figure out what I was doing wrong," he told the Minneapolis *Star-Tribune*. At one point he seriously considered quitting the game and moving back to Arkansas.

At a Glance . . .

Born Torii Kedar Hunter on July 18, 1975, in Pine Bluff, AR; son of Theotis (a cotton mill engineer) and Shirley (a schoolteacher) Hunter; married Katrina; four children.

Career: Gulf Coast League Twins, centerfielder, 1992-96; New Britain Rock Cats, centerfielder, 1996-98; Minnesota Twins centerfielder, 1999–.

Selected awards: Three Golden Glove awards, 2001, 2002, 2003.

Addresses: *Team office*—Minnesota Twins, Hubert H. Humphrey Metrodome, 900 S. Fifth St., Minneapolis, MN 55415.

But a freak occurrence restored Hunter's inspiration. In Baltimore during an East Coast road trip, a trade opened a temporary spot in the Twins' lineup for an outfielder. Rather than move a player across the country from their Salt Lake City farm team for just one or two days, the Twins turned instead to Hunter, who was within commuting distance of Baltimore. Hunter actually played in only one game, making an appearance as a pinch runner. But the excitement recharged Hunter's batteries. "It was an electric atmosphere," he told the *Star-Tribune*. "I saw how much fun those players were having, I saw all the people, I told myself, 'This is what you can dream about.'"

In 1998 Hunter's batting average jumped near the .300 mark, and after a stint at the Twins' AAA-level farm team, he was called up to the majors. He played in 19 games for the Twins in 1998 and became the team's starting centerfielder the following year. His hitting remained inconsistent, and during a bad slump early in 2000, batting only .207, he was sent back to Salt Lake City. After two months, however, he was back with the Twins, and he finished the season with a respectable .280 average.

In 2001 Hunter began to appear on fan radar screens, as he won his first Golden Glove award for fielding and added power to his repertoire at the plate, slamming 27 home runs. He hit his stride in 2002, winning another Golden Glove award, batting .289 with 29 home runs, and gaining tremendous visibility when he was named to the American League All-Star team for the first time. As it had before, excitement brought out the best in Hunter's abilities. He made a leaping catch on the outfield warning track that robbed star slugger Barry Bonds of a home run. "I had so much fun," Hunter told *Baseball Digest*. "It's something you dream of as a baseball player. It was a dream come true for me."

Fan-pleasing catches like the All-Star Game grab, along with Hunter's solid overall performance and the Twins' advance to the American League Championship series, made him a much more marketable player than he had been previously, and some tension marked his negotiations with the financially tight-fisted Twins' front office prior to the 2003 season. Hunter considered moving back to Texas in order to be closer to his family, but eventually signed a four-year contract with the Twins worth a reported $32 million.

The Twins made the playoffs once again in 2003, and Hunter went through another cycle of frustration followed by a hot streak in the spotlight. After a particularly bad slump in July of that year, Hunter shocked fans by smashing a bat to pieces in anger. He was quoted by *Knight-Ridder News Service* as saying, "I felt like I was falling back into 2000, when I got sent down [to Class AAA], and I was listening to everybody, and it hurt me." But he made several more razzle-dazzle catches in the outfield and roared back at the plate, finishing the season with a .250 average and a career-high 102 RBIs.

Hunter, who keeps a small wooden cross in his locker, has credited his religious faith for both his spirit of persistence and for the fact that he got the chance to play professional baseball in the first place. "I know the Lord is the main reason I didn't get shot or stay with a gang," he told the *Star-Tribune*. "He was one of the reasons I got out of the neighborhood and was able to get into the league and help my mother and my father." Still a developing player, Hunter looks forward to more seasons of spectacular fielding. Asked by *Sporting News* whether he was beginning to reconsider his penchant for running into fences, Hunter answered, "No. That's against my nature."

Sources

Periodicals

Baseball Digest, March 2003, p. 61.
Houston Chronicle, July 10, 2002, p. 5.
Knight Ridder/Tribune News Service, September 12, 2002, p. K0932; August 18, 2003, p. K3128.
Plain Dealer (Cleveland, OH), July 21, 2002, p. C7.
Sporting News, September 29, 2003, p. 59.
Sports Illustrated for Kids, March 1, 2003, p. 36.
Star Tribune (Minneapolis, MN), August 23, 1997, p. C7; March 9, 1998, p. C6; May 26, 2000, p. C11; September 15, 2000, p. C1; July 9, 2002, p. C1; March 30, 2003, p. S3; May 3, 2003, p. B6; September 28, 2003, p. C1; November 5, 2003, p. C2.

On-line

"Torii Hunter," *CBS Sports Line,* http://cbssports lihne.com/mlb/players/playerpage/10813 (December 11, 2003).

"Torii Hunter," *ESPN,* http://sports.espn.go.com/ mlb/players/stats?statsId=5884 (December 11, 2003).

—James M. Manheim

Thomas "T.D." Jakes

1957—

Entrepreneur, Pentecostal preacher, author

When T.D. Jakes first stepped into the pulpit, he trembled with nervousness and anxiety. Speaking in front of crowds was initially quite difficult for him due to a pronounced speech impediment. But judging from the reaction of his congregations, Jakes' preaching is very powerful, even "anointed," some would say. Jakes himself deflected attention to his spiritual gifts and well-honed abilities, saying in *Christianity Today*, "When a person flows into God's purpose and timing for his or her life, God can take a person with less ability and use his/her to extreme capacity, just because they are willing to be available."

Grew Up As "Bible Boy"

Born on June 9, 1957, and raised in Charleston, West Virginia, Jakes was "called" to preach at age 17. He could not have known then that his ministry would reach the entire nation and eventually effect millions of people through books, radio, television, and conferences. Jakes grew up in a community where it traditionally took a village to raise a child. Every adult in the community contributed to the children's upbringing. At an early age, he was described as opinionated, stubborn, and driven—traits that some still ascribed to the adult Jakes. He was also nicknamed "Bible Boy" due to his early habit of preaching to an imaginary congregation and always carrying his Bible to school. However, the nickname "T.D."—short for Thomas Dexter—is the one that stuck. He later gained the title "Bishop," which was conferred on him when the Higher Ground Assemblies elected him their regional prelate. (The

Higher Ground Always Abounding Assembly is an association of almost 200 Pentecostal Churches.)

Jakes' parents, Ernest and Odith, evidenced a strong work ethic and entrepreneurial spirit that would later characterize their preacher son. Odith, an economics teacher, taught all three of her children to cook, sew, and clean for themselves. Ernest, a self-made businessman, was entrepreneurial long before entrepreneurs were common among blacks. Ernest developed a janitorial business from one mop and bucket to include 42 employees who cleaned everything in the Charleston area—from the West Virginia Capitol building to grocery stores. This entrepreneurial drive left a mark on young Jakes, who delivered newspapers, Avon, and even products from his mother's garden.

Although working full-time at a chemical plant job with Union Carbide, Jakes was also involved as the part-time music director at the Baptist Church where he grew up and as a part-time street evangelist. When the Charleston-area chemical plant closed in 1982, and his father died of kidney disease, Jakes devoted all his time to his ministry as an evangelist and church-planter in the Charleston area.

Began a Church from Scratch

His first storefront church, Greater Emanuel Temple of Faith, had ten members in 1980. In a few short years that church grew enormously. Just as importantly, it transcended racial lines bringing together an integrated congregation and overcoming the diverse elements that traditionally divided the community.

At a Glance . . .

Born Thomas Dexter Jakes on June 9, 1957, in South Charleston, West Virginia; son of Ernest and Odith Jakes; married Serita Ann Jamison, 1981; five children. *Education:* Attended Center Business College, 1972; attended West Virginia State College, 1976; Friends University, BA, 1990, MA, 1990, Doctorate of Ministry, 1995.

Career: Held various positions in business and industry, 1976-82; Greater Emanuel Temple of Faith, pastor, 1982-93; "The Master's Plan," radio program, producer and on-air talent, 1982-85; "Bible Conference" ministry, creator and minister, 1983–; author, 1993–; T.D. Jakes Ministries, a non-profit conference and television ministry, founder and minister, 1994–; "When Shepherds Bleed" conference, founder and organizer, 1995–; Potter's House, founder and leader, 1996–.

Selected awards: Gospel Heritage Award for Ministry, 1996; Stellar Foundation Excellence Award, 1996; "Key to the City of Dallas" for his homeless ministry, Raven's Refuge, 1997; Gospel Music Association's Dove Seal for "Woman, Thou Art Loosed: The Songs of Healing and Deliverance," 1997; Grammy Award and Dove Award nomination for *Live at the Potter House,* 1999; Living Legend Award, National Professional Network, 2000; Named "America's Best Preacher," *CNN* and *Time,* 2001; Chairman's Award, National Religious Broadcasters, 2002; Grammy and Dove Award nominations and Stellar and NAACP Image Awards for *The Storm Is Over,* 2002.

Addresses: *Office*—The Potter's House, 6777 West Kiest Blvd., Dallas, Texas 75236.

In 1990 Jakes moved from Smithers to South Charleston, West Virginia, where his congregation grew from 100 to more than 300 members. And in 1993 he moved his Temple of Faith ministry to a renovated bank in Cross Lanes, West Virginia. There his congregation grew to more than 1,100 people of all races, including an unprecedented 40 percent Caucasian membership. In 1994 he established "T.D. Jakes Ministries," a non-profit organization that produced his nation-wide television and conference ministry. From 1995 to 1996, he hosted the nationally-syndicated weekly radio and television show, *Get Ready,* attended by millions of listeners and viewers throughout the United States and South Africa.

In May of 1996 Jakes' ministry grew once again when he and his wife, Serita, took their five children and 50-member staff to Dallas, Texas. There Jakes founded the Potter's House, a multi-racial, non-denominational megachurch, which grew from 7,000 worshipers to 14,000 in two years. Potter's House featured a 5,000-seat auditorium, enough space for its worship services, but its 34-acre hilltop campus in southwest Dallas seemed to be running out of space to house its multi-faceted ministries.

The hallmark of Jakes' ministry has been a deep spiritual healing with life-changing effects. He has described himself as a "spiritual physician," one who "has discovered some medicine in the Word of God.... As the physician, I am careful to always acknowledge that I am not the cure, but that I have been able to facilitate the cure because Jesus Christ lives in me."

Local civic leadership honored Jakes for his ministry to the greater Dallas/Fort Worth Metro Area by giving him and his wife the prestigious "Key to the City" in February of 1997. Jakes' ministry has engaged the community with various outreaches to needy people: including, the Raven's Refuge, a homeless ministry; Operation Rahab, an outreach to prostitutes; a G.E.D. tutoring and literacy program; Vessels of Clay and Ladies Choice, mentoring and job-training programs; S.A.L.T., a youth ministry program; Transformation Ministry, a ministry to drug and alcohol abusers; and weight-loss programs based on faith and his cookbook, *Lay Aside the Weight.*

Became a Best-Selling Author

Since the 1990s, Jakes has become a prodigious and popular author, cranking out 27 nonfiction books, six of which appeared on the national religious best sellers list, and one venture into fiction with the novel *Cover Girls.* Altogether, his books have sold well over one million copies since 1993. That distinction placed him among the most accomplished African-American authors in history.

His most popular book, *Woman, Thou Art Loosed,* sold more than 800,000 copies by 1996, making it the third best-selling religious book. The success of the book catapulted Jakes into a national conference ministry with its healing message. More than 18,000 women, mostly blacks, attended a 3-day event in Tampa Bay/St. Petersburg, Florida. The book *Woman, Thou Art Loosed* was adapted into a musical recording by Integrity Music, which received the Gospel Music Association's coveted Dove Award and was nominated for a Grammy in 1997.

Besides his most popular "Thou Art Loosed" conference for women, Jakes has also sponsored a variety of seminars, including the "When Shepherds Bleed" summit for pastors and their spouses, the "Manpower" series just for men, as well as "The Bible Conference" (first held at Greater Temple of Faith for 880 attendees in 1983, when it was called "Back to the Bible").

Numerous other books by Jakes have risen to the number one spot on various book lists, including the prestigious *New York Times* Bestseller List. His most recent book to top this list, *God's Leading Lady,* is yet another in a long line of non-fiction books intended to assist women in gaining confidence in themselves through belief in religion. Jakes told *Publishers Weekly,* "I wanted to provide women with tools to fortify themselves spiritually as they embark on new territories, whether in their public or private lives. This book focuses on the tremendous opportunities that are available to women today, and helps them to maximize those opportunities and live life to its fullest."

Greatly Expanded Ministry With Media

Since 1999 Jakes has continued to expand the reach of Potter's House through media. He launched a state-by state campaign for business and individuals to Adopt a Prison, allowing religious programming to be beamed into prisons via satellite. He also created the Prison Satellite Network, which allowed convicts to witness live conferences and receive bible study and church service directly from people outside of the prison system.

Continuing on the success of the musical adaptation of "Woman, Thou Art Loosed," Jakes produced *Sacred Love Songs,* an album that found many fans in the Gospel genre and was named the top Gospel Album of the year by *Billboard* magazine in 1999. A third album, *The Storm is Over* followed in 2001 with a new company founded by Jakes in collaboration with EMI Gospel, Dexterity Sounds. *The Storm is Over* received not only Dove and Grammy award nominations, but also NAACP Image and Stellar Gospel awards for Best Gospel Album in the Contemporary genre. In 2002 Jakes continued to produce music with Potter's House and other companies including an album of music inspired by his book *God's Leading Ladies,* and an album of Christmas songs entitled *Follow the Star.*

In addition to music, Jakes has also turned to the stage and screen to spread his message. 1999 saw the first theatrical staging of *Woman, Thou Art Loosed,* which quickly garnered the top Gospel Play Honors. A year later, he co-wrote *Behind Closed Doors,* which was produced by Touchdown Concepts, and like *Women, Thou Art Loosed,* was praised with Gospel Play Honors. By 2001 a televised version of *Woman, Thou Art Loosed* was broadcast into a billion homes around the world, bringing even the most remote of locations into the media web which Jakes had spun.

Blessed to Be a Blessing

When asked how he would define the rapid growth of his ministry Jakes said, "My assignment is to open the door of the Church for hurting people and refocus what the Church was meant to be in our society. The Church has become stereotyped as a 'spiritual club' for elitists and yuppies who portray themselves as persons who 'have arrived.' I believe the Church was meant to be a hospital for hurting people."

Despite his obvious success, or maybe because of it, the ministry of T.D. Jakes has not been universally accepted or appreciated. The *Gazette* criticized him for profiting from his revival/seminar ministry, leading the reader to infer that he was only in it for the money. Calculating $20 per person for the Tampa engagement, the *Gazette* noted "that's $360,000 for three days' work—more than Jakes might have earned in a lifetime at his chemical plant job." Such riches have allowed Jakes to buy a million-dollar mansion. As Jakes told *Christianity Today,* "I don't live in a mobile home. There's nothing wrong with being blessed and successful."

While he seemed abundantly blessed with the grace to sit on many different platforms, there were some people in the evangelical community who would not sit with him for either racial or doctrinal issues. Yet Jakes remained undaunted in his hope for the church, "As we come into healing and restoration, I would like to see the church rise up undaunted and be uncompromising in terms of our loyalty and covenant with one another."

Message Spoke of Human Needs

Jakes has delivered his message from the pulpit with Pentecostal fervor and poetic lyrics (e.g., "stop merely looking to the White house, and start turning back to the Church House"). His fervent messages typically focus on the restoration, reconciliation, and healing of hurting people. Contemporary illustrations, Bible stories, soulful praise, and joyful dancing are also common to his worship services.

His message of healing and restoration remained in demand by clergy and laity alike, and transcended every cultural and denominational barrier. According to Ken Walker of *Charisma* magazine, Jakes' message "is about God's supernatural ability, bestowed by a Lord who is color-blind and cares about each person.... He [Jakes] delivers the Word in such a lightening-rod fashion that he makes you believe that all things really are possible with God."

T. D. Jakes has earned renown for his deep commitment to bringing wholeness to men and woman. Compassionate in his understanding of human nature, Jakes sensed and has spoken to the basic human need for fulfillment and destiny. With the energy and drive of 50 men, Jakes has catapulted into the mainstream of speaking conferences and book sales nationwide. He met speaking engagements almost *every day*—often twice a day—to packed auditoriums and convention centers. His ability to captivate large audiences and hold their attention has been considered to be his distinctive speaking gift.

Though a black charismatic figure with Pentecostal theology, Jakes has been admired by people of all colors and most denominations. Many have long regarded him as a pastor to pastors and as a true father to the fatherless. His insights, many borrowed from his own life of peaks and valleys, have stirred within most readers, listeners, and viewers of his ministry a strong desire to fulfill their destiny, believing that "all things are possible with God."

Selected writings

Woman, Thou Art Loosed, Treasure House, 1993.
Can You Stand to Be Blessed? Destiny Image, 1995.
Help Me, I've Fallen, Pneuma Life, 1995.
Harvest, Pneuma Life, 1995.
Naked and Not Ashamed, Treasure House, 1995.
Loose That Man And Let Him Go, Albury Pub, 1995.
Daddy Loves His Girls, Creation House, 1996.
Help! I'm Raising My Children Alone, Creation House, 1996.
When Shepherds Bleed, Pnuema Life, 1997.
Lay Aside the Weight, Albury Pub, 1997.
The Lady, Her Lover and Her Lord, Putnam, 1998.
His Lady, Penguin/Putnam, 1999.
Maximize The Moment, Penguin/Putnam, 2000
The Great Investment, Penguin/Putnam, 2001.

God's Leading Lady, Penguin/Putnam, 2002.
Cover Girls, Warner Faith, 2003.

Sources

Books

Melton, Lucas, and Stone Melton, *Prime-Time Religion,* Oryx Press, 1997.

Periodicals

Christianity Today, January 12, 1998, p. 56.
Ebony, October 2002, pp. 24-5.
Economist, May 31, 1997, p. 28.
Essence, August 2003, p. 116.
Publishers Weekly, May 6, 2002, p. 54-5.

On-line

"Bishop T.D. Jakes-Published Works," *The Potter's House,* www.thepotterhouse.org/BJ_published.html (October 13, 2003).
"Bishop T.D. Jakes-Selected Honors," *The Potter's House,* www.thepotterhouse.org/BJ_honors.html (October 13, 2003).
"Bishop T.D. Jakes-Timeline," *The Potter's House,* www.thepotterhouse.org/BJ_timeline.html (October 13, 2003).
The News-Gazette Online, www.news-gazette.com (October 13, 2003).
The Potter's Touch-T.D. Jakes Ministries, www.td-jakes.org (October 13, 2003).

—Dietrich Gruen and Ralph G. Zerbonia

Edward P. Jones

1950—

Writer

In 1992 Edward P. Jones burst on the literary scene with his much-hailed collection of short stories *Lost in the City,* which was nominated for a National Book Award. Then after a decade-long silence, Jones published his first novel, *The Known World.* Initially catching reviewers' attention for its unusual subject matter—the ownership of slaves by a black master in the antebellum South—the novel soon demonstrated its literary qualities as well. Reviewers lauded Jones for the novel's epic grandeur, vernacular and lyrical prose, fully realized characters, and lively dialogue. Comparing Jones favorably with William Faulkner and Toni Morrison, several critics went so far as to dub Jones a major new force in Southern writing. For *The Known World* Jones earned a second National Book Award nomination in 2003, though the actual award continued to elude him.

Edward Paul Jones was born on October 5, 1950, in Arlington, Virginia. The only son of an illiterate hotel maid and kitchen worker, Jones grew up in his mother's sphere for his father had drifted out of his life when he was a preschooler. After attending Catholic school for kindergarten and part of first grade, Jones was educated in Washington public schools. His interest in literature was sparked early, yet it was some time before he realized that African Americans, like their white counterparts, were writing works of literary merit. "I always loved reading," Jones recalled to Robert Fleming of *Publishers Weekly.* Comic books formed the mainstay of his reading until as a thirteen year old, he discovered novels. "When I started reading black writers, I discovered two books that had a great

impact on me: Ethel Waters's *His Eye Is on the Sparrow* and Richard Wright's *Native Son.* I felt as if they were talking to me, since both books had people in them that I knew in my own life. I was shocked to learn black people could write such things."

Lost in the City Debuted

On a scholarship, Jones studied at Holy Cross College, in Worcester, Massachusetts. Many writers begin writing seriously during their college years, and Jones was no exception, writing his first fiction during his sophomore year. Although a professor encouraged his efforts, Jones did not consider writing as a possible career then, or even after his graduation in 1972, when he returned to Washington, D.C. Living with his terminally ill mother, he worked in various positions, including a stint with *Science* magazine. Once upon reading a short story in his sister's copy of *Essence,* Jones decided he could write better stories, and during the after-work hours at the American Association for the Advancement of Science, he typed them up. In 1975 he sold his first story to *Essence* at a particularly difficult time in his life—after his mother's death and when he was between jobs and living in a city mission.

Once after reading the collection of short stories *Dubliners* by James Joyce, Jones had decided to give Washington, D.C., a similar treatment. As he told Carole Burns in an online interview for the *Washington Post,* "I went away to college and people have a very narrow idea of what Washington is like. They don't know that it's a place of neighborhoods, for

At a Glance . . .

Born Edward Paul Jones on October 5, 1950, in Arlington, VA. *Education:* Holy Cross College, BA, 1972; University of Virginia, MFA, 1981.

Career: Columnist and proofreader for *Tax Notes,* 1990-2002; writer, 1992–; George Washington University, guest instructor, 2000s; University of Maryland, guest instructor, 2000s; Princeton University, guest instructor, 2000s.

Awards: National Book Award finalist, National Book Foundation, and Ernest Hemingway Foundation/PEN Award, for *Lost in the City,* 1992; grant, Lannan Foundation; grant, National Endowment for the Arts; nominated for the National Book Award for fiction for *The Known World,* 2003.

Addresses: *Home*—4300 Old Dominion Dr., No. 914, Arlington, VA 22207.

example, and I set out to give a better picture of what the city is like—the other city." While working at various jobs and attending graduate school at the University of Virginia, Jones wrote these realistic and personal stories over a period of three years, although he had been thinking about them for years before then. He wanted each story to be unique in its characters and situations, rather than linked to each other. "Every major character, and even most minor characters, would be different, so that each story would be distinct from the others," he recalled to Lawrence P. Jackson of *African American Review.* "I didn't want someone to come along and be able to say that the stories are taken out of the same bag. I suppose that is one of the reasons that it has taken me so long."

With stories bearing such titles as "The First Day," about a girl's first day of kindergarten, "The Girl Who Raised Pigeons," about a girl's relationship with her birds, "The Store," which tells of a man who tries to make a success of a neighborhood grocery, "His Mother's House," which recounts how a mother takes care of a home her son has bought by selling crack, and "Young Lions," about the criminal element in the District of Columbia, Jones clearly showed his talent. Although only one story, "The First Day," has a clearly autobiographical element, the others recapture the life Jones knew growing up in the 1950s and 1960s, especially the rich vernacular of his mother and her associates. "I remember black people's poetic language," he told Jackson. "Over years and years you absorb all of this stuff." Yet according to Jones, writers

must use such language judiciously: "I grew up with this wonderful way of talking. One of the things I remember about reading Zora Neale Hurston was that in certain novels you hear it too much. If you have lines like that in every paragraph, it's too rich."

Even the city itself, with its palpable presence, plays a character's role in the stories. As the title indicates, some of the characters in these stories become lost, engulfed in the city, while others "eventually find their way a bit." For these "insightful potraits" and "unsensationalized depictions of horrifying social ills," to quote a *Publishers Weekly* critic, Jones earned a National Book Award nomination.

Novel Required Long Gestation

Even with the prestigious nomination to his name, Jones struggled to earn a living, and when a steady, if dry, job presented itself, he did not refuse. For over a decade Jones, a confirmed bachelor who has never owned a car, worked full time as a freelance columnist and proofreader for *Tax Notes,* a newsletter for tax professionals. It was tedious work and thus left room for his imagination to wander to other topics. After publishing his short story collection, Jones had pondered his subjects for future pieces. He had even bought and read portions of more than a dozen books on slavery. However, it was an obscure fact that remained with him since his college days that charged his imagination—the fact that some free blacks had become slaveowners. Yet because he was not planning to become a writer at that time, he had mentally filed away this information.

Finally Jones let his imagination run and started mentally plotting in intricate detail the story of Henry Townsend, a Virginia slave who buys his freedom and then becomes a slave owner himself. However, this novel, told in omniscient point of view and in a nonlinear form, is more than the tale of Townsend. Townsend is the pivotal character around which the stories of myriad other characters revolve. *Winston-Salem Journal* reporter Ken Otterbourg, who likened the novel's structure to that of a tree whose branches intersect, remarked that "Jones' skill is in the weaving and in the telling." In concrete terms, there is no main character in *The Known World.* Yet in the abstract, the reader may consider the inhumane institution of slavery to be the novel's central "character." Structurally *The Known World* recalls *Lost in the City* for in both works various characters gather to tell a number of tales and consider the repercussions on the lives of those people somehow involved.

When Jones started writing *The Known World* after being laid off from Tax Notes in 2002, he began with the twelve pages he had at one time written down. He believed that he was writing a short story and was unaware that he was going to write a novel until he did. As Jones explained in a *Bookbrowse* interview, the novel's structure developed as he committed it to paper: "I always thought I had a linear story. Something happened between the time I began the real work in January [of] 2002 of taking it all out of my head and when I finished months later. It might be that because I, as the 'god' of the people in the book, could see their first days and their last days and all that was in between, and those people did not have linear lives as I saw all that they had lived." Compared with the years he had spent plotting the novel in his head, the actual writing of *The Known World* required a very short time, a mere two and a half months. After the work had been accepted for publication, Jones again spent that much time shortening it at the publisher's request.

Novel Earned Accolades

When it rolled off presses in 2003, *The Known World* quickly earned accolades from reviewers. Critics praised Jones for his use of language, well-drawn characterizations, and historical accuracy, nominating the novel for a National Book Award. While some readers may be drawn to the novel for the "hook" of its unusual subject matter, Jones did not have an agenda, an intent to say something particular about race. Rather, "It's about a person deciding to control another," he explained to Burns. "If someone reading it goes into it they'll see that I'm just not stuck on that topic. There are other things going on. There are relationships among people, of various kinds." Jones worked diligently to avoid creating stereotypical characters, a quality of the work that was not lost on reviewers.

Like he had in *Lost in the City*, Jones employed the colorful language that is a heritage of black Americans. He also enlivened the narrative with hints of humor and superstitions of his forebears. And although he wrote of some horrific events about slavery, he was able to remain emotionally detached from them because he had dealt with them during the novel's lengthy gestation period. "I had enough time to come to grips with what was going to be in the novel, so it didn't have that kind of immediacy," Jones told Edward Guthmann of the *San Francisco Chronicle*. This detachment is evident in Jones' narration, noted *Book World* reviewer Jonathan Yardley: "The pace of the novel is leisurely and measured, and Jones' lovely but unobtrusive prose is tuned accordingly." It is this "patient, insistent, sometimes softly sardonic, always wise" narrative thread that entices the reader to turn the next page, and the next.

While one reviewer pointed out several errors in fact in *The Known World*, many cited the work's verisimilitude as one of its strengths, praising Jones for his copious research. For his part, Jones admitted that the novel's setting, the fictional Manchester County, Virginia, is just that—fictional—and that his research efforts were limited. Originally he had planned to visit Lynchburg, Virginia. "But I never got around to going down there, and so I was forced to create my own place," he told Guthmann. "One can pick at its [the novel's] small faults without detracting from its overall importance," remarked Claude Crowley in a *Knight Ridder/Tribune News Service* review. What is the work's importance? Although only the passage of time will provide the ultimate answer, Yardley concluded: "Jones has woven nothing less than a tapestry of slavery, an artifact as vast and complex as anything to be found in the [world-famous French museum, the] Louvre. Every thread is perfectly in place, every thread connects with every other. The first paragraph connects, nearly 400 pages later, with the last. Against all the evidence to the contrary that American fiction has given us over the past quarter-century, *The Known World* affirms that the novel does matter, that it can still speak to us as nothing else can."

In 2003 Jones was working on another anthology of short fiction. Still intent on writing fiction "that matters", he told Flemming: "I want to write about the things which helped us to survive: the love, grace, intelligence and strength for us as a people."

Selected writings

Lost in the City, photographs by Amos Chan, Morrow, 1992.
The Known World, Amistad, 2003.

Sources

Periodicals

African American Review, spring, 2000, p. 95.
American Statesman (Austin, TX), September 21, 2003, p. K5.
Book, September-October, 2003, pp. 87-88.
Booklist, September 15, 2003, p. 211.
Entertainment Weekly, October 30, 1992, p. 80; August 22, 2003, p. 134.
Globe & Mail (Toronto, Canada), November 15, 2003, p. D8.
Journal (Winston Salem, NC), September 7, 2003, p. A24.
Knight Ridder/Tribune News Service, September 17, 2003, p. K3969; October 8, 2003, p. K1755.
Library Journal, May 15, 1992, p. 122; August, 2003, pp. 131-132.
Los Angeles Times Book Review, July 12, 1992, p. 6.
New York Times, June 11, 1992, p. C18; August 23, 1992, section 7, p. 16.
New York Times Book Review, August 23, 1992, p. 16; August 31, 2003, p. 9.
Newsweek, September 8, 2003, p. 57.
People, September 29, 2003, p. 45.
Post (Cincinnati, OH), August 21, 2003, p. B3.
Publishers Weekly, March 23, 1992, p. 59; August 11, 2003, pp. 253-255; August 11, 2003, pp. 253-254.

San Francisco Chronicle, October 30, 2003, p. E1.

School Library Journal, January, 1993, p. 144.

Times Literary Supplement, October 10, 2003, p. 24.

Washington Post, July 22, 1992, p. G1; October 6, 1992, p. B4.

Washington Post Book World, June 21, 1992, p. 3; August 29, 2003.

On-line

"Edward P. Jones," *BookBrowe,* www.bookbrowse. com/index.cfm?page=author&authorID=930 (November 10, 2003).

"Off the Page," *Washington Post,* www.washington-post.com/wp-dyn/articles/A11797-2003Oct24. html (October 30, 2003).

Other

"Fresh Air," interview with Edward P. Jones, *National Public Radio,* November 11, 2003.

—Jeanne M. Lesinski

John P. Kee

1962(?)—

Gospel singer, songwriter, choir leader

A number of gospel artists in the 1990s and early 2000s enriched the music's vocabulary with elements of hip-hop and R&B styles; figures such as Kirk Franklin and BeBe and CeCe Winans appealed to secular audiences and placed recordings in the top ranks of general sales charts. Perhaps no other gospel artist, however, absorbed urban styles as directly as John P. Kee, who lived the violent events described in many hip-hop pieces and then made sense of his experiences in gospel music. Kee and his New Life Community Choir were gospel favorites and consistent award winners over much of the 1990s.

John Prince Kee was born in Durham, North Carolina, around 1962 (that date is listed on the *All Music* website, but other accounts give ages for dates later in Kee's life that do not correspond with that birthdate). The 15th of 16 children, he grew up in a religious household where his father encouraged all his offspring to sing. The last of six boys, Kee put a lot of effort into getting his father's attention, and he developed into a child prodigy who quickly mastered the piano, flute, and drums. Kee was sent to the North Carolina School for the Arts in nearby Winston-Salem, and he gradu-

ated at age 14. He had already formed and led his first gospel choir.

Quickly Entered California Recording Scene

Together with his older brothers Al and Wayne, Kee headed for California to study music at the Yuba College Conservatory. His talents were noticed immediately, and he began to drift away from gospel and to perform with jazz musicians such as Donald Byrd and with pop acts like vocalist Phyllis Hyman and the funk group Cameo. Kee had both the musical chops and the adult demeanor to keep up, even though he was only in his mid-teens, but he lacked emotional maturity to handle the pressures of the music world.

"I was a spoiled brat," Kee told the New York *Daily News*. "I could call down from my room to a club and get any kind of money I wanted for what I did. I took advantage of it and I loved it. It was rewarding, and I really had my mind on my craft, but there was the sidetrack part: the clubs, the exposure." Soon, Kee recalled, he was "caught up in drugs and the whole nine." In 1980 Kee returned to North Carolina and

At a Glance . . .

Born c. 1962 in Durham, NC; married Felice Sampson, December of 1995; two children. *Education:* North Carolina School for the Arts, Winston-Salem, NC, 1970s; attended Yuba College Conservatory, Marysville, CA, 1970s; studied with Rev. James Cleveland in gospel music workshop, 1985. *Religion:* Christian.

Career: Cameo, Donald Byrd, and other acts, California, backup musician, late 1970s; Miss Black Universe beauty pageant, musical ensemble member, 1980s; New Life Community Choir, founder and choral leader, mid-1980s–; gospel recording artist, 1989–; New Life Fellowship Church, Charlotte, NC, founder and pastor, 1990s–.

Selected awards: Grammy nominations for *Show Up,* 1995, and *Strength,* 1997; numerous Stellar awards; gold record for *Show Up.*

Addresses: *Church offices*—New Life Fellowship Center, 1337 Samuel St., Charlotte, NC 28212; *Recording Studio*—New Life Productions, Suite 3101, 6425 Idlewild Rd., Charlotte, NY 28212.

settled in Charlotte, but the homecoming didn't put his life back on track. Indeed, it made things even worse.

For a time, Kee made money performing in the Ms. Black Universe beauty pageant, but he hungered for the easy money he had known as a teenage musical phenomenon. "In California, there was so much money to be made," he told the *Daily News.* "When I moved back East, it was a lifestyle change. I couldn't get work, so I got the lifestyle I was accustomed to in the street." Soon Kee was dealing cocaine out of a small grocery store in Charlotte's Double Oaks neighborhood.

Friend's Murder Sparked Return to Religion

The turning point in Kee's life came in June of 1981 when he witnessed the murder of his best friend in a drug deal gone bad. Kee announced a new commitment to Christianity at a Charlotte revival held by the Rev. Jim Bakker's PTL ministry, and soon he was making music in church once again and had founded the group of ex-addict and former prostitute singers that developed into the New Life Community Choir. An

early indication of things to come was visible when Kee showed up as vocalist on two separate tracks on the annual mass choir compilation of the Gospel Music Workshop of America—the first time any vocalist, let alone an unknown, had been so honored.

Kee was able to launch a national career after he penned a successful song called "Jesus Lives in Me" for gospel giant Edwin Hawkins and invested the profits in his own music. A debut album under the New Life Community Choir designation, *Yes Lord,* was followed by a solo debut, *Wait on Him,* in 1989. By the early 1990s Kee and the choir (he continued to mix solo and choral releases) were racking up gospel-industry Stellar Awards, of which he eventually earned more than a dozen. Numerous other awards flowed Kee's way, and gradually, as Kee moved from the small Tyscot label to the gospel industry leader Verity and finally recorded several albums for the secular label Jive, he began to gain fans from outside the usual gospel community.

The 1995 *Show Up* album, recorded with the New Life Community Choir, earned Kee the first of two Grammy nominations and was certified gold for sales of 500,000 copies. Around this time, Kee became one of the standard bearers for the trend of incorporating contemporary urban sounds, hip-hop above all, into gospel. "You need that," Kee explained to the *Daily News.* "Then you're still touching the lives of the masses. Keep a traditional vocal arrangement, add a back beat, and the babies enjoy the beat, grandma loves the lyrics, and we're all happy." Some compared Kee to earlier gospel crossover figures such as the Rev. James Cleveland, with whom Kee studied in a 1985 workshop, and even the father of gospel, Thomas A. Dorsey, whose music was strongly influenced by secular blues.

Songs Referred to Personal Experiences

Kee demurred at such comparisons, but there is no doubt that he used hip-hop effectively in order to communicate his personal voyage from street violence to Christian redemption. "It could have been me/Still selling drugs, pulling triggers on the street/Lighting up the night like a butane flicker/I was smooth and you couldn't trick the tricker," Kee rapped in "It Could Have Been Me," a song from his *Colorblind* album.

Kee and the New Life Community Choir continued as major forces in the gospel scene through the late 1990s and early 2000s. The 1997 album *Strength* gained Kee another Grammy nomination, and 2000's *Not Guilty ... The Experience* adapted the semi-dramatic, narrative structure of many contemporary hip-hop albums to a gospel message. The album, noted *All Music*'s Stacia Proefrock, was "a sort of gospel opera outlining the path to redemption through song." Kee followed that album up with 2002's *Blessed by Association.*

Increasingly, however, Kee was branching out into other activities. He applied his long years of musical experience as the producer of albums by other artists, including Vanessa Bell Armstrong, Inner City, and Drea Randle. Most importantly, he built and became pastor of the New Life Fellowship Center in Charlotte, expanding the church's ministry into community projects such as a homeless shelter, after-school tutoring, and food distribution for the hungry. "There is so much hurting and suffering in the world," the man now known as Pastor Kee observed on his website, "that the only way not to be overwhelmed by it, is to know that you are doing something about it."

Selected discography

Yes Lord, Verity, 1987.
There Is Hope, Tyscot, 1990.
Churchin' Christmas, Tyscot, 1992.
Never Shall Forget, Verity, 1994.
Show Up! Verity, 1995.
Stand, Jive, 1995.
Christmas Album, Verity, 1996.
Thursday Love, Verity, 1997.
Strength, Verity, 1997.
Any Day, Verity, 1998.
Not Guilty … The Experience, Verity, 2000.
Blessed by Association, Verity, 2002.

Sources

Periodicals

Chicago Sun-Times, June 8, 1994, p. 45.
Daily News (New York), June 9, 1996, p. 35; June 13, 1996, p. 47.
Washington Post, December 4, 1996, p. C4.

On-line

"Biography," *Official John P. Kee Website,* www.johnpkee.com (October 10, 2003).
"John P. Kee," *All Music,* www.allmusic.com (October 10, 2003).

—James M. Manheim

Rev. Dr. Samuel Kobia

1947—

Minister, church organization executive

A Kenyan religious leader committed to solving the problem of religious strife on the African continent, the Rev. Dr. Samuel Kobia was named general secretary of the World Council of Churches (WCC) in 2003. He was the first African and the first black minister to hold that position, heading an international organization of thousands of Protestant and Orthodox churches. As an ordained minister in the Methodist church of Kenya, Kobia brought to the post a lifetime of experience, not only with spiritual matters, but also with issues of development and economic inequity.

Kobia was born March 20, 1947, in the village of Miathene, Kenya, in the mountainous Meru district of the country. His parents were among the area's first adherents to the Christian religion, but otherwise his upbringing was similar to that of many other rural Kenyans, as he cared for the family livestock herd and did household chores. He finished secondary school in his home district and then enrolled in a Kenyan religious institution, St. Paul's United Theological College in the city of Limuru, near Nairobi. His gift for reaching out to members of other Christian sects first showed itself during this period, when he became involved with the Student Christian Movement and the World Students Christian Federation.

Time spent in two foreign countries, the United States and Ghana, shaped Kobia's faith and thinking. After graduating from St. Paul's with a theology degree in 1971, Kobia moved to Chicago and enrolled in the McCormick Theological Seminary in Chicago. His chosen field at McCormick, urban ministry, showed his interest in a career that was engaged with the problems of ordinary individuals in addition to purely theological questions. This broader set of interests was confirmed when Kobia augmented his religious education with a highly practical course of study, earning a master's degree from the Massachusetts Institute of Technology in 1978.

Kobia was awarded a Doctor of Divinity degree from the Christian Theological Seminary in Indianapolis, Indiana, in 1993, and completed coursework for a Ph.D. degree at Fairfax University in Louisiana in 2003. Alongside these studies, however, Kobia gained practical experience and became more and more involved in ecumenical organizations—cooperative en-

As his influence increased, Kobia became more active in social and political arenas. He became involved with several church-related peace and anti-racism groups and chaired peace talks in neighboring Sudan in 1991, working to promote a Christian-Muslim dialogue. He headed a monitoring team in Kenya's 1992 elections and the following year assumed the post of executive director of the WCC's Justice, Peace and Creation unit. Kobia wrote several books about Africa's problems. These included 1985's *Origins of Squatting and Community Organization in Nairobi* and 1993's *The Quest for Democracy in Africa,* with other works in progress.

Kobia's profile in the WCC was raised by a term spent in 2000 as a fellow at the Center for the Study of Values in Public Life at the prestigious Harvard Divinity School in Cambridge, Massachusetts. He was named to several other divisional leadership posts in the WCC, and began to win recognition outside of religious circles in 2001, when he criticized the U.S. invasion of Afghanistan in the wake of the September 11 terrorist attacks in New York City and Washington, D.C. "The world is being led on the warpath not because of the loss of 6,000 lives but because the security of the rich has been threatened," he was quoted as saying by *BBC Monitoring Africa.*

Observers were not surprised, therefore, when Kobia won election in 2003 over a European, Trond Bakkevig, to become the WCC's general secretary as well as its first African leader. "I consider my appointment as WCC General Secretary not as an individual honour," Kobia told the *Accra Mail.* "It is an honour to Africa, since I am the first African to assume this responsibility. I hope it will be a source of inspiration for many Africans within the ecumenical movement and beyond."

The historic nature of his appointment notwithstanding, Kobia inherited a set of high-intensity problems and controversies as he prepared to take over the reins of the WCC. Christian churches faced deeply rooted disputes over such issues as homosexuality, the degree to which churches should become politically engaged, and the decrease in membership among the organization's traditional "mainline" denominations—its financial lifeblood. This decrease highlighted the loss of many young people who had become more attracted to emotionally direct worship styles. Kobia was circumspect in addressing the homosexuality issue. "We've created an 'ecumenical space' for churches to engage in this issue, to share experiences of different churches," he told *United Press International (UPI).* "Human beings need to be understood, even if they choose lifestyles different from what we know."

"To the extent politics determines who gets what in the world, then churches can't run away from the politics," Kobia told *UPI.* On the potentially explosive issue of

terprises among various churches. In a project sponsored by the Christian Council of Ghana, Kobia worked as an industrial chaplain and did urban development work in the coastal city of Tema. Back in Kenya in 1974, Kobia joined the National Council of Churches of Kenya as an industrial advisor.

Married with four children, Kobia gradually became a more and more important figure among African Christians, who every year made up a greater and greater proportion of adherents to the faith worldwide. Over two decades, he divided his time between Nairobi and Geneva, Switzerland, the location of the WCC's headquarters. His first post with the WCC was as executive secretary for the organization's Urban Rural Mission from 1978 to 1984, during which period he also served as secretary of the WCC Africa Task Force. Kobia returned to the Kenya National Council of Churches (NCCK) in 1984 to take an administrative job relating to church-sponsored development projects. In 1987 he was named general secretary of the NCCK—the top post in Kenya's ecumenical hierarchy.

Christian-Muslim relations in Africa, Kobia offered visions of hope. "There is an African way of being Christian. And an African way of being Muslim," he argued in a *UPI* interview. "In situations where there is no outside interference, then you will find very harmonious multi-faith living between Christians and Muslims." Kobia used the examples of Sierra Leone and Malawi, as nations whose presidents each were Christians married to Islamic spouses. His appointment and his role as a dedicated peacemaker appear to hold promise for the often strife-torn continent of Africa.

Selected writings

Origins of Squatting and Community Organizations in Nairobi, NCCK, 1985.
The Quest for Democracy in Africa, NCCK, 1993.
Courage to Hope: The Roots for a New Vision and the Calling of the Church in Africa, Consul Oecumenique, 2004.

Sources

Periodicals

Accra Mail (Ghana, via Global News Wire), September 15, 2003.
Africa News, December 1, 2003.
BBC Monitoring Africa, October 14, 2001.
Deutsche Presse-Agentur (German Press Agency), August 28, 2003.
Guardian (London, England), September 13, 2003, p. 29.
New York Times, August 29, 2003, p. A7.
United Press International, October 29, 2003.

On-line

"Samuel Kobia—Director and Special Representative for Africa, General Secretary-elect of the WCC," *WCC Press Corner,* www.wcc-coe.org/wcc/press_corner/pc_kobiabio.html (January 2, 2004).

—James M. Manheim

Oni Faida Lampley

1959(?)—

Actor, playwright, essayist

Oni Faida Lampley permeates the world of theater as both a writer and performer. Working as an actor, Lampley has been in many movies, plays, and various television appearances. As an award-winning playwright, Lampley has explored the issues of race, identity construction, and cancer survivorship. Her performances move audiences to the heights and depths of emotion and her words speak to young and old alike.

Not much is known about Lampley's early life. She was born with the name Vera Lampley around 1959 in Oklahoma City, Oklahoma. She attended an all-white girls' Catholic school and this experience went on to influence her work and lay the foundations of one of her most acclaimed autobiographical plays, *The Dark Kalamazoo*. Lampley's mother was what she has labeled a SBW, Strong Black Woman. In *The Dark Kalamazoo* she depicts her mother with cigarette in one hand and Scotch glass in the other, sending letters to her full of what Isherwood called in his *Daily Variety* review "hard-won wisdom, motherly warmth and bitter defensiveness."

Study Abroad Influenced Early Work

Lampley graduated high school and went on to attend Oberlin College in Oberlin, Ohio, in the late 1970s and early 1980s. At Oberlin, Lampley majored in creative writing. During her second year of college, she sought out opportunities to study abroad, especially the possibility to travel to Africa. Oberlin had no programs that interested Lampley, so she sought an opportunity to travel abroad through Kalamazoo College in Kalamazoo, Michigan.

In 1979 Lampley departed on a study abroad trip to Ghana in West Africa. She expected to arrive in Africa and be accepted with open arms. Perceiving a warm welcome in "The Motherland," Lampley was shocked when she arrived and was met with prejudice. Being the only black student in the program of twenty students, she earned the hurtful nickname "Dark Kalamazoo," from the Africans she met—which would become the title of her autobiographical play about the experience. In America, she actively tried to escape the view society had of her as an African. However, upon arriving, she realized that the Africans viewed her as an American, an outsider.

A civil war in Ghana forced her to redirect plans and she traveled to Freetown, Sierra Leone. This affected her personal identity construction and her personal perception of herself as an African-American, and later went to influence her work as a writer. In a later interview with writer Zinta Aistars about her play *The Dark Kalamazoo*, Lampley stated, "Study abroad was a huge milestone for me. It was the biggest step away from my customary life that I have ever made, a step away to see how others saw me—from a distance—and step out of my own self-absorption." It was this breaking away from self-absorption that allows Lampley to have so much self-reflection in her work as a writer and actress.

After her travels to West Africa, and her graduation from Oberlin, the facts of her life begin to wane. After Oberlin, Lampley went on to attend Julliard's Lila

At a Glance . . .

Born Vera Lampley circa 1959, in Oklahoma City, OK. *Education:* Oberlin College, OH, BA, 1980s.

Career: Playwright, 1991–; actor, 1991–; essayist, 1993–.

Memberships: Drama Department, New York Theatre Workshop.

Awards: Helen Hayes Award for Outstanding New Play, 1991; Lincoln Center DeComte du Nouy Award.

Addresses: *Agent*—c/o Sarah Jane Leigh, International Creative Management, 40 West 57th Street, New York, NY 10019.

Acheson Wallace American Playwrights program. There she studied the craft of writing plays but also had the opportunity to experience poetry classes, literature lectures, and theater history classes. As the program only accepts four playwrights each year, this was quite an accomplishment. Her work at Julliard and the pieces that came out of her personal experience garnered her a Lincoln Center DeComte du Nouy Award.

Her first play, *Mixed Babies,* won her the 1991 Helen Hayes Award for Outstanding New Play. Her next play, *The Dark Kalamazoo,* received a nomination for a Barrymore Award for "Outstanding Leading Actress." This piece was based on her college travels to West Africa. The play began with 12-year-old Vera, learning what it meant to be black in an all-white, girls' Catholic school in Oklahoma City. The play then flashes to 19 year old Vera traveling to Freetown where she won the title "Dark Kalamazoo" from her African hosts. *The Dark Kalamazoo* garnered Lampley another Helen Hayes nomination in 1999, but did not win her the award.

Fought Cancer by Embracing Theater

In 1996 Lampley was diagnosed with breast cancer in her left breast. Where this tragic diagnosis would paralyze a lesser person, for Lampley it fueled her fire. In 2001 she scripted and performed "Shame the Devil" at a Carnegie Hall benefit, Artists for a Cure. She revived the piece for a 2003 performance in Brooklyn for the second installment of the series "My Soul To Keep," a cancer awareness show. When she took the stage in Brooklyn, she fearlessly showed her bald head, caused by chemo, and made the crowd aware of her age. This act showed Lampley's defiance in the face of adversity and strength of character—characteristics which have driven her career.

Out of her seven year struggle came her show *Tough Titty* in 2003. In a press release from the BRIC Studio in Brooklyn, Lampley explained her play as "part of digging out of the hole of seven years of breast cancer survivorship." She continued, "As an artist, my way of digesting life's events is to write. I've known for years, as events unfolded after diagnosis, that there is a useful story in this event." Useful it was. *Tough Titty* opened in late October and was well received among critics, audiences and cancer survivors.

However, one should not see Lampley as only a playwright. She is also an accomplished actor. She has made numerous appearances on the television shows *Law & Order*, *Third Watch*, *Oz*, *NYPD Blue*, and *Homicide: Life on the Streets*. She has also been seen on the silver screen in minor roles in such movies as *Money Train* with Woody Harrelson and Wesley Snipes, *Jungle2Jungle* with Tim Allen, *Bullet* with Tupac Shakur, Mickey Rourke, and Adrien Brody, and the Oscar nominated 1996 John Sayles' film *Lone Star*. In addition to this, she has performed in contemporary and classical material in regional theater and Off-Broadway. She has performed on Broadway in productions of *The Ride Down Mt. Morgan* and *Two Trains Running*. She was featured in the 1999 Peter Sellers' operatic staging of Stravinsky's *Biblical Pieces* premiering in Amsterdam.

With all of this in her life—her writing, her acting, her illness—Lampley continued to flourish and grow as an artist. She was a founding member of the Drama Department, a New York Theater project, and a Usual Suspect at New York Theatre Workshop. She began, in 1993, to write essays and columns for magazines like *Mirabella* and *ELLE*. Also, she was a participant in the 1998 Sundance Screenwriters Lab to develop *The Dark Kalamazoo* into a film. She has recently completed a screenplay based on a work of Robert Coles' about African-American migrant farm workers in the 1960s South. She will also appear in the 2004 release *Brother To Brother*, a film that explores the Harlem Renaissance through the conversations in a New York homeless shelter between an elderly black writer and a gay teen. It is clear that Lampley, while not a household name yet, has already made her impact on the world of entertainment.

Selected works

Film

Brother To Brother, 2004.
Jungle2Jungle, 1997.
Money Train, 1995.
The Keeper, 1997.
Lone Star, 1996.

Plays

Mixed Babies, 1990
The Dark Kalamazoo, 1997.
Tough Titty, 2003

Television

Law & Order, NBC, 2003, 2002, 1996, 1993.
Third Watch, NBC, 2001.
Oz, HBO, 1999-2000.
NYPD Blue, ABC, 1993.
Homicide: Life on the Streets, NBC, 1993.
One Life to Live, NBC, 1994, 1997.

Theatrical performances

Mule Bone, Ethel Barrymore Theater, 1991.
The Ride Down Mr. Morgan, Ambassador Theater,
  2000.
Two Trains Running, Broadway Production, 1990s.
Biblical Pieces, Amsterdam, 1999.

Other

Numerous essays for a variety of different magazines
including *Mirabella,* and *ELLE.*

Sources

Periodicals

Daily Variety, September 26, 2002, p.31
Entertainment Weekly, June, 28, 2002, p.100

Online

"Drama Department Official Bio," *Drama Department,* www.dramadept.org/who/bios/lampley-oni-
  faida.html (February 2, 2004).
"For 'Soul' Women, Age Will Never Take Center
  Stage," *Newsday,* www.newsday.com (February 2,
  2004).
"Oni Lampley," *Internet Movie Database,* www.imdb.
  com (February 2, 2004).
"So Fine She Causes Accidents," *Author's Den,*
  http://authorsden.com/visit/viewarticle.asp?
  AuthorID=2726&id=2541 (February 2, 2004).
"*Tough Titty* Press Release," *BRIC Studio,* www.
  brooklynx.org/pdf/bricstudio/bric_studio_toughtitty.
  pdf (February 2, 2004).

— Adam R. Hazlett

Alfred Liggins III

1965—

Radio executive

Alfred Liggins III is one of the most powerful African Americans in radio. As president and chief executive officer (CEO) of Radio One, he oversees the daily operations of the seventh largest radio broadcasting company in the United States, and the largest focused on urban radio. Under his reign are 66 stations in 22 markets nationwide, 2,000 employees, and nearly $300 million in revenue. He has come a long way since joining the company in 1985 as a salesman. At the time there were only two stations in the group, and they were stations that his mother, Washington, D.C., radio legend Cathy Hughes, had fought long and hard to establish. Over the next 15 years, working alongside his mother, Liggins went on a buying spree that culminated in the radio powerhouse that has become Radio One. "There is no question that I laid the foundation," Cathy Hughes told the *Washington Post*. "But every brick in the skyscraper that sits atop that foundation was laid by [my son]." And now, as the owner of cable channel TV One, Liggins seems determined to turn that skyscraper into a multi-media kingdom.

Grew Up Immersed in Radio

Alfred C. Liggins III was born in 1965 in Omaha, Nebraska, when Cathy Hughes was just 17. After two years of marriage to Alfred Liggins, Jr., Hughes divorced and moved to Washington, D.C., with her young son. She soon landed a job at WHUR, the radio station of Howard University, and began climbing up the ranks. Liggins was always by her side. "He came to the station after school, did his homework, and many nights we would have dinner right there at the station," she told *Ebony*. "I bought him his first tux at age eight, and he would go to all these black-tie events with me." In 1979, when he was a teenager, his mother bought her first station, WOL-AM in Washington, D.C., and the following year she founded Radio One. The $1 million purchase price put her in the red, and for a while she lived at the station to make ends meet. To save on the cost of staff, she took to the airwaves herself with a lively—and often controversial—talk show.

When not teaching her son the ins and outs of running a radio station, Hughes instilled in him a strong work

At a Glance . . .

Born Alfred C. Liggins III in 1965 in Omaha, NE; son of Cathy Hughes and Alfred Liggins, Jr. *Education:* University of Pennsylvania, MBA, 1995; attended University of California at Los Angeles; attended University of the District of Columbia.

Career: CBS Records, production assistant, 1984-85; Radio One, WOL-AM account manager, 1985-87, WOL-AM general sales manager, 1987-88, WOL-AM general manager, 1988-89, president, treasurer, and director, 1989–, CEO, 1995–.

Memberships: National Association of Broadcasters, board of directors; National Commission on Entrepreneurship, commissioner; FCC Advisory Committee on Diversity for Communications in the Digital Age, member.

Awards: National Black MBA Association, Outstanding Communicator of the Year, 2003; *Radio Ink* ranked Liggins as number one, 30 Most Influential African Americans in Radio; Ernst & Young, Arts and Entertainment, Top U.S. Entrepreneur (with Cathy Hughes), 2003; Broadcasters' Foundation, Golden Mike Award (with Cathy Hughes), 2002.

Addresses: *Office*—Radio One Inc, 5900 Princess Garden Pkwy., Lanham, MD, 20706-2925.

ethic and a determined self-reliance. As a result, Liggins was able to escape the gangs, drugs, and crime that plagued his poor D.C. neighborhood. "The bottom line is that I felt that if I worked hard and only made a marginal amount of money for all of my life, it would be better than making a large amount of money in a short time and spending the rest of my life in jail," he told the *Washington Post*. While still in junior high school, Liggins began working odd jobs, earning up to $100 a week. It was enough to buy himself some nice clothes—and earn another lesson from his mother. "One day, he comes home with a pair of designer jeans that he'd bought," Hughes told the *Washington Post*. "So I sat down with him and said if you are going to have someone's name plastered on your behind, it should be yours." He didn't understand, so Hughes explained, "Since you are actually going to pay somebody to be a walking advertisement for their jeans and help them build their business, you are also going to help me build mine." From then on the young Liggins

was required to pay $20 a week in rent. "People said I was so cruel," Hughes continued. "But that was my method of teaching responsibility."

After graduating from Woodrow Wilson High School in 1983, Liggins sold shoes and worked at a pet store, but he dreamed of working in the record industry. With his meager life savings, he set off for California, where he worked briefly as a sales executive with Light Records, a gospel recording company. He also attended classes at the University of California at Los Angeles. Soon he landed a job as a production assistant for CBS Records, where he booked talent and negotiated publishing rights. Just 19 years old, Liggins seemed destined for a bright future in the recording industry. However, his mother, who was having trouble keeping her radio station afloat, asked him to join her and work at the station. It was not a difficult decision for Liggins. He knew that one day the station could be his and, as he explained to *Broadcasting & Cable*, "My mother convinced me that if you're going to work your butt off, it's probably better to work for yourself."

Forged Success with Urban Format

In 1985, at age 21, Liggins joined WOL-AM as an account manager. After insisting that his mother focus on her morning show and leave the sales to him, he began knocking on doors. Selling advertising on the small AM station was not always easy. "I couldn't give away air time to advertisers," he recalled to the *Washington Post*. However, with the rising popularity of his mother's show, he began to secure accounts and to enjoy his work. "It was fun going out and talking to advertisers, helping them solve problems in how to grow their businesses, then going back and utilizing our programming to drive customers to them," he told *Black Enterprise*. By 1987 Hughes had acquired a second station in Washington. Originally a soft-rock station, Hughes changed the format of WMMJ to rhythm and blues, and within two years the station had attracted a large following in the African-American community and was making a profit. Meanwhile Liggins had become the general sales manager, overseeing both stations. Though he briefly studied business at the University of the District of Columbia, he later dropped out to focus on Radio One. It was not a bad decision. Just 23 years old, Liggins was already making over $100,000 a year.

In the early 1990s, as the Federal Communications Commission (FCC) eased regulations on the radio industry, Hughes purchased several more stations, including a popular FM station in Washington and an AM/FM station in Baltimore, Maryland. Meanwhile, Liggins moved up the ranks. After a one-year stint as general manager, he became president and director of the company in 1989, while Hughes retained the title of CEO. Liggins and his mother worked side by side building the business, in a relationship that Radio One's chief financial officer (CFO) Scott Royster described to *Broadcasting & Cable* as "very complementary." Liggins pointed out in the same article, "We've had knock-down, drag-out screaming matches. [But] it never was so bad that we were fractured at our foundation. ... The business is not so important to either one of us that we're going to ruin our personal relationship over it."

Liggins and Hughes built Radio One by purchasing low-wattage stations in primarily African-American markets. "We look for underperforming stations where we can either make their urban formats better or switch them to urban formats and grab higher audience shares," Liggins explained to the *Washington Post.* Radio One's success would come from reaching the African-American market through the promotion of an "urban format." This included anything designed to appeal to ethnic markets—particularly African-American—including rap, R&B, gospel, and jazz. It also included talk radio, a format that Hughes pioneered in the black community. "[The urban format is] our personal cultural heritage," Liggins told *Broadcasting & Cable.* "It's the format and the community we started out serving. It's the one we're comfortable serving. And we think we need to do it. And we think we can do it better than most people." It also made good business sense. As Liggins told the *New York Times,* "I call the African-American market the emerging market in the domestic market. As companies are looking to break into China and other countries around the globe, they should really be looking here."

Aggressively Developed Radio One

In 1995 Liggins earned a master's degree in business administration from the country's top-ranked business program, the Wharton School at the University of Pennsylvania. Though he did not have a bachelor's degree, the fact that he had brokered several multimillion dollar radio acquisitions assured him entry. The M.B.A. was a stipulation by his mother, who wouldn't hand him the company reigns without it, although Liggins pointed out to *Ebony,* "I would have gotten my MBA anyway." True to her word, Hughes promoted Liggins to CEO and stepped away from the daily operations of the station. "It's very hard for a parent, who changes the child's diaper, to then at a certain point, turn over their whole station and destiny and their career to that youngster," she told *Broadcasting & Cable.* However, she continued, "The best part has been that not only has Alfred turned out to be a highly competent manager, but he's embraced my dream."

After the passage of the Telecommunications Act in 1996 removed limitations on the number of radio stations that a single company could own, Liggins began buying. Over a 20-month period he negotiated

the purchase of 18 stations around the country. As a result, the company's revenues for 1998 topped $46 million. In May of 1999 Liggins took the company public, offering 6.5 million shares of Radio One on the stock market. The move was a huge boost for the company. The stock, initially offered at $24 a share, shot up to $62.13 in less than a year. A Wall Street insider explained some of this success to *Broadcasting & Cable:* "[Radio One is] a lot more savvy than a lot of other companies we take public. ... These guys know how to operate stations at peak performance."

Taking Radio One public brought the company a large cash flow and allowed Liggins to make some aggressive purchases. In 1999 he purchased 12 stations from Clear Channel, the country's biggest radio conglomerate. The $1.3 billion purchase gained Radio One footing in valuable markets in Houston, Dallas, Miami, and Los Angeles. The deal also made Radio One the seventh largest radio company in the country. However, Liggins was just heating up. "We're going to expand our reach throughout the country," he told *Washington Business Forward.* "Our goal is to be the dominant urban media company." In February of 2001 he reached that goal, brokering a deal to buy out Blue Chip Broadcasting and its 15 radio stations for almost $200 million. Along with Inner City Broadcasting, Blue Chip and Radio One were the top three companies vying for the urban market. With his purchase, not only did Liggins eliminate a major competitor, but he also gained stations that were already established in the urban market. The purchase put Radio One squarely at the top of the urban radio game. By 2003 the Radio One empire had grown to 66 stations reaching over nine million listeners in the top African-American markets in the country. Meanwhile, Liggins continued Radio One's tradition of building successful urban formats. One of his most popular developments was *The Steve Harvey Show* at Los Angeles's KBBT "The Beat." After conducting extensive research in the region, Liggins signed the popular actor and ratings began to soar.

In 2003 Liggins and Radio One joined forces with Comcast, the country's largest cable company, to launch TV One, a cable channel aimed at African-American audiences. "African-Americans are underserved in this space," Liggins told *Broadcasting & Cable.* "They are the single largest minority group, and there's only one service for them." He was referring to Black Entertainment Television (BET), founded by African-American media mogul Robert L. Johnson. Much has been made of the threat TV One may pose to BET, but Liggins has shrugged it off. In typical fashion, he has focused higher. "When I wake up in the morning and think of competing, I don't think of the next black guy," he told the *Washington Post.* "Bob [Johnson] is not the competition; Viacom and Clear Channel are. Those 200 guys above Bob on the Fortune 500 list, that's who I've got my sights on."

Sources

Periodicals

Black Enterprise, June 2000; June 2001.
Broadcasting & Cable, August 30, 1999; January 20, 2003.
Ebony, May, 2000.
New York Times, December 25, 2000.
Washington Post, April 26, 1988; January 26, 2003.

On-line

"Deals of the Year," *Washington Business Forward,* www.bizforward.com/wdc/issues/2002-04/deal-softheyear/acqlarge.shtml (December 23, 2003).
"The Next Network," *Washington Business Forward,* www.bizforward.com/wdc/issues/2000-10/next-network/page05.shtml (December 23, 2003).

—Candace LaBalle

Wangari Maathai

1940—

Environmental activist

Dr. Wangari Muta Maathai—an activist, feminist, mother, environmentalist, and member of the Kenyan parliament—was appointed Assistant Minister for Environment, Natural Resources and Wildlife in Kenya in 2003. Maathai is a qualified professor of veterinary medicine, and today she is internationally recognized as the founder of the Green Belt Movement in Kenya. The Movement is a grassroots, non-governmental organization (NGO) that concentrates on environmental conservation and community development by planting trees to protect the soil and empowers women by teaching them basic skills on environmentalism and creating jobs.

Maathai has not only had the courage to stand up for her beliefs, but she has risked her life for her beliefs. In 1992, Maathai was hospitalized after she was beaten unconscious by police during a hunger strike, which was not the first time she has been assaulted. Seven years later, when the Movement attempted to replace trees cut by real estate developers, Maathai and her group were attacked, leaving her head gashed and many of her supporters injured. On some occasions law enforcement officers have simply looked the other way. At one time Amnesty International sponsored a letter writing campaign to the Kenyan government and President Arap Moi to get her freed. Under constant threats so serious that for a time she was forced to go into hiding, she has never given up her cause. In *Currents Magazine* she reflects that "Despite continuing and constant opposition, the movement grows and expands. It shows that something can be done. Sometimes I marvel at the work we've done, despite the fact that maybe half of our time is spent just trying to survive. I wonder what we would have achieved if the government was supporting us instead of intimidating us."

Joined the Fight For Women's Rights

Maathai was born in Nyeri, Kenya, on April 1, 1940, and did not start school until she was eight years old. She was enrolled at Itithe Primary School, where she did very well. Four years later she was accepted at St. Cecilia's School, where she remained until 1955. The following year she was selected to attend Loreto Girls' School, in Lumuru, Kenya, graduating four years later. Maathai was very fortunate to have an opportunity to further her education in the United States following her completion of high school. She traveled to the United States to attend Mount St. Scholastica College, in Atchison, Kansas, earning a BA in 1964; the following year she earned a MA from the University of Pittsburgh.

In the 1960s the African continent was going through major political changes as the colonial powers were replaced by independence and black rule. During this time Maathai returned home to an independent Kenya, taking a position as a research assistant at the University of Nairobi in 1966. Soon afterward, she joined the National Council of Women of Kenya, (NCWK) an NGO whose focus was to educate women while advocating for their rights. Maathai's quest for advanced

studies continued as she found herself juggling her time as a mother, student, research assistant, and a women's rights advocate. She found time to study biological science and went on to obtain a doctorate degree at the University of Nairobi. She would later become head of the veterinary medicine faculty, the first woman in that capacity at any department at that university.

Like many women in lesser developed countries, Kenyan women were also struggling with their daily lives: tending the fields without access to running water or sanitation and walking for miles in search of firewood, a situation which has been worsened by deforestation. In 1989 a report by the United Nations noted that on the African continent, on average only 9 trees are planted to replace every 100 trees cut. The result of this magnitude of deforestation is soil erosion and water pollution, which, in turn interferes with animal nutrition and depletes firewood.

Surprisingly, Maathai's strong advocacy for women's rights did not sit too well with her husband or other critics. Early in her career, she had married a member of the Kenyan parliament. The marriage produced three children. According to the *Encyclopaedia of World Biographies,* in seeking a divorce, Matthai's husband complained that "she was too educated, too strong, too successful, too stubborn, and too hard to control." But what was really difficult for Maathai to understand was the criticism by other women from the ruling party who denounced her as a violator of African tradition for refusing to be submissive.

Founded Green Belt

Maathai's crusade began while she was doing field work, tracking down the life cycle of a tick. She realized that the mites were not the problem, rather, it was the degraded environment which was affecting the resistance of animals living in the habitat. She could not believe the loss of exotic species incurred by cutting down indigenous forests. A witness to soil erosion caused by treeless environments, she felt compelled to do something to save the earth. During a State of the World Forum conference, she told Marc Ian Barasch, "I went from purest academia to working directly with people." Soon afterward Maathai took over the leadership of National Council of Women of Kenya, (NCWK) and introduced the idea of planting trees as a way of conserving the environment. It was that simple, as she commented in *Currents:* "The earth was naked. For me the mission was to try to cover it up with green." The first tree planting campaign was called Save the Land Harambee, Swahili for "let's pull together." Community members were encouraged to plant trees in public land to form green belts of trees. This campaign was so successful and the idea spread so fast that the Green Belt Movement (GBM) was born. The GBM and NCWK have since worked hand-in-hand, promoting tree planting and providing a forum for women's leadership development training.

The Green Belt Movement's mission is "to raise community consciousness on self determination, equity, improved livelihood securities and environmental conservation using trees as an entry point." Thanks largely to the efforts of both the GBM and the NCWK, women learn to communicate assertively, change their environment, improve their lives, set goals, and make their own decisions. The movement also helps small scale farmers become agro-foresters through expert technology transfer, while public awareness is broadened to understand the relationship between population, food production and energy.

In the early 1980s, the Green Belt Movement focused on training its members to conserve the environment in order to improve the quality of their agricultural produce in order to alleviate hunger. This was initiated through a broad cross-Africa environmental grass roots campaign. By 1986 a Pan African Green Belt Movement was established in other countries, including Tanzania, Uganda, Malawi, Lesotho, Ethiopia, and Zimbabwe. An international chapter was also established to work outside the continent. Participants from other countries are taught to embrace the movement's vision and mission, and then concentrate on establishing similar tree planting initiatives in their own countries by using the Green Belt method.

In order to generate income and be able to meet the organization's expenses, Green Belt Safaris were introduced, offering field trips and home-stays for visitors and supporters. The objective is to engage guests in conservation through educational and cultural exchange programs and expose participants to the Kenyan fauna and flora. For a fee, visitors receive hands-on experience in conservation. Peace tree planting is another of the innovative projects introduced in the 1990s. Peace trees promote conflict resolution between communities with the goal of turning what would have been major disputes into peaceful negotiated cooperation.

Uphill Battle Against Government

Maathai and the Green Belt Movement have faced an uphill confrontation with the previous government, which have harassed her continuously and thrown her in jail. The movement has responded to these actions with civil disobedience. Asked by Barasch how she keeps from hating her enemies, Maathai responded, "The leaders don't know what they are doing. They are so blinded by greed they genuinely believe they should control all resources. They don't understand why we are willing to be abused, willing to put ourselves in danger."

In 1988, Matthai infuriated Arap Moi—then the president of Kenya—when she led an international campaign to prevent the government from erecting the tallest skyscraper on the entire continent. The project would have cost $200 million U.S dollars borrowed from foreign banks. The amount was equivalent to seven percent of Kenya's annual budget and it would have destroyed recreational space used by primarily the poor people. In an *Africa Society* profile, Maathai explained, "We already have a debt crisis owing billions to foreign banks. And people are starving, they need food, they need medicine and they need education. They did not need a skyscraper to house the ruling party and a 24-hr. television station. We can provide parks for rhinos and elephants; why can't we provide open space for people? Why are we creating an environmental havoc in urban areas?"

Currents noted that Moi was so outraged that he called Matthai "a mad woman who is a threat to the order and security of the country," and went on to urge the public "to stamp out trouble-makers." But when it appeared as if no one else cared, Maathai received support from the Kenyan National Museum and the Association of Architects; both opposed the erection of the government building. Above all, Maathai's opposition to the project prompted an international outcry and the withdrawal of foreign investors' support and eventually the government halted the plans.

Unfortunately, most of the accolades Maathai has received internationally have not contributed to the Movement's financial base. Australia and the Netherlands are the only governments that have provided needed financial support. However, the movement receives grant support from the Marion Foundation of Massachusetts. Other partners include Solar Electric Light Fund, which promotes rural solar power in developing nations, and the U.S.-based Lion-heart Foundation, which works with prisoners.

What started as primarily a women's grass-root organization to preserve the soil and the environment is today generating income for some 80,000 people, with more than 5,000 nurseries throughout Kenya and more than 20 million trees. These trees have had more than an aesthetic effect on Kenyan life and the impact on the environment cannot be denied. Most importantly, the project provides much needed income for women in rural communities, some of whom can hardly read or write. The efforts of Maathai and the movement have contributed to improving their living conditions as well as boosting their self esteem. The process is very simple. The women are trained to cultivate, plant, and properly care for seedlings. Complete orientation and support is provided, while the physical demands of successfully maintaining new seedlings are discussed. Everything must meet the movement's specifications. The seedlings are then sold to the movement, and the income generated enables the women to pay for their children's school fees or buy books and clothes.

Besides helping women, the Green Belt Movement under Maathai set out to integrate physically challenged young people by discouraging them from migrating to urban areas to seek employment. Instead they stay home to care for trees in their communities. They also receive training to become Green Belt Rangers, who monitor progress, care for the trees, and advise on local problems. This project has saved many physically challenged youth from winding up unemployed and living in squatter camps in the city. Instead, they are provided with a rewarding experience that also enhances their self-esteem. Involving the whole range of the population—school children, women, farmers, and the physically challenged—can and has made an immeasurable contribution to societal needs and conservation.

Fought Government By Joining It

As if her life was not complicated enough, Maathai decided to challenge the system once more by running for the Kenyan presidency. She was not only harassed, but she was displaced from the race when false reports of her withdrawal were widely distributed. In 1998 Maathai got involved in another worthy cause, chairing the Jubilee Africa Campaign in Kenya, which sought cancellation of foreign debt by poor countries of Africa by year 2000. Many poor governments take on huge loans usually geared for specific projects, but oftentimes because of mismanagement and embezzlement the projects are not completed and the citizens are shortchanged. In her acceptance speech at the 1991 laureate of the Africa Prize Leadership Maathai asked, "Why are the hungry masses forced to repay loans they never received and debts they never incurred? These repayments have become very heavy burdens, impoverishing them, driving them to slums, and creating internal conflicts. They are killing [the poor], through increasing poverty." Matthai seems unstoppable even after intimidation, harassment, ridicule, battering, and incarceration. Yet she defends the environment and women's rights tirelessly and passionately.

In 2001, the Green Belt Movement filed suit to prevent a forest clearance project by the Kenya government that included a plan to clear 69,000 hectares of woodland to house homeless squatters. Maathai believed that it was the government's deliberate ploy to gain support in the coming elections. Reuters reported that she commented, "It's a matter of life and death for this country, we are extremely worried. The Kenyan forests are facing extinction and it is a man-made problem."

Matthai's future plans include another worthy cause: she hopes to establish a center to house battered women and children. This is an enormous undertaking that will require a lot of support, education, and resources. Many African men will need to be persuaded as they might see this as an intrusion into their culture. Oftentimes they treat women as personal property, especially among those who have paid exorbitant amounts of money for the bride price. Successful programs in Europe and the United States include components for counseling both the victims and the perpetrators. Many Africans will have to change their mind-set and treat men who abuse women and children as law-breakers. On the other hand, African women should not be content to remain as victims; they should be aware that they have choices and human rights. Matthai was elected member of parliament in the new government and appointed Deputy Minister for the Environment, Natural Resources, and Wildlife. Now as she serves as a lawmaker, she is in a good position to support or enact laws that will protect women's rights as human rights.

Such commitment has earned Maathai many accolades and acclaim. Among the many prizes and recognitions bestowed upon her is the 1991 Goldman Environmental Prize, one of the most prestigious in the world. In that same year she also received the United Nations Africa Prize for Leadership. She received the Edinburgh Medal in 1992, and in 1997, she was elected by *Earth Times* as one of 100 persons in the world who have made a difference in the field of environmentalism. And what a difference she has made.

Sources

Books

Encyclopaedia of World Biographies, Gale, 1999.

Periodicals

Daily (University of Washington), October 28, 1999.
E Magazine, July/August 2002.
In Context, Spring 1991, p. 55.

On-line

"Acceptance Address by Professor Wangari Maathai," *The Hunger Project*, www.thp.org/prize/91/wm991.htm (January 21, 2004).
Amnesty International, www.amnesty.org (January 21, 2004).
"Bottle-Necks of Development in Africa," *Gift of Speech*, http://gos.sbc.edu/m/maathai.html (January 21, 2004).
"Dr. Wangari Maathai," *Africa Society Profile*, www.ualberta.ca/~afso/documents/maathai.pdf (January 21, 2004).
"Environmental Hero: Wangari Maathai," *Environmental News Network*, www.enn.com/features/2000/09/09252000/Maathai_30810.asp (January 21, 2004).
"Guerilla of the Week: Wangari Maathai," *Guerilla News Network*, www.guerrillanews.com/human%5Frights/doc949.html (January 21, 2004).
"Kenyan Greens File Suit to Stop Forest Clearance," *Planet Ark (Reuters Daily World Environment News)*, www.planetark.com/dailynewsstory.cfm/newsid/13379/newsDate/20-Nov-2001/story.htm (January 21, 2004).
"Saving the World Tree by Tree," *State of the World*

Forum, www.simulconference.com/clients/sowf/dis
patches/dispatch27.html (January 21, 2004).

"Wangari Maathai," *Goldman Prize Recipient Profile,* www.goldmanprize.org/recipients/recipientPro
file.cfm?recipientID=29 (January 21, 2004).

—Doris H. Mabunda

Felicia Mabuza-Suttle

1950—

Talk show host, businesswoman

Felicia Mabuza-Suttle is the most recognized woman in southern Africa thanks to her talk show. Filmed and aired on local television in South Africa, the show is appropriately called *Felicia*. Besides being a successful talk show host, she is also an internationally recognized business woman, columnist, public speaker, and a mother. She considers herself not just a celebrity but also a crusader whose mission is to bring South Africans together and encourage tourists to invest in the country.

Found Education and Romance Abroad

Mabuza-Suttle was born on June 3, 1950, in Sophiatown, a black community in Johannesburg, South Africa, during the apartheid era when every facet of life was racially segregated. She was raised by her grandfather Ben Mabuza whom she credits today as having been the force that influenced her to get where she is today. Ben Mabuza was a self-made business man, who owned and operated a butchery and a restaurant near downtown Johannesburg. Her website reported that when awakening the children in the morning her grandfather would remind them, "You are sleeping and the white man is making money…. Only people who work hard get rich." Even though Ben Mabuza was considered wealthy, he was down-to-earth and insisted on doing the cooking and waiting on his customers himself. Meanwhile, Mabuza-Suttle's dad owned one of the first driving schools in South Africa, which provided the family with a very good income.

Mabuza-Suttle enjoyed school but she also loved to dance, which led her to enroll in ballroom dancing. Glamour, as portrayed in popular black glossy magazines of the day, like *Zonk* and *Drum,* was highly publicized, and many young girls aspired to be cover girls, including Mabuza-Suttle. She did end up on the cover of *Drum*.

In the 1960s and the 1970s an exodus of black South Africans were going abroad into exile or to study. Mabuza-Suttle was one of the lucky ones who got the opportunity to study in the United States. Clinging to what her grandfather instilled in her, she wanted to be the first Mabuza to earn a college degree. Before leaving South Africa, Mabuza-Suttle had not been politically involved, but while working for the *World Newspaper,* she had a chance to meet many well known activists including Steve Biko, the leader of the Black Consciousness Movement who would tragically be murdered while under detention. Ironically, it is in the United States, many years later, that she would awaken politically as she joined the majority of African Americans to protest and advocate for sanctions against South Africa.

It is also in the United States that she would meet and marry the father of her two daughters, Earl Suttle. Suttle, then a school psychologist, was chaperoning a dance class in Milwaukee when he met Mabuza-Suttle, who, unbeknownst to him, was new in town. The two hit it off. Later, she sought his advice on where to attend college, and Suttle recommended Marquette University where he taught. It was the beginning of a long relationship.

At a Glance . . .

Born Felicia Mabuza on June 3, 1950, in Sophia-town, South Africa; married Earl Suttle, 1976; children: Lindi, Zani. *Education:* Marquette University, BA in Journalism, 1980s, MA in Mass Communication, 1980s.

Career: Radio Bophutatswana, on-air host, 1982; South African Airways, manger of Corporate Affairs, 1990-92; SABC, host of *Top Level,* 1992-1995, host of *The Felicia Show,* 1995-2000; Black O' Moon restaurant, partner, 1990s–; Felicia clothing and cosmetic line, owner and promoter, 1990s–; Pamodzi Investments, founder, 1996–; FMS Productions, founder and managing director, 1990s–; author and journalist, 1990s–; ETV, host of *Felicia,* 2000–.

Awards: The Star/Agfa Award for Popular Television Personality, 1995; Ralph Metcalfe Award, Marquette University, 1999; People's Choice Award for Entertainment, Vivid, 2000; People's Choice Award for Humanitarianism, Vivid, 2000; All University Alumni Merit Award, Marquette University, 2000; Tribute Achievers business category finalist, 2001; Soweto Legends Award, 2001; Prestige Rapport and City Press Achievers, 2001; Business Woman of the Year, 2001.

Addresses: *Publisher*—Struik Publishers, PO Box 1144, 8000; 80 McKenzie Street, Gardens, 8001, Republic of South Africa

Returned to South Africa

When Mabuza-Suttle returned briefly to South Africa to work for Radio Bophutatswana in 1982, she was criticized for being politically naive and incorrect. Bophutatswana was one of the artificially created black homelands by the South African apartheid government to disenfranchise blacks. Not a single nation in the world recognized the governments of the black homelands. Many felt she was working for the enemy. Dismissing her critics Mabuza-Suttle acknowledges that at least she was reaching South Africans and would do so by whatever means available including working for a "homeland radio" station.

Mabuza-Suttle went on to earn a BA degree in journalism and an MA in Mass Communication from Marquette University in Wisconsin. The first ten years of their marriage, the Suttles lived all over the United States,

including Fort Meyers, Fort Lauderdale, Houston, Charlotte, Atlanta. Many years later Mabuza-Suttle would settle in South Africa, and her husband would remain in the United States; theirs would be a long distance relationship.

The couple's saga began in 1990, when anti-apartheid activist Nelson Mandela, newly released from prison, made a plea encouraging South Africans living abroad to return and help to reshape the new democratic nation. Joining her other prodigal countrymen, Mabuza-Suttle returned to her country of birth. First she accepted a job as Manager of Corporate Affairs with the South African Airways. It was a very exciting time in South Africa, where complete political change was taking place. The hated apartheid regime and all traces of racial segregation had been eliminated and a newly elected popular government was opening doors to all kinds of opportunities and black empowerment.

Became Talk Show Host

Then opportunity came knocking in 1992, when the South African Broadcasting Corporation (SABC) offered Mabuza-Suttle a job to host a talk show that would engage audience participation in a manner similar to the *Donahue* and *Oprah* shows in the United States. The talk show was a new concept in South Africa, and Mabuza-Suttle's show became an overnight hit. She commented in *Ebony,* "I knew I could use television, a medium I had studied, to help in the rebuilding process." Today Mabuza-Suttle is commonly referred to as the "South African Oprah." At the beginning she was allocated a very small budget, hardly enough for an audience, but she took it as a challenge and went on to tape 3 shows every Sunday, which enabled her to build a loyal audience. Initially the program, featuring a mixed race audience, was called *Top Level,* with topics focused on the social issues driven by the political changes taking place in the country such as affirmative action, desegregation, capital punishment, etc. The timing was just right as the country was preparing for the first black vote and many citizens were taking a new pride in the state of the nation.

In 1995 *Top Level* was renamed *The Felicia Show* and the focus changed as Mabuza-Suttle set out to tackle social problems of the day while including forays into entertainment. The program was extended to an hour. One week she might feature "Prostitution," or "Rare Syndromes and Diseases," and the next might be "South Africa's Talented Kids." In this she believes she is both educating and entertaining. As she told Sean Houghton, "My dream has always been to try and unite South Africans through communication…. In South Africa, television tries to educate and inform too hard, they should also entertain…. Even information and education can be presented in such a way that it becomes entertaining…. We need to refocus and as far as Felicia Mabuza-Suttle is concerned, television has to entertain first, and inform and educate last."

The show has made a difference in some people's lives such as the families who have been reunited, the men whose paternity identity has been verified, and the doctors who have volunteered their services to perform complicated corrective surgeries. Some guests have found employment and shelter though Mabuza-Suttle's program. But her crusade has encountered a few barriers along the way, leading some to criticize her for making false promises. For example, a handicapped woman from Soweto, the largest black community in South Africa, appeared on the show. One week later the *Felicia* office informed the guest of an "American guy" who had offered to build a house for her. Weeks turned into months and nothing materialized. When questioned, a staff person from the show confirmed that an American guest had made a promise to build a house but unfortunately never came through. Mabuza-Suttle told *News24* that "we do get feedback from viewers who voice concerns on the various plights of our guests. But there is little we can do if guests don't fulfill their promises."

As Mandela was being ushered in as the first Black president, South Africa entered a black empowerment boom. New companies were being listed on the Johannesburg Stock Exchange and black representation on corporate boards was increasing. Mabuza-Suttle found herself serving on various boards. Together with a group of other women, she formed Pamodzi Investment Holding, South Africa, a consortium of investments that began with a small capital of three million rand. The estimated value in 2003 was approximately 100 million rands. The current exchange rate is 6.4 rands to 1 U.S. dollar.

Following her grandfather's footsteps in restaurant business, Mabuza-Suttle has capitalized on her show to create business ventures, becoming a skilled marketer. She is a partner in a successful restaurant called Back O' Moon, located at Gold Reef City, a five-star hotel in South Africa. The restaurant features international cuisine and a jazz club. She has also launched her own Mabuza-Suttle eyewear, shoes, and clothing, and says on her website, "Many of my fans have asked me when I am coming up with my own range of clothing or accessories, and I am happy to say it's here. The new range of clothing is a modest replica of the expensive suits I wear—simple, yet stylish and affordable." A portion of her eyewear proceeds go to the Felicia Mabuza-Suttle Trust, an anti-drug and anti-crime campaign she developed. In 2000 her show moved to ETV, the largest English speaking channel, in South Africa. The show is now simply called *Felicia* and is produced by her company, FMS.

Worked to Sustain Marriage and Crusade

Married to Earl Suttle since 1976, the two have remained together despite the enormous distance between Johannesburg, South Africa, and Atlanta, Georgia—8,421 miles. What has sustained them are periodic visits, long distance calls, and numerous e-mails. They have been doing this for a long time, so the hard part is behind them now. "The goodbyes are always the most haunting and troublesome," said Mabuza-Suttle in *Ebony*. "I love my husband and daughters more than anything in the world. No woman in her true mind, who loves children the way I do, who loves family the way I do, would leave the family for any crusade. You have to sacrifice something you cherish dearly. People don't understand the sacrifices. I made them because I [also] love my people."

The couple credit their Christian faith for keeping them grounded. They average three cross-Atlantic trips each per year, but they have had their share of stress, and even depression and loneliness. His friends wonder why Suttle has not given up. He lamented in *Ebony*, "I have thought about ending this relationship a few times.... But for me it's about my commitments to my family to see this journey through. We want to be role models for our daughters. We believe that how they see us love and respect each other will impact the kind of relationships they will develop in the future. So you have to hang in there through thick and thin."

Mabuza-Suttle seems determined as ever as she continues to confront controversial societal problems. Recent show topics have included xenophobia, Internet dating, run away street kids, and living with HIV/AIDS. Her sister, who told the *Independent Online* that "I am still HIV positive," shared her story with Mabuza-Suttle's viewers, exhibiting a strong will to keep on going and to try non-conventional medicines.

Through some luck, determination, and persistence, Mabuza-Suttle clung to the idea that the key to success was education, because with education, the sky is the limit. As she continues to inform, motivate and entertain, some of the world's best known individuals have appeared on her show—like Dr. Wayne Dyer, author John Maxwell, inspirational speaker Iyanda Vanzant, financial guru Suze Orman and jazz singer Al Jarreau. She considers Nelson Mandela's appearance on her show as one of the most memorable ever, as he was interviewed by children, he seemed to enjoy every minute.

At present Mabuza-Suttle is working on a doctorate degree, is in demand as a speaker, and writes a newspaper column. Her autobiography, *Felicia: Dare to Dream* was published a few years ago, and is described on her website as being about "a girl from the dusty, daring and dangerous streets of Soweto, South Africa, who dared to dream." According to the website, her message is simple, "If I can, you too can because I come from the same neighborhood."

Selected writings

Felicia: Dare to Dream, Struik Publishers, 1990s.

Sources

Periodicals

Ebony, October 2000.
Essence, March 2002.

On-line

"Felicia Mabuza-Suttle Wins Prestigious Award," *ETV,* www.etv.co.za/PRESSLIST/0176.html (January 22, 2004).
Felicia Online, www.feliciaonline.co.za (January 22, 2004).
"Felicia Zeal Is Almost Missionary," *Sunday Times,* (South Africa), www.suntimes.co.za (January 22, 2004).

"15 Minutes with Felicia," *Dispatch Online,* www. dispatch.co.za/2001/11/17/features/FELICIA. HTM (January 22, 2004).
"I'm Still HIV Positive says Felicia's Sister," *Independent Online,* www.iol.co.za/index.php?set_id=1& click_id=13&art_id=vn20030721011355267C74 8076 (January 22, 2004).
"It's Felicia the Fashion Queen," *Sunday Times,* (South Africa), www.suntimes.co.za/1999/12/12/ arts/gauteng/aneg02.htm (January 22, 2004).
"Promises, Promises," *News 24* www.NEWS24.com (January 22, 2004).
"The Challenges Facing Diaspora Africans Who Return to Africa," *The Perspective,* www.theperspec tive.org/diaspora.html (January 22, 2004).

—Doris H. Mabunda

Darnell Martin

1964—

Filmmaker

Darnell Martin, writer and director of 1994's *I Like It Like That,* attained a momentous first in the entertainment industry with her debut film: she became the first African-American woman to make a movie with the sponsorship of a major Hollywood studio. Martin's film, a tale of love and hardship set in the South Bronx, won critical plaudits, but she has faced difficulties in building her subsequent career.

Inspired by Faulkner Novel

Born on January 7, 1964, Martin was the daughter of an unconventional set of parents: she rarely saw her African-American father, an attorney, when she was growing up, while her mother, of Irish heritage, was often busy performing with her African fire-dance troupe. Martin and her two older sisters grew up in various New York neighborhoods, including Morrisania in the South Bronx, and there were times when the family had to depend on public assistance. Morrisania in the early 1970s was a rough area, but as the future filmmaker told *New York Times* journalist Jan Hoffman, "When you're a kid you don't think *drugs.* You just notice that everyone seems kind of laid-back and tired."

Martin's mother tried to pave a way for her daughters out of Morrisania. Once, she found a job selling commodities and moved the family out of the boroughs and into Manhattan. She sought a scholarship so that Martin could attend the Barnard College School for Girls, and another time she was able to send her to a Greenwich, Connecticut, boarding school. It was there that Martin first read William Faulkner's 1932 novel, *Light in August.* In it, an orphan named Joe Christmas is accused of being part African American even before he is born, and that rumor follows him for the rest of his lonely, isolated life, culminating in a shocking act of violence. She explained in an interview with Kate Meyers of *Entertainment Weekly* that the novel had inspired her deeply. "That a white man from the South, from a different period and a different social structure than I, could write something that was more close to me than anything I have ever read in my life says we're all ... human."

At Sarah Lawrence College, Martin studied theater and literature, and decided to pursue filmmaking for her graduate education. She was rejected by all the film schools to which she applied, and instead took a job as a technician in a film laboratory in Manhattan. At other times she tended bar and worked for a camera-rental business. Through the film lab job, however, she met cinematographer-director Ernest Dickerson, best known for his work on a number of Spike Lee films. Dickerson helped Martin land a job doing second-assistant camera work on Lee's 1989 movie *Do the Right Thing,* as well as for an Anita Baker video. Still formally untrained, Martin was hired for commercial and video work, but only made it into New York University's (NYU) film school when Lee, an alumnus, made a phone call on her behalf.

At a Glance . . .

Born on January 7, 1964, in NY; daughter of Marilyn (a dancer) and an attorney; married Giuseppe Ducret (an artist). *Education:* Sarah Lawrence College, BA, 1980s; New York University Film School, MA, 1990s. *Religion:* Christian Scientist.

Career: Technician at film laboratories in New York City, 1980s; *Do the Right Thing;* second assistant camera person, 1989; film director, screenwriter, film producer, 1992–; television director, 1993–.

Memberships: Writers Guild of America.

Awards: Directing fellowship, Sundance Institute, Utah.

Addresses: *Office*—c/o Columbia Pictures, 3400 Riverside Dr., Los Angeles, CA 90027.

Courted by Columbia TriStar

Martin's NYU student film, *Suspect,* was showcased in the New York Public Theater's Young Black Cinema event in 1992, and helped win her a fellowship in directing at actor-director Robert Redford's prestigious Sundance Institute in Utah. She had already begun writing *I Like It Like That* while at NYU, originally calling it "Blackout," and her timing was fortuitous. She took the finished script around to the studios, who were suddenly eager to take on work from young, untested African-American filmmakers. The box office success of movies like *Boyz in the Hood,* with their urban themes and already-known musical stars, awakened studios to the profit potential in courting a new generation of visual storytellers, and Martin was the first female among this first wave of black filmmakers to achieve success.

The road to making her debut feature film was not an easy one, however. New Line Cinema initially offered Martin $2 million to make it, which meant she would have had to shoot the entire movie in just seven weeks. As she recalled in the *New York Times,* at the time the offer came through she was out of money. "I was about to be evicted, and I was eating spaghetti and oil for dinner," she told Hoffman. "But I thought 'If I shot that film in seven weeks, it wouldn't be a good movie.'" She turned it down, and then Columbia TriStar Pictures offered her $5 million. The finished product, which starred newcomers Jon Seda and Lauren Vélez, earned strong reviews when shown at the 1994 Cannes Film Festival, and also did well at the box office.

I Like It Like That is set in a Hispanic-American community in the South Bronx. Vélez plays Lisette, who is of mixed African-American and Latino heritage. She and Seda's Chino, a bike messenger, have three young children. During a blackout, Chino tries to steal a stereo for her and is sent to prison. Lisette must find a job and rely on her family and community for help, which proves to be a mixed blessing. Her subtly racist mother-in-law, played by Rita Moreno, brags that their Puerto Rican family has only pure Spanish Castilian blood; Lisette's brother is a transvestite who encourages her to model. Instead she finds work at a Manhattan record company. When her wealthy white boss drives her home one night, the neighbors assume she is cheating on Chino. "Like Martin's own childhood, Lisette's world is crowded with rakish relatives and friends who drop by uninvited, often to deliver unwelcome messages," noted Hoffman in the *New York Times.*

The record company plot line aside, music was a key element in Martin's debut film, and she noted later that some objected, claiming it was overpowering. She defended the soundtrack in an interview with *American Visions,* telling writer Steve Monroe that it reflected the world in which she grew up. "In New York you have people of all cultures—black, white, Latino—living on top of each other. You hear them talking and shouting, and you hear their music all the time." She was eager to stress elsewhere, however, that the film was certainly not autobiographical, save for the South Bronx neighborhood. Her background was far closer to that of the movie's oldest son, Li'l Chino, than to Lisette, she told Hoffman in the *New York Times.* "You're a kid trying to break up a fight between the people who are taking care of you."

Found Work in Television

Critics applauded both *I Like It Like That* and its creator. *Cineaste* writer Alvina Quintana asserted that the movie "offers viewers its share of familiar … stereotypes, images of virtuous and loose women, macho men, dysfunctional families, drug dealing gangs, poor barrio homes, and so forth. But other aspects of the film suggest that Martin's portrayal of the young multiracial married couple exemplifies the struggle between the visions of the past and those of the future, representing the filmmaker's attempt to challenge outdated cultural models." Leah Rozen of *People* commented on the respect that Martin seemed to have for the characters she created, noting that she "doesn't pretend anyone in this neighborhood has it easy but demonstrates the sense of belonging that can be had there." Writing for *Entertainment Weekly,* Lisa Schwarzbaum called Martin's status as Hollywood's first black woman filmmaker an impressive achievement, but conceded that Martin was "not the one who needs the certificate. Columbia deserves the attaboy clap on the back for having latched on to such an intelligent, confident filmmaker at the start of her career."

Despite such praise, Martin had a difficult time with her next project. The story came out of a film class she taught for underage offenders at New York City's Spofford Correctional Facility, and she collaborated on the project with rapper Q-Tip, once a member of A Tribe Called Quest. The result was a musical called *Prison Song*, which never made it to theatrical release despite a solid performance by Mary J. Blige. Since then, Martin has worked primarily in television, finding a home as the director of episodes for the bleak HBO prison drama *Oz*, and for spin-offs of the network drama *Law & Order*.

Martin married Giuseppe Ducret, an artist from Italy, whom she met when she was 17 and traveling in Europe. She was pragmatic about her success in an *Essence* interview with Deborah Gregory. "The only reason I am living my dreams now is because my mother raised me to believe that I could be whoever I wanted to be," she reflected. "A lot of people aren't that lucky."

Selected works

Films

Suspect, 1992.
I Like It Like That, 1994.
Prison Song, 2001.

Television

Homicide, Life on the Street, NBC, 1993.
ER, NBC, 1994.
Oz, HBO, 1997.
Law & Order: Special Victims Unit, NBC, 1997.
Law & Order: Criminal Intent, NBC, 2001.
Dragnet, ABC, 2003.

Sources

American Visions, October-November 1994, p. 43.
Black Collegian, October 1994, p. 8.
Cineaste, Summer 1996, p. 30.
Entertainment Weekly, October 21, 1994, p. 47; April 14, 1995, p. 72.
Essence, December 1994, p. 52; March 2000, p. 82.
Nation, November 14, 1994, p. 592.
New York Times, October 9, 1994, p. H28.
People, October 31, 1994, p. 20.
Variety, July 14, 1997, p. 34.

—Carol Brennan

Curtis Mayfield

1942-1999

Singer, guitarist, songwriter, record company executive

Curtis Mayfield was an early comer to the world of music. When he was barely ten years old he was already writing music, and by the time he was fifteen he was invited to join the group the Impressions, a group that would come to be known world-wide for its rhythm and blues sound found in such songs as "Gypsy Woman," the song for which the group was eventually honored with a place in the Rock & Roll Hall of Fame. Mayfield went on to an incredibly successful solo career during which he became famous for such popular songs as "Superfly" and "Freddie's Dead." He was a political man, many of whose songs, such as "We're a Winner," "I'm So Proud," and "People Get Ready," were unofficially associated with the Civil Rights Movement of the 1960s. In 1990 Mayfield was injured during a concert rehearsal and paralyzed. He didn't let that stop him, however, and before his death in 1999 Mayfield wrote more music and was admitted as a solo artist into the Rock & Roll Hall of Fame.

Joined the Impressions

Born on June 3, 1942, Curtis Lee Mayfield grew up in a poor family that moved from neighborhood to neighborhood in Chicago. By the time he was in high school, his family had settled in the Cabrini-Green projects on Chicago's North Side. Mayfield's strongest early musical influence came from his membership in a local gospel group called the Northern Jubilee Gospel Singers, which included three cousins and Jerry Butler. But young Mayfield was also interested in his own music. As Mayfield told the *Detroit News* in 1974, "I was writing music when I was 10 or 11 years old." Mayfield's grandmother was a preacher in the Traveling Souls Spiritualist Church, and traces of church and gospel music are evident in many of his compositions. Mayfield attended Wells High School on Chicago's North Side along with another popular singer, Major Lance, but he left when he was in the tenth grade to begin performing with the Impressions.

The Impressions began playing around 1956 as the Roosters in Chattanooga, Tennessee, with Fred Cash, Sam Gooden, Emanuel Thomas, and the brothers Richard and Arthur Brooks. Seeking to advance their musical careers, Gooden and the Brooks brothers went north to Chicago in 1957 and moved to the North Side in the Cabrini-Green projects. Jerry Butler was a senior in high school at the time, and he acted as a replace-

At a Glance . . .

Born Curtis Lee Mayfield on June 3, 1942, in Chicago, IL; died on December 26, 1999, in Atlanta, GA of natural causes; married three times; children: eleven.

Career: The Impressions, lead singer and songwriter, 1958-70; Curtom Record and Publishing Co., owner, 1970-99; solo performer, 1970-99.

Awards: Rock & Roll Hall of Fame, inductee with the Impressions, 1990; Nat. Acad. of Recording Arts & Sciences Lifetime Achievement Award, 1994; Rock & Roll Hall of Fame, inductee as a solo artist, 1998; Songwriters' Hall of Fame, inductee, 2000.

ment for the vocalists who had stayed in Tennessee. Butler encouraged Mayfield to join the group, saying they needed someone "who could play an instrument and who could help us get our harmony together," as quoted by Robert Pruter in *Chicago Soul*. By this time, Mayfield was writing gospel-influenced songs and had learned how to play the guitar.

The group made some early recordings for the Bandera label and were then discovered by Eddie Thomas of Vee Jay records, who became their manager and changed their name to the Impressions. Vee Jay and Chess records were two of Chicago's major rhythm and blues labels of the time, and the Impressions made their first record for Vee Jay about six months after Mayfield joined the group. Released on the company's subsidiary label, Falcon, "For Your Precious Love" featured Jerry Butler's lead vocals. Its first issue sold over nine hundred thousand copies. Vee Jay's A&R man Calvin Carter signed them immediately after hearing the song, which he reportedly liked for its spiritual feel, a genuine departure from the doo-wop harmonies of the day.

Vee Jay promoted the group as "Jerry Butler and the Impressions" and developed Butler as a solo artist. After three singles, Butler left the group to go out on his own. As Mayfield told Pruter, "When Jerry left … it allowed me to generate and pull out my own talents as a writer and a vocalist." Mayfield's soprano singing contrasted with Butler's baritone leads. The group released a few singles with Mayfield as leader and then was dropped by Vee Jay. From 1959 to 1961, the Impressions temporarily split up, and Mayfield began writing songs and playing guitar for Butler in 1960.

Gospel Influence Proved Popular

By 1961 Mayfield had saved enough money—about a thousand dollars—to regroup the Impressions and take them to New York to arrange a recording session. In July they recorded "Gypsy Woman" for ABC-Paramount. Mayfield was only 18 when the group signed with ABC-Paramount, and it was the beginning of a seven-year string of popular and rhythm and blues hits that were all composed by Mayfield. Mayfield, Sam Gooden, Fred Cash, and Arthur and Richard Brooks sang on "Gypsy Woman." The Brooks brothers left the Impressions in 1962, and the remaining members continued as a trio throughout the 1960s.

In 1963 the group recorded "It's All Right," which Pruter termed "the first single to define the classic style of the 1960s Impressions." Producer Jerry Pate "lifted the energy level considerably, adding blaring horns and a more forceful, percussive bottom," wrote Pruter. "It's All Right" was a crossover hit that went to Number Four on the pop charts and Number One on the rhythm and blues charts in the fall of 1963. The song featured "the lead switching off from among the three and the two others singing in harmony with the lead," Pruter commented in *Chicago Soul*. It was a fresh new sound in rhythm and blues, but critics have noted that it came directly from Mayfield's gospel singing experience.

In 1964 the Impressions became a major act with a series of strong singles that included "I'm So Proud," "Keep On Pushing," and "Amen." Mayfield was apparently inspired by the emergence of the civil rights movement. The Reverend Martin Luther King, Jr., and Jesse Jackson adopted "Keep On Pushing" as an unofficial theme song for the movement. Dan Kening, writing in the *Chicago Tribune*, proclaimed that Mayfield's "inspirational lyrics reflected a strong black consciousness while preaching the tenets of hard work, persistence, and faith as the key to achieving equality."

The group peaked with their best material in 1965 when they released "People Get Ready," a song with heavy gospel imagery and feeling. The album of the same name included such songs as "Woman's Got Soul" and the churchy "Meeting Over Yonder." Following this peak, the group was less successful and had fewer hits. In 1967 "We're a Winner" managed to reach Number 14 on Billboard's pop charts, in spite of the fact that many white radio stations, including Chicago's WLS, would not play it. That song, and its follow-up "We're Rolling On," also caused black radio stations problems in the late 1960s. As Pruter wrote, "Surprisingly at that time, black radio had not kept pace with its black constituency and there was a lot of resistance by programmers over playing such 'overtly' political songs. The popularity of those songs ["We're a Winner" and "We're Rolling On"] had the effect of pushing black radio in the direction its listeners were going."

In addition to composing, singing, and playing the guitar, Mayfield was also interested in setting up his own record label. In 1960, at the age of 21, he made the unprecedented move of establishing his own music publishing company, Curtom, while recording at Vee Jay. Mayfield began setting up two labels in 1966, Mayfield and Windy C., but it was in 1968 that he established his most successful label, also named Curtom. He took the Impressions away from ABC and also recorded and produced such artists as Major Lance, Baby Huey and the Babysitters, and the Five Stairsteps. Mayfield's songwriting and producing abilities were a key factor in the label's success, which enjoyed distribution by Buddah from 1968 to 1975 and by Warner Brothers from 1975 until Mayfield folded the label in 1980.

Found Success With Solo Career

Mayfield announced his departure from the Impressions in August of 1970. He began his solo career in 1971, offering "a biting commentary of the American scene and impressions of oppressed people," according to a review in *Billboard*. A *New York Times* music critic said of his first solo album, *Curtis:* "Mayfield himself continues to be a kind of contemporary preacher-through-music. He sings in a breathlessly high, pure voice, breaking his phrases into speech-like patterns, his rhythms pushed by the urgency of his thought.... He is not a lyrical singer, and his message seems as important to him as his melody." Including songs of up to ten minutes in length, *Curtis* established Mayfield as an album rather than a singles artist.

Mayfield began a successful career writing soundtracks for films with the 1972 movie, *Superfly.* Somewhat controversial, the film glorified the life of a drug pusher and was part of the then-popular genre of "blaxploitation" films. According to a *New York Times* review, "Mayfield's music is more specifically anti-drugs than the philosophical content of the movie, and it is also considerably more stylish in design and execution." Two top-ten hit singles resulted from the soundtrack: "Freddie's Dead" and "Superfly."

Throughout the 1970s, Mayfield continued to write soundtracks for several films and solidified his reputation as a solo artist. Mayfield's solo career featured harder sounding songs than he wrote for the Impressions, with didactic lyrics and social commentary. In spite of adverse criticism, Pruter assessed Mayfield's 1970s output positively, writing, "Some of the very best black popular music of the 1970s came from Mayfield, who despite the many misses during the decade was one of the creative leaders in establishing a new contemporary style of rhythm and blues, one with a militant, harder edge."

The Impressions regrouped in 1983 for a reunion tour. Original members Butler, Mayfield, Gooden, and Cash performed the 1960s hits of the Impressions along with the solo hits of Butler and Mayfield. As reviewed by Robert Palmer in the *New York Times,* the performances "amounted to a capsule history of recent black popular music, from the slick doo-wop and grittier gospel-based vocal group styles of the 1950s to Mr. Butler's urbane pop-soul, Curtis Mayfield's soul message songs and later funk, and the styles the Impressions have tackled as a group." Palmer continued: "The Impressions were one of the two top rhythm-and-blues vocal groups of the 1960s; the other was the Temptations. Both were rooted in the rich traditions of black gospel music."

Mayfield's influence on a new generation of listeners was evident in many ways. His 1960s compositions for the Impressions have enjoyed numerous cover versions from a wide range of popular singers. And some critics have suggested that his anti-drug messages, most emphatically expressed in the songs for *Superfly,* fit well with the new films created by young black filmmakers. Popular rap singer and actor Ice-T, who sang on "Superfly 1990" with Mayfield, said in tribute to the artist, "There's only been a couple of people I've met [in the music business] that to me are really heavy. Curtis is one of them."

Continued Career After Paralyzing Accident

A native Chicagoan who moved to Atlanta in 1980, Curtis Mayfield was enjoying the best comeback year of his career in 1990. His soul vocal group the Impressions, was nominated for a place in the Rock & Roll Hall of Fame, and a successful cover version of their 1961 hit "Gypsy Woman," was recorded by Santana. *Take It to the Streets,* Mayfield's first album in more than five years, was released in early 1990, and he toured the United States, Europe, and Japan to promote it. Capitol Records was set to release the soundtrack to *The Return of Superfly,* a rap sampler featuring four original songs written and performed by Mayfield.

Then tragedy struck. On a windy summer night in August of 1990, Mayfield was getting set to start a concert at Wingate Field in Brooklyn. As he was plugging in his guitar, a gust of wind toppled a light tower near the stage, striking him in the head. The accident resulted in three broken vertebrae and paralysis for Mayfield from the neck down. After spending a week in a Brooklyn hospital, he was transferred to the Shepherd Spinal Center in Atlanta. Keeping his spirits up, Mayfield began physical therapy in September of 1990 and made his first public appearance in February of 1991, when he donated $100,000 to set up the Curtis Mayfield Research Fund at the Miami Project to Cure Paralysis in Florida. His family was reportedly hopeful that his physical therapy would enable him to make at least a partial recovery.

Mayfield might have been injured, but he wasn't forgotten. Various artists got together in 1994 to put out a tribute album in honor of the great Curtis Mayfield, including Eric Clapton, Phil Collins, Stevie Wonder, Whitney Houston, Aretha Franklin, B.B. King, Lenny Kravitz, the Isley Brothers, and Bruce Springsteen. Mayfield himself got back into the recording studio to do "All Men Are Brothers" for the album. He told *Guitar Player* magazine that the album meant a lot to him. "I was just overwhelmed. It brought tears to my eyes. As they would record them, they would send me copies of each. I'd play them over and over, and there wasn't a song I didn't like. It just goes to show you that no matter how bad things might get, there's always room for something good to happen."

And Mayfield's music stayed alive. Rhino Records came out with a three-CD boxed set of Mayfield's music in 1996. It included music from his days with the Impressions through to his later solo career. In 1997 Mayfield released the new album *New World Order.* When asked how his music writing had changed since his accident, Mayfield told *People Weekly,* "It's difficult simply because when an idea hits me, I can't just up and grab a guitar or recorder or a pencil and write it down.... But I'm happy to know I can still lock in lyrics, and I have enough voice and strength in my lungs to sing a song." As an even greater tribute to the man and his music, Mayfield was inducted into the Rock & Roll Hall of Fame in 1998 for his solo recordings.

On December 26, 1999, Mayfield died in Atlanta, Georgia of natural causes. Even though he had passed on, his music and career continue to be influential. In 2000 a two-hour musical celebration was held to commemorate Mayfield's life and career at the First AME Church in Los Angeles. Performers such as Stevie Wonder, Lauryn Hill, the Impressions, Mayfield's old band, and Danny Glover led the event. Also in 2000, Mayfield was posthumously inducted into the Songwriters' Hall of Fame. It is a great tribute to a man who led many in their paths to musical art. As Eric Clapton told *Guitar Player* magazine, "Curtis changed the course of modern music, bringing refinement, cool, and social comment to R&B and leading the way for songwriters, players, and singers in all fields of music. He [was] a great talent and inspiration to us all.

Selected discography

(With The Impressions) *The Impressions,* ABC-Paramount, 1963.
(With The Impressions) *The Never Ending Impressions,* ABC-Paramount, 1964.
(With The Impressions) *Keep On Pushing,* ABC-Paramount, 1964.
(With The Impressions) *People Get Ready,* ABC-Paramount, 1965.
(With The Impressions) *Ridin' High,* ABC-Paramount, 1966.
(With The Impressions) *The Fabulous Impressions,* ABC-Paramount, 1967.
(With The Impressions) *This Is My Country,* Curtom, 1968.

(With The Impressions) *Young Mods' Forgotten Story,* Curtom, 1969.
(With The Impressions) *Check Out Your Mind,* Curtom, 1970.
(With The Impressions) *The Vintage Years: Featuring Jerry Butler and Curtis Mayfield,* Sire, 1976.
Curtis, Curtom, 1970.
Curtis Live, Curtom, 1971.
Roots, Curtom, 1971.
Superfly (soundtrack), Curtom, 1972.
Back to the World, Curtom, 1973.
Sweet Exorcist, Curtom, 1974.
Got to Find a Way, Curtom, 1974.
There's No Place Like America, Curtom, 1975.
Give Get Take and Have, Curtom, 1976.
Never Say You Can't Survive, Curtom, 1977.
Short Eyes (soundtrack), Curtom, 1977.
Do It All Night, Curtom, 1978.
Heartbeat, RSO/Curtom, 1978.
Something to Believe In, RSO/Curtom, 1979.
The Right Combination, RSO/Curtom, 1980.
Honesty, Boardwalk, 1982.
Take It to the Streets, Curtom, 1990.
The Return of Superfly (soundtrack), Capitol, 1990.
New World Order, 1996.

Sources

Books

Albert, George, and Frank Hoffman, editors, *The Cashbox Black Contemporary Singles Charts, 1960-1984,* Scarecrow, 1986.
Pruter, Robert, *Chicago Soul,* University of Illinois Press, 1991.
St. James Encyclopedia of Popular Culture, 5 Volumes, St. James Press, 2000.
Whitburn, Joel, *Joel Whitburn's Top Pop Singles 1955-1990,* Record Research, 1991.
——, *Joel Whitburn's Top R&B Singles 1942-1988,* Record Research, 1988.

Periodicals

Billboard, August 29, 1970; February 6, 1971; January 22, 1994, p. 1; January 13, 1996, p. 7; August 16, 1997 p. 12.
Chicago Tribune, September 2, 1990.
Detroit News, January 27, 1974.
Down Beat, November, 1999, p. 70; January, 2001, p. 72.
Ebony, July 1973.
Entertainment Weekly, October 11, 1996, p. 91; March 9, 2001, p. 80.
Guitar Player, August, 1991; June, 1994, p. 71; December, 1996, p. 29; April, 2000, p. 35.
Indianapolis Star, May 15, 1983.
Jet, March 14, 1994, p. 56; April 7, 1997, p. 42; July 13, 1998, p. 35; April 5, 1999, p. 26; March 13, 2000, p. 32; July 3, 2000, p. 34.

Los Angeles Times, October 23, 1989; August 26, 1990.

Michigan Chronicle, June 19, 1976.

Newsweek, October 14, 1996, p. 75; January 10, 2000, p. 9.

New York Times, December 6, 1970; May 6, 1983.

People Weekly, August 5, 1996, p. 24; February 17, 1997, p. 111; March 17, 1997, p. 41; January 1, 2000, p. 118.

—David Bianco and Catherine V. Donaldson

Gay J. McDougall

1947—

Lawyer, civil rights activist

Gay McDougall made history in 1994 as the first African American to be appointed to the Washington, D.C.-based International Human Rights Law Group. Such landmark achievements have been typical for McDougall, however. A civil rights activist and international lawyer, she has perhaps been most noted for her role in loosening the grip of apartheid—legally sanctioned racial discrimination—on South Africa. Recently, she has been at work on behalf of the oppressed peoples of other countries as well, including Haiti, Nicaragua, Paraguay, and Bosnia.

McDougall was born in Dixie Hills, a northwest neighborhood of Atlanta, Georgia, on August 13, 1947, just as the civil right movement was gaining momentum. Her mother, Inez Gay Johnson, was a high school mathematics teacher active in the church, and her father, Louis Johnson, was a hospital cook. McDougall and her mother had several aunts who were employed as social workers. These female role models sowed the seeds of McDougall's desire to weave social concerns into her professional life. These women were not her only mentors. Growing up in Atlanta during the height of the civil rights era, she saw prominent figures of the movement such as Stokely Carmichael, Julian Bond, and Martin Luther King, Jr., working practically down the street.

Began Law Career

McDougall attended English Avenue and Anderson Park elementary school and then attended Booker T. Washington High School. McDougall enrolled in Agnes Scott College, a women's school in Decatur, Georgia, in 1965. Every year Booker T. Washington High School applied for one black student to go to the all-white school, but no one was ever accepted. So, McDougall was stunned when she discovered she had been chosen to attend the elite school. The only black student on campus, she was lonely, and so frustrated by the conservative and highly traditional attitudes and curriculum of the school that, in 1968, she transferred to Bennington College, in Bennington, Vermont. After graduating from Bennington in 1969, she enrolled in Yale Law School and received her law degree in 1972. At both Bennington and Yale, she found a far freer atmosphere that nurtured her growing social conscience. She took an enthusiastic part in voter registration drives and civil rights projects and developed a keen interest in the proliferating African independence movements as well as the United States' march towards true racial equality.

Upon graduation from Yale in 1972, McDougall put her civil rights activities on hold for a short time, while she worked for the New York City-based corporate law firm of Debevoise, Plimpton, Lyons & Gates. "I really was there to learn to be the best professional that I could be, because I thought that the issues that I cared about deserve that," she told the *Washington Post*. The training she wanted took her two years to achieve. She also trained as a legal clerk while still in law school at Cravath, Swaine, and Moore, another New York law firm. After that, having saved a large proportion of her salary, she was able to follow her true wish and work as

At a Glance . . .

Born on August 13, 1947, in Atlanta, GA. *Education:* Attended Agnes Scott College, 1965-67; Bennington College, BA, 1969; Yale Law School, JD, 1972; London School of Economics, MA, 1978.

Career: Debevoise, Plimpton, Lyons & Gates, legal aide, 1972-74; National Conference of Black Lawyers, general counsel, 1970s; City of New York, Board of Corrections, 1980; Lawyers' Committee for Civil Rights Under Law, Southern Africa Project, director, 1980-94; International Human Rights Law Group, executive director, 1994–.

Memberships: National Conference of Black Lawyers; Black Forum on Foreign Policy; International Federation of Women Lawyers.

Selected awards: Candace Award, National Coalition of 100 Black Women, 1990.

Addresses: *Office*—International Human Rights Law Group, 1601 Connecticut Ave., NW, Ste. 700, Washington, DC 20009.

an unpaid employee for the non-profit National Conference on Black Lawyers (NCBL) in Washington, D.C.

The NCBL was formed in 1968, partly to help minorities and the poor with legal problems, racial issues, and matters concerning voters' rights. The NCBL also addressed international civil rights concerns. Perfectly in tune with the organization's mission, McDougall soon became the NCBL representative to the United Nations (UN), and gained a unique opportunity to fuse her legal training and her civil rights interests by forming a task force to study the increasingly visible African liberation movements. Working for the NCBL was a stimulating experience that she enjoyed.

After two years with the NCBL, McDougall took a job with the New York City Board of Corrections. The Board of Corrections was formed shortly after 43 inmates were killed in the Attica Prison riot in September of 1971. An adjudicating body, the board dealt with the issues that had led to the uprising: inadequate medical attention, poor work wages, unresolved dietary concerns, and insufficient fresh air and exercise. McDougall tackled these issues with zest, then decided to return to the international human rights arena.

McDougall believed that further education would ease her transition into international law so, in 1978, she

obtained her Master's degree from the London School of Economics. Long favored as an educational institution by international humanitarian and liberation movements, the London School had trained Jomo Kenyatta, eventual president of Kenya as well as the contemporary leaders of the struggle for independence in Zimbabwe and South Africa whom she met when she arrived. "It was one of the best moves I've made in my life, in terms of the people I met, who inspired me and centered me and helped me find exactly what I think in many ways," McDougall explained in the *Washington Post.*

Led Southern Africa Project

In 1980 McDougall returned to the United States to find a new challenge on her home turf ably provided by the Lawyers' Committee for Civil Rights Under Law. The civil rights group was formed in the early 1960s to provide legal backing for racial equality issues. Using its connections to human rights groups based in other parts of the world, the Lawyers' Committee tried to help counteract the South African government's increasingly sinister record of detentions, tortures, and bannings.

As a result, the Lawyer's Committee formed the Southern Africa Project, charged with the responsibility of making contact with South African lawyers for the purpose of providing them legal assistance to aid South African victims of racism or torture. The Southern Africa Project also provided reports for both the U.S. government and the UN regarding situations in other southern African countries. For example, in 1979, the organization released a 72-page report that played a large part in then U.S.-President Jimmy Carter's decision against unilaterally lifting sanctions against Rhodesia. The sanctions had been set in place because Rhodesia's white minority government had illegally declared independence from Great Britain, but many felt the penalties were hurting the black citizens as well as the government.

McDougall was asked to direct the Southern Africa Project, a post she kept until 1994. She took part in symposiums and accessed reports that documented a horrifying record of tortures and murders, all aimed at keeping apartheid intact. However, as McDougall noted in a paper called "Proposals for a New United States Policy Towards South Africa," delivered during a 1988 human rights symposium, South Africa was not confining its policies to its own borders. The African country of Namibia, whose "independence" from South Africa had just been announced, was also under pressure by the South African government, which was attempting to maneuver the upper hand in the upcoming Namibian elections.

McDougall saw to it that the aggression of the South African government towards Namibia was thwarted by the Southern Africa Project. She founded a new group called the Commission on Independence for Namibia that consisted of 31 distinguished policymakers from the community. She supervised the commission's monitoring of a UN-mandated system instituted to ensure ethical voting in the 1989 Namibian elections. Her efforts at securing a fair election were successful, as 96 percent of the people of Namibia cast their ballots. Discussing the success of the Southern Africa Project McDougall was quoted in the *Washington Post* as having said, "I would say we have been responsible for getting literally thousands of people out of jail. We helped to mount cases that challenged a lot of apartheid laws and caused many of them to be overturned.... We helped communities who were being forcibly removed to get legal counsel to resist, and a lot of them won."

The beginning of the 1990s found McDougall married to John Payton, a partner in the law firm of Wilmer, Cutler, and Pickering who went with McDougall to Africa to support her in her endeavors there. It also found her with even more challenging duties. Sanctions against South Africa, plus a rising red tide of anti-apartheid violence were now making majority rule in that country inevitable. With the prison release of South African political activist Nelson Mandela, McDougall began to spend long periods in South Africa, unraveling constitutional knots and helping to dismantle the hundreds of laws that had locked apartheid into place. Additionally, she was asked to join 15 other experts on the Independent Electoral Commission, that was given the task of supervising the country's first multiracial election process. The commission's duties varied widely, dealing with the logistics of setting up more than 150,000 voting booths and other electoral equipment nationwide, plus printing and transporting more than 80 million voting ballots from England. Communications projects were needed to persuade the country's estimated 22 million voters to come to the polls. Also, strategic methods needed to be designed to best ensure fairness in the election.

Not all South Africans were convinced the 1994 election would go smoothly. Primarily Zulu, the Inkatha Political Party, lead by Mangosuthu Gatsha Buthulezi, refused to take part in the elections until a scant five days before the polling began. Reasons for the boycott included a fear that, if the party lost the election to Nelson Mandela's African National Congress (ANC), the Zulu homelands would be abolished as prescribed by the new constitution, and Buthulezi's power would be removed. Despite the threatened boycott, and a wave of violence surrounding the political parties involved, McDougall remained confident. "We are committed to pulling off this election on April 26, 27, and 28," she said in *USA Today.* Her efforts were successful.

Conquered New Turf

After playing such a large role in setting South Africa firmly on its course towards majority rule, McDougall

began to focus her attention on other tragic corners of the world. In September of 1994, she accepted a new position as executive director of the International Human Rights Law Group (IHRLG), a Washington-based international advocacy organization devoted to helping frontline advocates protect human rights around the world. Under McDougall's direction, one of the IHRLG's initiatives involved monitoring the repressive military regime of Haiti and its subsequent U.S.-led occupation.

During her illustrious career, McDougall has practiced law before the U.S. District Court of the Southern District of New York, the U.S. Supreme Court, and the Court of Appeals of the State of New York. She has written numerous articles concerning human rights around the world and she has served on the board of such organizations as CARE, Africa Watch, the International Human Rights Law Group, and the Robert F. Kennedy Memorial Foundation. In 1990 the National Coalition of 100 Black Women presented McDougall with a Candace Award. In 1999 McDougall was one of 32 distinguished individuals who received MacArthur Fellowships. She received a $350,000 fellowship. According to *Jet* magazine, "The fellows are selected by the Chicago-based John D. and Catherine T. MacArthur Foundation, a private independent grant-making institution dedicated to helping groups and individuals foster lasting improvement in the human condition."

McDougall's IHRLG appointment was just one of the latest in a long list of accomplishments that have positively impacted the international human rights arena. Influenced early in her life by family members, as well as major civil rights activists, she developed quite a consciousness with regard to social issues. This sense of commitment has served her well during her career as advocate for those world citizens that have been forced to live under less than humane conditions.

Selected writings

Deaths in Detention and South Africa's Security Laws, Lawyers' Committee for Civil Rights Under Law, 1983.
Nambia: UN Resolution 435 and the Independence of Namibia, 1989.
South Africa's Death Squads, Lawyers' Committee for Civil Rights Under Law, 1990.

Sources

Books

Notable Black American Women, Book 2, Gale Research, 1996.
Writers Directory, 19th edition, St. James Press, 2003.

Periodicals

Jet, July 12, 1999, p. 6.
New Pittsburgh Courier, November 5, 1994, p. A2.
New York Amsterdam News, October 29, 1994, p. 22.
USA Today, March 31, 1994, p. 6A.
Washington Informer, November 9, 1994, p. 18.
Washington Post, December 7, 1989, p. B3., April 26, 1994, p. E1.

Other

Additional information for this biography was obtained from *Annual Report,* Southern Africa Project, 1979-80.

—Gillian Wolf and Catherine V. Donaldson

Frank Mercado-Valdes

1962—

Television executive

Once a Junior Olympic boxer and Golden Gloves Lightweight Champion, Frank Mercado-Valdes used guts, determination, and passion to turn his love for African-American cinema into The Heritage Networks (THN), the most powerful syndicate of ethnic television programming in the United States, and a company worth nearly one-half billion dollars. "As a business owner, I believe that if you simply transform that which you really have a lot of passion about and like into a workable plan for business and capitalism, you can do well," he told *Black Enterprise*. It is hard to argue with his success.

Sought Business Opportunities

Born on May 18, 1962, in New York, Frank Marcelino Mercado-Valdes was raised by his mother, Lidia Valdes, and her Cuban grandparents. His Puerto Rican father, Frank Mercado, was absent from the picture. At the age of 11, Mercado-Valdes and his mother left their tough South Bronx neighborhood for an equally tough barrio in Miami, Florida, where the young man ran into drug dealers, crime and gangs. "If you live in the ghetto, you can't avoid people like that," he told the *Knight-Ridder/Tribune Business News*. Yet Mercado-Valdes managed to stay out of trouble by throwing his own punches. In 1978 he became the Junior Olympic boxing champion of Florida and in 1979 gained the state's Golden Gloves Lightweight Championship. A year later he made it to the quarter-finals for the U.S. Olympic boxing trials. The boxing ring was good schooling for Mercado-Valdes. Years later he would tell

the *Network Journal,* "When I reflect on my career, it is the training I received as a competitive boxer that has led to my foundation as a businessman."

Mercado-Valdes did a two-year stint in the U.S. Marines beginning in 1980. After his military service he headed for Miami-Dade College, where he earned an associate's degree in 1983. The following year, with his sights set on becoming a lawyer, Mercado-Valdes enrolled in the University of Miami as a political science major. However, somewhere between his classes and his 1985 graduation, his plans to go to law school were shelved. Blame it on a beauty pageant. In 1984 he made up his mind to create the Miss Collegiate African-American Pageant. Local entrepreneurs helped sponsor the event, and it was quite successful. When several people suggested that it would do well on television, Mercado-Valdes's interest in media programming was aroused. After earning a bachelor's degree from the University of Miami in 1985, he moved back to New York where, as he recalled to *Black Enterprise,* "I didn't even have a personal checking account." But Mercado-Valdes was able to land his first big break when he was hired as a media coordinator for the 1988 Bush-Quayle presidential campaign. According to *Black Enterprise,* Mercado-Valdes became the "point man for black media."

Following his stint in the world of politics, Mercado-Valdes turned back to television and sought out syndication for his pageant. Using the determination that would come to characterize his future business dealings, Mercado-Valdes got his show on the air in 1990 and became the youngest African American to serve as

At a Glance . . .

Born Frank Marcelino Mercado-Valdes on May 18, 1962, in NY; son of Lidia Valdes and Frank Mercado. *Education:* Miami-Dade College, AA, 1983; University of Miami, BA, 1985. *Military Service:* U.S. Marine Corps, 1980-82.

Career: Bush/Quayle presidential campaign, media coordinator, 1988; The Heritage Networks (African Heritage Network), CEO, 1990–.

Memberships: National Association of Television Program Executives; African-American Film and Television Association; Golden Gloves of Florida Benefit Committee, 1987; Kappa Alpha Psi Scholarship Foundation, 1989-92; African-American Anti-Defamation Association, 1991–.

Awards: Junior Olympic Boxing Champion, FL, 1978; Golden Gloves Lightweight Champion, FL, 1979; *Black Enterprise,* one of the Top 50 Black Power Brokers In Entertainment, 2002.

Addresses: *Office*—The Heritage Networks, 50 Broadway, Suite 1003, New York, NY, 10004-3840.

executive producer of a television program. "Through this event I began to realize the economics of ethnic markets," he told *Entrepreneur Magazine.* He soon produced a second television special, *Stomp,* about the practice of stepping among black fraternities and sororities. But business turned sour, and within three years Mercado-Valdes was broke. For a time he was without a home, sleeping in the doorways of New York City. It was a dire time for Mercado-Valdes, and he even entertained thoughts of suicide. However, his old fighting spirit would not abandon him. Described by *Hollywood Reporter* as "one of those people who seems to be genetically wired to be an entrepreneur," it was not long before Mercado-Valdes was planning his next move.

Launched African Heritage Network

"I loved watching old black movies," he told *Black Enterprise,* "but I never could find any of them on local television." Nor on video store shelves. An idea began to form. If he could buy the syndication rights to films such as *Cotton Comes to Harlem, Porgy 'n Bess,* and *Shaft,* he could package them into a movie-of-the-month format and offer them to television stations in

African-American markets across the country. It would be a perfect sell to advertisers who wanted to reach those markets. Mercado-Valdes named his venture African Heritage Network, and set about the grueling task of making it real.

"Many studios didn't want to give up their product to an unknown company," Mercado-Valdes told *Black Enterprise.* "In fact, many of them have a general policy that says that they don't give up their projects to subdistributors who compete with them. So the first challenge for me was to convince them that I was not competing with them." To do that, he chose films that were at least 20 years old, knowing that competitors would not be interested in showing them. To finance the syndication deal, Mercado-Valdes relied heavily on a $350,000 loan from the Pro-Line Corporation, which had been an advertiser on the pageant program. He also did a lot of sweet-talking. "I had to convince them to go ahead and let me license the movie and that I would pay them when the time came, before the movie aired," he told *Black Enterprise.* It was not a problem for a man *Crain's New York Business* described as "the kind of guy who makes an impression very quickly." Thus, the African Heritage Network's "Movie of the Month" series, hosted by African-American screen legends Ossie Davis and Ruby Dee, was launched in 1993.

By the end of its first year, the African Heritage Network had films showing in 80 markets across the country, reaching 88 percent of all African-American households. It also generated $1 million in revenue. In 1994 the network served as executive producer of *A Tribute to Alex Haley,* a program highlighting the accomplishments of the author of *Roots.* The following year Mercado-Valdes's company had syndicated its movie package to more than 100 markets and had reached revenues of $8 million. It was only the beginning. "I am constantly thinking of the next idea," he told *Black Enterprise.* "If I have any skill or gift as an entrepreneur, it's that I never actually enjoy what's happening now. I'm always thinking about what could happen in the future."

Started Ethnic Television Empire

Mercado-Valdes's next coup came in 1996, when he successfully negotiated the weekend syndication rights of the popular police drama *New York Undercover.* With the $8.5 million purchase, the African Heritage Network made history, becoming the first minority-owned company to purchase a major network series for syndication. By 1998 Mercado-Valdes had sold the show to 140 stations across the country, with the expectation that it would boost the network's sales to $20 million over the next several years. By 2000 his predictions had come true. The company earned $35.5 million in revenue. It also earned syndication rights to another top television show, the comedy *Moesha.* The following year was dismal throughout the broadcasting industry, due to a recession and to the terrorist attacks of September 11 in New York City and Washington, D.C., but although the African Heritage Network lost millions of dollars, none of its 48 employees lost their jobs.

By 2002 Mercado-Valdes's entrepreneurial drive had pushed African Heritage Networks into original programming. Top shows under the network's banner included *The Source: All Access,* based on the popular hip-hop magazine, and *N'Gear,* a behind-the-scenes look at urban fashions, designers, and models. That same year the company changed its name to The Heritage Networks (THN). "It was a business decision based on who's watching our so-called black shows," Mercado-Valdes told *Black Enterprise.* "When we got into original programming ... we found very consistently that 40 to 50 percent of our audience was not black. So we realized that our name wasn't accurately reflecting the audience base, although it certainly reflected the cultural base upon which the programming was created." The change also positioned them to strike new deals with Hollywood heavyweights. One result was *Livin' Large,* a hip-hop version of *Lifestyles of the Rich and Famous,* produced in conjunction with the creators of *The Cosby Show.* "We are very fortunate because they don't do these types of partnerships very often," Mercado-Valdes told *Black Enterprise.* "But we came to them with the right idea at the right time."

Mercado-Valdes seemed to possess a knack for having the right idea at the right moment. By focusing on the African-American market, he was able to build the largest black-owned marketing, sales, and distribution company in broadcast television. "We're a company that has learned to succeed off of ratings that other people would starve on," he told *Hollywood Reporter.* That success rang in revenues of $61.5 million for the year 2002. It also launched Heritage 215 Entertainment, a Washington-based production company, and Alto-Marc Communications, a Mercado-Valdes-fronted specialty advertising sales group that he eventually merged with the distribution company of Baruch Entertainment. Meanwhile THN landed syndication rights to such popular programs as *The Steve Harvey Show, The Hughleys,* and *The Cosby Show.*

Focused on the Future

Mercado-Valdes had developed THN into a force to be reckoned with. Some high-powered media players in Harlem discovered this in 2003, when the entrepreneur wrested syndication and production control of the long-running *Showtime at the Apollo* from its original creators. Percy Sutton was considered an icon in Harlem for having restored the historic Apollo Theater and for creating *Showtime at the Apollo,* the country's number one syndicated show for black audiences. However, the Apollo Theater Foundation was not happy with the low profit margins they were seeing,

and when Sutton's contract came up in 1998, they sought out new syndicators. Mercado-Valdes stepped up, and found himself in the middle of a political war. There were many Sutton loyalists on the board of directors, and in the end Sutton was awarded the contract once again. Public outcry and a subsequent investigation by the district attorney resulted in an overhaul of the board. In 2002, when Sutton's contract expired once again, the foundation was determined to open bidding for the show to other contenders. Mercado-Valdes again emerged as the leader, but this time he had additional cash and clout to back him up, and eventually landed the contract on a one-year provisional trial. He told *Knight-Ridder/Tribune Business News* that, with the help of Emmy Award-winning producer Suzanne de Passe, they turned the show from a "Kmart to a Bergdorf Goodman." The theater saw higher profits as well. Yet Sutton was not ready to give up.

When Mercado-Valdes's original contract with the Apollo expired in 2003, Sutton was there. And like the champion boxer he was trained to be, Mercado-Valdes was also ready, this time with media heavyweight Warner Brothers on his side. THN soon landed a five-year contract, with the show expected to push the network's revenues up to $85 million. However, in typical fashion, Mercado-Valdes stayed focused on the future. According to *Black Enterprise,* "That future could include millions in advertising revenue and an extension of the Apollo brand that could eventually birth everything from CDs and Internet merchandising to TV programs." By the end of 2003 THN had penetrated 212 television markets across the country and Mercado-Valdes was considering branching out into cable, film production, and soundtracks. Considering his history of knock-outs in the television arena as well as his own burning ambition, there is little reason to doubt that Mercado-Valdes will one day no longer be known as an African-American media mogul, but rather as a media-mogul, period.

Sources

Periodicals

Black Enterprise, February 2001; January 2003.
Crain's New York Business, August 31, 1998, p. 9.
Hollywood Reporter, January 28, 2002, p. 12.
Knight Ridder/Tribune Business News, February 18, 2003.

On-line

"40 under 40," *Network Journal,* www.tnj.com/articless/tnjevent/40/mercado.html (December 23, 2003).
"African Heritage Movie Network Finds Niche," *Black Enterprise,* www.blackenterprise.com/Archiveopen.asp?source=/archive1997/08/0897-08.htm (December 23, 2003).

"Black Programming By Any Other Name," *Black Enterprise,* www.blackenterprise.com/Archiveopen .asp?source=/articles/01232002jj.html (December 23, 2003).

"Young Millionaires Part II," *Entrepreneur Magazine,* www.entrepreneur.com/mag/article/0,1539,2670 52----5-,00.html (December 23, 2003).

—Candace LaBalle

Laura W. Murphy

1955—

Organization executive

As director of the Washington, D.C., office of the American Civil Liberties Union (ACLU), Laura W. Murphy is responsible for implementing the goals of that organization in the American legislative arena. She works to mobilize the ACLU's national membership on civil liberties matters, supervises a 35-person staff, and generally serves as the organization's public face, appearing on television and radio discussion programs and writing opinion pieces for numerous publications. After the terrorist attacks of September 11, 2001, Murphy became a tireless defender of established civil liberties laws and practices, as they came under pressure from a presidential administration that was intent on expanding the powers of law enforcement and intelligence agencies.

Murphy was born on October 3, 1955, in Baltimore, Maryland. Her family background made her a natural for political activism. Her great-grandfather John Henry Murphy was an ex-slave who founded the *Afro-American* newspaper, on whose board of directors Murphy still sits. Her uncle George Murphy was a union organizer and an associate of the famed actor and activist Paul Robeson. Both of Murphy's parents ran for political office several times, and in 1970 her father, William H. Murphy, Sr., became the second African American in Baltimore to gain election to a judgeship, winning over a white incumbent. "I've been handing out literature since the age of 7," Murphy told *Ebony.* "My brother and I would take a block. He would be on one side of the street, and I would be on the other. I learned how to get over my shyness and just speak to adults in a way that would engage them at a very early age."

Dissatisfied with the educational conditions prevailing at local schools in Murphy's segregated South Baltimore neighborhood of Cherry Hill, her mother enrolled her in Pimlico Junior High School, on the city's northwest side, when she was 12 years old. At the time, Murphy was one of only a few African-American students in a heavily Jewish student body. The negative attitudes of her middle-class schoolmates toward the neighborhood where she grew up made a strong impression on Murphy. "I really got an education about class and how cruel Americans can be to their own countrymen, black and white," she told the Baltimore *Sun.* However, the change in environment didn't slow Murphy down scholastically. She graduated from Northwestern High School in 1972 at age 16 and entered Wellesley College in Massachusetts. Elite Wellesley presented Murphy with yet another set of new circumstances, but she continued to flourish, majoring in history and winning a summer internship in a Capitol Hill legislative office in Washington, D.C.

During that summer Murphy found her calling, when she discovered that she enjoyed the rough-and-tumble world of politics. "I loved the action," she told *Ebony.* "I loved the law-making process. I got to work on things that really affected people's lives." Murphy served as president of the Black Student Union at Wellesley and headed into the political world after her graduation in

At a Glance . . .

Born on October 3, 1955, in Baltimore, MD; daughter of Judge William H. and Madeline Murphy; divorced; children: Bertram M. Lee, Jr. *Education:* Wellesley College, BA, 1976.

Career: Office of Rep. Parren J. Mitchell, legislative assistant, 1976-77; office of Rep. Shirley Chisholm, legislative assistant, 1977-79; ACLU of Southern California, legislative representative, 1979-82; ACLU Foundation of Southern California, director of development, 1983-84; Mixner Scott Inc., project manager, 1984-87; office of California Assembly Speaker Willie Brown, chief of staff, 1986-87; Jesse Jackson presidential campaign, national finance director, 1987-88; private fundraising consultant, 1988-90; Washington, DC, mayor's office, tourism consultant, 1990-92; Government Office of Tourism, Washington, DC, director, 1992-93; ACLU, Washington, DC, office, director, 1993–.

Selected memberships: Leadership Conference on Civil Rights, 1993–; DC Committee to Promote Washington, acting chair, 1993-95; Public Defenders Service of Washington, board member, 1993-95.

Selected awards: ACLU, Washington Office, Human Rights Award, 1982; NAACP Black Women of Achievement Award, 1987; Washington, DC, mayor's office, Distinguished Public Service Award, 1994; Congressional Black Caucus, William L. Dawson Award, 1997.

Addresses: *Office*—American Civil Liberties Union, 122 Maryland Ave. NE, Washington, DC 20002.

1976. She moved to California and worked for several legislators, including the pioneering African-American U.S. Representative Shirley Chisholm, in the late 1970s. In 1979 she was hired by the California branch of the American Civil Liberties Union (ACLU) as a legislative aide, and she soon landed in the thick of the ultimately successful fight over the 1982 extension of the federal Voting Rights Act.

Murphy's next position was concerned with the financial underpinnings of activism. She took a position as development director for the ACLU Foundation of Southern California in 1983. In the late 1980s she moved on to other finance-oriented posts, after a stint in private industry and a two-year term as chief of staff to California Assembly Speaker and future San Francisco mayor Willie Brown. "So I learned the legislative process inside and out," she told *Ebony.* Murphy then moved into the national spotlight, as finance director for the presidential campaign of the Rev. Jesse Jackson in 1988, and subsequently worked as an independent fundraising consultant.

Divorced and with one son, Murphy moved to Washington and worked as a tourism consultant for the District of Columbia city government, becoming director of the city's tourism office in 1992. The following year she was named director of the ACLU's Washington office, merging the organizational and activist sides of her career. By 1998 her legislative prowess had been recognized by the congressional newsletter *Roll Call,* which named her one of the 50 most influential people in congressional politics. Murphy worked mostly behind the scenes, although after the 2000 elections she took a more visible role in opposing President George W. Bush's nomination of John Ashcroft as U.S. Attorney General. "It's not like throwing a bone to the religious right, it's like throwing a carcass," Murphy was quoted as saying on the *CNN* website.

It was the September 11, 2001, terrorist attacks in New York City and Washington, D.C., and their aftermath that presented Murphy with her greatest challenge, as the nation struggled to reconcile the constitutional guarantees of civil liberties with a new tight security environment. About three months after the attacks, Murphy responded to Attorney General Ashcroft's contention that the civil liberties community was aiding America's enemies. In a *CounterPunch* essay, she wrote that "free and robust debate is one of the main engines of social and political justice." Murphy became a familiar face on the talk show circuit, appearing on such programs as the *PBS News Hour with Jim Lehrer, NBC Nightly News,* and CNN's *Crossfire.* She also worked to broaden the ACLU's traditional civil liberties concerns, as the organization began to address such issues as racial profiling and immigrants' rights.

By 2003 Murphy was part of a reinvigorated civil liberties movement. The ACLU now numbered about 400,000 members, a new record, drawing a variety of new members from various ethnic groups and different parts of the political spectrum. Charismatic and energetic, Murphy could claim a share of the credit. She commanded respect from legislators of both major political parties, and her position as a bulwark against further erosion in civil liberties seemed a formidable one. "Rights are only as good as their reach to those in the minority," she told *Ebony.* "People in the majority don't need much protection. ... It's those dissenting voices, those going against popular opinion, who need the protection of the Bill of Rights."

Sources

Periodicals

Ebony, September 2003, p. 148.
Sun (Baltimore, MD), October 6, 2001, p. A10.

On-line

"Ashcroft's Jihad," *CounterPunch,* www.counter-punch.org/murphy1.html (December 29, 2003).
"Laura Murphy—Director of the DC Office of the ACLU," *American Civil Liberties Union,* http://archive.aclu.org/about/murphy.html (December 29, 2003).
"Liberals, Conservatives Clash on Bush's Nomination for Attorney General," *CNN,* www.cnn.com/2001/LAW/12/22/ashcroft.profiling.pol/ (December 29, 2003).

—James M. Manheim

António Agostinho Neto

1922-1979

Politician

António Agostinho Neto became Angola's first president in 1975, after one of the African continent's bloodiest and most protracted wars for independence. As head of the Movimento Popular de Libertação de Angola (MPLA) since the early 1960s, Neto, who died in 1979, led the struggle to break free from Portuguese colonial rule. Trained as a physician in Portugal as a young man, he was also a published poet whose *Times* of London obituary termed him "a man of outstanding intellectual abilities who took advantage of the opportunities offered by the colonial authorities to emerge as their principal opponent."

Neto was born on September 17, 1922, in Icolo-e-Bengo, in what was then known as Portuguese West Africa. Icolo-e-Bengo was located in an area called Catete, near Luanda, the capital city of this southwestern African land. His family was of Mbundu heritage, descendants of a once powerful kingdom that was brutally suppressed in 1902 by the Portuguese, who had established a lucrative economic presence in the area that dated back to 1575. Neto's father was a Methodist minister who headed a local church, and his mother taught at a kindergarten. In his teens, he was one of only a few African students admitted to the prestigious Liceu Salvador Carreia, a high school that educated the country's Portuguese elite. After high school, with his hopes to become a physician temporarily set aside, he worked for the government health services beginning in 1944. In 1947 he was offered a Methodist scholarship to study in Portugal, and enrolled at the University of Coimbra. Once there, he joined a group of students from African countries who opposed the entrenched dictatorship of António de Oliveira Salazar in Portugal.

Unlike many European countries in the post-World War II era, Portugal held on to its African colonies like Angola and Mozambique. The Salazar socialist regime formally declared Angola an overseas province in 1951, and made plans for a massive industrialization of the country. It did, however, attempt to extend more political rights to some native-born Angolans, granting *assimilado* status to a select few, which would provide full citizenship rights once educational credentials were submitted and an income level attained. Neto would eventually become one of the assimilado, who made up just one percent of Angola's six million blacks. But while still abroad, he began to write poetry that questioned Portuguese rule in Angola, and from there he took an increasing role in student demonstrations. He was jailed three times for participating in political rallies, but was so well-known that a group of Portuguese and African dissidents organized a petition drive for his release.

Neto earned a medical degree from the University of Lisbon in 1958, and returned to Angola with his Portuguese-born wife, Maria Eugénia da Silva. Outside Luanda, in the Museques slum area, he opened a medical practice in which, holding true to his political ideals, he treated all regardless of income. He also continued to write verse, and his first volume, *Colectânea de Poemas,* was published in 1961. Most of the poems were "despairing portraits of Africans under the colonial yoke," noted a *New York Times* report by Michael T. Kaufman. Not surprisingly, the

At a Glance . . .

Born on September 17, 1922, in Icolo-e-Bengo, Portuguese West Africa; died on September 10, 1979, in Moscow, Union of Soviet Socialist Republics; son of Agostinho Pedro (a clergyman) and Maria (a kindergarten teacher; maiden name, de Silva) Neto; married Maria Eugénia da Silva, 1958; children: one son, two daughters. *Education:* Attended University of Coimbra; University of Lisbon, MD, 1958. *Politics:* Marxist.

Career: Worked for Angolan government health services, 1944-47; poet and student activist in Lisbon and Coimbra, Portugal, 1950s; physician in Luanda, Angola, 1959-62; writer, 1961-79; Movimento Popular de Libertação de Angola, president, 1962-79; president of Angola, 1975-79.

poems landed him in trouble with colonial authorities, who declared them seditious, but Neto was already becoming a well-known figure in Luanda as well. Finally he was arrested at his office, and a crowd gathered in his home village. Soldiers fired when the crowd erupted, and some 30 people were killed. The incident was part of a much larger political foment that year, which the Portuguese harshly suppressed.

Neto was exiled to the Cape Verde Islands, and from there he was sent to Portugal, where he was placed under house arrest, before escaping to Morocco in 1962. He made his way to Zaire (now the Democratic Republic of the Congo), and in its capital, Kinshasa, he became involved in an Angolan exile group that sought political sovereignty for the country. Marxist in tone, the MPLA dated back to 1956 and had become popular with many middle-class Angolans who had been educated abroad, like Neto. He was quickly elected to lead the party.

Neto went back into Angola, and led the MPLA for the next twelve years during its struggle to gain independence for the country. The group's strategy involved guerrilla raids from outside the country by both MPLA units and those of the Front for the Liberation of Angola (FNLA). A third group, the União Nacional para a Independência Total de Angola (UNITA), emerged in 1966 to join the existing resistance movement. The leaders of all three groups, Neto included, sought help from Western and Communist nations, as well as other African countries, in order to obtain both funding and international sympathy for Angolans in their plight against Portuguese domination. Neto traveled to the Soviet Union in 1964, and to Cuba to seek

assistance from the government of Communist leader Fidel Castro.

By the early 1970s, Portugal's determination to hold onto Angola and other overseas provinces was forcing some 40 percent of its meager national budget into military expenditures. Widespread dissatisfaction inside Portugal itself finally helped end the Angolan war for independence, when a 1974 military coup in Lisbon brought down the dictatorship, and the new government declared a truce with the Angolan rebel groups. By late 1975, negotiations were concluded that finally granted Angola its independence, and the People's Republic of Angola was declared at midnight on November 11, 1975. Neto was sworn in as the country's first president on the same night.

Neto faced numerous obstacles in bringing peace to the newly independent country, ravaged after years of war that had decimated the countryside and cities. Within weeks, FNLA and UNITA forces had teamed up to fight the MPLA in what became a civil conflict that endured until 2002. Neto's MPLA government was recognized by the international community, however, and in a historic step he managed to gain admittance for Angola to the United Nations in 1977. He continued to seek help from Cuba, and Angola became a Cold War battleground for a time, with Communist nations funding the MPLA and Western powers and South Africa's apartheid government providing aid to the UNITA group.

Neto traveled once more to Moscow in 1979, to receive treatment for cancer. He died there on September 10, 1979. The sole volume of his poetry that has appeared in English translation is titled *Sacred Hope.*

Selected writings

Colectânea de Poemas (poems), Edição da Casa dos Estudantes du Império, 1961.
Sagrada esperanca (poems), Livraria Sa da Costa Editora, 1974, published as *Sacred Hope,* Marga Holness trans., Tanzania Publishing, 1974.
Poemas de Angola, Superbancas, 1976.

Sources

Books

Encyclopedia of World Biography, 2nd edition, Gale, 1998.

Periodicals

New York Times, December 23, 1975, p. 6; September 16, 1979, p. E3.
Times (London, England), January 11, 1977, p. 7; November 23, 1979, p. III.

On-line

"António Agostinho Neto," *Contemporary Authors Online,* reproduced in *Biography Resource Center,* http://galenet.galegroup.com/servlet/BioRC (December 16, 2003).

—Carol Brennan

Annetta Nunn

1959—

Police chief

In 1963 Birmingham, Alabama, made worldwide headlines as the site of some of the most vicious attacks of the civil rights movement, when notorious police chief Eugene "Bull" Connor unleashed attack dogs and fire hoses on protestors in an effort to enforce segregation. Connor also instructed his officers to look the other way as white-cloaked Ku Klux Klan members viciously beat black Birmingham residents. One of those members went so far as to toss a bomb into an African-American church, killing four young black girls who were attending Sunday school. Those living through this reign of terror could not have imagined that a successor to Connor's seat was in their very midsts—a four-year-old African-American girl named Annetta Watts Nunn. Yet, 40 years later, Nunn did just that, becoming the first African-American female to don the police chief's badge in Birmingham. A student of local history, Nunn brought to the position not only a reputation for dedicated crime fighting, but also a belief in her ability to change things for the better. After a stellar 23-year career spent on the Birmingham police force, Nunn's promotion was indeed well-deserved.

From Coal Miner's Daughter to Police Captain

A native of Birmingham, Nunn was born Annetta Watts in 1959, the daughter of a coal miner and a nurse. A dedicated student early on, Nunn graduated as class valedictorian from Jackson-Olin High School. She went on to study at the University of Alabama, where she majored in criminal justice and minored in history. After earning a bachelor of arts degree with the honors distinction of magna cum laude, she was commissioned as an officer in the Birmingham Police Department. The year was 1980 and the police department had just begun a massive minority recruitment campaign in response to a racial discrimination suit. As a result, Nunn had to endure suggestions that she had succeeded on the force only because of her skin color, accusations that were unfair considering the level of education she brought to the position. "When I took the job, I told people to judge me by my character, not by the color of my skin or by my sex," she told the *New York Times*. She then set about earning what *American Police Beat* called "a reputation for quietly getting things done."

At a Glance . . .

Born Annetta Watts in 1959, in Birmingham, AL; married Robert Nunn, Sr.; children: Robert Jr., Stephen. *Education:* University of Alabama, BA, criminal justice, 1980; graduate, FBI National Academy. *Religion:* Baptist.

Career: Birmingham Police Department, officer, 1980-83, sergeant, 1983-91, lieutenant, 1991-95, captain, 1995-2000, deputy chief, 2000-03, police chief, 2003–.

Memberships: Leadership Birmingham, member; Workshops, Inc., board of directors.

Awards: Drum Major For Justice award, 2003.

Addresses: *Office*—1710 1st Avenue North, Birmingham, AL, 35203.

Nunn's hard work steadily propelled her up the ranks in the police force. In 1983 she was promoted to sergeant. She became a lieutenant in 1991, and then a captain in 1995. Her ascent through the ranks was aided by her graduation from the FBI National Academy. During this time she married Robert Nunn, Sr., and gave birth to two sons. A devout Baptist, Nunn also became heavily involved with the work of her church, most notably through its choir. She also sang in the choir of the Alabama Christian Movement for Human Rights. Nunn's close alliance with the Baptist church has had an impact on the way she fights crime. "[Nunn] brings to her job a strong belief in the church's potential, and responsibility, for solving the social problems that breed crime," noted the *New York Times*. To that end, Nunn has recruited ministers from some of the most crime-ridden neighborhoods in Birmingham to step forward and help, urging them to offer job training and drug counseling, as well as alternatives to gang activity. "If people want to change, they need the resources. That's where the church comes in," she told *Essence*.

Her conviction proved right in 1997, when she was serving as a precinct captain in the north end of Birmingham. The mayor had proposed a city-wide goal of reducing crime by 15 percent. Nunn was the only precinct commander to meet—and exceed—that goal, cutting crime by 16 percent in her precinct. However, the gains did not always come easily. Many ministers refused to become involved out of fear. "People say to me, 'I can't get involved, because I'm afraid something may happen to me,'" Nunn told the *New York Times*.

"And I tell them, 'Thank God those who came 40 years before acted in spite of their fears, or we would not have the gains we have today.'"

Promoted to Police Chief

In March of 2000 Nunn continued her upward climb through Birmingham's police ranks, becoming the first African-American woman to serve as a deputy chief. In that role she headed up the department's Field Operations Bureau, a position she held until February of 2003, when Nunn was promoted to the position of police chief. In her new role she would become the first woman to head Birmingham's police department, and only the second African-American to hold that post. It was as if her life had come full circle. As a child she had borne witness to the racial intolerance of a police chief bent on keeping African Americans down. Now she wore that same badge, overseeing a police department that was "committed to serving all citizens and one another with dignity and respect," as she noted on the official *City of Birmingham* website.

Nunn's appointment drew nationwide news coverage in both the black and mainstream presses. Besides the historical significance of the fact that an African-American mother and Baptist choir singer was now occupying the seat once held by Bull Connor, the fact also remained that Nunn had earned her position during 23 years with the department. Birmingham's Mayor Bernard Kincaid, in an official press release on the *City of Birmingham* website, declared that "in naming a new chief, the first consideration was qualifications. Based on her education, her experience, and the level of respect she commands within the department, Chief Nunn was a natural choice...."

As the fanfare of Nunn's promotion quieted down, the new chief eagerly took on her job, including the management of more than 1,100 officers and employees and a $70 million annual budget. However, her real challenge lay not in the daily operations of the department but in the increasing problem of what she described to the *New York Times* as "the scourge of black-on-black violence."

Fought Crime Through Community Effort

In 2002 73 percent of Birmingham's 243,000 citizens were African-American, and the majority of the city's crime occurred amid this population. As chief of police, Nunn faced a rising homicide rate, with nearly all of the victims and most of those indicted being African American. "We are our own worst enemy," she told the *New York Times*. "My job would be much easier if we would stop killing each other, if we would stop stealing and burglarizing each other." In her efforts to combat this epidemic, Nunn turned once again to black churches and ministers, and implored local citizens to become involved. "The whole community must be involved in fighting crime," she told the London, England, *Sun*. "People must not only report crime and make sure their property is safe but also help clean up an area once crime has been eased there."

Nunn has also not been afraid to use hardball tactics, including a crackdown on drug crimes. "We practice zero tolerance but call it 100 percent enforcement," she told the *Sun*. "If you see a violation of any sort, however trivial, you take action immediately and enforce the law." Since Nunn's tenure began, arrests have increased and crime has decreased. In addition she has instituted new policies that reduce the amount of paperwork police officers must file, thus freeing them to spend more time on the streets.

Nunn's first six months in office were met with praise, from both local city leaders and from police units as far away as Birmingham, England, where Nunn was interviewed on her crime reduction efforts in August of 2003. However, she has also met with controversy. After the police shooting of a suspected criminal, several prominent Birmingham ministers—including the Rev. Abraham L. Woods, one of Birmingham's most revered civil rights leaders—publicly criticized the police department. Nunn turned the tables on the critics, asking why they chose to criticize a police officer when they had turned their backs at shootings committed by civilians in their own neighborhoods. Her fearlessness in the face of these powerful local leaders drew praise from her officers as well as the local community.

Sources

Periodicals

Ebony, August 2003, p. 10.
Essence, October 2003, p. 36.
Jet, March 3, 2003, p. 20.
New York Times, May 3, 2003.
Sun (London, England), August 27, 2003, p. 6.

On-line

"Birmingham, Alabama's Top Cop Brings Talent and a Sense of History to the Job," *American Police Beat,* www.apbweb.com/articles-z40.htm (December 23, 2003).
"Chief," *City of Birmingham Official Website,* www.informationbirmingham.com/police/chief.htm (December 23, 2003).
"Mayor Kincaid Taps Nunn as Birmingham's First Female Police Chief," *City of Birmingham Official Website,* www.informationbirmingham.com/press-rele/nunn.htm (December 23, 2003).

—Candace LaBalle

Ouattara

1957—

Painter

West African painter Ouattara has achieved an international reputation for works that combine African and Western themes, symbols, and materials. Incorporating found objects, ritual elements, and artifacts from popular culture, his paintings express the need for balance between technology and spirituality. "My vision," he stated in an interview in the catalog *West African Artists at the Venice Biennale,* "is not based only on a country or a continent. ... Even though I localize it to make it understood better, it's wider than that. It refers to the cosmos."

Raised With Traditions of Healing

Ouattara was born Ouattara Watts in 1957 in Abidjan, a modern multicultural city that is the capital of Ivory Coast. His father was trained as a Western surgeon but also practiced traditional African healing, and these traditions were central to the young artist's upbringing. The family spoke both French and the local language, Bambara; they also practiced a mix of various religions including Christianity, Islam, Judaism, and indigenous religions. As he explained to the catalog interviewer, Thomas McEvilley, "We tried everything, we believed in everything. That's voodoo. If you try Catholicism or Protestantism by itself in Africa it causes problems. So you mix them all with African traditional religion. ... My father was a shaman whose practice was based on a religion with the widest possible scope."

Though Ouattara attended formal schools from the age of six, his first education was the initiation school, or spirit school. This spiritual initiation, he told McEvilley,

began at age seven. "The spiritual school permits you to understand the world," he explained. "You are allowed a vision that is cosmic rather than a nationalistic or village-oriented one." His spiritual education included rituals and symbolic objects, such as the bullroarer that Ouattara still uses in his work. Even today, he noted, he still begins his work with a spiritual ceremony.

Indeed, Ouattara's art and his spirituality cannot be separated. His talent, he explained, was first recognized at his initiation ceremony when he created images used in the ritual. He loved to draw, and made works that he described to McEvilley as "very bizarre, very strange drawings, very mysterious, close to surrealism." With little art instruction at his French school, the boy pursued his talent at home, teaching himself from the African images around him and from the bits of Western popular culture—such as advertisements and cars—to which the city exposed him.

Studied in Paris

At age sixteen Ouattara, whose family expected him to complete his education and become a doctor, dropped out of school to focus on his art. His father disapproved, but let the young man continue with his paintings. During this period Ouattara also discovered books at Abidjan's French Cultural Center that introduced him to the work of such Western artists as Picasso. At age nineteen the young artist went to Paris, attracted by the city's rich artistic history and by the fact that Picasso and his group lived there.

At a Glance . . .

Born in 1957 in Abidjan, Ivory Coast. *Education:* Attended the Ecole des Beaux-Arts, Paris.

Career: Painter 1980s–.

Addresses: *Agent*—Gagosian Gallery, 980 Madison Ave., New York, NY 10021.

In Paris Ouattara studied at the Ecole des Beaux-Arts. He also went to museums to see the actual paintings whose reproductions in books had first interested him. He has cited Picasso, Miro, Brancusi, and Duchamp as particular influences on his own work from this time. Ouattara's early years in Paris were difficult. Though he worked steadily he was reluctant to show his work because he felt that it wasn't yet ready. "I needed to make a synthesis of everything I had learned in Africa and everything that I was learning in the West," he told McEvilley. "I had to assimilate it all." It took nine years before the artist had his first gallery show. The exhibit was widely reviewed, and Ouattara sold every piece. From then on, interest in his work grew.

In 1988 Ouattara met artist Jean-Michel Basquiat at the latter's exhibition in Paris. Basquiat asked to visit Ouattara's studio and was so impressed by what he saw that he bought the whole series of paintings, which he then showed to art dealers in New York City. At Basquiat's invitation Ouattara went to New York, where he had a group show in 1988 and a one-man show the following year. Since 1989 Ouattara has lived and worked in New York, but he also maintains homes in Paris and Abidjan.

"Inscriptions for the World to Discern"

Critics have found much to admire and debate in Ouattara's work. Many have noted the narrative elements in his pieces, which often include written words and printed material. As a writer in *St. James Guide to Black Artists* observed, "Words in Arabic, German, English, French, and other languages cut swaths in open fields of blue, yellow, and red." Found objects and symbolic artifacts, often of wood or metal, are also often attached to the surface of a work, adding complexity to its story. Indeed, according to the *St. James Guide,* Ouattara has described his works as "personal and spiritual documents filled with inscriptions for the world to discern." In an on-line article critic Christian Rattemeyer calls the paintings "messengers between the diverse cultures and societies of [the artist's] experience."

Ouattara often makes strong political references in his work. The painting "Nkroumah, Berlin, 1885," for example, bases its title on both the conference where European powers debated the division of Africa among them, and on Kwame Nkrouma, the first president of the first nation in Africa to achieve post-colonial independence that later became Ghana. "Dark Star" presents a skeleton drummer against a background of hundreds of handprints, footprints, and prints from Nike sneakers—a symbol of capitalism. "Untitled," as associate curator Dana Self observes in an exhibit catalog from Kemper Museum of Contemporary Art, can be seen as "a commentary on consumer culture and Africa's long and troubled history of slavery." As Self points out, the figures in the painting and their sack of coffee beans indicate colonial exploitation, but the fact that the coffee is labeled "naturally decaffeinated" suggests a more contemporary circumstance in which colonization "through economic dominance and penury is as destructive as slavery."

According to *New York Times* critic Holland Cotter, Ouattara's work grapples with the major question facing African art today: the conflict between traditional and modern approaches. "In the West," Cotter wrote, "'African' and 'modern' were mutually exclusive terms from the start. Modern meant movement, change, cities, technology, cultural adulthood. Africa meant stasis, timelessness, tribes, magic, and childlike naivete." To be authentic, in this view, African art had to be tribal, exotic. Yet modern African artists have refused to be limited by this view. Ouattara, for one, creates paintings that, as Cotter described them, "couch archaic-looking personal symbols in a suave modern style." In the view of *New York Times* critic Roberta Smith, Ouattara's works reveal both his African roots and more modernist "buoyant abstractions."

Ouattara emphasizes that his work does not posit spirituality only in Africa or technology only in the West. He sees spirituality as well as modernism in both worlds. But he does believe that spirituality is necessary to help humankind manage technology for good instead of destruction. In this sense, he believes, he is carrying on the healing traditions of his father and his native culture. As he told McEvilley, "When you talk about freedom, art is the liberator."

Sources

Books

St. James Guide to Black Artists, St. James Press (Detroit, MI), 1997.

Periodicals

Fusion: West African Artists at the Venice Biennale, Museum of African Art, 1992.
New York Times, February 17, 2002; May 10, 2002.

On-line

"Ouattara," *Culturebase,* www.culturebase.net (January 6, 2004).

"Ouattara," *Kemper Museum of Contemporary Art,* www.kemperart.org/exhibits/ (January 6, 2004).

—E. M. Shostak

Robert Parish

1953—

Professional basketball player

Robert Parish holds the distinction of playing in more games than any other player in the history of the National Basketball Association (NBA). In an outstanding career that spanned a record 21 seasons, Parish's remarkable endurance and skilled playing brought him numerous awards and four national NBA championship crowns. It also landed him in the Basketball Hall of Fame in what *Celtic Nation* called "the culmination of a career unparalleled in its length and unquestioned in its brilliance." Considering that Parish, after only four years of professional play, had seriously considered retiring, this was quite an achievement.

Coaxed into Playing Basketball by Coach

Robert Lee Parish was born on August 30, 1953, in Shreveport, Louisiana. Though he soon shot up to a gangly six-foot eight-inch junior high school student, Parish was not the least bit interested in basketball. He even admitted many years later to the *Boston Herald,* "I really didn't like basketball growing up." Parish focused instead on football, baseball, and track. Then

Coleman Kidd, the basketball coach at Union Junior High School, noticed Parish, and knew from his incredible height that he had potential on the court. Parish was not so sure. "[Coleman would] come to my house and take me to practice *every* day until I had to start showing up myself," Parish told the Shreveport, Louisiana, *Times.* "I give all the credit to him." However, Parish was far from the Hall-of-Famer he would become. He was uncoordinated and lacked confidence. Still, Kidd didn't give up on him. He gave Parish a basketball to practice with at home, and continued to nurture his skills. Parish continued to grow, topping out at seven-foot one-inch in height, and his skill on the court grew along with him. Parish started at Woodlawn High School in 1968, where he became a state champion. He was named All-American, All-State, All-District, and All-City in 1972. That same year he led his team to the state championships.

Colleges soon came calling, but Parish preferred to remain close to home, choosing to attend Shreveport's Centenary College. "The reason why I chose Centenary is because of their coaches," Parish told the *Times.* "I was very impressed with the coaches. They

At a Glance . . .

Born Robert Lee Parish on August 30, 1953, in Shreveport, LA; married Nancy Saad, early 1980s (divorced, 1990); one child. *Education:* Centenary College, Shreveport, LA, BA, 1976.

Career: Golden State Warriors, center, 1976-80; Boston Celtics, center, 1980-94; Charlotte Hornets, center, 1994-96; Chicago Bulls, center, 1996-97; USBL Maryland Mustangs, coach, 2000-01.

Awards: Centenary College, Freshman of the Year, 1972; World University Games, Gold Medallist, 1975; Louisiana Collegiate Player of the Year, 1974-76; nine-time NBA All-Star, 1981-87, 1990-91; four NBA championships, Boston Celtics, 1981, 1984, 1986, and Chicago Bulls, 1997; 50 greatest players in NBA history, 1996; USBL Coach of the Year, 2001; elected to Naismith Memorial Basketball Hall of Fame, 2003.

Addresses: *Office*—Chicago Bulls, 1901 W. Madison St, Chicago, IL 60612.

didn't try to sell me on the material things. They sold me on the school. That's what I was impressed with." Parish's decision was a coup for the small school. "It was critical for us to find someone talented but we also needed a good person to go with it, and Rob filled the bill," Centenary's former coach told the *Times*. "Rob allowed our program to really take off. We had lots and lots of packed houses in [our stadium] and he was the primary reason."

Parish took the court with the Centenary College team in 1972, and promptly began setting records for scoring and rebounding. He was named Freshman of the Year and Louisiana Collegiate Player of the Year three times in a row. In 1975 he was named captain and starting center for the U.S. Pan-Am team, and in 1976 *Sporting News* named him to their All-American team. In his senior year he led the nation in rebounds with an average of 15.4 rebounds per game. His efforts helped Centenary earn a spot in the top 25-ranked teams in the nation. They also made Parish a top draft choice for the 1976 NBA draft. However, Parish was never a player to seek the limelight for himself. He preferred winning. "He was very unselfish," one of Parish's college teammates told the *Times*. "If he didn't have a shot, he had a great outlet pass and would wing it back out to me."

Found Fame With Celtics

Following his graduation in 1976, Parish immediately went pro. The Golden State Warriors picked him up during the first round of the draft and made him their star player. It was a mistake. "He didn't fit into the Warrior system, which placed most of the scoring burden on the young seven-footer," wrote *Celtic Nation*. "He was regarded as a leading man, when his true calling was that of supporting actor." As a result, Parish floundered for four years with the team. It was a difficult time for Parish, and he was soon ready to give it up. "I was contemplating retiring because I was losing my passion for the game," he told the *Boston Herald*. "I didn't enjoy playing and the guys I played with were very selfish and individualistic. We weren't playing as a team, we weren't going anywhere, so I thought about giving it up." That all changed on June 9, 1980, when the Boston Celtics organized a trade that picked up not only Parish but top draft pick Kevin McHale. "Once I got traded, I felt rejuvenated, with a new lease on life," Parish told the *Boston Herald*. "It was a shot in the arm and I needed that. That change recharged my batteries."

Wearing jersey number 00, Parish became the Celtics' starting center and went on to make some impressive statistics his first year out, including 18.9 points and 9.5 rebounds per game. The *Boston Globe* noted that "Parish found the perfect atmosphere in which to blend, which had always been his idea of hoop nirvana. He could be himself, cede the spotlight, and go about his business." He did this very well, landing on the NBA All-Star team for 1981, and earning a spot on the All-Star team eight more times during his career. Meanwhile Parish would form, along with McHale and superstar Larry Bird, the formidable "Big Three" of the Boston Celtics. "We were focused, very professional and everything fell into place," Parish told the *Boston Herald*. "I came into my own as a player. We put our egos aside because the name on the front of the jersey was more important than the name on the back of the jersey." The strategy paid off and the powerhouse trio led the Celtics to 13 playoffs, nine Atlantic Division titles, and five trips to the NBA championships. They captured the title in three of those years, 1981, 1984, and 1986.

"It's hard for me to even believe how good we were," Parish later told the *NBA* website. "Some nights I'd be out there just kicking some guy's butt, really feeling it, and then I'd look over and see what Kevin was doing, and what Larry was doing, and I'd say, 'Man, this is something. This is special.'" Coaches and teammates had nothing but praise for Parish's on-court demeanor. "Robert was special because he knew his place on the team," Parish's former coach K.C. Jones told *Celtic Nation*. "He knew that there were only so many basketballs to go around, and that Larry and Kevin were going to get the majority of the shots. ... He just understood what was expected from him and he went out and did his job. Robert was awesome." Hall-of-Famer Bill Walton told the *NBA* website, "He's probably the best medium-range shooting big man in the history of the game."

Inducted to Hall of Fame

By 1994 Bird and McHale had retired and the Celtics' run at the top of the NBA was winding down. Though 40 years old, Parish was averaging 11.7 points and 7.3 rebounds per game, and still had a lot to contribute to the team. He has credited that energy to his off-court hobbies, including Tae Kwon Do, a martial arts discipline. "I did a lot of stretching and meditation and I think that's the reason I played so long," he told the *Boston Herald.* "The stretching and meditation did a lot to keep the body loose and relaxed. I had longevity, durability and dependability." In fact, during all his years of play, Parish never once suffered a serious injury. After the 1994 season came to a close, Parish decided to leave the Celtics and sign on as a free agent with the Charlotte Hornets, a new expansion team. He served two seasons as a reserve center with the team, and during a 1996 game he became the NBA's leader in number of games played, totalling 1,560, and surpassing the previous record-holder, NBA superstar Kareem Abdul-Jabbar. The high of this achievement was dampened by the dissolution of his decade-long marriage to Nancy Saad amid allegations of spousal abuse. Though the charges didn't hold, Parish was left with the first negative press of his stellar career.

In 1996 Parish was named by the NBA as one of the 50 greatest players of all time. In September of that same year, he made headlines again when he became the oldest player in the NBA to land another free agent contract, this time with the top-seated Chicago Bulls. He had been a professional basketball player for 20 years by that time, and became the first to launch into a 21st season. Though his role with the Bulls was described by the *Boston Globe* as that of a "bench warmer/guru," Parish played in 43 games during the 1996-97 season, starting three times. He also shared in the victory when the Bulls took home the 1997 NBA Championship. It was his fourth and final championship game.

With 1,611 games under his belt, Parish finally decided to hang up his uniform. A few days shy of his 44th birthday, he announced his retirement during an interview with ESPN. "I know in my heart that it's time to walk away," *Jet* quoted him as saying. "I'm just tired of it, not playing, but the other things like training camp." He added, "I'm going to miss all the players that I've played with." And with that he was gone. At his retirement Parish was 13th in the NBA in points with 23,334, sixth in rebounds with 14,715, sixth in blocked shots with 2,361, and eighth in field goals with

9,614. His record for most games played continued to stand through the end of 2003, as did records for most seasons played (21), most offensive rebounds (571), and most defensive rebounds (10,117). He was also second in playoff appearances and fourth in total playoff games played. In 2000 he enjoyed a stint as coach for the Maryland Mustangs of the United States Basketball League (USBL), and was named that league's Coach of the Year.

Parish enjoyed an amazing career, and was admired by basketball insiders, observers, and fans alike. "Robert is an extraordinary individual, a unique person who will go down as one of the greatest centers to ever play the game of basketball," a former teammate told *Celtic Nation.* In September of 2003, the Naismith Memorial Basketball Hall of Fame agreed with this assessment and inducted Parish into their revered ranks. "I was never one to be conscious of single awards but this has got to be the ultimate single award there is," Parish told the *Boston Herald.* "This is just a very humbling day for me. I am truly flattered and honored by this." In the Hall of Fame he joined former teammates Bird and McHale, and "The Big Three" were together again. It was a fitting end to his career. As Parish told the *NBA* website, "I will always be a Celtic at heart."

Sources

Periodicals

Boston Herald, April 8, 2003, p. 90; September 6, 2003, p. 46.
Jet, September 15, 1997, p. 46.
Times (Shreveport, LA), April 13, 2003, p. 8, p. 16; September 5, 2003, p. A1; September 6, 2003, p. C5.

On-line

"Chief Achieves Fame in Boston," *Boston Globe,* www.boston.com/sports/basketball/celtics/articles/2003/09/07/chief_achieves_fame_in_boston/ (December 23, 2003).

"Chief Appointment," *Celtic Nation,* www.celtic-nation.com/news/2003_2004_news/08_19_2003_chief_appointment.htm (December 23, 2003).

"Chief Gets His Due," *Celtic Nation,* www.celtic-nation.com/news/2003_2004_news/09_07_2003_chief_gets_his_due.htm (December 23, 2003).

"Robert Lee Parish," *NBA Website,* www.nba.com/history/players/parish_bio.html (December 23, 2003).

"Robert Parish, Hall of Famers," *Naismith Memorial Basketball Hall of Fame,* www.hoophall.com/halloffamers/parish_robert.htm (December 23, 2003).

—Candace LaBalle

Lenrie Peters

1932—

Poet, author, surgeon

Lenrie Peters is considered to be one of the most original of modern African poets, as well as one of the most intellectual. He is a member of the founding generation of African poets writing in English, and is a pioneer of Gambian literature in English. He has written three critically acclaimed collections of poetry and a novel, published in the 1960s and 1970s. His subject matter is wide-ranging but centers on the past, the post-colonial present, and the precarious future of the African continent. Peters is a Pan-Africanist, concerned with the African continent as a whole, rather than with tribal or national affiliations. The imagery and metaphors in his writings draw heavily on his background in science and medicine.

Educated in England

Lenrie Leopold Wilfrid Peters was born on September 1, 1932, in Bathurst (now Banjul), Gambia, to parents from a privileged background. His father, Lenrie Peters, had studied Greek and Latin at the Fourah Bay College of the University of Sierra Leone. He worked as an accountant at the import-export firm of S. Madi Ltd., and edited a weekly newspaper, the *Gambia Echo*. Peters's mother, Keziah Peters, had been raised in England. Both parents were Anglicans who had emigrated from Sierra Leone and met and married in Gambia. The Peters family was among the most highly respected families in the country. Peters had four sisters: Bijou became a nurse and a journalist, Florence Mahoney became a distinguished historian, Ruby retired as a United Nations administrator, and, prior to

her death, his sister Alaba was prominent in business and the film industry.

The Peters family also nurtured their young son's intellectual interests. Peters attended St. Mary's Primary School and the Methodist Boys' High School in Bathurst. In 1949 he entered a two-year science program at the Prince of Wales School in Freetown, Sierra Leone, where he earned his higher school certificate.

Moving to England, Peters studied Latin and physics at the Cambridge Technical College. In 1953 he began studying natural sciences at Trinity College, Cambridge, graduating with honors in 1955. As an undergraduate, Peters was elected president of the African Students' Union at Cambridge. In an interview with the *Africa News Service,* Peters explained why he became a doctor: "Strangely enough when I was a young man there were only two professions that were acceptable. One was Medicine, the other was Law. People used to say I would be a doctor and I sort of inherited that concept." Peters trained at the University College Hospital in London, earning an M.D. degree in 1959. He completed an advanced course in surgery in Guildford, England, in 1967, and practiced surgery at Northampton General Hospital.

During his years in England, Peters worked as a freelance broadcaster for the African Service and the World Service of the British Broadcasting Corporation (BBC). Among other BBC radio broadcasts, he hosted *African Forum* and *Calling West Africa.* Peters also sang in various amateur musicals and operas, and musical rhythms became integral to his later free-form verse. He met his English wife, Rosemary, while performing in an opera for which she was the pianist. They divorced in the late 1960s after two years of marriage.

Began Writing at Cambridge

Even as an undergraduate at Cambridge, Peters was determined to become a writer as well as a physician. While still in school he wrote poetry and plays and began a novel, *The Second Round*, which was pub-lished in 1965. The book is a semi-autobiographical novel about a young doctor who, after years of studying and practicing medicine in England, returns to Free-town, Sierra Leone. Both he and Africa have changed and he finds himself alienated from his native culture and from African society.

Early reviews of the *The Second Round* were mixed, and the novel fell into neglect, at least among African readers. Unlike much African fiction of the 1960s, *The Second Round* was not focused on African culture and tradition, nor was it a protest against colonialism. In fact, Peters was one of the first African novelists to criticize his own country and the decline of its culture.

Critics of the book complained that it focused on individuals rather than African society, and used poetic language to convey his characters' emotions. In particular, Peters appeared to portray male-female relationships in a westernized context, and some critics claimed that he sounded more British than African. In his book *The Emergence of African Fiction*, Charles R. Larsen wrote, "The problem is apparently that there is a more heightened demand being placed on black artists that their work be a frontal attack on the race situation as it involves them—depending on their culture—that is, protest, and protest in a manner which may be appreciated by the masses." However, Larsen felt that "Peters has simply written the first African horror story, the first African Gothic novel."

Poems Expressed African Themes

Peters's first collection of 33 poems was published in Ibadan, Nigeria, in 1964. These were primarily poems of youthful love and melancholy, lacking the irony and anger of his later work. Nevertheless, they expressed the grief, loneliness, and hopelessness of exiled Africans who were alienated from both traditional African and modern western cultures.

Peters's poetry, much of which deals directly with African themes, has been taken more seriously than was his novel. *Satellites,* published in London in 1967, included 21 poems from his first collection, as well as 34 new poems. In contrast to the post-colonial optimism of many writers from newly independent African nations, Peters's poems expressed themes that were pessimistic and bleak.

According to Peters, colonialism, westernization, and corrupt African politicians have destroyed the African soul. In an unpublished 1976 essay, quoted by Romanus N. Egudu in *New West African Literature,* Peters wrote, "Africa has slept too long at the geographical centre of the world, a mere plaything eternally castrated." One poem in *Satellites* opens with, "Wings my ancestors used/to fly from oppression, slavery/tincture of skin, arid birth and death/hang limp on my shoulders/with guilt of the oppressor."

Returned to Gambia

British colonial rule of Gambia ended in 1965. Peters returned to the Gambian capital of Banjul in 1969, to practice surgery as a government employee at the Bansang Hospital. In 1972 Peters and a partner, Dr. Samuel J. Palmer, opened the Westfield Clinic in Kanifing, the nation's first private medical clinic.

Katchikali, a collection of 69 poems, appeared in 1971. The poems in the book address the modern human condition and world problems as they relate to Africa. Katchikali is the Gambian god of fertility, procreation, and protection. In the title poem, the powers of Katchikali, symbolizing the African cultural heritage, are undermined and finally destroyed by colonialism, and by the new black elite, development, and tourism. "But the new people do not understand/will not understand Katchikali/and all the institutions crumble.//As the mud hut crumbles/withers, all is base/seething self-interest and corruption/and the demon of gain/in your waters Katchikali."

Peters's poetry is full of medical and scientific imagery. A poem in *Katchikali* begins, "Love is juxtaposed to the Ego,/competes with the Ego;/stands between it and life/like a dark photographic screen, inverted;/ ... nibbles at resistance with haze of spectroscopic light." In a poem that begins, "I am thinking about time;" Peters wrote, "An infant thrusts an organ/at me for circumcision—/mother would have it deprived./The anaesthetist reads his comics,/other eye asleep./This serious business of living/makes the flesh creep."

Selected Poetry Included Best Work

The publication of *Selected Poetry* in 1981 was considered to be a milestone in the development of African literature. The collection included 48 new poems, as well as poems from *Satellites* and *Katchikali.* In his new poems Peters attempts to integrate traditional African culture and a hopeful future into the shattered present of post-colonial Africa. Peters has remained a Pan-Africanist, addressing issues of disunity and instability within and among African nations, and focusing on the problems of underdevelopment and social injustice and the need for original, African-based solutions.

In Poem 85 of *Selected Poetry* Peters writes: "I shout beating my fist/against the foreign gates/of your conscience./ ... as all fall to their knees/not in supplication/but in anger and despair/against injustice and oppression/outside and within their ranks;/against the schism where union is blessed/fanatics of tribe, cast, religion;/against blank indolence, incompetence."

In Poem 76 Peters writes of his search for his African identity, with reference to Alex Haley, the American author of *Roots:* "The first Africa/the early dawn/of ancestral Gods/and naming ceremonies/of ritual sacrifice/and burial rites/are lost even to me for good/irrecoverable!//My two faces/move sideways/groping for identity/or re-identity/with group or tribe/from tribe to tribe/nation to nation/continent to continent/world among worlds.//How much more so/for you Mr. Haley/with wall-street/hammering in your brain/moon-flights in your dreams." The Gambian poet and writer Tijan M. Sallah, in his essay "The Dreams of Katchikali," quoted a speech by Peters given at the Berlin Horizon Conference on World Cultures: "My family has been detribalized for several generations. I am like Alex Haley. I am searching for my roots." Other references to America in *Selected Poetry* include the vitality of New Orleans jazz, the crassness and obscenity of Las Vegas, the Ku Klux Klan, and the destruction of native American cultures.

Over the years Peters has contributed to numerous anthologies, periodicals, and professional journals. His work has appeared in the *African Literature Association Magazine, Afro-Asian Magazine, Black Orpheus, Presence Africaine, Prism,* and the *Transatlantic Review,* among other publications. He has encouraged and inspired young Gambian writers and was the founding editor of *Ndanaan,* a literary magazine published by the Gambian Writers Club between 1971 and 1976. Peters's satiric monologue, "The Local Party Secretary," was performed in 2001.

Worked to Improve Gambia

From 1981 until 1999 Lenrie served as chair and chief executive of Farato Farms Export Ltd. This company grew Irish potatoes for the local market and exported vegetables and mangoes to the United Kingdom. In 1994 Yahya Jammeh took power in Gambia in a military coup. He appointed Peters as chairman of the National Consultative Committee (NCC), which Jammeh hoped would reinforce his demand for a four-year transition period to constitutional democracy. In January of 1995, less than two months after its formation, the NCC submitted its report. Contrary to Jammeh's hopes, the NCC called for a transitional civilian government with elections to be held in two years' time.

When asked how he would like to be remembered by society, Peters told the *Africa News Service,* "If they remember me at all it's just that I try to do the best things to help the people of The Gambia and to leave the world a better place than I found it."

Selected writings

Fiction

The Second Round, Heinemann, 1965.

Poetry

Poems, Mbari Press, 1964.
Satellites, Heinemann, 1967.

Katchikali, Heinemann, 1971.
Selected Poetry, Heinemann, 1981.

Other

"Qua Vadis Africa: No More Executive Presidents in Africa" (article), *Africa News,* May 7, 2001.

Sources

Books

Contemporary Poets, 7th ed., St. James, 2001.
Dictionary of Literary Biography, Volume 117: Twentieth-Century Caribbean and Black African Writers, First Series, Gale, 1992, pp. 252-257.
Egudu, Romanus N., in *New West African Literature,* Ogungbesan, Kolawole, ed., Heinemann, 1979, pp. 60-70.
Larson, Charles R., *The Emergence of African Fiction,* Indiana University Press, 1971, pp. 227-241.

Periodicals

Africa News Service, February 2, 2001.

On-line

"Dreams of Katchikali: The Challenge of a Gambian National Literature," *University of Berne (Switzerland) Dept. English,* www.cx.unibe.ch/ens/cg/africanfiction/gambia/sallah/sallah.html (December 20, 2003).
"Lenrie (Leopold Wilfred) Peters," *Biography Resource Center,* www.galenet.com/servlet/BioRC (November 16, 2003).
"Passionate Spaces: African Literature and the Post-Colonial Context," *Murdoch University (Perth, Australia),* www.mcc.murdock.edu.au/ReadingRoom/listserv/Webb/contents.html (November 19, 2003).

—Margaret Alic

Margaret and Matilda Roumania Peters

Tennis players, teachers

Professional women's tennis has not had many African-American players, let alone champions. Althea Gibson made history as the first African-American woman to play against whites and she went on to win six Grand Slam championships in the 1950s. In 1990 Zina Garrison was the next African-American woman to succeed Gibson as a finalist at the prestigious Wimbledon championship. In 1999 history was made again when Serena Williams became the first African-American woman to win the U.S. Open since Gibson. Since then Serena and her older sister Venus have been dominating women's tennis in both the singles and the doubles competitions. However, they were not the first African-American siblings to succeed at the game of tennis.

Decades before Venus and Serena Williams overpowered the sport, two other talented African-American women changed the face of women's tennis. Margaret and Matilda Peters, affectionately known as "Pete" and "Repeat" Peters, made history with their doubles record from the 1930s to the 1950s. At a time when African Americans were not allowed to compete against whites, the Peters sisters played in the American Tennis Association, which was created specifically to give blacks a forum to play tennis competitively.

Margaret Peters was born in 1915 in Washington, D.C., and Matilda Roumania Peters was born two years later in the same city. The girls began playing tennis for fun when Margaret was about ten years old. They played in a park across from their home in Georgetown. They began to play competitively when they were teenagers in the 1930s. The Peters sisters played for the American Tennis Association (ATA), which was created in 1916 to organize Negro Tennis Clubs across the country and to provide competitions for African-American tennis players.

At that time tennis, like most other sports, was segregated so African Americans were not allowed to compete against whites. Prior to the ATA, African-American tennis players could only participate in invitational and interstate tournaments. At one such event in New York in 1916 the organizers came up with the idea of a national association for African-American tennis players. The ATA was officially formed on November 30, 1916, in Washington, D.C. The first tournament sponsored by the ATA did not even offer a competition for women's doubles. The 1917 national championship tournament in Baltimore

At a Glance . . .

Born Margaret Peters in 1915 in Washington, DC; born Matilda Roumania Peters in 1917 in Washington, DC; *Matilda:* died on May 16, 2003, in Washington, DC; *Matilda:* married James Walker, 1957; children: Frances Della, James George. *Education: Margaret:* Tuskegee University, BS in physical education, 1941; New York University, MS in physical education; *Matilda:* Tuskegee University, BS in physical education, 1941; New York University, MS in physical education.

Career: Tennis players, 1935-1953; teachers 1941-1981.

Memberships: American Tennis Association.

Awards: Tuskegee Hall of Fame, 1997; USTA Achievement Award, 2003; USTA Mid-Atlantic Section Hall of Fame, 2003.

only had three events, which were men's singles, women's singles, and men's doubles.

In 1935 Margaret Peters was offered a full scholarship to attend Tuskegee University. She had been recruited by the athletic director Cleveland Leigh Abbott, who noticed her playing in the ATA. Margaret was reluctant to leave her family in Washington, D.C., so she waited for Matilda to finish high school and then the two sisters went to Tuskegee in 1937. They both graduated from college in 1941 with degrees in physical education. The sisters then moved to New York where they earned master's degrees in physical education from New York University.

During and after college, the Peters sisters dominated the ATA. Between 1938-1941 and 1944-1953 they won 14 ATA doubles championships, a record which has not yet been broken. As of 2003 Venus and Serena Williams have won ten Women's Tennis Association (WTA) doubles titles together. Matilda Peters also won two singles ATA titles in 1944 and 1946. For the second title she defeated the legendary Althea Gibson. Gibson later went on to make history of her own when she became the first African-American woman to play competitive tennis against whites in 1950. This was exactly a decade after Jimmy McDaniel became the first African-American man to play against a white man, tennis legend Don Budge, at a match held in New York.

The sisters played mainly on clay courts and many of their matches were held in the evenings under flood-

lights. They were known for their slice serves, strong backhands, and quick chop shots. They traveled to regional and national ATA tournaments, which were usually held at black colleges across the country. Despite their successes on the court, the Peters sisters did not make a living from tennis. At that time tennis was an amateur sport. Not only did the players receive no compensation, but they also had to pay for their own equipment and travel expenses. In order to continue funding their tennis careers, the Peters sisters got teaching certificates and worked as teachers.

Both Margaret and Matilda lived in Washington, D.C., during their ATA and teaching careers. Margaret never married and had a career as a special education teacher. Matilda married James Walker in 1957. He was a math professor at Tuskegee University and he died in 1992. They had two children together, a daughter named Frances Della and a son named James George. Matilda also worked as a teacher. In the 1950s she taught at Howard University and from 1964 to 1981 she taught for the Washington, D.C., public school system. For many years she worked at Dunbar High School. She also directed tennis camps for the department of recreation to expose underprivileged children to the game.

During their reign as ATA champions, the Peters sisters were quite famous. They were often asked to pose for publicity photographs and they even played exhibition matches for English royalty. Compared to the other successful African-American women tennis players such as Althea Gibson and the Williams sisters, the Peters sisters had not received much recognition for their accomplishments. However, there has been some renewed interest in their role in tennis history. In 1977 the Peters sisters were inducted into the Tuskegee Hall of Fame. In 2003 they were given an achievement award by the United States Tennis Association (USTA) and inducted into the USTA's Mid-Atlantic Section Hall of Fame. Matilda Peters died on May 16, 2003, from pneumonia. Margaret Peters is 88 years old and suffers from Alzheimer's disease.

Sources

Periodicals

Black Issues in Higher Education, August 28, 2003.
Jet, September 8, 2003.
Washington Post, May 21, 2003.

On-line

"Know Your History and Grow," *American Tennis Association,* www.atanational.com/about.htm (January 4, 2004).
"Legendary Tuskegee Tennis Titans To Be Honored at Federation Cup (July 9, 2003)," *Onnidan Online,* www.onnidan.com/03-04/news/july/tusk0709.htm (January 4, 2004).

"Trailblazing Sisters Finally Recognized (July 19, 2003)," *News-Star,* www.news-star.com/stories/ 071903/spo_38.shtml (January 4, 2004).

—Janet P. Stamatel

Willa B. Player

1909-2003

College president, administrator, educator

The first African-American woman to become president of a four-year college in the United States, Willa B. Player was a quiet but crucial contributor to the struggle for civil rights in the South. When students at Bennett College, the North Carolina school she presided over for ten years in the 1950s and 1960s, were jailed during lunch counter sit-ins, Player brought their assignments to their jail cells, insuring that their studies would not be interrupted. Widely known for her bold decision to host an important early speech by the Rev. Martin Luther King, Jr., Player served as an inspiration to several generations of female students during her 35-year career at Bennett.

The youngest of three children, Willa Beatrice Player was born on August 9, 1909, in Jackson, Mississippi. The Player family moved north to Akron, Ohio, in 1916 or 1917, and as a teenager Willa was actively involved with the Methodist church the family attended. She reaped rewards for the hours she spent in the church's youth choir, for her church involvement opened up one of the few paths to a college education available to a black woman at the time. After graduating from Akron's West High School, Player was accepted at Ohio Wesleyan University in Delaware, Ohio,

a Methodist school. She was one of three black students who, because of their race, were not permitted to stay in campus dormitories.

Player graduated from Ohio Wesleyan in 1929 and earned a master's degree at Oberlin College the following year. From there, the 21-year-old Player was hired to teach French and Latin at Bennett College in Greensboro, North Carolina, a new Methodist-affiliated school oriented toward the education of African-American women. She would spend most of her career at Bennett, rising through the college's administrative hierarchy and holding the posts of director of admissions, dean, coordinator of instruction, and vice president. She added to her educational credentials, studying on a Fulbright fellowship in France in 1935, doing graduate work at the Universities of Chicago and Wisconsin, and earning a doctorate in education from Columbia University in 1948.

In 1956 she was named Bennett's president, becoming the first black woman president of a four-year college in the United States. Player herself didn't focus on the historic nature of the appointment. "All I was thinking was that I had a job to do," she said in an interview

At a Glance . . .

Born on August 9, 1909, in Jackson, MS; died on August 27, 2003, in Greensboro, NC. *Education:* Ohio Wesleyan University, BA; Oberlin College, MA; University of Grenoble, France, post graduate studies; University of Chicago, post-graduate studies; University of Wisconsin, post graduate studies; Columbia University, PhD, education, 1948.

Career: Bennett College, Greensboro, NC, instructor in Latin and French, 1930-1940s, director of admissions, dean, coordinator of instruction, and vice president, 1940s-1950s, president, 1956-66; Division of College Support, Department of Education, Washington, DC, director, 1966-77; higher education consultant and lecturer, 1970s-1990s.

Selected awards: Ford Fellowship for study tour of 12 colleges and universities in United States; Frank Ross Chambers Fellow, Columbia University, 1948; numerous honorary doctorates.

quoted in *Notable Black American Women.* To students at Bennett, Player was an inspiring and even awesome figure. Elegantly dressed and commanding in manner, Player took a personal interest in student life. "Many nights, as students lingered by the magnolias saying goodbye to their dates, a quiet figure passed by," Bennett alumna Mary Ann Scarlette recalled to the Greensboro *News & Record.* Player raised Bennett's academic profile, and the institution became one of the first historically black schools to win accreditation from the Southern Association of Colleges and Schools.

The changes that were beginning to stir in the South in the late 1950s thrust Player into a critical position. In 1958 a proposed appearance by the Rev. Martin Luther King, Jr. to the Greensboro area carried with it the possibility of violent retaliation by terrorist elements of the Southern white population, and no organization in Greensboro seemed willing to take the chance of playing host to the famous activist. Player, however, organized a campus appearance by King, arguing, as quoted by the *News & Record,* "Bennett College is a liberal arts school where freedom rings, so Martin Luther King Jr. can speak here." Player herself later ranked King's visit as one of the key moments in the college's history.

King's speech at Bennett helped make central North Carolina a focal point for the growing civil rights movement. In 1960 students from nearby North Caro-

lina A&T University organized a sit-in aimed at desegregating a downtown Greensboro Woolworth's lunch counter. The students were quickly joined in similar protests by Bennett students who, though not urged on by Player, received her unequivocal support. Asked by city leaders to order the students back to campus, Player's niece Linda Brown recalled in a *Winston-Salem Journal* interview that Player responded, "We don't teach our students what to think. We teach them how to think. If I have to give exams in jail, that's what I'll do."

Player made good on that promise, when up to 40 percent of Bennett's students were jailed at various times. Students remembered that Player visited them in jail and on protest picket lines, negotiated on their behalf for better treatment, and made sure that their educational careers were not interrupted. Current Bennett president Johnnetta Cole told the *News & Record* that Player played a "quiet but piercingly effective role in the struggle for civil rights in Greensboro ... She was incapable of being ordinary."

Player retired from Bennett's presidency in 1966 to take a position in the federal Department of Education under President Lyndon Johnson. As director of the Division of College Support she was instrumental in directing increased financial support toward historically underfunded black colleges through a program called Strengthening Developing Institutions. In later life, Player moved back to Akron for a time and remained active on numerous church and educational advisory boards. She was the recipient of numerous honorary degrees and was named to the Ohio Women's Hall of Fame in 1984. She never married. According to the *Akron Beacon-Journal,* Player remarked to a friend, "I didn't have time for men. I was too busy educating the youth."

Player understood that the gains made by black women over the years did not mean they had achieved equality in society. According to the *Akron Beacon-Journal,* she remarked in a 1985 speech in Wooster, Ohio, that "the black woman is expected to be a superwoman without acting like one." Player suffered a stroke in 1995 and died in Greensboro on August 27, 2003, at the age of 94. Looking back on her own accomplishments in a 1997 interview quoted by the *News & Record,* Player recalled the straightforward energy with which she had approached every problem she had encountered over her career: "There were people who said, 'How did that one lone little woman do this?'. ... I wonder how I ever did it without being afraid, but it never occurred to me to be afraid."

Sources

Books

Smith, Jessie Carney, ed., *Notable Black American Women,* Book 1, Gale, 1992.

Periodicals

Akron Beacon-Journal, November 29, 2003.
News & Record (Piedmont Triad, NC), August 28, 2003,p. B1; August 29, 2003, p. A16; September 5, 2003, p. B1.
New York Times, August 30, 2003, p. B7.
Winston-Salem Journal, August 28, 2003, p. B1.

—James M. Manheim

John Shippen

1879-1968

Professional golfer

When he was born in 1879, there was no reason to think that John Matthew Shippen, Jr. would ever become the first golf professional to be born in the Unites States. In a family of well-educated and degreed professionals, Shippen would ignore the family focus on education and would instead become the first African American to play golf. Equally importantly, and in an elitist sport where golfers were either British or Scottish, Shippen would become the first American player to compete in a U.S. Open tournament. Shippen was neither educated or born to privilege, but he did have a natural talent for the game of golf.

Shippen was the fourth of the nine children born to John Shippen, Sr., and Eliza Spotswood Shippen on December 5, 1879, in Washington, D.C. At the time of Shippen's birth, the family lived in the Hillsdale section of Anacostia, Maryland, just outside Washington, D.C. His parents valued the privileged education in their lives, and even though his father had received a certificate of education that permitted him to teach school, which he did at the elementary level, he returned to school in an effort to better provide for his family. Shippen's father received a degree in theology from Howard University, and when Shippen was just four years old, the family moved to Fayetteville, Arkansas, for the first of the elder Shippen's church positions. The next move took the family to Florence, Alabama, where they lived for the next few years. By the time Shippen was nine years old, the family was again on the move when in 1889 his father was assigned as pastor to the Presbyterian mission on the Shinnecock Indian reservation in Southampton on New York's Long Island.

Began Golfing Early

Shippen spent the remainder of his childhood on the Shinnecock reservation, where he attended school and played with his classmates. When Shippen was 12 years old, a nearby piece of land was purchased and developed into a premier golf course that was designed to rival the famous British courses that were then the model of excellence in the golfing world. Shippen was one of the many young boys who were hired to help clear the land and construct the course. By 1895 the new course was nearing completion, and soon a Scottish golfer named Willie Dunn arrived to oversee the completion of the course's final 18 holes. Dunn decided to teach some of the local boys how to caddie, and Shippen was among the first and most promising of these golfing novices.

In a chapter that related Shippen's accomplishments for his 1998 book, *Forbidden Fairways: African Americans and the Game of Golf*, author Calvin H. Sinnette told of how all thoughts of completing his education disappeared as Shippen became thoroughly captivated by the game of golf. Sinnette described Shippen as having "spent every waking moment on the golf course practicing under the watchful eye of Willie Dunn." Even though education was so important to his parents, Shippen dropped out of school and concentrated on golf to the exclusion of all else. He was soon an assistant to Dunn and was even giving lessons to

At a Glance . . .

Born on December 5, 1879, in Washington, DC; died on July 15, 1968, in Newark, NJ; married Effie Walker, late 1890s (died early 1900s); married Maude Elliot Lee, May 27, 1901 (died 1957); children: six.

Career: Maidstone Golf Club, professional golfer, 1898-1900, 1902-1913; Aronomink, professional golfer, 1900-1902; private golf instructor 1913-1915; Spring Lake Golf & Country Club, professional golfer, late 1910s; Marine and Field Club, professional golfer, late 1910s; Shinnecock Hills, greenskeeper, 1920-21; National Golf Links, course maintenance foreman, 1921; Citizens Golf Club, professional golfer, 1921-1927; National Capital Golf Club, professional golfer, 1927-1931; Shady Rest Golf Club, professional golfer, 1931-1957.

Awards: Fifth place, U.S. Open, 1896, 1902; John Shippen Foundation, established in 1990.

some club members. Teaching was not Shippen's only duty. He arose early every day and arrived at the club to repair clubs and assist the maintenance staff. Shippen also served as a starter for some tournaments and as a scorekeeper. Shippen was still a teenager, according to Sinnette, when it became clear that his skill as a golfer "warranted an opportunity for the sixteen-year-old caddie to match his prowess with the top-ranked golfers of the day." A year later, in July 1896, the Shinnecock Hill club was selected as the site for the U.S. Open Championship.

In a June 2002 interview, Thurman Simmons, the Chairman of the John Shippen Foundation, told Peter Aviles of the *Black Athlete Sports Network,* that Shippen did not actually enter the second U.S. Open of his own accord. Instead, his name was entered by some of the members of the Shinnecock club, whom Shippen had been teaching. These members—people like the Rothchilds, the Mellons, and the Carnegies—entered Shippen's name and paid his entrance fees. However just entering Shippen in this prestigious tournament was not enough to guarantee that he would be able to play. Shippen wanted to play, but prejudice and racism were still a very significant issue within all levels of American sporting events. Golf was no exception.

Although not all of the details are known, the story was that a number of the English and Scottish golfers threatened to withdraw if an African American was permitted to play. The tournament director, Theodore F. Havemeyer, refused to have Shippen and his friend, Oscar Bunn, who was a Shinnecock Indian, removed from the tournament. Sinnette stated that one account of this incident has Havemeyer claiming that "Shippen was only 'half black,' implying that he would have prohibited the ministers son from playing if he were a full-blooded African American." When the tournament director would not agree to Shippen and Bunn's removal, the protesting golfers returned to the course and began playing as scheduled. Thus Shippen became not only the first African American to play in the U.S. Open, but he and Bunn became the first Americans of any ancestry to play. In the first U.S. Open all of the players had been either English or Scottish, but now at the second U.S. Open at least two players would be American, and thus the tournament attracted large crowds who came to see these two young men play.

Shippen acquitted himself well in the first round of play, and in fact was tied with four others at the end of the first round. On the second round he was leading during the first nine holes, but at the thirteenth hole, Shippen's ball became stuck in the sand trap to the far right of the hole. Shippen described the hole in Pete McDaniel's *Uneven Lies: The Heroic Story of African-Americans in Golf* as "a little, easy par-four. I'd played it many times and I knew I just had to stay on the right side of the fairway with my drive. Well, I played it too far to the right and the ball landed in a sand trap road. Bad trouble in those days before sand wedges. I kept hitting the ball along the road, unable to lift it out of the sand and wound up with an unbelievable eleven for the hole." As a result, Shippen lost the U.S. Open, seven strokes behind the Scottish winner. He tied for fifth place with a 159 and won ten dollars. While Shippen often was quoted as saying it was just an honor to play in the tournament, he told McDaniel in *Uneven Lies,* "You know, I've wished a hundred times I could have played that little par-four again."

Although he did not win in his first professional debut, Shippen so impressed tournament observers that he was invited to play an exhibition match against the golf professional at the newly constructed Maidstone Club in nearby East Hampton. Shippen won that match, and Sinnette quoted a leading sporting magazine as claiming that Shippen should be "given every opportunity to show what he can do."

Made Golfing a Career

Shippen's family returned to Washington, D.C., in 1898, but Shippen decided to remain in Shinnecock on his own. With his victory at Maidstone, Shippen earned the position of club professional at the club. He held this position for the next two years and then moved on to the Aronomink Golf Club near Philadelphia. During this period Shippen also married. His first marriage, to a Shinnecock woman, Effie Walker, ended early when his bride died soon after their marriage. Then on May 27, 1901, Shippen married again. His second wife was also a Shinnecock woman, Maude Elliot Lee. Shippen moved back to the Maidstone club in 1902 and continued as the golf professional at the club until 1913. During this time, Shippen and his wife had six children during their first nine years of marriage. Shippen also continued to play golf and played in several more U.S. Open tournaments—in 1899, 1900, 1902, and 1913. His best finish was in 1902, when he again finished in fifth place. Shippen did achieve an important success when he tutored Walter J. Travis, who won the 1904 British Amateur. This victory added to Shippen's reputation because at that time the amateur players were more highly regarded than the professional golfers.

According to Sinnette's book, Shippen worked as a private instructor to a few wealthy businessmen from 1913 to 1915. Over the next few years, Shippen's movements became less exact. He left his family on the Shinnecock reservation, where his wife was left to her own resources to support and raise their children. In the meantime, Shippen continued to move about on his own during the period from 1915 to 1921. Sinnette stated that Shippen was briefly a professional at Spring Lake Golf & Country Club in New Jersey and was for a time the professional at the Marine and Field Club in Brooklyn, New York. During this period Shippen was also briefly back at Shinnecock Hills as a greenskeeper, where he spent two years. After a brief stay as the course maintenance foreman at the National Golf Links on Long Island, Shippen moved back to Washington, D.C., and briefly took a civil service job with the federal public works department. Sinnette's biography noted that Shippen failed to support his family and that he may have had a problem with alcohol that led to his many moves and frequent employment changes, but this latter allegation could not be proved definitively. Whatever the cause of these frequent job turnovers, Shippen's next employment was as a golf professional and an instructor at the Citizens Golf Club in Washington, D.C., from 1921 to 1927. Then he worked at the National Capital Country Club in Laurel, Maryland from 1927 until 1931. During these years, Shippen also competed in the United Golfers Association, a professional association for African American players, during the 1920s and 1930s.

Eventually Shippen settled in Scotch Plains, New Jersey, where he would become the head golf professional at the Shady Rest Golf Club. Shady Rest, established in 1925, was the first African-American golf course in the United States. In 1931 when Shippen arrived at Shady Rest, the economy was suffering from the effects of the depression. Money was tight, but Shippen found a way to earn extra money. According to Sinnette, Shippen "gave golf lessons, served as caddie master, repaired clubs, sold golf equipment, and gave greenkeeping consultations to nearby golf courses." According to McDaniel, when Shippen arrived at Shady Rest, the club had already achieved notice as an important stop for many important scholars and social reformers such as W.E.B. DuBois. Shippen arrived as the club superintendent and golf professional, a position he held for the next 26 years. Shippen's reputation was enhanced by his association with the club, just as the club gained through Shippen's reputation as a talented golfer. Through the next few years, Shippen also helped to build golf courses in Maryland and in Washington, D.C.

A Legacy Remembered

After his wife's death in 1957, Shippen apparently reconciled with some of his children. Even though his health was not always good, he still continued to play golf even into his 80s. Shippen died in a Newark, New Jersey, nursing home on July 15, 1968. After his death a committee was formed of friends and admirers who wanted to remember and honor Shippen's contributions to golf. The committee began honoring Shippen in a very public way in 1990 by staging golf tournaments as a way to raise money for scholarships for deserving African American students. Then, in 1996, this committee created a foundation to honor Shippen's legacy in a more permanent manner. Shippen, himself, never completed school, but shortly after his death, he was quoted in a 1969 Tuesday magazine article as saying, "I wonder if I did the right thing when I quit school and went into golf. Maybe I should have kept going and gone to Yale like my brother who's a teacher." However, Shippen never regretted his decision for more than a few moments, and so the establishment of a scholarship in his name suggested both the paradox inherent in Shippen's lack of education and the promise that today a young athlete need not choose between education or athletics.

For many years there was no mention of Shippen as the first African American to play in a U.S. Open. Often times his ancestry was confused with that of Bunn's, and Shippen was lauded as an early American Indian golfer and not as an African American. There was some added confusion based on the supposed remarks attributed to Havemeyer that Shippen was only half-black. In John H. Kennedy's book, A Course of Their Own: A History of African American Golfers, Shippen's daughter reiterated the point that Shippen's parents had both been black: "'My father was a Negro,' said Clara Johnson, 'Every time I meet somebody, I have to correct that story.'" In fact it was Shippen's daughter who first pointed out that her father had been an African American, when she told a reporter for the Pittsburgh Post-Gazette that her father was black. In an August 2000 article for the Pittsburgh Post-Gazette, reporter Monica L. Haynes recalled that the first time that Shippen's daughter had asserted her father's race was to a Post-Gazette reporter in 1986. That 1986 reporter, Marino Parascenzo, alerted the United States Golf Association with the need to correct Shippen's ethnicity in their official records. It had only taken 90 years for Shippen to receive the acclaim he so richly deserved, as the first black man to play in a professional golfing tournament.

Sources

Books

Kennedy, John H., *A Course of Their Own: A History of African American Golfers*, Stark Books, 2000, pp. 7-12.

McDaniel, Pete, *Eneven Lies: The Heroic Story of African-Americans in Golf*, The American Golfer, 2000, pp. 23-27, 59-62.

Sinnette, Calvin H., *Forbidden Fairways: African Americans and the Game of Golf*, Sleeping Bear Press, 1998, pp. 15-25.

Periodicals

Pittsburgh Post-Gazette, August 22, 2000, p. D-1.

On-line

"An Interview With Thurman Simmons," *Black Athlete Sports Network,* www.blackathlete.net/Interviews/int062302.html (November 13, 2003).

—Dr. Sheri Elaine Metzger

Alice Walker

1944—

Writer

Recognized as one of the leading voices among black American women writers, Alice Walker has produced an acclaimed and varied body of work, including poetry, novels, short stories, essays, and criticism. Her writings portray the struggle of black people throughout history, and are praised for their insightful and riveting portraits of black life, in particular the experiences of black women in a sexist and racist society. Her most famous work, the award-winning and best-selling novel *The Color Purple,* chronicles the life of a poor and abused southern black woman who eventually triumphs over oppression through affirming female relationships. Walker has described herself as a "womanist"—her term for a black feminist—which she defines in the introduction to her book of essays, *In Search of Our Mothers' Gardens: Womanist Prose,* as one who "appreciates and prefers women's culture, women's emotional flexibility … women's strength" and is "committed to [the] survival and wholeness of entire people, male *and* female."

A theme throughout Walker's work is the preservation of black culture, and her women characters forge important links to maintain continuity in both personal relationships and communities. According to Barbara T. Christian in *Dictionary of Literary Biography,* Walker is concerned with "heritage," which to Walker "is not so much the grand sweep of history or artifacts created as it is the relations of people to each other, young to old, parent to child, man to woman." Walker admired the struggle of black women throughout history to maintain an essential spirituality and creativity in their lives, and their achievements serve as an inspiration to others. In *Our Mother's Gardens,* Walker wrote: "We must fearlessly pull out of ourselves and look at and identify with our lives the living creativity some of our great-grandmothers were not allowed to know. I stress *some* of them because it is well known that the majority of our great-grandmothers knew, even without 'knowing' it, the reality of their spirituality, even if they didn't recognize it beyond what happened in the singing at church—and they never had any intention of giving it up."

Influenced by Roots

Walker was born on February 9, 1944, in the small rural town of Eatonton, Georgia, where she was the youngest of eight children of impoverished sharecrop-

At a Glance . . .

Born Alice Malsenior Walker on February 9, 1944, in Eatonton, GA; daughter of Willie Lee and Minnie Tallulah (Grant) Walker (sharecroppers); married Melvyn Rosenman Leventhal (a civil rights lawyer), March 17, 1967 (divorced, 1976); children: Rebecca Grant. *Education:* Attended Spelman College, 1961-63; Sarah Lawrence College, BA, 1965.

Career: Voter register in Liberty County, GA, c. 1965; New York City welfare department, employee, c. 1966; poet, 1968–; Friends of the Children of Mississippi, black literature consultant, 1967; Jackson State College, Jackson, MS, writer in residence 1968-69; novelist, 1970–; Tougaloo College, Tougaloo, MS, writer in residence, 1970-71; Wellesley College, Wellesley, MA, lecturer in literature, 1972-73; University of Massachusetts-Boston, lecturer in literature, 1972-73; essayist, 1973–; University of California-Berkeley, Afro-American studies department, distinguished writer, 1982; Brandeis University, Waltham, MA, Fannie Hurst Professor of Literature, 1982; Wild Trees Press, Navarro, CA, co-founder and publisher, 1984-88.

Memberships: Board of trustees, Sarah Lawrence College.

Selected awards: Bread Loaf scholar, 1966; National Book Award nomination and Lillian Smith Award from Southern Regional Council, both for *Revolutionary Petunias and Other Poems,* 1973; Richard and Hinda Rosenthal Foundation Award from American Academy and Institute of Arts and Letters, for *In Love and Trouble: Stories of Black Women,* 1974 National Book Critics Circle Award nomination, 1982, Pulitzer Prize, 1983, and American Book Award, 1983, all for *The Color Purple;* O. Henry Award, for *Kindred Spirits,* 1986; Sheila Award, Tubman African American Museum, 1997.

Addresses: *Office*—c/o Random House, 299 Park Ave, New York, NY, 10171.

described in *Our Mothers' Gardens* as "a walking history of our community." A childhood accident at the age of eight left Walker blind and scarred in one eye, which, partially corrected when she was fourteen, left a profound influence on her. "I believe ... that it was from this period—from my solitary, lonely position, the position of an outcast—that I began really to see people and things, really to notice relationships and to learn to be patient enough to care about how they turned out.... I retreated into solitude, and read stories and began to write poems." Walker has commented that as a southern black growing up in a poor rural community, she possessed the benefit of "double vision." She explained in *Our Mothers' Gardens:* "Not only is the [black southern writer] in a position to see his own world, and its close community ... but he is capable of knowing, with remarkably silent accuracy, the people who make up the larger world that surrounds and suppresses his own."

Walker was an excellent student, and received a scholarship to Spelman College in Atlanta, and later to Sarah Lawrence College in the Bronx, New York. While in college, she became politically aware in the Civil Rights Movement and participated in many demonstrations. Her first book of poems, *Once,* was written while she was a senior at Sarah Lawrence and was accepted for publication the same year. Walker wrote many of the poems in the span of a week in the winter of 1965, when she wrestled with suicide after deciding to have an abortion. The poems recount the despair and isolation of her situation, in addition to her experiences in the Civil Rights Movement and of a trip she had made to Africa. Though not widely reviewed, *Once* marked Walker's debut as a distinctive and talented writer. Carolyn M. Rodgers in *Negro Digest* noted Walker's "precise wordings, the subtle, unexpected twists ... [and] shifting of emotions." Christian remarked that already in *Once,* Walker displayed what would become a feature of both her future poetry and fiction, an "unwavering honesty in evoking the forbidden, either in political stances or in love."

Walker returned to the South after college and worked as a voter register in Georgia and an instructor in black history in Mississippi. She recounted in *Our Mothers' Gardens* that she was inspired by Martin Luther King, Jr.'s message that being a southern black meant "I ... had claim to the land of my birth." Walker continued to write poetry and fiction, and began to further explore the South she came from. She described in *Our Mothers' Gardens* of being particularly influenced by the Russian writers, who spoke to her of a "soul ... directly rooted in the soil that nourished it." She was also influenced by black writer Zora Neale Hurston, who'd wrote lively folk accounts of the thriving small, southern black community she grew up in. Walker stated in *Our Mothers' Gardens* how she particularly admired the "racial health" of Hurston's work: "A sense of black people as complete, complex, *undimin-*

pers. Both of her parents were storytellers, and Walker was especially influenced by her mother, whom she

ished human beings, a sense that is lacking in so much black writing and literature."

Explored Male Violence and Sexism

Critics have often objected to her portrayal of black males. With the help of a 1967 McDowell fellowship, Walker completed her first novel, *The Third Life of Grange Copeland,* published in 1970. The novel depicts cycles of male violence in three generations of an impoverished southern black family (the Copelands), and displays Walker's interest in social conditions that affect family relationships, in addition to her recurring theme of the suffering of black women at the hands of men. The novel revolves around a father (Grange) who abandons his abused wife and young son (Brownfield) for a more prosperous life in the North, and returns years later to find his son similarly abusing his own family. Christian wrote that the men in the novel are "thwarted by the society in their drive for control of their lives—the American definition of manhood—[and] vent their frustrations by inflicting violence on their wives." Critics praised the realism of the novel, *CLA Journal* contributor Peter Erickson, who noted that Walker demonstrated "with a vivid matter-of-factness the family's entrapment in a vicious cycle of poverty." However, Walker was also faulted for her portrayal of black men as violent, an aspect which is frequently criticized in her work. Walker responded to such criticism in an interview with Claudia Tate in *Black Women Writers at Work:* "I know many Brownfields, and it's a shame that I know so many. I will not ignore people like Brownfield. I want you to know I know they exist. I want to tell you about them, and there is no way you are going to avoid them."

Walker frankly depicted the "twin afflictions" of racism and sexism. Walker's women characters display strength, endurance, and resourcefulness in confronting—and overcoming—oppression in their lives, yet Walker is frank in depicting the often devastating circumstances of the "twin afflictions" of racism and sexism. "Black women are called, in the folklore that so aptly identifies one's status in society, 'the mule of the world,' because we have been handed the burdens that everyone else—*everyone* else—refused to carry," Walker stated in *Our Mothers' Gardens.* Mary Helen Washington in *Sturdy Black Bridges: Visions of Black Women in Literature* noted that "the true empathy Alice Walker has for the oppressed woman comes through in all her writings.... Raising an ax, crying out in childbirth or abortion, surrendering to a man who is oblivious to her real name—these are the kinds of images which most often appear in Ms. Walker's own writing." Washington added that the strength of such images is that Walker gives insight into "the intimate reaches of the inner lives of her characters; the landscape of her stories is the spiritual realm where the soul yearns for what it does not have."

Walker's short story collections, *In Love and Trouble* and *You Can't Keep a Good Woman Down* expound upon the problems of sexism and racism facing black women. *In Love and Trouble* features thirteen black women protagonists—many of them from the South—who, as Christian notes, "against their own conscious wills in the face of pain, abuse, even death, challenge the conventions of sex, race, and age that attempt to restrict them." In *Our Mothers' Gardens,* Walker stated that her intent in the stories was to present a variety of women—"mad, raging, loving, resentful, hateful, strong, ugly, weak, pitiful, and magnificent"—as they "try to live with the loyalty to black men that characterizes all of their lives." Barbara Smith in *Ms.* praised the collection, stating it "would be an extraordinary literary work if its only virtue were the fact that the author sets out consciously to explore with honesty the textures and terror of black women's lives." Smith added: "The fact that Walker's perceptions, style, and artistry are also consistently high makes her work a treasure."

The stories in *You Can't Keep a Good Women Down* represented an evolution in subject matter, as Walker delved more directly into mainstream feminist issues such as abortion, pornography, and rape. Although a number of critics remarked that the polemic nature of the stories detracted from their narrative effect, Walker again demonstrated, according to Christian, "the extent to which black women are free to pursue their own selfhood in a society permeated by sexism and racism."

Walker explored similar terrain in her acclaimed 1976 novel, *Meridian,* in which she recounts the personal evolution of a young black woman against the backdrop of the politics of the Civil Rights Movement. Structurally complex, the novel raised questions of motherhood for the politically-aware female, and the implications for the individual of being committed to revolution. Writing in the *New York Times Book Review,* Marge Piercy praised *Meridian* as "a fine, taut novel that accomplishes a remarkable amount" and noted that Walker "writes with a sharp critical sense as she deals with the issues of tactics and strategy in the civil rights movement, with the nature of commitment, the possibility of interracial love and communication, the vital and lethal strands in American and black experience, with violence and nonviolence." The novel received much critical recognition and was praised for its deft handling of complex subject matter. Years after its publication, Robert Towers commented in the *New York Review of Books* that *Meridian* "remains the most impressive fictional treatment of the 'Movement' that I have yet read."

During this time period, Walker moved to San Francisco in order to escape the world of everyday work as an editor at *Ms.* magazine. It was here that she rekindled a relationship with Robert Allen, shortly after her divorce from Melvyn Rosenman Leventhal in 1976. She and Allen would move in together in Mendocino, California, and in later years would start a publishing company together called Wild Tree Press.

Struck A Chord With Color Purple

In her 1982 novel, *The Color Purple,* Walker brought together many of the characters and themes of her previous works in a book which Peter S. Prescott in *Newsweek* proclaimed "an American novel of permanent importance." *The Color Purple* is a series of letters written by a southern black woman (Celie), reflecting a history of oppression and abuse suffered at the hands of the men. The book was resoundingly praised for its masterful recreation of black folk speech, in which, as Towers noted, Walker converts Celie's "subliterate dialect into a medium of remarkable expressiveness, color, and poignancy." Towers added: "I find it impossible to imagine Celie apart from her language; through it, not only a memorable and infinitely touching character but a whole submerged world is vividly called into being."

The novel charts Celie's resistance to the oppression surrounding her, and the liberation of her existence through positive and supportive relations with other women. Christian noted that "perhaps even more than Walker's other works, [*The Color Purple*] especially affirms that the most abused of the abused can transform herself. It completed the cycle Walker announced a decade ago: the survival and liberation of black women through the strength and wisdom of others." The novel won both the Pulitzer Prize and the American Book Award, and was made into a popular motion picture which received several Academy Award nominations.

While *The Color Purple* garnered much success for Walker, it also brought about a good deal of controversy. Many critics attacked the book as well as the movie adaptation for being "degrading to Black men and promoting lesbianism among Black women," according to *Essence.* Many people also felt that Walker had degraded the story of *The Color Purple* when she had allowed Steven Spielberg to adapt the film. According to *Essence,* many readers of her book felt that she had "'betrayed' Blacks by joining forces with a Jewish male director who epitomized Tinseltown's 'feel-good' cinematic traditions." It took a long time for Walker to respond to this criticism but in 1995 she shot back with *The Same River Twice: Honoring the Difficult,* a book that was aimed at answering a lot of the criticism of both the book and the movie as well as documenting both the writing and the movie making process that Walker went through. Her hope was that by showing the difficulty in compiling a story such as *The Color Purple,* by fleshing out why she wrote the book and certain scenes as she did, as well as explaining exactly how much control she had over the movie version of her story, she would give readers a better understanding of her motivations. The book also included Walker's original screenplay for the movie adaptation that was much truer to the book, another flaw many fans of the book had with the movie.

Flipped Between Critical Opinion and Fiction

During the process of turning *The Color Purple* into a movie, Walker continued to be prolific. In 1983 she put out *In Search of Mother's Garden,* her first collection of nonfiction essays that touched on the themes of feminism and the theories of the feminist movement. She returned to poetry in 1984 with *Horses Make the Landscape More Beautiful,* which again explored the themes of the past, family, and ancestry. Shortly after the release of *The Color Purple* on movie screens, Walker turned to children's literature with *To Hell With Dying* which focuses on the mortality of the physical world and how memory conquers this mortality. Many people felt that the book was too heavy handed for a children's book, but many critics saw it as one of the few books that was able to tactfully deal with such an important subject.

Her 1989 novel, *The Temple of My Familiar,* described by Walker as "a romance of the last 500,000 years," represents a departure of sorts for the author, and critical opinion was mixed upon its publication. J. M. Coetzee in the *New York Times Book Review* described it as "a mixture of mythic fantasy, revisionary history, exemplary biography and sermon" which is "short on narrative tension, long on inspirational message." In the novel, Walker features six characters, three men and three women, who relate their views on life through recounting memories of ancestors and spirits from past cultures. While a number of reviewers faulted the ideological weight of the novel, others commented that the book remained faithful to the concerns of Walker's works. Luci Tapahonso noted in the *Los Angeles Times Book Review* that the novel focused on familiar Walker themes, such as "compassion for the oppressed, the grief of the oppressors, acceptance of the unchangeable and hope for everyone and everything."

While Walker's works speak strongly of the experiences of black women, critics have commented that the messages of her books transcend both race and gender. According to Gloria Steinem in *Ms.,* Walker "comes at universality through the path of an American black woman's experience.... She speaks the female experience more powerfully for being able to pursue it across boundaries of race and class." Jeanne Fox-Alston in the *Chicago Tribune Book World* called Walker "a provocative writer who writes about blacks in particular, but all humanity in general." In her 1988 prose collection, *Living by the Word: Selected Writings, 1973-1987,* Walker discussed, through essays and journal entries, topics such as nuclear weapons and racism in other countries. Noel Perrin in the *New York Times Book Review* wrote that although Walker's "original interests centered on black women, and especially on the ways they were abused or underrated ... now those interests encompass all creation." Derrick Bell commented in the *Los Angeles Times Book Review* that

Walker "uses carefully crafted images that provide a universality to unique events." *Living by the Word* presents "vintage Alice Walker: passionate, political, personal, and poetic."

Brought Mutilation Into Consciousness

The early 1990s were a difficult time for Walker, for she ended her 13 year relationship with Robert Allen and contracted Lyme disease. But none of these things stopped her from writing. Shortly before addressing the controversy of *The Color Purple* in *The Same River Twice: Honoring the Difficult,* Walker produced another book which brought about much controversy in the critical world, *Possessing the Secret of Joy,* in 1992. The book focused on Tashi, a young woman living in the fictional African country of Olinka, who is forced by her tribe to take part in the rituals of female circumcision, a process which ruins the rest of Tashi's life. The novel describes graphically the process of female genital mutilation and the repercussions of such actions, including not only physical and psychological problems, but also an inability to keep intact gender. Before the book is finished, Tashi loses all pleasure from sexual encounters, gives birth to a mentally-challenged son, and due to the traumatic nature of the chain of events, is driven to murder the woman who initially circumcised her.

A year later, Walker continued to bring female genital mutilation to the forefront of social consciousness by producing a book and movie called *Warrior Marks: Female Genital Mutilation and the Sexual Blindings of Women.* Much like *Possessing the Secret of Joy, Warrior Marks,* looks at the repercussions of the mutilation traditions in many societies, but instead of fictionalizing the issue as she did in *Possessing the Secret of Joy* Walker instead decided to work from a documentary standpoint. The film and the book attempted to search out the meanings behind the traditional ceremonies of female genital mutilation and in turn looked for reasons why the tradition was still carried on in modern times.

What impressed many people about both the movie and the book is that it took a complete look at the issue, from both a cultural standpoint as well as a psychological standpoint. Many people were also surprised to learn that Walker was the driving force behind the movie version of *Warrior Marks,* for she used all of the money that was advanced to her by her publisher Harcourt for the non-fiction documentary book on the subject to produce the movie herself. Walker made it clear in both the movie and the book that her intent with these projects was to make the world-wide public aware that such practices were still going on and according to *Publishers Weekly* she was "determined to do what she could to rid the world of that barbaric, and often deadly, centuries-year-old tradition."

Turned to Own Life For Inspiration

By the late 1990s Walker had turned to her own experiences in the world for subject matter for her essays and novels. In 1998 she put out a collection of essays entitled *Anything We Love Can Be Saved: A Writer's Activism* which aimed at showing how through writing activism occurred and vice-versa. This idea had begun with Walker during her time making *Warrior Marks* and carried over into her becoming more socially and politically active on subjects such as the treatment of women in Ghana, the defense of Winnie Mandela, and the role of parents in the lives of children.

In 1999 Walker released *By the Light of My Father's Smile,* a novel that examines how a person's sexuality can influence the way in which people respond to them. This was an issue that Walker dealt with directly in her own life when she made it publicly known that she was homosexual in the mid-1990s. *By the Light of My Father's Smile* is also concerned with the idea of cultural diversity and spirituality, with the ghost of the father of the main character, Magdalena, unable to rest in the afterworld until he is able to accept the love between his daughter and a person of a mixed heritage.

In an attempt to chronicle many of the events of her life, Walker turned to the essay filled *The Way Forward Is With a Broken Heart.* In this book Walker examined her early marriage to a white man as well as, according to *Black Issues Book Review,* exploring the "complexity of love and race and family ... the contradictory nexus of sexual response and sexual responsibility and worries about past loves, unfamiliar therapists and weeping children." In a response to this book, Walker's daughter Rebecca wrote *Black, White and Jewish: Autobiography of a Shifting Self,* which revealed a very different side to Walker's personal life, about how she often treated her daughter poorly and how she was often selfish in her pursuit of her writing. Walker has taken a good deal of criticism since the release of *Black, White and Jewish: Autobiography of a Shifting Self,* but in response she told *Black Issues Book Review,* "In general, I don't seem to care very much about what people think ... I'm pretty clear about what I'm supposed to be doing here, and I do that."

In 2003 Walker returned to poetry, a medium she had not used since the mid-1980s, with her book *Absolute Trust in the Goodness of the Earth.* Written in response to events such as the terrorist attacks of September 11, 2001, the poems in the book focus on healing the spirit through experience and age in a world that is attempting to kill freedom. She told *Black Issues Book Review,* "I think that with time, we begin to understand a little better that some things we thought were horrible, unbearable ... can be bearable as we grow older. For instance, in my early poetry ... I wrote poems about suicide. And now I don't think about that very much. It's interesting because I think that to wage continuous war in the world is a kind of suicide. In a sense, the suicide that I see now is a global one. It's humanity that seems to be interested in ending itself. But I don't feel interested in ending myself. I think that's progress."

Walker continues to make the public aware of views, not only in media, but in her actions as well. In March of 2003 she joined with Maxine Hong Kingston and a group known as CodePink to protest the United States military action in Iraq and was arrested for demonstrating in a closed area in front of the White House and crossing police lines. Many critics have wondered whether the writer will ever slow down, but she told *Black Issues Book Review*, "I think all I can say is that now I'm an older person. I'm someone who has had much more experience than in the beginning. But in some ways, I'm concerned about the same issues, the same emotions. I'm concerned with the safety of our people, the planet, people who are in deep trouble around the world."

Selected works

Fiction

The Third Life of Grange Copeland, Harcourt, 1970.
In Love and Trouble: Stories of Black Women, Harcourt, 1973.
Meridian, Harcourt, 1976.
You Can't Keep a Good Woman Down, Harcourt, 1981.
The Color Purple, Harcourt, 1982.
To Hell with Dying, Harcourt, 1988.
The Temple of My Familiar, Harcourt, 1989.
Possessing the Secret of Joy, Harcourt, 1992.
By the Light of My Father's Smile, Random House, 1998.

Nonfiction

Langston Hughes: American Biography (for children), Crowell, 1973.
(Editor) *I Love Myself When I'm Laughing ... and Then Again When I Am Looking Mean and Impressive: A Zora Neale Hurston Reader*, Feminist Press, 1979.
In Search of Our Mothers' Gardens: Womanist Prose, Harcourt, 1983.
Living by the Word: Selected Writings, 1973-1987, Harcourt, 1988.
Warrior Marks: Female Genital Mutilation and the Sexual Blinding of Women, Harcourt, 1993.
The Same River Twice: Honoring the Difficult, Scribner, 1996.
Banned, Aunt Lute Books, 1996.
Anything We Love Can Be Saved: A Writer's Activism, Random House, 1997.
The Way Forward Is With a Broken Heart, Random House, 2000.
Sent By Earth: A Message From the Grandmother Spirit After the Bombing of the World Trade Center, Seven Stories Press, 2001.

Poetry

Once: Poems, Harcourt, 1968.
Revolutionary Petunias and Other Poems, Harcourt, 1973.
Goodnight, Willie Lee, I'll See You in the Morning, Dial, 1979.
Horses Make a Landscape Look More Beautiful, Harcourt, 1984.
Her Blue Body Everything We Know: Earthling Poems, Harcourt, 1991.
Absolute Trust in the Goddess of the Earth: New Poems, Random House, 2003.

Other

Contributor to numerous books, anthologies, and periodicals; contributing editor to periodicals, including *Freedomways* and *Ms.* Media adaptations—*The Color Purple* was made into a film and released by Warner Bros. in 1985.

Sources

Books

Bell, Roseann P., Bettye J. Parker, and Beverly Guy-Sheftall, editors, *Sturdy Black Bridges: Visions of Black Women in Literature*, Anchor Press, 1979.
Bestsellers 89, Issue 4, Gale, 1989.
Contemporary Authors New Revision Series, Volume 27 (entry contains interview), Gale, 1989.
Contemporary Literary Criticism, Gale, Volume 5, 1976; Volume 6, 1976; Volume 9, 1978; Volume 19, 1981; Volume 27, 1984; Volume 46, 1988.
Dictionary of Literary Biography, Volume 6: "American Novelists since World War II," 2nd series, Gale, 1980; Volume 33: "Afro-American Fiction Writers after 1955," Gale, 1984.
Evans, Mari, editor, *Black Women Writers (1950-1980): A Critical Evaluation*, Anchor Press/Doubleday, 1984.

Periodicals

Biblio, January 1999, p. 61.
Black Issues Book Review, November 2000, p. 17; March-April 2003, pp. 34-38.
Chicago Tribune Book World, August 1, 1982; September 15, 1985.
CLA Journal, September 1979.
Essence, February 1996, pp. 84-88.
Lancet, February 13, 1993, p. 423.
Los Angeles Times Book Review, May 29, 1988; May 21, 1989.
Ms., February 1974; June 1982.
Negro Digest, September/October 1968.
Newsweek, June 21, 1982.

New York Review of Books, August 12, 1982.
New York Times Book Review, May 26, 1976; June 5, 1988; April 30, 1989.
Publishers Weekly, October 25, 1993, p. 13; December 18, 1995, p. 38.

On-line

Book www.bookmagazine.com (October 24, 2003).
"Walker's Complete Works," *Living By Grace,* http://members.tripod.com/chrisdanielle/completeworks.html (October 24, 2003).

—Michael E. Mueller and Ralph G. Zerbonia

J. Ernest Wilkins, Jr.

1923—

Mathematician, physicist, nuclear engineer

J. Ernest Wilkins, Jr., is well known for his important contributions in the fields of nuclear engineering and theoretical and applied mathematics and physics. He has had an unusually varied career, moving in and out of academia, government, and industry. His teaching and mentoring at historically black universities has encouraged young blacks to choose careers in science, mathematics, and engineering. During World War II Wilkins worked on the Manhattan Project that developed the atomic bomb. Later he served as president of the American Nuclear Society (ANS). Wilkins is best known for his work on radiation shielding and his contributions to early nuclear reactor design and the development of optical instruments for space exploration. He is also a distinguished professor of Applied Mathematics and Mathematical Physics at Clark Atlanta University in Atlanta, Georgia.

Proclaimed a Child Prodigy

Jesse Ernest Wilkins, Jr., was born in Chicago on November 27, 1923. His father, J. Ernest Wilkins, Sr., was a well-known lawyer who held a bachelor's degree in mathematics from the University of Illinois and a law degree from the University of Chicago. In 1941 and 1942 the elder Wilkins served as president of the Cook County Bar Association in Chicago. President Dwight D. Eisenhower appointed him Assistant Secretary of Labor in 1954, the first black American to hold a sub-cabinet position. In 1958 he was appointed to the Civil Rights Commission. Wilkins's mother, Lucile Beatrice Robinson Wilkins, held bachelor's and master's degrees in education from the University of Chicago, and taught in Chicago public schools. Wilkins maternal grandfather had founded St. Mark's Methodist Church in New York City, and the family were active churchgoers.

Given their backgrounds, it is hardly surprising that Wilkins's parents stressed the importance of education and achievement. An extremely bright child, Wilkins entered Willard Elementary School at the age of four, skipping grades until he found himself in the fifth grade at the age of seven. Although his two brothers became lawyers, Wilkins was more interested in mathematics. His parents encouraged his early interests, and soon he was solving a variety of mathematical puzzles. At Parker High School, Wilkins's math teacher recognized

At a Glance . . .

Born Jesse Ernest Wilkins, Jr., on November 27, 1923, in Chicago, IL; son of J. Ernest and Lucile Beatrice (Robinson) Wilkins, Sr.; married Gloria Louise Stewart (deceased); married Maxine G. Malone (deceased); children: (first marriage) Sharon Wilkins Hill, J. Ernest III. *Education:* University of Chicago, BS, 1940, MS, 1941, PhD, 1942; New York University, BME, 1957, MME, 1960.

Career: Institute for Advanced Study, Princeton, NJ, postdoctoral research fellow, 1942-43; Tuskegee Institute, mathematics instructor, 1943-44; University of Chicago, Metallurgical Laboratory, physicist, 1944-46; American Optical Co., mathematician, 1946-50; NDA (UNC), numerous positions, 1950-59, manager, 1959-60; General Dynamics Corp., General Atomic div., Theoretical Physics dept., 1960-65, John Jay Hopkins Laboratory, asst. dir., Defense Science and Engineering Center, dir., computational research, 1965-70; Howard Univ., distinguished prof., 1970-77; Argonne National Laboratory, visiting scientist, 1976-77, fellow, 1984-85, consultant 1985-90; EG&G Idaho, various positions, 1977-84; Clark Atlanta University, distinguished prof., 1990–; Georgia Institute of Technology, adjunct prof., 1995–.

Selected memberships: American Society of Mechanical Engineers; ANS, board of directors, 1967-77, president, 1974-75; NRC, Advisory Committee on Reactor Safeguards, chairman, 1990-94; Oak Ridge Assn. Univ., council, 1990; U.S. Army Science Board, chairman, 1970-2001.

Selected awards: U.S. Army Outstanding Civilian Service Medal, 1980; NAM, Honorary Life Member, Lifetime Achievement Award, 1994; QEM Network, Giant in Science Award, 1994; DOE, Special Recognition Award, 1996; Univ. of Chicago Alumni Association, Professional Achievement Citation, 1997.

Addresses: *Home*—587 Virginia Avenue NE, No. 612, Atlanta, GA 30306. *Office*—Department of Mathematics, Box J, Clark Atlanta University, James P. Brawley Dr. at Fair St. SW, Atlanta, GA 30314-4839.

his talent and accelerated his coursework. He also participated in track, tennis, and baseball.

Wilkins entered the nearby University of Chicago at the age of 13—the youngest student ever admitted. University scholarships covered his tuition. He lived at home and tutored other students to earn spending money. While majoring in mathematics, Wilkins took extra courses and graduated Phi Beta Kappa in 1940 at the age of 16. That same year he ranked in the top ten in the prestigious William Lowell Putnam Mathematical Competition for undergraduates. In addition, Wilkins won the boys' state table tennis championship in 1938 and was the university's champion for three years. Using the graduate credits he had earned as an undergraduate, Wilkins was awarded his master's degree in mathematics in 1941. The following year, at the age of 19, Wilkins earned a doctoral degree from the University of Chicago. Newspapers around the country proclaimed him the "Negro genius."

Published His First Mathematical Papers

Wilkins's dissertation, completed under Magnus R. Hestenes, was titled *Multiple Integral Problems in Parametric Form in the Calculus of Variations.* He was the eighth black American, and one of the youngest Americans ever, to earn a Ph.D. degree in mathematics. A Rosenwald Scholarship enabled Wilkins to spend 1942 at the Institute for Advanced Study in Princeton, New Jersey, as a postdoctoral research fellow.

Despite his outstanding credentials, Wilkins could not find a position at a research university. During 1943 and 1944 he was a mathematics instructor at the Tuskegee Institute (now Tuskegee University), a historically black school in Tuskegee, Alabama. It was the first year that the institute offered graduate-level courses.

Wilkins published his first two research papers, both on geometry, in 1943. During the following year he published four more papers, three on differential and integral equations and problems, including his revised Ph.D. dissertation, and one on statistics.

Joined the Manhattan Project

Wilkins returned to work at the University of Chicago in 1944, first as an associate mathematical physicist and then as a physicist, in the Metallurgical Laboratory. Under Arthur Holly Compton and Enrico Fermi, the laboratory was developing a method for producing fissionable material for a nuclear bomb—plutonium 239. It was not until August 6, 1945, when the atomic bomb was dropped on Hiroshima, Japan, that Wilkins understood the goal of his research.

While at Chicago, Wilkins taught mathematics and collaborated with the Nobel Prize-winning physicist

Eugene Wigner. Their research on the absorption of neutrons led to the Wigner-Wilkins approach for estimating the distribution of neutron energies within nuclear reactors. Their joint paper, written in 1944 and declassified in 1948, eventually was published in Wigner's *Collected Works*.

In 1946 Wilkins moved to industry, as a mathematician for the American Optical Company in Buffalo, New York. There he tested optical techniques for the development of lenses for large telescopes. Wilkins married Gloria Louise Stewart on June 22, 1947, and the couple had two children. In 1947 Wilkins was invited to attend the American Mathematical Society (AMS) meeting at the University of Georgia. The committee informed him that they had found a black family with whom he could stay and take his meals, since he would not be able to join the other delegates in the segregated hotel. Offended by their racism, Wilkins never attended an AMS meeting in the Southeast.

Became a Nuclear Engineer

Like many scientists who worked on the Manhattan Project, Wilkins was fascinated by the potential peaceful applications of atomic energy. In 1950 he became a senior mathematician at the Nuclear Development Corporation of America (NDA), later United Nuclear Corporation (UNC), in White Plains, New York. In 1955 he became manager of the Physics and Mathematics department and in 1958 he was promoted again, first to assistant manager and then to manager of research and development. Between 1950 and 1957 NDA's scientific staff grew from seven to more than 300. In 1955 Wilkins was a delegate to a conference on the peaceful uses of atomic energy. The following year he was elected a fellow of the American Association for the Advancement of Science (AAAS).

Realizing that many of his engineering colleagues at NDA were not consulting with the mathematicians, Wilkins decided that he should become an engineer. He earned a bachelor's degree in mechanical engineering, magna cum laude, in 1957, and a master's degree in mechanical engineering in 1960, both from New York University. He now was qualified to work on the design and construction of nuclear facilities.

In 1960 Wilkins moved to the General Atomic division of General Dynamics Corporation in San Diego, California, first as administrator and then as assistant chairman of the Theoretical Physics department. He later became assistant director of the Atomic division. In 1965 Wilkins was promoted, first to assistant director of the John Jay Hopkins Laboratory, then to director of the Defense Science and Engineering Center, and finally to director of Computational Research.

Moved From Academia to Industry

Wilkins remained with General Dynamics until 1970, when he moved to Howard University in Washington, D.C., as distinguished professor of Applied Mathematical Physics. At Howard, Wilkins was instrumental in establishing a doctoral program in mathematics, the only such program at a historically black university. During his seven years at Howard, Wilkins directed four doctoral dissertations. He spent his 1976-77 sabbatical as a visiting scientist at the U.S. Department of Energy's (DOE) Argonne National Laboratory in Argonne, Illinois.

After being elected a fellow of the American Nuclear Society (ANS) in 1964, Wilkins held various offices in the society, serving on the board of directors from 1967-77 and as president from 1974-75. In recognition of his contributions to the design and development of nuclear reactors for peaceful purposes, in 1976 Wilkins became only the second black American to be elected to the National Academy of Engineering (NAE). This academy advises the federal government on issues of science and technology. Wilkins also served on advisory committees on science and engineering education for the NAE, the National Research Council, and various other organizations and universities. He was a council member of the AMS from 1975-77. In 1980 Wilkins was awarded the U.S. Army's Outstanding Civilian Service Medal.

In 1977 Wilkins became vice president and associate general manager for science and engineering at EG&G Idaho, Inc., in Idaho Falls, Idaho. EG&G Idaho operated the Idaho National Engineering Laboratory for the DOE, developing new uses for nuclear energy and designing low-cost nuclear power plants. While remaining a vice president, in 1978 Wilkins was promoted to deputy general manager for science and engineering.

In addition to his other activities, Wilkins was the joint owner of a company that designed and developed nuclear reactors for generating electrical power. He also worked with the Nuclear Regulatory Commission on issues of reactor safety. On June 2, 1984, Wilkins married Maxine G. Malone.

After retiring from EG&G Idaho in 1984, Wilkins spent a year as a fellow at Argonne National Laboratory. He continued as a consultant there until 1990, when he was appointed as distinguished professor of Applied Mathematics and Mathematical Physics at Clark Atlanta University. In 1995 Wilkins also became an adjunct professor at the Woodruff School of Mechanical Engineering at Georgia Institute of Technology.

Known for Research on Radiation Shielding

During the course of his career Wilkins published some 100 research papers in the fields of pure and applied mathematics, optics and optical optimization problems, and nuclear engineering. He also wrote 22 unpublished reports for the Atomic Energy Commission. His nuclear engineering research led to publications on the design, operation, and heat transfer of nuclear reactors.

Wilkins may be best known for his research on the penetration of gamma-rays, conducted in collaboration with Herbert Goldstein and published in *Physical Review* in 1953. Wilkins developed mathematical models for the calculation of the amount of gamma radiation absorbed by a given material. This work was crucial for the development of shielding to absorb gamma radiation emitted by the sun and other nuclear sources and was instrumental for both nuclear reactor design and space research.

Between 1943 and 1997 Wilkins published 46 mathematical research papers. As a theoretical mathematician he made contributions in the fields of Bessel functions, differential and integral equations, and the calculus of variations. In addition, he has published papers on the estimation of the number of real roots of random polynomials.

Recruited Young Blacks to Scientific Careers

Wilkins has been involved with the Urban League for many years, working for racial equality in all areas of life. In 1992 he gave a lecture to a joint meeting of the AMS and the Mathematical Association of America (MAA) in Baltimore, Maryland. His lecture was on heat transfer—specifically on the mathematics of designing fins for expelling heat from an engine. The AMS produced a video of the lecture and an interview with Wilkins, in which he described some of the mathematical problems that have interested him during his career. He also spoke about the difficulties of recruiting underrepresented groups, including blacks, for careers in science and mathematics. The AMS banquet honored Wilkins as the longest-term AMS member, with a tenure of 61 years.

Wilkins was the keynote speaker at the First Annual Conference for African-American Researchers in the Mathematical Sciences (CAARMS1) in 1995, and in 1999 he was an invited speaker at CAARMS5 in Ann Arbor, Michigan. In 1994 Wilkins gave the inaugural lecture at the Undergraduate MATHfest, a mathematics research conference for minority undergraduates sponsored by the National Association of Mathematicians (NAM). Since then the J. Ernest Wilkins Lecture has been presented annually at MATHfest. The J. Ernest Wilkins, Jr. Award for Life Sciences, an oral research competition, is given at EMERGE conferences. EMERGE stands for Empowering Minority Engineers/Scientists to Reach for Graduate Education. Morgan State University in Baltimore has established the J. Ernest Wilkins, Jr. Distinguished Professorship in Physics.

In 1998 Wilkins gave a presentation at the Scholarly Productivity Workshop for Junior Faculty from Historically Black Colleges and Universities, sponsored by the Quality Education for Minorities (QEM) Network and the National Association for Equal Opportunity in Higher Education. Wilkins is on the advisory board for the *Spelman Science and Mathematics Journal* and has continued to give invited lectures and pursue mathematical research.

Selected writings

Books

(With Robert L. Hellens and Paul E. Zweifel) "Status of Experimental and Theoretical Information on Neutron Slowing-Down Distributions in Hydrogenous Media," in *Proceedings of the International Conference on the Peaceful Uses of Atomic Energy,* United Nations, 1956.

"The Landau Constants," in *Progress in Approximation Theory,* Nevai, Paul and Allan Pinkus, eds., Academic Press, 1991.

(With E. P. Wigner) "Effect of the Temperature of the Moderator on the Velocity Distribution of Neutrons With Numerical Calculations for H as a Moderator," in *The Collected Works of Eugene Paul Wigner,* Springer-Verlag, 1992.

"Mean Number of Real Zeroes of a Random Trigonometric Polynomial. II," in *Topics in Polynomials of One or Several Variables and Their Applications,* World Scientific Publishing, 1993.

Periodicals

(With Herbert Goldstein and L. Volume Spencer)" Systematic Calculations of Gamma-Ray Penetration," *Physical Review,* 1953.

"The Silverman Necessary Condition for Multiple Integrals in the Calculus of Variations," *Proceedings of the American Mathematics Society,* 1974.

"A Variational Problem in Hilbert Space," *Applied Mathematics and Optimization,* 1975-76.

(With Keshav N. Srivastava) "Minimum Critical Mass Nuclear Reactors, Part I and Part II," *Nuclear Science and Engineering,* 1982.

(With J. N. Kibe) "Apodization for Maximum Central Irradiance and Specified Large Rayleigh Limit of Resolution, II," *Journal of the Optical Society of America A, Optics and Image Science,* 1984.

"A Modulus of Continuity for a Class of Quasismooth Functions," *Proceedings of the American Mathematics Society,* 1985.

"An Asymptotic Expansion for the Expected Number of Real Zeros of a Random Polynomial," *Proceedings of the American Mathematics Society,* 1988.

"An Integral Inequality," *Proceedings of the American Mathematics Society,* 1991.

(With Shantay A. Souter) "Mean Number of Real Zeros

of a Random Trigonometric Polynomial. III," *Journal of Applied Mathematics and Stochastic Analysis,* 1995.

"The Expected Value of the Number of Real Zeros of a Random Sum of Legendre Polynomials," *Proceedings of the American Mathematics Society,* 1997.

"Mean Number of Real Zeros of a Random Trigonometric Polynomial IV," *Journal of Applied Mathematics and Stochastic Analysis,* 1997.

"Mean Number of Real Zeros of a Random Hyperbolic Polynomial," *International Journal of Mathematics and Mathematical Sciences,* 2000.

Other

Optimization of Extended Surfaces for Heat Transfer, video recording, American Mathematical Society, 1994.

Sources

Books

Agwu, Nkechi and Asamoah Nkwanta, in *African Americans in Mathematics: DIMACS Workshop, June 26-28, 1996,* Dean, Nathaniel, ed., American Mathematical Society, 1997, pp. 195-205.

"J. Ernest Wilkins, Jr.," in *Notable Scientists from 1900 to the Present,* Gale, 2001.

Kessler, James H., J. S. Kidd, Renée A. Kidd, and Katherine A. Morin, *Distinguished African American Scientists of the 20th Century,* Oryx Press, 1996, pp. 331-334.

On-line

"J. Ernest Wilkins, Jr.," *Biography Resource Center,* www.galenet.galegroup.com/servlet/BioRC (November 16, 2003).

"J. Ernest Wilkins, Jr.," *MAA Online,* www.maa.org/summa/archive/WilkinsJ.htm (November 19, 2003).

"J. Ernest Wilkins, Jr.," *Mathematicians of the African Diaspora,* www.math.buffalo.edu/mad/PEEPS/wilkns_jearnest.html (November 19, 2003).

"J. Ernest Wilkins, Jr.," *Princeton University Website,* www.gopher.princeton.edu/~mcbrown/display/wilkins.html (November 19, 2003).

"Jesse Ernest Wilkins Jr.," *Mac Tutor History of Mathematics archive,* www-history.mcs.st-and.ac.uk/Mathematicians/Wilkins_Ernest.html (November 19, 2003).

—Margaret Alic

Tyrone Willingham

1953—

College football coach

Just after the 2001 college football season Tyrone Willingham became the first African-American coach to lead one of college football's highest profile programs, the University of Notre Dame. His career has followed the trajectory of many coaches, going from one job to another until finally garnering the contacts and experience to get a head coaching position. Willingham's first opportunity to lead a program was at Stanford University where he was known as 'The Sheriff.' In his time at Stanford he led the school with perhaps the most demanding academic requirements in Division 1-A to its first Rose Bowl Championship in thirty years and was twice named PAC-10 Coach of the Year in his seven years at Stanford. It was this ability to succeed at a university with rigorous academics which led Notre Dame to name Willingham to one of the top positions in American sports.

Lionel Tyrone Willingham was born on December 30, 1953, in Kinston, North Carolina, to Nathaniel and Lillian Willingham, the oldest of the four Willingham children. Though his father only had a fifth grade education, the elder Willingham worked hard buying and maintaining rental properties to support his family.

His mother was an elementary school teacher who earned a master's degree from Columbia University. In a time of immense social change in the south, Lillian Willingham served as an example for all the people of her community serving on the school board and on the Kinston city council. The Willingham children were raised in an environment where segregation still existed, but they were taught there were no excuses for not achieving a high standard in the classroom and on the sports field.

Played for MSU Against Odds

Willingham gained a desire to lead from his parents early on, integrating his peewee football team as the quarterback and team captain. At Jacksonville High he became the starting quarterback, even though he was only just over five feet tall. Willingham also played basketball and baseball in high school, and though by the time he graduated he stood only five-feet-seven inches tall, he had his mind set on playing Division 1-A football. He wrote over 100 letters to programs around the country, but only Toledo and Michigan State University (MSU) replied. MSU assistant and recruiter

At a Glance . . .

Born Lionel Tyrone Willingham on December 30, 1953, in Kinston, NC; married Kim, 1970s; children: Cassidy, Kelsey, Nathaniel. *Education:* Michigan State University, BS in physical education, 1977.

Career: Michigan State University, graduate assistant, 1977, secondary and special teams coach, 1980-82; North Carolina State, secondary and special teams coach, 1983-85; Rice, receivers and special teams coach, 1986-88; Stanford, running backs coach, 1989-91, head coach, 1995-2001; Minnesota Vikings, running backs coach, 1992-94; Notre Dame University, head coach, 2002–.

Awards: Second team all Big Ten in baseball, 1977; Big Ten Medal of Honor, 1977; Pac-10 Coach of the Year, 1995, 1999; Eddie Robinson Distinction Award, 2000; Home Depot National Coach of the Year, 2003; *The Sporting News'* Sportsman of the Year, 2003.

Addresses: *Office*—Football Office, University of Notre Dame, Notre Dame, Indiana 46556.

Jimmy Raye told the *Knight Ridder Newspaper's* Ann Killion about recruiting Willingham to MSU: "I couldn't convince them to give a scholarship to a 5-foot-7 quarterback. I had to arrange for a make-good situation. If he walked on, he could have the chance to play quarterback. I could see all the intangibles. He was committed, dedicated, he had the heart of a lion."

Willingham chose to attend MSU and, despite being the smallest player on the team, got a chance to play during his freshman year when the two quarterbacks in front of him were injured. In the 1973 season he started four games and led the Spartans to three wins, completing 10 of 19 passes for 124 yards and a touchdown. His efforts earned him a scholarship for the following year.

Though he would not complete another pass in his career at MSU, Willingham did contribute as a receiver and as a punt and kickoff returner. In addition to football, he also played baseball. In his senior year he was named a co-captain of the football team and earned second-team All-Big Ten honors. By the end of his time at MSU he had won three varsity letters in football and baseball and, along with his awards in baseball, was named the football team's most inspirational player and received the Big Ten Conference Medal of Honor as a scholar athlete. This was also the

year Willingham met his wife Kim.

Rode Coaching Carousel

Willingham graduated with a degree in physical education and then stayed at MSU for the 1977 season to begin his career as a football coach, signing on as a graduate assistant. After a year at MSU, Willingham spent two years as a secondary coach at Central Michigan University and then returned to MSU to coach the secondary and the special teams for three years. Willingham then went back home to coach at North Carolina State where Kim worked as a television anchor until their first child Cassidy was born in 1984. Second daughter Kelsey was born in 1988 in Houston when Willingham was coaching the receivers and special teams at Rice University. Kim Willingham told *Knight Ridder's* about their lifestyle in those years: "We moved every three years like clockwork. By Year 2, I started to wonder whether or not I should paint the house because I knew we'd just move again."

Willingham spent three years at Rice and then moved on to Stanford in 1989 to coach under Dennis Green. Green had been a coach with the San Francisco 49ers and met Willingham at a coaching clinic. When Green was named head coach at Stanford, he brought in Willingham the following year to coach his running backs. In 1992 when Green was hired by the Minnesota Vikings of the National Football League (NFL), Willingham went with him to Minnesota to coach the NFL team's running backs. Willingham stayed in Minnesota for two years until he finally got his chance to be a head coach.

Stanford coach Bill Walsh had left the university after a 3-7-1 season. The program lacked talent and lacked discipline and Stanford Athletic Director Ted Leland remembered the quiet, intense man who had coached with Green. On the sidelines Willingham has the demeanor of an iceberg, never yelling, never out of control or upset whether his team is down by 20 or up by 20. Willingham told Alan Grant of *ESPN The Magazine* why he has adopted his steely demeanor: "When I was at Rice, we'd often be getting our butts beat at halftime. I remember coaches trying to get guys to play by yelling and screaming. But young people don't need to be screamed at. What they need is a plan."

Found Success at Stanford

Willingham was brought in to restore order to the Stanford program, and he succeeded brilliantly in his first year despite the fact that skeptics complained all year long that he was a life-long assistant and that he did not have the experience to be a head coach. Willingham led the previously rudderless ship that was Stanford football to a 7-4-1 record in 1995 and was voted the PAC-10 Coach of the Year. He followed up that season with a 7-5 campaign and a 38-0 win over his alma mater MSU in the Sun Bowl.

Willingham then endured two losing seasons, but in 1999 his team won the PAC-10 and made its first Rose Bowl appearance since 1972. Willingham became the first black coach ever to lead a team to the Rose Bowl. He commented about this milestone to Gage Harter of *The Orange County Register,* "I think it does carry some significance. I don't know whether it's important or as important to me as I think it is to some others. I think my first responsibility is to my football team. I don't think my football team cares what color I am as long as I can provide them with the leadership that they need. Probably my sense and feeling on the situation is I'm probably saddened to a great degree that it's coming to this day. My question is, why not sooner?"

The Cardinal lost 17-9 to Wisconsin, but the team with the strictest academic standards in Division 1-A finished with an 8-4 record and a major bowl appearance. Willingham had brought back the Stanford program and quieted those doubters who claimed that teams from universities that require their athletes to also perform in the classroom would never be able to field a decent football team. Willingham's team finished 5-6 in 2000, but the following season saw the Cardinals win nine games for only the second time in 50 years.

Moved on to Coach Notre Dame

While Willingham was succeeding at an academically demanding school, another similarly rigorous school was floundering, but this time it was not a brainy west coast institution, but the most storied program in college football. Notre Dame was experiencing another year of mediocrity and critics were beginning to question whether big-time football and an exacting academic environment could coexist at the same place. After firing coach Bob Davie, Notre Dame interviewed Willingham, but he did not get the job. Willingham was not the rah-rah coach who was filled with awe about the history of the institution. Notre Dame ended up hiring Georgia Tech coach George O'Leary, an Irish Catholic who remained on the job for five days and then resigned when it came to light that he had made false claims on his resume. When it seemed that there was no one else to turn to, Notre Dame turned to Willingham to pull the program out of the mire.

From the first meeting with Willingham, the players knew that they were in for a completely different experience than what they had been used to. Willingham introduced himself to his team with a detailed power point presentation, which layed down the expectations that he had for all of his football players. Senior wide receiver Arnaz Battle told Wayne Drehs on the *ESPN* website, "You could tell instantly that he was going to change things. He had this list of what he wanted, what his demands were, and you could just feel

the anticipation in the room. You could tell he was as good as advertised." Everything about playing football at Notre Dame changed—workouts at 6:30 in the morning became mandatory, practices were planned down to the minutest detail, and any effort less than 100 percent by any member of the program was now intolerable.

In his first season the greatest change in the Notre Dame program was in the win column. Against all odds the Fighting Irish started the season 8-0, with wins over many of the top programs in college football. The Irish knocked off Maryland, Pittsburgh, Air Force, Michigan, Michigan State, Florida State, and Willingham's former school, Stanford. The team moved up the polls from being unranked before the season to the number four team in the nation. Suddenly Willingham was the most prominent college football coach in the nation appearing on the covers of *Sports Illustrated* as "The Savior of Notre Dame" and being compared to great Irish coaches of the past like Ara Parseghian and Knute Rockne. Through it all, Willingham kept the same cool intensity that he has maintained throughout his career. Notre Dame cooled off at the end of the season losing to USC and then losing to North Carolina State 28-6 in the Gator Bowl, but the Irish finished the season with a 10-3 record and a number 17 national ranking. Willingham was named the Home Depot National Coach of the Year and the *Sporting News'* Sportsman of the Year for his turnaround miracle at Notre Dame.

In the second year of his tenure, Willingham discovered the type of negative scrutiny that can come along with the head coach's job at Notre Dame. The Irish ended the season with a 5-7 record and no bowl game, and in certain games during the 2003 campaign the team was completely overmatched. Internet sites such as *Fire Tyrone Willingham* popped up and critics were calling his previous winning season a fluke. But through all the turmoil Willingham remained the same person. Notre Dame receiver Maurice Stovall told *The Houston Chronicle* about Willingham's demeanor: "Coach Willingham is very humble about things. He's always the same whether we win or lose. I think any other coach more likely would yell at the team or scream at them. But Coach Willingham, on the other hand, will tell you what you're doing wrong and tell you to fix it."

Though everything about Notre Dame football had changed from one season to the next, the man at the center of it all remained the same coach he always had been. Willingham told Jonathon Okanes from *Knight Ridder Newspapers* about his focus through whatever conditions surround him: "I'm not capable of really trying to develop something for five years, because I don't know what's promised to me for five years. As I understand it, I have today. My focus is to be absolutely the best you can today. That's always been my focus. If you do the best you can today, that gives you the best chance to be the best you can tomorrow."

Sources

Periodicals

Houston Chronicle, October 5, 2003.
Knight Ridder/Tribune News Service, December 25, 1999; January 9, 2003.
Orange County Register, December 20, 1999.

On-line

"Irish Eyes on Willingham's Changes," *ESPN,* http://espn.go.com/ncf/s/Willingham/notredame.html (January 26, 2004).
"Player Bio: Tyrone Willingham," *Official Athletic Site, Notre Dame,* http://und.ocsn.com/sports/m-footbl/mtt/Willingham_tyrone00.html (January 26, 2003).

—Michael J. Watkins

CeCe Winans

1964—

Gospel recording artist, performer, author

CeCe Winans burst forth from her large, talented musical family, like a shooting star out of a twinkling sky being marveled at by stargazers on a mission to laud their maker. Insisting that, all her life, she has sought only to be a "server of Christ" and "server of people," Winans has shimmered brightly in the Gospel and Christian Contemporary markets while also warming audiences both secular and religious. Winans' stardom is a byproduct of what she has done instinctively since she was a tot—sing praises to God. And with 5 Grammys, eighteen Dove awards, and numerous gold and platinum albums, Winans credits her musical success entirely to God's handiwork in her life. Describing Gospel music to *Jet* Magazine as "God's words set to music." Winans explained, "...it is all about love; it is all about peace; it's all about joy; it's all about happiness. It's all about answers."

Sang Praises with the Family

CeCe Winans, originally named Priscilla, was born on October 8, 1964, by David and Dolores Winans who had long awaited a daughter after seven boys—David, Ronald, Marvin, Carvin, Daniel, Michael, and Ben-

jamin (BeBe). A few years later, Winans was joined by two more female Winans, sisters Angelique and Debbie. According to Winans' 1999 memoirs, *On a Positive Note,* no one remembers for certain how Priscilla Winans came to be called CeCe, but the nickname is most likely traced to Winans' beloved paternal grandmother, Laura Howze, who called her "Sister" since her birth. Referring to Grandmother Howze her childhood "best friend," Winans recalled her grandmother's good advice in her memoir: "God's got His hands on you, CeCe. Just keep your hands in His hands, and you'll be all right."

Winans' parents were truly dedicated to God and family. The ten children were fed and housed with the income David Winans earned as a barber and taxi driver combined with what Dolores earned in her employment at Metropolitan Hospital. Always musical and involved in the church, Winans' parents had met in 1950 as members of Detroit's Lemon Gospel Chorus. Their love for music and God became central to their lifestyle and to their parenting.

A quiet, shy girl, Winans began singing God's words publicly as a small child of seven, when she performed "Fill My Cup" for her congregation. But this boldness

At a Glance . . .

Born Priscilla Winans on October 8, 1964, in Detroit, MI; married Alvin Love, II on June 23, 1984; children: Alvin III, Ashley.

Career: *PTL*, singer, 1982-84; beauty shop owner and beautician, 1984-86; Sparrow Records, recording artist, 1987-98; Pioneer Records, recording artist, 1998-99; Wellspring Gospel, founder, recording artist, 1999–.

Selected awards: Five Grammy Awards, including Best Pop Contemporary Gospel Album, *Andrae Crouch* (various artists), 1996, and Best Pop/Contemporary Gospel Album, *CeCe Winans*, 2001; 18 Dove Awards, including Contemporary Gospel Recorded Song, "Take Me Back," Female Vocalist of the Year, Special Event Album, *Tribute: The Songs of Andrae Crouch* (various artists), 1997, Contemporary Gospel Recorded Song, "Up Where We Belong," Special Event Album, *God With Us: A Celebration of Christmas Carols* (various Artists), 1998, and Contemporary Gospel Album, *CeCe Winans,* Contemporary Gospel Recorded Song, "Anybody Wanna Pray?" 2002; three Soul Train awards including a Soul Train Lady of Soul Award, Best Gospel Album, *His Gift,* 1999.

Addresses: *Home*—P.O. Box 877, Brentwood, TN 37024. *Management*—TBA Entertainment, 300 Tenth Ave., South, Nashville, TN 37203.

should not have surprised worshippers acquainted with the Winans family, for whom singing was as natural as walking, even breathing. Winans grew up singing daily among her family of 12 in their three-bedroom Westside Detroit house on Woodingham Street. "Our house was always filled with music," Winans wrote. "It was nothing for Mom to strike up a song while standing in the kitchen cooking dinner, or for Dad to line a song as he stood in the mirror on Sunday morning, shaving and reading to himself for Sunday school. Singing was the way we communicated, the way we entertained ourselves, and the way we made sense of the world."

Celebrating Christmas as they celebrated life, the family of 12 performed an annual Christmas concert for their community in lieu of exchanging gifts. "Our parents were always striving to bring home to us the real meaning of Christmas," Winans told the *Family* website. Her parents advertised the show, and the major surprise for the family then each holiday season would be how large their audience would be at Mercy Hall.

Rose to Fame With BeBe

At age 17, Winans joined BeBe as a singer on the television program *Praise the Lord (PTL)*. The duo recorded their platinum-certified album *Lord Lift Us Up* which they performed on *PTL*, allowing them to break into the national Christian market. The rest of the family continued on in the fields of music and religion as well. Winans four oldest brothers—David, Ronald, Marvin and Carvin—would become the award-winning Gospel quartet The Winans. Her brother Daniel would perform and record as a solo artist as well. And from a small group of believers, Marvin would also found the 3,000-member Perfecting Church in Detroit and lead it as pastor.

In June of 1984, at age 19, Winans married Alvin Love, 16 years her senior. A friend of Ronald Winans, Love had met his future wife when he joined the family for an evening of bowling. Later, Love traveled with Ronald to North Carolina for a visit to BeBe and CeCe, where they were working for *PTL*. About a year later Love and Winans were married, and Winans moved back to Detroit, leaving BeBe behind.

While settling into marriage, Winans completed beauty school training and continued singing with BeBe a bit on the road. She and Alvin, who was employed at Xerox, opened a beauty salon, where her father worked as a barber. Alvin and her father ran the salon for Winans while she continued performing with BeBe.

In the spring of 1985, Winans gave birth to her first child, Alvin III. By then the demand for her to record and perform with BeBe had increased. Fortunately, Love was able to arrange for a job transfer with Xerox to Nashville, the heart of the Gospel- and Christian Contemporary music-recording industry and where BeBe had already made his home.

The couple together developed Winans musical career as partners. In an article in *Marriage Partnership*, Love and Winans explained that they were able to grow closer in their marriage despite a hectic newlywed period because they have always been true companions. "The friendship made our marriage easier," Love declared. Growing in marriage "boils down to whether you love God more than you love yourself," Winans remarked.

In 1987 Winans and Love's daughter, Ashley Rose, was born. Winans told the *Family* website that being a wife and mother is her "favorite job." She learned from her parents that the key to raising a family well is by putting God first and to "make sure you're in church and your kids are in church." Winans told the *Women in Faith* website, "When you put God first, he gives you wisdom to balance the rest of your life."

Even while caring for a young family, Winans enjoyed increased success with BeBe. The duo recorded their self-titled album in 1987 and *Heaven* in 1988, which earned them heightened popularity in the Gospel and Christian Contemporary sectors. Their 1991 work, *Different Lifestyles,* was embraced enthusiastically by Christian audiences and was sought after in the secular market as well — particularly due to the chart-climbing tracks "Addictive Love" and "I'll Take You There." *Different Lifestyles* earned BeBe and CeCe a Grammy and Soul Train Award for best Gospel album, as well as Dove Awards for Best Song ("Addictive Love") and Group of the Year.

Went Solo, Founded Record Company

In 1995 Winans launched her solo career with the debut release, *Alone in His Presence.* Showcasing covers of traditional hymns, such as "Great Is Thy Faithfulness," "Blessed Assurance," and "I Surrender All," the album won Winans a Grammy for best Gospel album. However, the downside of her solo success was missing working with BeBe. "My favorite spot is singing next to BeBe," Winans admitted to *Essence* in 1999, "...but I have to say this: By our splitting, I've grown a whole lot, as an artist, as a person, and I didn't realize I needed that."

She acknowledged that her earlier recording and performing with BeBe had prepared her to handle music-industry business matters well as a solo artist. However, Love came to assist her in that arena when he left Xerox to become her business manager. The young family of four then went on the road together until travel became problematic. Though Winans and Love home-schooled the children on the road—and continued to do so even after rooting themselves firmly at a home base—the children's extra-circular activities, such as scouts and sports, made travel too difficult. Later, Love gave up managing his wife's career so that the couple's time together would not be dominated by business talk.

Quite remarkably, Winans's career continued to blossom as she dedicated herself further to raising her children. She was able to write, record, and perform, as well as venture into different kinds of television work. She hosted the variety show, *CeCe's Place,* on the Odyssey Network for one season between 1997 and 1998, during which she interviewed close friend Whitney Houston, with whom she recorded the 1996 hit "Count on Me" for the *Waiting to Exhale* soundtrack. And Winans' 1998 release, *His Gift,* earned her a 1999 Soul Train Lady of Soul Award for best Gospel album.

In 1999 Winans and Love founded their own label, Wellspring Gospel, a subsidiary of their company, CW Wellspring Entertainment. Winans told the *Crosswalk* website that founding the label was something that she felt the industry needed. "We just need more God-fearing companies to put out music," she said. The same year, the new label released Winans' fourth solo work, *Alabaster Box,* a gold-certified album of praise songs. She told the *Praise TV* website that she carefully selected the songs in a quest "to bring His [God's] people into a higher place of praise—that place where you lose yourself, that place where you can see his purpose and why you're going through certain things." *Alabaster Box* featured other industry greats, including Take 6, who sang "One and the Same" with CeCe, the Brooklyn Tabernacle Choir, who backed CeCe in "Comforter," and the Nashville Symphony Orchestra, which accompanied the title cut.

Alabaster Box speaks to spiritual brokenness, a reflection of Winans' own internal struggles, as well as a way for her to minister to those who had criticized her professional choices or those close to her who were facing difficulties. She explained that, emotionally speaking, "Nothing really came easy … I say that more in a spiritual sense than in a natural sense." According to Winans, a state of "brokenness" is where one needs to be in order to find true worship of God, to be "elevated" to a "higher place."

Moved into TV and Writing

Winans' 2001 self-titled, gold-certified and Grammy-winning album was followed by a major tour that was co-billed with Gospel dynamo Donnie Mcclurkin. Immediately following, Winans joined her siblings in "The Winans Family Tour" in 2002. That same year, Winans fulfilled guest roles on WB's *7th Heaven* and Pax's *Doc.* Other television appearances have included several appearances on *Soul Train* and *Trinity Broadcast Network (TBN),* as well as *Oprah, Live with Regis and Kathie Lee, Vibe, The Today Show, Good Morning America,* and many others. Remarking on her television gigs, Winans told *Christianity Today,* "It's always humbling to see when doors begin to open and show you how to reach an even broader audience than before."

In September of 2003, Winans released her album *Throne Room,* a collection of worship songs. She stated in a *Christianity Today* interview that she felt called to the project "because of the urgency of true worship," which she calls a Christian's "hiding place" in the world. "When you're a true worshipper, you're always reminded of who God is and how great He is," she said. "… I have changed because of it (*Throne Room*)."

Throne Room's title cut was co-written with Gospel living legend Andrae Crouch, a friend of the Winans family. Winans recorded "Mercy Said No," written by Greg Long, as a dedication to her brother Ronald who had a few years earlier undergone emergency heart surgery, during which he was clinically dead for four minutes during the 14-hour procedure.

In January of 2004, *Throne Room,* a companion

devotional text to the album written by Winans and songwriter Claire Cloninger, was released by Integrity Publishers. Winans, who prays and reads the Bible each morning, sought to offer people an additional tool to music for growing a relationship with God. "Worship is so important to me and my desire is that *Throne Room* will help usher people into the presence of the almighty," Winans said in a release announcing the new title.

At the close of 2003 Winans was also busy promoting artists signed to her label and also working within a partnership agreement with Sony to record a mainstream album. She also spent time performing with her home church choir, Born Again Choir, who released an album featuring other well-known Gospel artists, including Desmond Pringle and Israel Haughton.

Making time for good works besides singing, Winans is known to surprise fans in need of a kind word and prayer with a phone call or note. She is also a World Vision artist—a promoter for the charitable organization that links sponsors to needy children around the world,—as well as a spokesperson for Project Teen Save—a teen-suicide-prevention initiative. Winans founded the non-profit organization, Sharing the Vision—designed to meet needs in her local community, as well as extend financial support to other worthy charitable organizations. "The smile, the glow that drew me to CeCe, that's her big heart showing," Love told *Marriage Partnership*. "... I have to share her with her fans and stand off in the background."

Winans is still a force in the Gospel music industry and many people wonder what area she might take on next, whether it will be a full time radio show or something outside of show business completely. Regardless of what her venture is, however, Winans is hopeful that all of her actions will reflect that which is most important to her, her values and her religion. "Without Him [God], I would be just another voice singing just another song," Winans told *Christianity Today*. "I'm just grateful that He's able to use me."

Selected works

Discography

(With BeBe Winans) *Lord Lift Us Up,* Sparrow, 1985.
(With BeBe Winans) *BeBe & CeCe Winans,* Sparrow, 1987.
(With BeBe Winans) *Heaven,* Sparrow, 1988.
(With BeBe Winans) *Different Lifestyles,* Sparrow, 1991.

(With BeBe Winans) *First Christmas,* Sparrow, 1993.
(With BeBe Winans) *Relationships,* Sparrow, 1994.
Alone in His Presence, Sparrow, 1995.
(With BeBe Winans) *Greatest Hits,* Sparrow, 1996.
(With Whitney Houston) "Count on Me," Arista, 1996.
Everlasting Love, Pioneer,1998.
His Gift, Pioneer, 1998.
Alabaster Box, Wellspring Gospel, 1999.
CeCe Winans, Wellspring Gospel, 2001.
Throne Room, Wellspring Gospel, 2003.

Writings

(with Renita J. Weems) *On a Positive Note,* Simon & Schuster, 1999.
(with Claire Cloninger) *Throne Room,* Integrity, 2004.

Sources

Books

Winans, CeCe, and Claire Cloninger, *Throne Room,* Integrity, 2004.
Winans, CeCe, and Renita J. Weems, *On a Positive Note,* Simon & Schuster, 1999.

Periodicals

Essence, June 1999.
Jet, October 22, 2001.
Marriage Partnership, Spring 2000.

On-line

"A Christmas conversation with CeCe Winans," *Family,* www.family.org (December 31, 2003).
"CeCe Winans," *Jamsline,* www.jamsline.com (December 31, 2003).
"CeCe Winans," *Women of Faith,* www.womenoffaith.com (December 31, 2003).
"CeCe Winans—*Alabaster Box,*" *Praise TV,* www.praisetv.com (December 31, 2003).
"CeCe Winans: inside the alabaster box," *Crosswalk,* www.crosswalk.com (December 31, 2003)
"Thoughts from the throne room," *Christianity Today,* www.christianitytoday.com (December 31, 2003).
The Throne Room, www.cecewinans.com (December 31, 2003).

—Melissa Walsh

George C. Wolfe

1954—

Playwright, stage director, producer

In the spring of 1993 George C. Wolfe was named the new head of the New York Shakespeare Festival, one of Manhattan's most influential theater projects. At the time he took over the New York Shakespeare Festival, Wolfe was still a young man, but he had nevertheless compiled a body of work that lifted him to national prominence. He was the author of *The Colored Museum,* a satirical comedy, and *Jelly's Last Jam,* a production that began a long Broadway run in the early 1990s. Wolfe also forged a reputation as a premier director, working with the Shakespeare Festival and at other venues on such pieces as German playwright Bertolt Brecht's *Caucasian Chalk Circle* and Tony Kushner's epic drama *Angels in America: Millennium Approaches.* These and other plays bearing Wolfe's influence have established him as "one of the leaders of a new generation ... in the American theater—one whose work raises provocative questions about racial culture, history, and identity," to quote *Los Angeles Times* contributor Hilary De Vries.

The New York theatrical community reserves its greatest respect for those people who can merge the sometimes conflicting considerations of art and com-

merce—those who can craft a hit play that also pleases the critics. Wolfe's *Jelly's Last Jam* was one such play, selling out on Broadway while garnering eleven Tony Award nominations and winning three. Observers expected Wolfe to bring this concept of heightened commercialism without artistic sacrifice to the Shakespeare Festival. Wolfe himself told the *Los Angeles Times:* "I don't think you have to compromise edge for entertainment; in my life, they've gone hand in hand.... When you go to the theater, you can experience somebody trying to deal with his own vulnerability, and it's affirming to see the struggle and the attempt to survive. I think that's what good theater does."

Found Love of Theater Early

Wolfe was born on September 23, 1954, the third of four children in a middle-class Frankfort, Kentucky, family. His mother was a teacher who rose to be principal of an elementary school. His father worked for the Kentucky state government. In his early youth, Wolfe lived in "a very insular world" that included little contact with those outside his race. "There were white people, but I didn't feel they had any severe impact on me," he told the *Los Angeles Times.* "The church was all black, the grade school was all black. I knew I couldn't go down to the local movie theater and see '101 Dalmatians,' but it was a nice and polite little world."

Wolfe's parents and teachers groomed him to move beyond the "polite little world," and in his teen years he discovered his life's passion. At the age of thirteen he traveled to New York City and saw the Broadway staging of *Hello, Dolly!*. Afterward he was determined to become an actor. Part of Wolfe's drive came from his parents, who instilled in him a need to succeed in a white dominated field. Wolfe told the *New York Times:* "I was 13 or 14 before I was thrust into the white world. And ever since then it's become clearer and clearer to me that I was part of a generation of black children who were raised like integration soldiers, who were groomed to invade white America. I don't know how conscious it was, but with my parents it was definitely: 'They think you're less than; you've got to be better than.'"

Wolfe joined theater workshops in Frankfort and continued to pursue acting in college, first at Kentucky State University and later at Pomona College in California. After earning a Bachelor's degree in theater arts, he settled in Los Angeles, where he wrote, directed, and acted in plays. For a time in the 1970s he was associated with the Inner City Cultural Center in Los Angeles as a playwright and director, but he gradually became disenchanted with California. "The goal of success in L.A. was not theater, but movies and

TV, and I knew that wasn't right for me then," he told the *Los Angeles Times.*

Made a Name as Playwright and Director

In 1979 Wolfe moved to New York City. He enrolled in the Master's degree program in musical theater at New York University and continued to write, act, and direct. "I struggled for six or seven years," he admitted in the *New York Times.* Amidst the years of struggle he saw his first play produced, a work called *Paradise* that was presented Off-Off Broadway at Playwrights Horizons in 1985. The *Los Angeles Times* noted that the play, "a musical about a family that escapes to an island, was largely savaged by area critics." A better reception awaited Wolfe's next production.

Wolfe told the *Los Angeles Times* that he wrote *The Colored Museum* as a personal "exorcism" of black cultural myths. The work was an outrageous, satirical look at black people that dared to challenge some of black Americans' most cherished icons, including Lorraine Hansberry's play *A Raisin in the Sun* and political activist Eldridge Cleaver's *Soul on Ice.* The piece, modeled on a revue, includes skits in which a young black woman must choose between two hairpieces, one an Afro, one a Euro; a segment in which a hefty black woman reminiscent of Aunt Jemima stirs a cauldron of unidentified stew; a monologue from a black transvestite; and a sketch in which a flight attendant takes her passengers through three centuries of African-American history. *New York* magazine columnist John Simon called the work "young in spirit, gifted in most aspects ... a sophisticated, satirical, seriously funny show that spoofs white and black America alike. It is remarkably unafraid of lampooning black foibles, which is a sign of artistic maturity. We come of age—all of us, black or white—when we can laugh at ourselves."

The Colored Museum had its premier at the Crossroads Theater in New Jersey in 1986. The show's New Jersey producers hailed Wolfe in the *Los Angeles Times* as "a courageous and fresh voice, ... a new voice." Within a year the play moved to New York's Public Theater—home of the Shakespeare Festival—and later it was broadcast on public television as part of the *Great Performances* series. "That's when my career started to feed me," Wolfe told the *New York Times.*

Not everyone greeted *The Colored Museum* with enthusiasm, however. The play's content and mordant satire drew charges of reverse racism from some critics. Wolfe told the *Los Angeles Times:* "When [the play] opened, the self-appointed black crowd said, 'This is horrifying. This is horrifying. I can't believe he is actually saying that'…. And that was painful. Because that was exactly the place where I was coming from…. All the whites went into programmed guilt and the black people went into programmed rage and the play kept saying, 'You can't do that.' It was really a play about self-empowerment. About how I am now going to define myself the way that I am capable of." In a sense, *The Colored Museum* prefigured other popular black satires such as *In Living Color* that dared to explode black cultural myths.

The success of *The Colored Museum* brought Wolfe other opportunities under the aegis of the Shakespeare Festival. He became a resident director at the Public Theater and worked on a number of projects there. Most notable among these was *Spunk,* a series of three vignettes he adapted from short stories by renowned author Zora Neale Hurston, and *The Caucasian Chalk Circle,* an adaptation of a Brecht play done by Thulani Davis. Both works premiered at the Public Theater in 1990 and received good reviews. *New Yorker* critic Mimi Kramer wrote of *The Caucasian Chalk Circle:* "The production is uplifting and exhilarating in a way that *New York Shakespeare Festival* theater hardly ever is: through simply showing a work to its best advantage and giving the audience a good time." Likewise, *New Yorker* columnist Edith Oliver praised *Spunk* for its "powerful injection of irony and wit," and concluded that the piece was "a beautiful show."

Wolfe directed other plays and performance art pieces at the Shakespeare Festival, but in the early 1990s he sought to produce a musical for Broadway. This was a risky undertaking because musicals are expensive to mount and require extensive preparation and rehearsal. Wolfe's musical, for which he wrote the book and helped to write the lyrics, was based on the life of Ferdinand Joseph LeMenthe "Jelly Roll" Morton, a 1920s New Orleans jazz musician. In the play, Jelly Roll is given a supernatural opportunity—like the one afforded Ebenezer Scrooge—to review the important and formative moments of his life. The show features songs and tap dancing as well as a portrait of a man uncomfortable with his racial origins. Wolfe not only wrote the play but directed it as well.

Jelly's Last Jam had its premiere in Los Angeles in 1991 and moved to Broadway in 1992 with Gregory Hines in the leading role. Edith Oliver called the play "an ironic, tough evocation of the complex, embittered, and anything but heroic man who wrote and played [jazz]," adding that "The book, strong enough to justify the narrative and the characters, the music and the emotions, is Mr. Wolfe's accomplishment. There has never been anything like it, on or off Broadway." And E. R. Shipp commented in *Emerge* that the depth and boldness of *Jelly's Last Jam* made Wolfe "the hope for the future of American theater…. He [shows] theatergoers that so much that is referred to as black culture is really about being human."

On the "A-List"

A *New York Times* reporter claimed that the success of *Jelly's Last Jam* "propelled [Wolfe] onto producers'

A-lists and garnered him the choicest of this [1993] season's assignments on Broadway." That "choice assignment" was Pulitzer Prize-winner Tony Kushner's epic drama *Angels in America,* a sweeping look at gay America, AIDS, and politics for which a sequel was almost immediately planned. Wolfe directed *Angels in America,* which opened on Broadway in May of 1993. In a review of the three-and-a-half-hour play, *Newsweek* correspondent Jack Kroll called the work "the most intelligent, most passionate American play in recent memory," adding that Wolfe was "the perfect director for the play's ricochet rhythm between realism and fantasy." Of his success Wolfe told *American Theatre* "When I did *Jelly* on Broadway, I said to myself, 'Okay it's going to be three or four years before I come back to this arena.' All of a sudden I was back the next year with *Angels.* All of a sudden, the next season I was back with Part 2…. It's fun and exciting and dangerous to work on Broadway, but it's also extraordinarily exhausting because of the warrior energy you have to have."

Just before *Angels in America* opened, the board of directors of the New York Shakespeare Festival announced that Wolfe would be the new head of the Festival. Wolfe took the reins of the institution from JoAnne Akalaitis, a producer-director who had run it for eighteen months. In making the change in leadership, the Festival's board of directors cited declining revenues and waning corporate support for the program and its Public Theater. *American Theatre* magazine said that part of the decision to make Wolfe the new head had to have been the fact that Wolfe had "become one of the most sought-after directors in the country by making the cultural leap from *Jelly's Last Jam* to *Angels.*" Wolfe, who had for years half-jokingly called himself "the Negro at the Public," enthusiastically embraced the opportunity to revive the flagging fortunes of the Shakespeare Festival. He planned to accent diversity in programming and casting, to invite more participation from minority playwrights, and to produce "a theater that looks, feels, and smells like America," to quote Wolfe in the *New York Times.*

Asked about his vision for the Shakespeare Festival, Wolfe told *Newsweek:* "I see a brilliant, dangerous new musical on one of the main stages [at the Public Theater]. Upstairs, a workshop of a play by a writer who failed last season but has come back with a marvelous play. On the top floor, a young director is staging his first Shakespeare. On the other large stage, I'm directing a Restoration comedy because by now the endowment is so large I can relax. And downstairs, there's a series of solo artists, white, Asian, and Hispanic." Wolfe hoped to attract new sponsors for the Festival and revive former sources of revenue, all the while maintaining artistic control over the institution's offerings. One big concern was that the theatre had been supported by its sale of "A Chorus Line" years before and that money had started running out. He began with a 1994 budget of roughly four million dollars.

He started out, much as his dream, with the play "Blade to the Heat" in rehearsal on one floor, on another floor the Young Playwright's Festival was going on, Hal Prince was planning a new musical by Michael John LaChiusa called "The Wild Party" in which Toni Collette played the lead Queenie, a jazz-age hostess, and Barry Edelstein was doing "Merchant of Venice." Wolfe won a Tony Award nomination for directing "The Wild Party." Wolfe also put on the famous show "Bring In 'Da Noise, Bring In 'Da Funk." He started his reign with a bang and never looked back.

"Topdog/Underdog" came out in 2001 with Wolfe directing the play about a duo of brothers who were abandoned by their parents when they were teenagers. *Variety* said of the show, "With director George C. Wolfe displaying his typical showmanship and style, they … bring a sort of vaudevillian energy and style to some of the livelier physical set pieces. Among these are Cheadle's dance of disrobement, as he takes off two complete layers of clothes he's 'boosted' from a store, and a sort of impromptu Southern song routine celebrating Lincoln's payday." In 2002 Wolfe wrote and directed a permanent production for the Apollo Theater—"Harlem Song." The show dealt with significant historical moments in Harlem's history and had original music written by the same team that did the music for "Bring In 'Da Noise, Bring In 'Da Funk," Daryl Waters and Zane Mark.

In 2003 Wolfe put on the play "Radiant Baby," a story that centered around graffiti artist Keith Haring who became amazingly popular and then at age 30 was diagnosed with AIDS and at age 31 died. Wolfe said of the play, "Working on this show was like reactivating a decade—how people looked and how people walked and what crowds were like. Doing theater and doing art, it's always so hard. And doing it in New York, it feels especially hard. The work takes something from you, but it also gives something to you. For me, it rekindled certain memories—very sad ones but at the same time very joyful and foolish ones." He also directed and produced the musical "On the Town." The play was met with mixed reviews and seemed rather controversial because Wolfe changed the original dance scenes and some purists didn't approve. Among the long list of other productions Wolfe has been involved with, Wolfe has been responsible for bringing "Julius Ceasar," and "The Taming of the Shrew" to Broadway. He also directed the Tony Kushner musical "Not Just Pocket Change."

Rich of the *New York Times* hailed Wolfe as a producer-director-playwright who "crossed over from the American to the African, from drama to satire to musical theater, from verbal elegance to visual dash. He is one to try anything rather than take no for an answer." Assessing his own capacity to create new directions for American theater, Wolfe told the *Los Angeles Times:* "I'm a warrior…. I know the right conditions under which good work happens. And there are a number of artists who may not be as good at being warriors as I am, but they're good artists. If I can use my connections and the force of my personality to create structures for other artists, great, because other people did that for me."

Selected works

Plays

Paradise, produced Off-Off Broadway at the Playwrights Horizons, 1985.
The Colored Museum, first produced at the Crossroads Theater, New Jersey, 1986; produced at Public Theater, New York, 1986; broadcast on PBS-TV as part of *Great Performances series,* 1991.
(Adapter) *Spunk* (three one-act plays based on stories by Zora Neale Hurston), produced at Public Theater, 1990.
(Director) *The Caucasian Chalk Circle,* 1990.
(Director) *Fires in the Mirror,* 1991.
Jelly's Last Jam (musical), first produced in Los Angeles, 1991; produced on Broadway at the Virginia Theater, 1992.
Angels in America: Millennium Approaches, 1993.

Other

Also author of *Queenie Pie, Hunger Chic,* and *Minimum Wage.*

Sources

Books

Contemporary Dramatists, Sixth edition, St. James Press, 1999.

Periodicals

Advocate, April 15, 2003, p. 52.
American Theatre, May-June, 1993, p. 43; December, 1994, p. 14; December, 2003, p. 32.
Emerge, November 1993, pp. 63-66.
Entertainment Weekly, December 4, 1998, p. 87; August 24, 2001, p. 127.
Essence, February, 1991, p. 35.
Jet, May 29, 2000, p. 54; May 27, 2002, p. 52.
Los Angeles Times, March 3, 1991, p. Calendar-6; November 24, 1992, p. Calendar-1.
National Review, January 24, 1994, p. 71.
New Criterion, January, 1999, p. 43.
New Leader, May 9, 1994, p. 23; December 14, 1998, p. 30.
New Republic, January 21, 1991, p. 28; May 24, 1993, p. 29.
Newsweek, May 7, 1990, p. 62; March 29, 1993, p. 63; May 17, 1993, p. 70.

New York, November 17, 1986, p. 119; May 18, 1992, p. 61; May 17, 1993, pp. 102-03.

New Yorker, November 10, 1986, p. 120; May 7, 1990, p. 83; December 17, 1990, p. 110; May 11, 1992, p. 78; October 26, 1992, pp. 117-18.

New York Times, March 13, 1993, p. 14; March 21, 1993, p. H-1; March 22, 1993, p. C-1.

Time, December 22, 2003, p. 123.

Variety, November 30, 1998, p. 73; July 12, 1999, p. 46; October 18, 1999 p. 50; August 28, 2000, p. 48; October 30, 2000; August 6, 2001, p. 25; April 15, 2002, p. 36; June 17, 2002, p. 43; March 10, 2003, p. 40; December 8, 2003, p. 63.

Other

Additional information for this profile was provided by the New York Shakespeare Festival.

—Anne Janette Johnson and
Catherine V. Donaldson

Lewin Wright

1962—

Naval Commander

Occasionally a child knows exactly what he will do with his life even while still very young. Perhaps some childhood experience or the goals of a parent will inform a young man's choice and he will create a life plan in fulfillment of some youthful dream. Such was not the case for the first African-American commander of the naval ship, the USS *Constitution*, also known as "Old Ironsides." Commander Lewin Wright never set out to command the most historically significant vessel in the U.S. Navy; indeed he never set out to join the navy, and no doubt, never dreamed of such a future when he was a child growing up in London, England.

Family Encouraged Pursuit of Education

Lewin C. Wright was born in London in April of 1962. He was one of four children born to Lenworth and Melvina Wright, who had immigrated to England from Jamaica during the 1950's, bringing with them one son from an earlier marriage. In a December 2003 statement provided to *Contemporary Black Biography* (*CBB*), Wright stated that his family was part of the post World War II influx of West Indians into England. During World War II, his father had served in the British Royal Air Force, and after the war ended, London was a destination for many of the Caribbeans who had fought on behalf of the British during the war years. After they moved to London the family settled in North London, where earlier West Indian emigrants had already established a community. Wright's father worked as a bus driver and his mother found employment as a nurse's aid. Wright attended public schools and was in every way what he called an "average young boy."

In 1975 the Wright family immigrated to the United States and settled into the Flatbush section of Brooklyn, New York. Wright was 12 years old when the family moved, and while he did notice significant differences between his old West Indian neighborhood in London and his new neighborhood in Brooklyn, he easily settled into the family's new American life. When he was old enough, Wright attended the prestigious Brooklyn Technical High School, which required that entering students pass a rigorous entrance exam before they could be accepted. While at Brooklyn Technical, Wright focused on chemistry and prepared for college.

At a Glance . . .

Born in April of 1962 in London, England; married Sharon Greene, 1989. *Education:* Brandeis University, BS, 1984; Surface Warfare Officers Department Head Course, 1993; Officer's Candidate School, Newport, RI, 1995; Army Command and General Staff College, Leavenworth, KS, completed Joint Professional Military Education, phase one, 1999; Benedictine College, MBA, 1999. *Military Service:* U.S. Navy, 1986–.

Career: U.S. Navy, electrical officer and electronic warfare officer onboard the USS Vancouver, 1986-1989, navigator onboard the USS Buchanan, 1989-1991, recruiter, 1991-1992, operations officer onboard the USS Lewis B., 1993-1995, pre-commissioning unit for the USS Robin, 1995-1996, executive officer onboard the USS Robin, 1996-1998, executive officer onboard the USS Samuel Eliot Morison, 1999-2000, Chief of Naval Operations, Washington DC, assistant for strategy, 2001-2003, USS Constitution, commander, 2003–.

Awards: Navy Commendation Medal, 1995, 1998, 2001; Meritorious Service Medal, 2003.

Addresses: *Office*—USS Constitution, Charlestown Navy Yard, Charlestown, MA 02129-1797.

There was never any question that Wright would attend college once he had completed high school. In his interview with *CBB*, Wright mentioned that "Going to college was not a decision—it was a fact. By this I mean that in my family, there was never a question as to whether you would go to college. The question was what profession would you pursue." Wright discovered Brandeis University at a college fair that he attended while still in high school, and so after his graduation from Brooklyn Technical in 1980, he headed to Waltham, Massachusetts, to begin his college studies. In August of 2003 Wright told interviewer Dennis Nealon of the *Brandeis University News* that it was Wright's mother who liked the idea of his attending the university. But Wright noted that he agreed with his mother that attending was "one of the best things I've done with my life." For Wright, attending Brandeis was only one of many careful decisions to be made, each time with conscientious thought. Although he had not conceived of a specific plan, he gave each decision about schooling very careful thought before proceeding.

Joined the Navy

As he neared the completion of his degree at Brandeis, Wright had no plans to enter the military. His degree was in computer science, and there were many job opportunities for careers in this growing field. But during his final year in college, Wright decided that he did not want to spend the rest of his life working in the computer field. Wright told *CBB* that during a job fair in Boston he was waiting for the line at one of the computer company kiosks to shorten when he began to speak with the Navy recruiter. Wright said it was nothing specific that the recruiter said that convinced him to join, and in fact, they just discussed the navy in general, but the more he thought of it the more he thought that becoming a Surface Warfare officer, someone who drives the ship, was "something I could do for a few years." After he spoke with the recruiter, Wright made the decision to enter the navy as an officer. Even then he did not intend to make the navy a career. He signed up for four years but would stay much longer. Just as they had previously done when he had made other important life decisions, Wright's family supported his decision to join the navy. In his statement to *CBB*, Wright noted that his parents "approached this the way they approached most of my decisions. By this I mean that as long as my decision was well thought out and what I was doing was meaningful then they supported me." And so just as he had earlier when choosing to attend Brooklyn Technical or Brandeis University, Wright chose a path that presented the best opportunities but that also recognized his own talents and the likelihood for a significant contribution to the navy.

After his graduation from Brandeis in 1984, Wright was sent to Officer's Candidate School in Newport, Rhode Island, from which he graduated in September of 1985. At that time Wright was commissioned into the United States Navy as an ensign. Wright's first navy assignment was as an electrical and electronic warfare officer onboard the USS Vancouver, an amphibious transport dock ship, which was homeported in San Diego, California. Wright was assigned to the USS Vancouver from June of 1986 until May of 1989. During his time on the USS Vancouver, he was also promoted to lieutenant junior grade. His next assignment was as a navigator on board the USS Buchanan, a guided missile destroyer that was also homeported in San Diego, California. While assigned to the USS Buchanan, Wright married Sharon Greene in late 1989. This second assignment lasted from July of 1989 to March of 1991, during which time Wright was promoted to lieutenant. Wright's third assignment took him to the Navy Recruiting District in San Francisco, California, where he functioned as a navy recruiter from May of 1991 until October of 1992.

After his tenure as a navy recruiter, Wright's next assignment was to complete the Surface Warfare Officers Department Head Course, which he did in 1993. With this additional training out of the way, Wright was assigned as the Operations Officer onboard the USS *Lewis B. Puller*, a frigate that was homeported in Long Beach, California, from June of 1993 until January of 1995. Wright received the first of three Navy Commendation Medals for his service aboard the USS *Lewis B. Puller*. With his duty onboard this vessel completed, Wright spent the next year attached to the precommissioning unit for the USS *Robin*, a coastal minehunter that was nearing completion in New Orleans, Louisiana. After the USS *Robin* was completed and commissioned, Wright became the Executive Officer, a position that he held from January of 1996 until May of 1998. Shortly after assuming the position of executive office, Wright was promoted to lieutenant commander. He was also rewarded with the second of his three Navy Commendation Medals, earned during his service on the USS *Robin*.

When Wright headed off to Army Command and General Staff College, in Leavenworth, Kansas, in June of 1998, he had already spent 14 years in the navy. In a December 2003 statement Wright told *CBB* that he had "no master plan" for what he had done with his life. He had never planned to make the navy a career; instead he said, "I have simply been doing what I think most people do which is trying to find myself. Whenever I have come to a 'fork in the road' in my life I have examined my choices and based on my experiences, thoughts, and recommendations from friends and family and trusting my gut, made what I thought would be the best decision at that point in time."

As they had in the past, Wright's thoughtful choices had served him well during his early career in the navy. He completed the Joint Professional Military Education, phase one in June of 1999. At the same time, he also completed the coursework for a master's degree in business administration from Benedictine College. With this phase of his education completed, Wright was assigned to the USS *Samuel Eliot Morison*, a frigate that was homeported in Mayport, Florida. Wright reported to his new assignment in September of 1999 and assumed the duties of the executive officer until December of 2000, when he was once again reassigned.

Assigned Command of USS Constitution

At the conclusion of his tenure onboard the USS *Samuel Eliot Morison*, Wright received his third Navy Commendation Medal, and then in February of 2001, he was assigned to the staff of the Chief of Naval Operations in Washington, D.C. While in Washington Wright served as the section head for strategy for the director of the Surface Warfare Division. Four months after his arrival in Washington, Wright was promoted to Commander. As he neared the completion of his Washington assignment, Wright was awarded the Meritorious Service Medal for his contributions to the navy during the previous two years. Then just over two years after he was promoted to commander, Wright received what he considered to be the most significant achievement of his career—command of the USS *Constitution*, homeported in Boston. According to the USS *Constitution*'s website, Commander Wright's own comments at the ceremony relayed the importance of this assignment. As he prepared for the change of command ceremony, Wright thought about the ship's history and of those who had captained it in the past. Wright said that it was hard to believe that he was "taking over this historical ship, with all its tradition, and great captains." Although he would join an illustrious list of naval officers as commander of the USS *Constitution*, Wright would also achieve much more, since he also became the first African American commander of this historical vessel. And so it is of little surprise that he felt "a little awe struck" at receiving the honor he so clearly had earned.

Wright's duties on the USS *Constitution* were very different than they would be on any other Naval vessel. The oldest warship in the navy does not sail of its own accord, and Wright's office is not onboard but is located in a building overlooking the ship. As Commander Wright told *CBB,* the USS *Constitution*'s most important function is to "keep the flame of our nation's rich naval heritage burning brightly in the hearts and minds of Americans." As commander, Wright took charge of some 50-60 navy men and women who worked to preserve the ship's history as well as educate the public. And as commander, Wright also made many public speeches and appearances in connection with the ship's history. One of the very special duties that Wright undertook in connection with his new command occurred in October of 2003 when a replica of the *La Amistad* made a historic visit to Boston. Wright was asked to take part in the official welcoming of the schooner. He told *CBB* that the captain of the *Amistad*, Bill Pinkney, had an early naval career and that he had been denied entry into the Navy officer program, although he would have been qualified. Even though the Navy had been officially desegregated in 1948, discrimination still existed in some areas. Wright said that because it was very difficult for blacks to make it into the officer ranks, his attendance, "as commander of the Navy's most historical ship," meant a lot to Pinkney, since Wright's command made clear how much the navy had changed. The Amistad's arrival and the subsequent honors accorded to Pinkney also meant a great deal to Wright, who told *CBB* that he "was touched and extremely gratified to participate in such a significant event that meant so much to a man who means so much to our maritime heritage." As the commander of the USS *Constitution*, Wright had many opportunities to welcome dignitaries, but welcoming the *Amistad* to Boston was one event that had great personal meaning to Wright.

When Wright was interviewed by *CBB* in December of 2003, he had only been commander of the USS *Constitution* for six months. When asked about how his life experiences would influence his command decisions, Wright replied that to be a successful commander he would have to call upon all of his experiences, good and bad, and draw from those the necessary lessons to command. Wright noted that he is "a combination of all the commanding officers for whom I have worked on the five ships on which I have been stationed." His tenure onboard the USS *Constitution* will last into 2005, when he will again be reassigned to other duties. As had been the case throughout his naval career, Wright was prepared for the inevitable move. Wright explained to *CBB* that the navy life was hard on marriages. The frequent moves and the time at sea, with the long separations from loved ones can make a marriage difficult to sustain. Yet of his 14 year marriage to Sharon Greene-Wright, Wright said that he "felt blessed to have such a wonderful partner with whom to share his life." It is hard to imagine what sort of command might follow that of the USS *Constitution*, but certainly Commander Lewin Wright will be prepared for whatever follows "Old Ironsides."

Sources

On-line

"In the Lap of History: Brandeis alum becomes 68th commander of 'Old Ironsides,'" *Brandeis University,* www.my brandeis.edu/item?news_item_id=10 1873 (November 14, 2003).

"USS *Constitution* Change of Command 2003," USS *Constitution Official Website,* www.ussconstitution. navy.mil/COC2003.htm (November 14, 2003).

Other

Additional information for this profile was obtained from a telephone interview with *Contemporary Black Biography,* on December 22, 2003, as well as from a personal statement and Curriculum Vitae provided by Lewin Wright on December 19, 2003.

—Dr. Sheri Elaine Metzger

Cumulative Nationality Index

Volume numbers appear in **bold**

Wilson, Phill **9**
Wilson, Sunnie **7**
Wilson, William Julius **20**
Winans, Angie **36**
Winans, BeBe **14**
Winans, CeCe **14, 43**
Winans, Debbie **36**
Winans, Marvin L. **17**
Winans, Vickie **24**
Winfield, Dave **5**
Winfield, Paul **2**
Winfrey, Oprah **2, 15**
Winkfield, Jimmy **42**
Witherspoon, John **38**
Witt, Edwin T. **26**
Wolfe, George C. **6, 43**
Wonder, Stevie **11**
Woodard, Alfre **9**
Woodruff, Hale **9**
Woods, Granville T. **5**
Woods, Sylvia **34**
Woods, Tiger **14, 31**
Woodson, Carter G. **2**
Woodson, Robert L. **10**
Worrill, Conrad **12**
Wright, Bruce McMarion **3**
Wright, Charles H. **35**
Wright, Deborah C. **25**
Wright, Lewin **43**
Wright, Louis Tompkins **4**
Wright, Richard **5**
Wynn, Albert R. **25**
X, Malcolm **1**
Yancy, Dorothy Cowser **42**
Yarbrough, Camille **40**
Yoba, Malik **11**
York, Vincent **40**
Young, Andrew **3**
Young, Coleman **1, 20**
Young, Jean Childs **14**
Young, Lester **37**
Young, Roger Arliner **29**
Young, Whitney M., Jr. **4**
Youngblood, Johnny Ray **8**
Youngblood, Shay **32**
Zollar, Alfred **40**
Zollar, Jawole Willa Jo **28**

Angolan
Bonga, Kuenda **13**
dos Santos, José Eduardo **43**
Neto, António Agostinho **43**
Savimbi, Jonas **2, 34**

Antiguan
Williams, Denise **40**

Australian
Freeman, Cathy **29**

Austrian
Kodjoe, Boris **34**

Bahamian
Ingraham, Hubert A. **19**

Barbadian
Arthur, Owen **33**
Brathwaite, Kamau **36**
Clarke, Austin C. **32**
Flash, Grandmaster **33**
Foster, Cecil **32**
Kamau, Kwadwo Agymah **28**
Lamming, George **35**

Batswana
Masire, Quett **5**

Belizian
Jones, Marion **21**

Beninois
Hounsou, Djimon **19**
Joachim, Paulin **34**
Kerekou, Ahmed (Mathieu) **1**
Mogae, Festus Gontebanye **19**
Soglo, Nicéphore **15**

Bermudian
Gordon, Pamela **17**
Smith, Jennifer **21**

Brazilian
da Silva, Benedita **5**
Nascimento, Milton **2**
Pelé **7**
Pitta, Celso **17**

British
Abbott, Diane **9**
Adjaye, David **38**
Akomfrah, John **37**
Amos, Valerie **41**
Armatrading, Joan **32**
Bassey, Shirley **25**
Berry, James **41**
Blackwood, Maureen **37**
Boateng, Ozwald **35**
Breeze, Jean "Binta" **37**
Campbell, Naomi **1, 31**
Carby, Hazel **27**
Christie, Linford **8**
David, Craig **31**
Davidson, Jaye **5**
Emmanuel, Alphonsia **38**
Henriques, Julian **37**
Henry, Lenny **9**
Jean-Baptiste, Marianne **17**
Jordan, Ronny **26**
Julien, Isaac **3**
Kay, Jackie **37**
King, Oona **27**
Lewis, Denise **33**
Lewis, Lennox **27**
Lindo, Delroy **18**
Markham, E.A. **37**
Newton, Thandie **26**
Pitt, David Thomas **10**
Seal **14**
Taylor, John (David Beckett) **16**
Walker, Eamonn **37**

Burkinabé
Somé, Malidoma Patrice **10**

Burundian
Ndadaye, Melchior **7**
Ntaryamira, Cyprien **8**

Cameroonian
Beti, Mongo **36**
Biya, Paul **28**
Kotto, Yaphet **7**
Milla, Roger **2**
Oyono, Ferdinand **38**

Canadian
Bell, Ralph S. **5**
Brand, Dionne **32**

Brathwaite, Fred **35**
Carnegie, Herbert **25**
Clarke, Austin **32**
Clarke, George **32**
Cox, Deborah **28**
Curling, Alvin **34**
Elliot, Lorris **37**
Foster, Cecil **32**
Fox, Rick **27**
Fuhr, Grant **1**
Hammond, Lenn **34**
Harris, Claire **34**
Iginla, Jarome **35**
Isaac, Julius **34**
Johnson, Ben **1**
Mayers, Jamal **39**
McKegney, Tony **3**
Mollel, Tololwa **38**
O'Ree, Willie **5**
Philip, Marlene Nourbese **32**
Reuben, Gloria **15**
Richards, Lloyd **2**
Senior, Olive **37**
Williams, Denise **40**

Cape Verdean
Evora, Cesaria **12**
Pereira, Aristides **30**

Chadian
Déby, Idriss **30**
Habré, Hissène **6**

Congolese
Kabila, Joseph **30**
Lumumba, Patrice **33**

Costa Rican
McDonald, Erroll **1**

Cuban
Ferrer, Ibrahim **41**
León, Tania **13**
Quirot, Ana **13**

Dominican
Charles, Mary Eugenia **10**
Sosa, Sammy **21**

Dutch
Liberia-Peters, Maria Philomena **12**

Ethiopian
Gerima, Haile **38**
Haile Selassie **7**
Meles Zenawi **3**

French
Baker, Josephine **3**
Baldwin, James **1**
Bonaly, Surya **7**
Noah, Yannick **4**
Tanner, Henry Ossawa **1**

Gabonese
Bongo, Omar **1**

Gambian
Jammeh, Yahya **23**
Peters, Lenrie **43**

German
Massaquoi, Hans J. **30**

Cumulative Occupation Index
Volume numbers appear in **bold**

Russell, Herman Jerome **17**
Russell-McCloud, Patricia **17**
Saint James, Synthia **12**
Samara, Noah **15**
Sanders, Dori **8**
Scott, C. A. **29**
Sengstacke, John **18**
Siméus, Dumas M. **25**
Simmons, Russell **1, 30**
Sims, Naomi **29**
Sinbad, **1, 16**
Smith, B(arbara) **11**
Smith, Clarence O. **21**
Smith, Jane E. **24**
Smith, Joshua **10**
Smith, Willi **8**
Sneed, Paula A. **18**
Spaulding, Charles Clinton **9**
Steinberg, Martha Jean "The Queen" **28**
Steward, David L. **36**
Stewart, Ella **39**
Stewart, Paul Wilbur **12**
Sullivan, Leon H. **3, 30**
Sutton, Percy E. **42**
Taylor, Karin **34**
Taylor, Kristin Clark **8**
Taylor, Susan L. **10**
Terrell, Dorothy A. **24**
Thomas, Franklin A. **5**
Thomas, Isiah **7, 26**
Thomas-Graham, Pamela **29**
Thompson, John W. **26**
Tribble, Israel, Jr. **8**
Trotter, Monroe **9**
Tyson, Asha **39**
Ussery, Terdema, II **29**
Utendahl, John **23**
Van Peebles, Melvin **7**
VanDerZee, James **6**
Walker, A'lelia **14**
Walker, Cedric "Ricky" **19**
Walker, Madame C. J. **7**
Walker, Maggie Lena **17**
Walker, T. J. **7**
Ward, Lloyd **2**
Ware, Carl H. **30**
Washington, Alonzo **29**
Washington, Val **12**
Wasow, Omar **15**
Watkins, Donald **35**
Watkins, Walter C. Jr, **24**
Wattleton, Faye **9**
Wek, Alek **18**
Wells-Barnett, Ida B. **8**
Wharton, Clifton R., Jr. **7**
White, Walter F. **4**
Wiley, Ralph **8**
Williams, Armstrong **29**
Williams, O. S. **13**
Williams, Paul R. **9**
Williams, Terrie **35**
Williams, Walter E. **4**
Wilson, Phill **9**
Wilson, Sunnie **7**
Winfrey, Oprah **2, 15**
Woods, Sylvia **34**
Woodson, Robert L. **10**
Wright, Charles H. **35**
Wright, Deborah C. **25**
Yoba, Malik **11**
Zollar, Alfred **40**

Dance
Ailey, Alvin **8**
Alexander, Khandi **43**

Allen, Debbie **13, 42**
Atkins, Cholly **40**
Babatunde, Obba **35**
Baker, Josephine **3**
Bates, Peg Leg **14**
Beals, Jennifer **12**
Beatty, Talley **35**
Byrd, Donald **10**
Clarke, Hope **14**
Collins, Janet **33**
Davis, Chuck **33**
Davis, Sammy Jr. **18**
Dove, Ulysses **5**
Dunham, Katherine **4**
Ellington, Mercedes **34**
Fagan, Garth **18**
Falana, Lola **42**
Glover, Savion **14**
Guy, Jasmine **2**
Hall, Arthur **39**
Hammer, M. C. **20**
Henson, Darrin **33**
Hines, Gregory **1, 42**
Horne, Lena **5**
Jackson, Michael **19**
Jamison, Judith **7**
Johnson, Virginia **9**
Jones, Bill T. **1**
King, Alonzo **38**
McQueen, Butterfly **6**
Miller, Bebe **3**
Mills, Florence **22**
Mitchell, Arthur **2**
Moten, Etta **18**
Muse, Clarence Edouard **21**
Nicholas, Fayard **20**
Nicholas, Harold **20**
Nichols, Nichelle **11**
Powell, Maxine **8**
Premice, Josephine **41**
Primus, Pearl **6**
Rhoden, Dwight **40**
Ribeiro, Alfonso **17**
Richardson, Desmond **39**
Robinson, Bill "Bojangles" **11**
Robinson, Cleo Parker **38**
Robinson, Fatima **34**
Rodgers, Rod **36**
Rolle, Esther **13, 21**
Tyson, Andre **40**
Vereen, Ben **4**
Walker, Cedric "Ricky" **19**
Washington, Fredi **10**
Williams, Vanessa L. **4, 17**
Zollar, Jawole Willa Jo **28**

Education
Achebe, Chinua **6**
Adams, Leslie **39**
Adams-Ender, Clara **40**
Adkins, Rutherford H. **21**
Aidoo, Ama Ata **38**
Ake, Claude **30**
Alexander, Margaret Walker **22**
Allen, Robert L. **38**
Allen, Samuel W. **38**
Alston, Charles **33**
Amadi, Elechi **40**
Anderson, Charles Edward **37**
Archer, Dennis **7**
Aristide, Jean-Bertrand **6**
Asante, Molefi Kete **3**
Aubert, Alvin **41**
Awoonor, Kofi **37**
Bacon-Bercey, June **38**

Baiocchi, Regina Harris **41**
Baker, Augusta **38**
Baker, Gwendolyn Calvert **9**
Baker, Houston A., Jr. **6**
Ballard, Allen Butler, Jr. **40**
Bambara, Toni Cade **10**
Baraka, Amiri **1, 38**
Barboza, Anthony **10**
Bath, Patricia E. **37**
Beckham, Barry **41**
Bell, Derrick **6**
Berry, Bertice **8**
Berry, Mary Frances **7**
Bethune, Mary McLeod **4**
Biggers, John **20, 33**
Black, Keith Lanier **18**
Blassingame, John Wesley **40**
Blockson, Charles L. **42**
Bluitt, Juliann S. **14**
Bogle, Donald **34**
Bolden, Tonya **32**
Bosley, Freeman, Jr. **7**
Boyd, T. B., III **6**
Bradley, David Henry, Jr. **39**
Branch, William Blackwell **39**
Brathwaite, Kamau **36**
Braun, Carol Moseley **4, 42**
Briscoe, Marlin **37**
Brooks, Avery **9**
Brown, Claude **38**
Brown, Joyce F. **25**
Brown, Sterling **10**
Brown, Uzee **42**
Brown, Wesley **23**
Brown, Willa **40**
Bruce, Blanche Kelso **33**
Brutus, Dennis **38**
Bryan, Ashley F. **41**
Burke, Selma **16**
Burke, Yvonne Braithwaite **42**
Burks, Mary Fair **40**
Burroughs, Margaret Taylor **9**
Burton, LeVar **8**
Butler, Paul D. **17**
Callender, Clive O. **3**
Campbell, Bebe Moore **6, 24**
Campbell, Mary Schmidt **43**
Cannon, Katie **10**
Carby, Hazel **27**
Cardozo, Francis L. **33**
Carnegie, Herbert **25**
Carruthers, George R. **40**
Carter, Joye Maureen **41**
Carter, Warrick L. **27**
Carver, George Washington **4**
Cary, Lorene **3**
Cary, Mary Ann Shadd **30**
Catlett, Elizabeth **2**
Cayton, Horace **26**
Cheney-Coker, Syl **43**
Clark, Joe **1**
Clark, Kenneth B. **5**
Clark, Septima **7**
Clarke, Cheryl **32**
Clarke, George **32**
Clarke, John Henrik **20**
Clayton, Constance **1**
Cleaver, Kathleen Neal **29**
Clements, George **2**
Clemmons, Reginal G. **41**
Clifton, Lucille **14**
Cobb, Jewel Plummer **42**
Cobb, W. Montague **39**
Cobbs, Price M. **9**
Cohen, Anthony **15**

Parker, Kellis E. **30**
Parks, Suzan-Lori **34**
Patterson, Frederick Douglass **12**
Patterson, Orlando **4**
Payton, Benjamin F. **23**
Peters, Margaret and Matilda **43**
Pickett, Cecil **39**
Pinckney, Bill **42**
Player, Willa B. **43**
Porter, James A. **11**
Poussaint, Alvin F. **5**
Price, Florence **37**
Price, Glenda **22**
Primus, Pearl **6**
Prophet, Nancy Elizabeth **42**
Puryear, Martin **42**
Quarles, Benjamin Arthur **18**
Rahman, Aishah **37**
Ramphele, Mamphela **29**
Reagon, Bernice Johnson **7**
Reddick, Lawrence Dunbar **20**
Redding, J. Saunders **26**
Redmond, Eugene **23**
Reid, Irvin D. **20**
Ringgold, Faith **4**
Robinson, Sharon **22**
Robinson, Spottswood **22**
Rogers, Joel Augustus **30**
Rollins, Charlemae Hill **27**
Russell-McCloud, Patricia **17**
Salih, Al-Tayyib **37**
Sallee, Charles Louis, Jr. **38**
Satcher, David **7**
Schomburg, Arthur Alfonso **9**
Senior, Olive **37**
Shabazz, Betty **7, 26**
Shange, Ntozake **8**
Shipp, E. R. **15**
Shirley, George **33**
Simmons, Ruth J. **13, 38**
Sinkford, Jeanne C. **13**
Sisulu, Sheila Violet Makate **24**
Sizemore, Barbara A. **26**
Smith, Anna Deavere **6**
Smith, Barbara **28**
Smith, Jessie Carney **35**
Smith, John L. **22**
Smith, Mary Carter **26**
Smith, Tubby **18**
Sowande, Fela **39**
Soyinka, Wole **4**
Spikes, Dolores **18**
Stanford, John **20**
Steele, Claude Mason **13**
Steele, Shelby **13**
Stephens, Charlotte Andrews **14**
Stewart, Maria W. Miller **19**
Stone, Chuck **9**
Sudarkasa, Niara **4**
Sullivan, Louis **8**
Swygert, H. Patrick **22**
Tanksley, Ann **37**
Tatum, Beverly Daniel **42**
Taylor, Helen (Lavon Hollingshed) **30**
Taylor, Susie King **13**
Terrell, Mary Church **9**
Thomas, Alma **14**
Thurman, Howard **3**
Tillis, Frederick **40**
Tolson, Melvin **37**
Tribble, Israel, Jr. **8**
Tucker, Rosina **14**
Turnbull, Walter **13**
Tutu, Desmond **6**
Tutuola, Amos **30**

Tyson, Andre **40**
Tyson, Asha **39**
Tyson, Neil de Grasse **15**
Usry, James L. **23**
van Sertima, Ivan **25**
Wade-Gayles, Gloria Jean **41**
Walcott, Derek **5**
Walker, George **37**
Wallace, Michele Faith **13**
Wallace, Phyllis A. **9**
Washington, Booker T. **4**
Watkins, Shirley R. **17**
Wattleton, Faye **9**
Weaver, Afaa Michael **37**
Wedgeworth, Robert W. **42**
Wells-Barnett, Ida B. **8**
Wells, James Lesesne **10**
Welsing, Frances Cress **5**
Wesley, Dorothy Porter **19**
West, Cornel **5, 33**
Wharton, Clifton R., Jr. **7**
White, Charles **39**
White, Lois Jean **20**
Wilkens, J. Ernest, Jr. **43**
Wilkins, Roger **2**
Williams, Fannie Barrier **27**
Williams, Gregory **11**
Williams, Patricia J. **11**
Williams, Sherley Anne **25**
Williams, Walter E. **4**
Wilson, William Julius **22**
Woodruff, Hale **9**
Woodson, Carter G. **2**
Worrill, Conrad **12**
Yancy, Dorothy Cowser **42**
Young, Jean Childs **14**

Fashion
Bailey, Xenobia **11**
Banks, Jeffrey **17**
Banks, Tyra **11**
Barboza, Anthony **10**
Beals, Jennifer **12**
Beckford, Tyson **11**
Berry, Halle **4, 19**
Boateng, Ozwald **35**
Bridges, Sheila **36**
Brown, Joyce F. **25**
Burrows, Stephen **31**
Campbell, Naomi **1, 31**
Dash, Damon **31**
Davidson, Jaye **5**
Henderson, Gordon **5**
Iman **4, 33**
Jay-Z **27**
John, Daymond **23**
Johnson, Beverly **2**
Jones, Carl **7**
Kodjoe, Boris **34**
Kani, Karl **10**
Kelly, Patrick **3**
Lars, Byron **32**
Malone, Maurice **32**
Michele, Michael **31**
Onwurah, Ngozi **38**
Powell, Maxine **8**
Rhymes, Busta **31**
Robinson, Patrick **19**
Rochon, Lela **16**
Rowell, Victoria **13**
Sims, Naomi **29**
Smaltz, Audrey **12**
Smith, B(arbara) **11**
Smith, Willi **8**
Steele, Lawrence **28**

Taylor, Karin **34**
Walker, T. J. **7**
Webb, Veronica **10**
Wek, Alek **18**

Film
Aaliyah **30**
Akomfrah, John **37**
Alexander, Khandi **43**
Allen, Debbie **13, 42**
Amos, John **8**
Anderson, Eddie "Rochester" **30**
Awoonor, Kofi **37**
Babatunde, Obba **35**
Baker, Josephine **3**
Banks, Tyra **11**
Barclay, Paris **37**
Bassett, Angela **6, 23**
Beach, Michael **26**
Beals, Jennifer **12**
Belafonte, Harry **4**
Bellamy, Bill **12**
Berry, Halle **4, 19**
Blackwood, Maureen **37**
Bogle, Donald **34**
Braugher, Andre **13**
Breeze, Jean "Binta" **37**
Brooks, Hadda **40**
Brown, Jim **11**
Brown, Tony **3**
Burnett, Charles **16**
Byrd, Michelle **19**
Byrd, Robert **11**
Calloway, Cab **14**
Campbell, Naomi **1, 31**
Campbell-Martin, Tisha **8, 42**
Carroll, Diahann **9**
Carson, Lisa Nicole **21**
Cash, Rosalind **28**
Cedric the Entertainer **29**
Cheadle, Don **19**
Chestnut, Morris **31**
Clash, Kevin **14**
Cliff, Jimmy **28**
Combs, Sean "Puffy" **17, 43**
Cortez, Jayne **43**
Cosby, Bill **7, 26**
Crothers, Scatman **19**
Curry, Mark **17**
Curtis-Hall, Vondie **17**
Dandridge, Dorothy **3**
Daniels, Lee Louis **36**
Dash, Julie **4**
David, Keith **27**
Davidson, Jaye **5**
Davidson, Tommy **21**
Davis, Guy **36**
Davis, Ossie **5**
Davis, Sammy, Jr. **18**
de Passe, Suzanne **25**
Dee, Ruby **8**
Devine, Loretta **24**
Dickerson, Ernest **6, 17**
Diesel, Vin **29**
Diggs, Taye **25**
DMX **28**
Dourdan, Gary **37**
Dr. Dre **10, 14, 30**
Driskell, David C. **7**
Duke, Bill **3**
Duncan, Michael Clarke **26**
Dunham, Katherine **4**
Dutton, Charles S. **4, 22**
Edmonds, Kenneth "Babyface" **10, 31**
Elder, Lonne, III **38**

Williamson, Mykelti **22**
Wilson, Debra **38**
Winfield, Paul **2**
Winfrey, Oprah **2, 15**
Witherspoon, John **38**
Woodard, Alfre **9**
Yoba, Malik **11**

Government and politics--international
Abacha, Sani **11**
Abbott, Diane **9**
Achebe, Chinua **6**
Ali Mahdi Mohamed **5**
Amadi, Elechi **40**
Amin, Idi **42**
Amos, Valerie **41**
Annan, Kofi Atta **15**
Aristide, Jean-Bertrand **6**
Arthur, Owen **33**
Awoonor, Kofi **37**
Azikiwe, Nnamdi **13**
Babangida, Ibrahim **4**
Baker, Gwendolyn Calvert **9**
Banda, Hastings Kamuzu **6**
Bedie, Henri Konan **21**
Berry, Mary Frances **7**
Biko, Steven **4**
Bishop, Maurice **39**
Biya, Paul **28**
Bizimungu, Pasteur **19**
Bongo, Omar **1**
Boye, Madior **30**
Bunche, Ralph J. **5**
Buthelezi, Mangosuthu Gatsha **9**
Charlemagne, Manno **11**
Charles, Mary Eugenia **10**
Chissano, Joaquim **7**
Christophe, Henri **9**
Conté, Lansana **7**
Curling, Alvin **34**
da Silva, Benedita **5**
Dadié, Bernard **34**
Davis, Ruth **37**
Déby, Idriss **30**
Diop, Cheikh Anta **4**
Diouf, Abdou **3**
dos Santos, José Eduardo **43**
Ekwensi, Cyprian **37**
Eyadéma, Gnassingbé **7**
Fela **1, 42**
Gbagbo, Laurent **43**
Gordon, Pamela **17**
Habré, Hissène **6**
Habyarimana, Juvenal **8**
Haile Selassie **7**
Haley, George Williford Boyce **21**
Hani, Chris **6**
Houphouët-Boigny, Félix **4**
Ifill, Gwen **28**
Ingraham, Hubert A. **19**
Isaac, Julius **34**
Jagan, Cheddi **16**
Jammeh, Yahya **23**
Jawara, Sir Dawda Kairaba **11**
Ka Dinizulu, Mcwayizeni **29**
Kabbah, Ahmad Tejan **23**
Kabila, Joseph **30**
Kabila, Laurent **20**
Kabunda, Kenneth **2**
Kenyatta, Jomo **5**
Kerekou, Ahmed (Mathieu) **1**
King, Oona **27**
Liberia-Peters, Maria Philomena **12**
Lumumba, Patrice **33**
Luthuli, Albert **13**

Maathai, Wangari **43**
Mabuza, Lindiwe **38**
Machel, Samora Moises **8**
Mamadou, Tandja **33**
Mandela, Nelson **1, 14**
Mandela, Winnie **2, 35**
Masekela, Barbara **18**
Masire, Quett **5**
Mbeki, Thabo Mvuyelwa **14**
Mbuende, Kaire **12**
Meles Zenawi **3**
Mkapa, Benjamin **16**
Mobutu Sese Seko **1**
Mogae, Festus Gontebanye **19**
Moi, Daniel **1, 35**
Mongella, Gertrude **11**
Mugabe, Robert Gabriel **10**
Muluzi, Bakili **14**
Museveni, Yoweri **4**
Mutebi, Ronald **25**
Mwinyi, Ali Hassan **1**
Ndadaye, Melchior **7**
Neto, António Agostinho **43**
Ngubane, Ben **33**
Nkomo, Joshua **4**
Nkrumah, Kwame **3**
Ntaryamira, Cyprien **8**
Nujoma, Samuel **10**
Nyanda, Siphiwe **21**
Nyerere, Julius **5**
Nzo, Alfred **15**
Obasanjo, Olusegun **5, 22**
Obasanjo, Stella **32**
Okara, Gabriel **37**
Oyono, Ferdinand **38**
Pascal-Trouillot, Ertha **3**
Patterson, P. J. **6, 20**
Pereira, Aristides **30**
Perkins, Edward **5**
Perry, Ruth **15**
Pitt, David Thomas **10**
Pitta, Celso **17**
Poitier, Sidney **36**
Ramaphosa, Cyril **3**
Rawlings, Jerry **9**
Rawlings, Nana Konadu Agyeman **13**
Rice, Condoleezza **3, 28**
Robinson, Randall **7**
Sampson, Edith S. **4**
Sankara, Thomas **17**
Savimbi, Jonas **2, 34**
Sawyer, Amos **2**
Senghor, Léopold Sédar **12**
Smith, Jennifer **21**
Soglo, Nicephore **15**
Soyinka, Wole **4**
Taylor, Charles **20**
Taylor, John (David Beckett) **16**
Touré, Sekou **6**
Toure, Amadou Toumani **18**
Tsvangirai, Morgan **26**
Tutu, Desmond **6**
Vieira, Joao **14**
Wharton, Clifton Reginald, Sr. **36**
Wharton, Clifton R., Jr. **7**
Zuma, Jacob G. **33**
Zuma, Nkosazana Dlamini **34**

Government and politics--U.S.
Adams, Floyd, Jr. **12**
Alexander, Archie Alphonso **14**
Alexander, Clifford **26**
Ali, Muhammad **2, 16**
Allen, Ethel D. **13**
Archer, Dennis **7, 36**

Arrington, Richard **24**
Avant, Clarence **19**
Baker, Thurbert **22**
Ballance, Frank W. **41**
Barden, Don H. **9, 20**
Barrett, Andrew C. **12**
Barrett, Jacqueline **28**
Barry, Marion S. **7**
Bell, Michael **40**
Belton, Sharon Sayles **9, 16**
Berry, Mary Frances **7**
Berry, Theodore M. **31**
Bethune, Mary McLeod **4**
Blackwell, Unita **17**
Bond, Julian **2, 35**
Bosley, Freeman, Jr. **7**
Boykin, Keith **14**
Bradley, Jennette B. **40**
Bradley, Thomas **2**
Braun, Carol Moseley **4, 42**
Brazile, Donna **25**
Brimmer, Andrew F. **2**
Brooke, Edward **8**
Brown, Cora **33**
Brown, Corrine **24**
Brown, Elaine **8**
Brown, Jesse **6, 41**
Brown, Lee Patrick **24**
Brown, Les **5**
Brown, Ron **5**
Brown, Willie L., Jr. **7**
Bruce, Blanche K. **33**
Bryant, Wayne R. **6**
Buckley, Victoria (Vicki) **24**
Bunche, Ralph J. **5**
Burke, Yvonne Braithwaite **42**
Burris, Chuck **21**
Burris, Roland W. **25**
Butler, Jerry **26**
Caesar, Shirley **19**
Campbell, Bill **9**
Cardozo, Francis L. **33**
Carson, Julia **23**
Chavis, Benjamin **6**
Chisholm, Shirley **2**
Christian-Green, Donna M. **17**
Clay, William Lacy **8**
Clayton, Eva M. **20**
Cleaver, Eldridge **5**
Cleaver, Emanuel **4**
Clyburn, James **21**
Coleman, Michael B. **28**
Collins, Barbara-Rose **7**
Collins, Cardiss **10**
Colter, Cyrus J. **36**
Connerly, Ward **14**
Conyers, John, Jr. **4**
Cook, Mercer **40**
Cose, Ellis **5**
Crockett, George, Jr. **10**
Cummings, Elijah E. **24**
Cunningham, Evelyn **23**
Currie, Betty **21**
Davis, Angela **5**
Davis, Artur **41**
Davis, Benjamin O., Jr. **2, 43**
Davis, Benjamin O., Sr. **4**
Davis, Danny K. **24**
Days, Drew S., III **10**
Delany, Martin R. **27**
Delco, Wilhemina R. **33**
Dellums, Ronald **2**
Diggs, Charles R. **21**
Dinkins, David **4**
Dixon, Julian C. **24**

Gates, Sylvester James, Jr. **15**
Gayle, Helene D. **3**
Gibson, Kenneth Allen **6**
Gibson, William F. **6**
Gourdine, Meredith **33**
Granville, Evelyn Boyd **36**
Gray, Ida **41**
Gregory, Frederick D. **8**
Griffin, Bessie Blout **43**
Hall, Lloyd A. **8**
Hannah, Marc **10**
Harris, Mary Styles **31**
Henderson, Cornelius Langston **26**
Henson, Matthew **2**
Hinton, William Augustus **8**
Imes, Elmer Samuel **39**
Irving, Larry, Jr. **12**
Jackson, Shirley Ann **12**
Jawara, Sir Dawda Kairaba **11**
Jemison, Mae C. **1, 35**
Jenifer, Franklyn G. **2**
Johnson, Eddie Bernice **8**
Johnson, Lonnie G. **32**
Jones, Randy **35**
Julian, Percy Lavon **6**
Just, Ernest Everett **3**
Knowling, Robert E., Jr. **38**
Kountz, Samuel L. **10**
Latimer, Lewis H. **4**
Lawless, Theodore K. **8**
Lawrence, Robert H., Jr. **16**
Leevy, Carrol M. **42**
Leffall, LaSalle, Jr. **3**
Lewis, Delano **7**
Logan, Onnie Lee **14**
Lyttle, Hulda Margaret **14**
Manley, Audrey Forbes **16**
Massey, Walter E. **5**
Massie, Samuel P., Jr. **29**
Mays, William G. **34**
Mboup, Souleymane **10**
McCoy, Elijah **8**
McNair, Ronald **3**
Millines Dziko, Trish **28**
Morgan, Garrett **1**
Murray, Pauli **38**
Neto, António Agostinho **43**
O'Leary, Hazel **6**
Person, Waverly **9**
Peters, Lenrie **43**
Pickett, Cecil **39**
Pitt, David Thomas **10**
Poussaint, Alvin F. **5**
Prothrow-Stith, Deborah **10**
Quarterman, Lloyd Albert **4**
Riley, Helen Caldwell Day **13**
Robeson, Eslanda Goode **13**
Robinson, Rachel **16**
Roker, Al **12**
Samara, Noah **15**
Satcher, David **7**
Shabazz, Betty **7, 26**
Shavers, Cheryl **31**
Sinkford, Jeanne C. **13**
Staples, Brent **8**
Staupers, Mabel K. **7**
Stewart, Ella **39**
Sullivan, Louis **8**
Terrell, Dorothy A. **24**
Thomas, Vivien **9**
Tyson, Neil de Grasse **15**
Wambugu, Florence **42**
Washington, Patrice Clarke **12**
Watkins, Levi, Jr. **9**
Welsing, Frances Cress **5**

Wilkins, J. Ernest, Jr. **43**
Williams, Daniel Hale **2**
Williams, O. S. **13**
Witt, Edwin T. **26**
Woods, Granville T. **5**
Wright, Louis Tompkins **4**
Young, Roger Arliner **29**

Social issues
Aaron, Hank **5**
Abbot, Robert Sengstacke **27**
Abbott, Diane **9**
Abdul-Jabbar, Kareem **8**
Abernathy, Ralph David **1**
Abu-Jamal, Mumia **15**
Achebe, Chinua **6**
Adams, Sheila J. **25**
Agyeman, Jaramogi Abebe **10**
Ake, Claude **30**
Al-Amin, Jamil Abdullah **6**
Alexander, Clifford **26**
Alexander, Sadie Tanner Mossell **22**
Ali, Muhammad, **2, 16**
Allen, Ethel D. **13**
Andrews, Benny **22**
Angelou, Maya **1, 15**
Annan, Kofi Atta **15**
Anthony, Wendell **25**
Archer, Dennis **7**
Aristide, Jean-Bertrand **6**
Arnwine, Barbara **28**
Asante, Molefi Kete **3**
Ashe, Arthur **1, 18**
Auguste, Rose-Anne **13**
Azikiwe, Nnamdi **13**
Ba, Mariama **30**
Baisden, Michael **25**
Baker, Ella **5**
Baker, Gwendolyn Calvert **9**
Baker, Houston A., Jr. **6**
Baker, Josephine **3**
Baker, Thurbert **22**
Baldwin, James **1**
Baraka, Amiri **1, 38**
Bass, Charlotta Spears **40**
Bates, Daisy **13**
Beals, Melba Patillo **15**
Belafonte, Harry **4**
Bell, Derrick **6**
Bell, Ralph S. **5**
Bennett, Lerone, Jr. **5**
Berry, Bertice **8**
Berry, Mary Frances **7**
Bethune, Mary McLeod **4**
Betsch, MaVynee **28**
Biko, Steven **4**
Blackwell, Unita **17**
Bolin, Jane **22**
Bond, Julian **2, 35**
Bonga, Kuenda **13**
Bosley, Freeman, Jr. **7**
Boyd, John W., Jr. **20**
Boyd, T. B., III **6**
Boykin, Keith **14**
Bradley, David Henry, Jr. **39**
Braun, Carol Moseley **4, 42**
Broadbent, Hydeia **36**
Brooke, Edward **8**
Brown, Cora **33**
Brown, Eddie C. **35**
Brown, Elaine **8**
Brown, Jesse **6, 41**
Brown, Jim **11**
Brown, Lee P. **1**
Brown, Les **5**

Brown, Llyod Louis **42**
Brown, Tony **3**
Brown, Willa **40**
Brown, Zora Kramer **12**
Brutus, Dennis **38**
Bryant, Wayne R. **6**
Bullock, Steve **22**
Bunche, Ralph J. **5**
Burks, Mary Fair **40**
Burroughs, Margaret Taylor **9**
Butler, Paul D. **17**
Butts, Calvin O., III **9**
Campbell, Bebe Moore **6, 24**
Canada, Geoffrey **23**
Carby, Hazel **27**
Carmichael, Stokely **5, 26**
Carter, Mandy **11**
Carter, Rubin **26**
Carter, Stephen L. **4**
Cary, Lorene **3**
Cary, Mary Ann Shadd **30**
Cayton, Horace **26**
Chavis, Benjamin **6**
Chideya, Farai **14**
Childress, Alice **15**
Chissano, Joaquim **7**
Christophe, Henri **9**
Chuck D **9**
Clark, Joe **1**
Clark, Kenneth B. **5**
Clark, Septima **7**
Clay, William Lacy **8**
Claytor, Helen **14**
Cleaver, Eldridge **5**
Cleaver, Kathleen Neal **29**
Clements, George **2**
Cobbs, Price M. **9**
Cole, Johnnetta B. **5, 43**
Collins, Barbara-Rose **7**
Comer, James P. **6**
Cone, James H. **3**
Connerly, Ward **14**
Conté, Lansana **7**
Conyers, John, Jr. **4**
Cook, Toni **23**
Cooke, Marvel **31**
Cooper, Anna Julia **20**
Cooper, Edward S. **6**
Cosby, Bill **7**
Cosby, Camille **14**
Cose, Ellis **5**
Creagh, Milton **27**
Crockett, George, Jr. **10**
Crouch, Stanley **11**
Cummings, Elijah E. **24**
Cunningham, Evelyn **23**
da Silva, Benedita **5**
Dash, Julie **4**
Davis, Angela **5**
Davis, Artur **41**
Davis, Danny K. **24**
Davis, Ossie **5**
Dawson, Matel "Mat," Jr. **39**
DeBaptiste, George **32**
Dee, Ruby **8**
Delany, Martin R. **27**
Dellums, Ronald **2**
Diallo, Amadou **27**
Dickerson, Ernest **6**
Diop, Cheikh Anta **4**
Divine, Father **7**
Dixon, Margaret **14**
Dodson, Howard, Jr. **7**
Dove, Rita **6**
Drew, Charles Richard **7**

Richardson, Nolan **9**
Richmond, Mitch **19**
Rivers, Glenn "Doc" **25**
Robertson, Oscar **26**
Robinson, David **24**
Robinson, Eddie G. **10**
Robinson, Frank **9**
Robinson, Jackie **6**
Robinson, Sugar Ray **18**
Rodman, Dennis **12**
Rudolph, Wilma **4**
Rubin, Chanda **37**
Russell, Bill **8**
Sampson, Charles **13**
Sanders, Barry **1**
Sanders, Deion **4, 31**
Sapp, Warren **38**
Sayers, Gale **28**
Scott, Stuart **34**
Scott, Wendell Oliver, Sr. **19**
Scurry, Briana **27**
Sharper, Darren **32**
Sheffield, Gary **16**
Shell, Art **1**
Shippen, John **43**
Showers, Reggie **30**
Sifford, Charlie **4**
Silas, Paul **24**
Simmons, Bob **29**
Simpson, O. J. **15**
Singletary, Mike **4**
Smith, Emmitt **7**
Smith, Hilton **29**
Smith, Tubby **18**
Solomon, Jimmie Lee **38**
Sosa, Sammy **21**
Sprewell, Latrell **23**
St. Julien, Marlon **29**
Stackhouse, Jerry **30**
Stargell, Willie **29**
Stearns, Norman "Turkey" **31**
Steward, Emanuel **18**
Stewart, Kordell **21**
Stone, Toni **15**
Strahan, Michael **35**
Strawberry, Darryl **22**
Stringer, C. Vivian **13**
Stringer, Korey **35**
Swann, Lynn **28**
Swoopes, Sheryl **12**
Taylor, Lawrence **25**
Thomas, Debi **26**
Thomas, Derrick **25**
Thomas, Frank **12**
Thomas, Isiah **7, 26**
Thompson, Tina **25**
Thrower, Willie **35**
Thugwane, Josia **21**
Tyson, Mike **28**
Unseld, Wes **23**
Upshaw, Gene **18**
Ussery, Terdema, II **29**
Vick, Michael **39**
Walker, Herschel **1**
Ware, Andre **37**
Washington, MaliVai **8**
Watson, Bob **25**
Watts, J. C., Jr. **14, 38**
Weathers, Carl **10**
Webber, Chris **15, 30**
Westbrook, Peter **20**
Whitaker, Pernell **10**
White, Bill **1**
White, Jesse **22**
White, Reggie **6**

Whitfield, Fred **23**
Wilkens, Lenny **11**
Williams, Doug **22**
Williams, Serena **20, 41**
Williams, Natalie **31**
Williams, Venus Ebone **17, 34**
Willingham, Tyrone **43**
Wilson, Sunnie **7**
Winfield, Dave **5**
Winkfield, Jimmy **42**
Woods, Tiger **14, 31**

Television
Alexander, Khandi **43**
Allen, Byron **3**
Allen, Debbie **13, 42**
Allen, Marcus **20**
Amos, John **8**
Anderson, Eddie "Rochester" **30**
Arkadie, Kevin **17**
Babatunde, Obba **35**
Banks, William **11**
Barclay, Paris **37**
Barden, Don H. **9**
Bassett, Angela **6, 23**
Beach, Michael **26**
Beaton, Norman **14**
Beauvais, Garcelle **29**
Belafonte, Harry **4**
Bellamy, Bill **12**
Berry, Bertice **8**
Berry, Halle **4, 19**
Blackwood, Maureen **37**
Blake, Asha **26**
Boston, Kelvin E. **25**
Bowser, Yvette Lee **17**
Bradley, Ed **2**
Brady, Wayne **32**
Brandy **14, 34**
Braugher, Andre **13**
Bridges, Todd **37**
Brooks, Avery **9**
Brooks, Hadda **40**
Brown, James **22**
Brown, Joe **29**
Brown, Les **5**
Brown, Tony **3**
Brown, Vivian **27**
Burnett, Charles **16**
Burton, LeVar **8**
Byrd, Robert **11**
Campbell, Naomi **1, 31**
Campbell Martin, Tisha **8, 42**
Carroll, Diahann **9**
Carson, Lisa Nicole **21**
Carter, Nell **39**
Cash, Rosalind **28**
Cedric the Entertainer **29**
Cheadle, Don **19**
Chestnut, Morris **31**
Chideya, Farai **14**
Christian, Spencer **15**
Clash, Kevin **14**
Clayton, Xernona **3**
Cole, Nat King **17**
Cole, Natalie Maria **17**
Coleman, Gary **35**
Corbi, Lana **42**
Cornelius, Don **4**
Cosby, Bill **7, 26**
Crothers, Scatman **19**
Curry, Mark **17**
Curtis-Hall, Vondie **17**
Davidson, Tommy **21**
Davis, Ossie **5**

Davis, Viola **34**
de Passe, Suzanne **25**
Dee, Ruby **8**
Devine, Loretta **24**
Dickerson, Eric **27**
Dickerson, Ernest **6**
Diggs, Taye **25**
Dourdan, Gary **37**
Dr. Dre **10, 14, 30**
Duke, Bill **3**
Dutton, Charles S. **4, 22**
Elder, Larry **25**
Elise, Kimberly **32**
Emmanuel, Alphonsia **38**
Ephriam, Mablean **29**
Erving, Julius **18**
Esposito, Giancarlo **9**
Eubanks, Kevin **15**
Evans, Harry **25**
Falana, Lola **42**
Fields, Kim **36**
Fishburne, Larry **4, 22**
Fox, Rick **27**
Foxx, Jamie **15**
Foxx, Redd **2**
Freeman, Al, Jr. **11**
Freeman, Morgan **2**
Freeman, Yvette **27**
Gaines, Ernest J. **7**
Givens, Robin **4, 25**
Glover, Danny **3, 24**
Glover, Savion **14**
Goldberg, Whoopi **4, 33**
Goode, Mal **13**
Gooding, Cuba, Jr. **16**
Gordon, Ed **10**
Gossett, Louis, Jr. **7**
Greely, M. Gasby **27**
Grier, David Alan **28**
Grier, Pam **9, 31**
Guillaume, Robert **3**
Gumbel, Bryant **14**
Gumbel, Greg **8**
Gunn, Moses **10**
Guy, Jasmine **2**
Haley, Alex **4**
Hampton, Henry **6**
Hardison, Kadeem **22**
Harper, Hill **32**
Harrell, Andre **9, 30**
Harris, Robin **7**
Harvey, Steve **18**
Hatchett, Glenda **32**
Hayes, Isaac **20**
Haysbert, Dennis **42**
Hemsley, Sherman **19**
Henriques, Julian **37**
Henry, Lenny **9**
Henson, Darrin **33**
Hickman, Fred **11**
Hill, Dulé **29**
Hill, Lauryn **20**
Hinderas, Natalie **5**
Hines, Gregory **1, 42**
Horne, Lena **5**
Hounsou, Djimon **19**
Houston, Whitney **7, 28**
Howard, Sherri **36**
Hughley, D.L. **23**
Hunter-Gault, Charlayne **6, 31**
Hyman, Earle **25**
Ice-T **6, 31**
Ifill, Gwen **28**
Iman **4, 33**
Ingram, Rex **5**

Curtis-Hall, Vondie **17**
Dadié, Bernard **34**
David, Keith **27**
Davis, Ossie **5**
Davis, Sammy, Jr. **18**
Davis, Viola **34**
Dee, Ruby **8**
Devine, Loretta **24**
Diggs, Taye **25**
Dodson, Owen Vincent **38**
Dourdan, Gary **37**
Duke, Bill **3**
Dunham, Katherine **4**
Dutton, Charles S. **4, 22**
Elder, Lonne, III **38**
Emmanuel, Alphonsia **38**
Esposito, Giancarlo **9**
Europe, James Reese **10**
Falana, Lola **42**
Fishburne, Larry **4, 22**
Freeman, Al, Jr. **11**
Freeman, Morgan **2, 20**
Freeman, Yvette **27**
Fuller, Charles **8**
Glover, Danny **1, 24**
Glover, Savion **14**
Goldberg, Whoopi **4, 33**
Gordone, Charles **15**
Gossett, Louis, Jr. **7**
Graves, Denyce **19**
Greaves, William **38**
Grier, Pam **9, 31**
Guillaume, Robert **3**
Gunn, Moses **10**
Guy, Jasmine **2**
Hansberry, Lorraine **6**
Harris, Robin **7**
Hayes, Teddy **40**
Hemsley, Sherman **19**
Hill, Dulé **29**
Hill, Errol **40**
Hines, Gregory **1, 42**
Holder, Laurence **34**
Holland, Endesha Ida Mae **3**
Horne, Lena **5**
Hyman, Earle **25**
Hyman, Phyllis **19**
Ingram, Rex **5**
Jackson, Millie **25**
Jackson, Samuel L. **8, 19**
Jamison, Judith **7**
Jean-Baptiste, Marianne **17**
Jones, James Earl **3**
Jones, Sarah **39**
Joyner, Matilda Sissieretta **15**
King, Woodie, Jr. **27**
King, Yolanda **6**
Kitt, Eartha **16**
Kotto, Yaphet **7**
Lampley, Oni Faida **43**
Lathan, Sanaa **27**
La Salle, Eriq **12**
Lee, Canada **8**
Lemmons, Kasi **20**
LeNoire, Rosetta **37**
Leon, Kenny **10**
Letson, Al **39**
Lincoln, Abbey **3**
Lindo, Delroy **18**
Mabley, Jackie "Moms" **15**
Marrow, Queen Esther **24**
Martin, Helen **31**
Martin, Jesse L. **31**
McDaniel, Hattie **5**
McDonald, Audra **20**

McKee, Lonette **12**
McQueen, Butterfly **6**
Mickelbury, Penny **28**
Mills, Florence **22**
Milner, Ron **39**
Mitchell, Brian Stokes **21**
Mollel, Tololwa **38**
Moore, Melba **21**
Moses, Gilbert **12**
Moss, Carlton **17**
Moten, Etta **18**
Muse, Clarence Edouard **21**
Nicholas, Fayard **20**
Nicholas, Harold **20**
Norman, Maidie **20**
Orlandersmith, Dael **42**
Parks, Suzan-Lori **34**
Payne, Allen **13**
Perry, Tyler **40**
Powell, Maxine **8**
Premice, Josephine **41**
Primus, Pearl **6**
Ralph, Sheryl Lee **18**
Randle, Theresa **16**
Rashad, Phylicia **21**
Reese, Della **6, 20**
Rhames, Ving **14**
Richards, Beah **30**
Richards, Lloyd **2**
Richardson, Desmond **39**
Robeson, Paul **2**
Rolle, Esther **13, 21**
Rollins, Howard E., Jr. **16**
Rotimi, Ola **1**
Schultz, Michael A. **6**
Shabazz, Attallah **6**
Shange, Ntozake **8**
Smith, Anna Deavere **6**
Smith, Roger Guenveur **12**
Snipes, Wesley **3, 24**
Soyinka, Wole **4**
St. Jacques, Raymond **8**
Talbert, David **34**
Taylor, Meshach **4**
Taylor, Regina **9**
Taylor, Ron **35**
Thigpen, Lynne **17, 41**
Thompson, Tazewell **13**
Thurman, Wallace **16**
Toussaint, Lorraine **32**
Townsend, Robert **4, 23**
Tyson, Cicely **7**
Uggams, Leslie **23**
Underwood, Blair **7, 27**
Van Peebles, Melvin **7**
Vance, Courtney B. **15**
Vereen, Ben **4**
Walcott, Derek **5**
Walker, Eamonn **37**
Ward, Douglas Turner **42**
Washington, Denzel **1, 16**
Washington, Fredi **10**
Waters, Ethel **7**
Whitaker, Forest **2**
Whitfield, Lynn **18**
Williams, Bert **18**
Williams, Billy Dee **8**
Williams, Clarence, III **26**
Williams, Samm-Art **21**
Williams, Vanessa L. **4, 17**
Williamson, Mykelti **22**
Wilson, August **7, 33**
Winfield, Paul **2**
Wolfe, George C. **6, 43**
Woodard, Alfre **9**

Writing
Adams-Ender, Clara **40**
Abrahams, Peter **39**
Abu-Jamal, Mumia **15**
Achebe, Chinua **6**
Aidoo, Ama Ata **38**
Ake, Claude **30**
Al-Amin, Jamil Abdullah **6**
Alexander, Margaret Walker **22**
Allen, Debbie **13, 42**
Allen, Robert L. **38**
Allen, Samuel W. **38**
Amadi, Elechi **40**
Ames, Wilmer **27**
Andrews, Raymond **4**
Angelou, Maya **1, 15**
Ansa, Tina McElroy **14**
Anthony, Michael **29**
Aristide, Jean-Bertrand **6**
Arkadie, Kevin **17**
Asante, Molefi Kete **3**
Ashe, Arthur **1, 18**
Ashley-Ward, Amelia **23**
Atkins, Cholly **40**
Aubert, Alvin **41**
Awoonor, Kofi **37**
Azikiwe, Nnamdi **13**
Ba, Mariama **30**
Baiocchi, Regina Harris **41**
Baisden, Michael **25**
Baker, Augusta **38**
Baker, Houston A., Jr. **6**
Baldwin, James **1**
Ballard, Allen Butler, Jr. **40**
Bambara, Toni Cade **10**
Bandele, Asha **36**
Baraka, Amiri **1, 38**
Barrett, Lindsay **43**
Bass, Charlotta Spears **40**
Bates, Karen Grigsby **40**
Beals, Melba Patillo **15**
Beckham, Barry **41**
Bell, Derrick **6**
Bell, James Madison **40**
Bennett, Lerone, Jr. **5**
Benson, Angela **34**
Berry, James **41**
Berry, Mary Frances **7**
Beti, Mongo **36**
Bishop, Maurice **39**
Bland, Eleanor Taylor **39**
Blassingame, John Wesley **40**
Blockson, Charles L. **42**
Bluitt, Juliann S. **14**
Bolden, Tonya **32**
Bontemps, Arna **8**
Booker, Simeon **23**
Borders, James **9**
Boston, Lloyd **24**
Boyd, Gerald M. **32**
Bradley, David Henry, Jr. **39**
Bradley, Ed **2**
Branch, William Blackwell **39**
Brand, Dionne **32**
Brathwaite, Kamau **36**
Breeze, Jean "Binta" **37**
Bridges, Sheila **36**
Brimmer, Andrew F. **2**
Briscoe, Connie **15**
Britt, Donna **28**
Brooks, Gwendolyn **1, 28**
Brown, Claude **38**
Brown, Elaine **8**
Brown, Les **5**
Brown, Llyod Louis **42**

Cumulative Subject Index

Volume numbers appear in **bold**

Black Alliance for Educational Options
Fuller, Howard L. **37**

Black American West Museum
Stewart, Paul Wilbur **12**

Black Americans for Family Values
Foster, Ezola **28**

Black Academy of Arts & Letters
White, Charles **39**

Black and White Minstrel Show
Henry, Lenny **9**

Black arts movement
Barrett, Lindsay **43**
Cortez, Jayne **43**
Dumas, Henry **41**
Gayle, Addison, Jr. **41**
Giovanni, Nikki **9, 39**
Neal, Larry **38**

Black Cabinet
Hastie, William H. **8**

Black Caucus of the American Library Association (BCALA)
Josey, E. J. **10**

Black Christian Nationalist movement
Agyeman, Jaramogi Abebe **10**

Black Coaches Association (BCA)
Freeman, Marianna **23**

Black Consciousness movement
Biko, Steven **4**
Muhammad, Elijah **4**
Ramaphosa, Cyril **3**
Ramphele, Maphela **29**
Tutu, Desmond **6**

Black culturalism
Karenga, Maulana **10**

Black Economic Union (BEU)
Brown, Jim **11**

***Black Enterprise* magazine**
Brimmer, Andrew F. **2**
Graves, Earl G. **1, 35**
Wallace, Phyllis A. **9**

***Black Enterprise* Corporate Executive of the Year**
Chenault, Kenneth I. **5, 36**
Steward, David L. **36**

Black Entertainment Television (BET)
Ames, Wilmer **27**
Gordon, Ed **10**
Greely, M. Gasby **27**
Johnson, Robert L. **3, 39**
Jones, Bobby **20**
Smiley, Tavis **20**

Black Filmmaker Foundation (BFF)
Hudlin, Reginald **9**
Hudlin, Warrington **9**
Jackson, George **19**
Williams, Terrie **35**

Black Filmmakers Hall of Fame
McKinney, Nina Mae **40**

Black Gay and Lesbian Leadership Forum (BGLLF)
Wilson, Phill **9**

Black Guerrilla Family (BGF)
Jackson, George **14**

Black History Month
Woodson, Carter G. **2**

Black Horizons on the Hill
Wilson, August **7, 33**

Black Liberation Army (BLA)
Shakur, Assata **6**
Williams, Evelyn **10**

Black literary theory
Gates, Henry Louis, Jr. **3, 38**

Black Manifesto
Forman, James **7**

Black Music Center
Moore, Undine Smith **28**

Black Muslims
Abdul-Jabbar, Kareem **8**
Ali, Muhammad **2, 16**
Farrakhan, Louis **2**
Muhammad, Elijah **4**
Muhammed, W. Deen **27**
X, Malcolm **1**

Black nationalism
Baker, Houston A., Jr. **6**
Baraka, Amiri **1, 38**
Carmichael, Stokely **5, 26**
Farrakhan, Louis **2**
Forman, James **7**
Garvey, Marcus **1**
Innis, Roy **5**
Muhammad, Elijah **4**
Turner, Henry McNeal **5**
X, Malcolm **1**

Black Oscar Awards
Daniels, Lee Louis **36**

Black Panther Party (BPP)
Abu-Jamal, Mumia **15**
Al-Amin, Jamil Abdullah **6**
Brown, Elaine **8**
Carmichael, Stokely **5**
Cleaver, Eldridge **5**
Cleaver, Kathleen Neal **29**
Davis, Angela **5**
Forman, James **7**
Hampton, Fred **18**
Hilliard, David **7**
Jackson, George **14**
Neal, Larry **38**
Newton, Huey **2**
Pratt, Geronimo **18**
Rush, Bobby **26**
Seale, Bobby **3**
Shakur, Assata **6**

Black Power movement
Al-Amin, Jamil Abdullah **6**
Baker, Houston A., Jr. **6**
Brown, Elaine **8**
Carmichael, Stokely **5, 26**
Dodson, Howard, Jr. **7**
Dumas, Henry **41**
Giovanni, Nikki **9, 39**
McKissick, Floyd B. **3**
Stone, Chuck **9**

Blackside, Inc.
Hampton, Henry **6**

Black theology
Cone, James H. **3**

Blackvoices.com
Cooper, Barry **33**

Black Writers Conference
McMillan, Rosalynn A. **36**

"Blood for Britain"
Drew, Charles Richard **7**

Blessed Martin House
Riley, Helen Caldwell Day **13**

Blood plasma research/preservation
Drew, Charles Richard **7**

Blues
Ace, Johnny **36**
Austin, Lovie **40**
Barnes, Roosevelt "Booba" **33**
Bland, Bobby "Blue" **36**
Brown, Charles **23**
Clarke, Kenny **27**
Collins, Albert **12**
Cox, Ida **42**
Cray, Robert **30**
Davis, Gary **41**
Davis, Guy **36**
Dixon, Willie **4**
Dorsey, Thomas **15**
Estes, Sleepy John **33**
Evora, Cesaria **12**
Freeman, Yvette **27**
Gaines, Grady **38**
Guy, Buddy **31**
Handy, W. C. **8**
Harris, Corey **39**
Hemphill, Jessie Mae **33**
Holiday, Billie **1**
Hooker, John Lee **30**
House, Son **8**
Howlin' Wolf **9**
Hunter, Alberta **42**
Jean-Baptiste, Marianne **17**
Jackson, John **36**
James, Skip **38**
Johnson, Buddy **36**
King, B. B. **7**
Little Mitlon **36**
Little Walton **36**
Mahal, Taj **39**
Martin, Sara **38**
Mo', Keb' **36**
Moore, Johnny B. **38**
Muse, Clarence Edouard **21**
Odetta **37**
Owens, Jack **38**
Parker, Charlie **20**

Julien, Isaac **3**
Lane, Charles **3**
Lee, Spike **5, 19**
Lemmons, Kasi **20**
Lewis, Samella **25**
Martin, Darnell **43**
Micheaux, Oscar **7**
Morton, Joe **18**
Moses, Gilbert **12**
Moss, Carlton **17**
Mwangi, Meja **40**
Onwurah, Ngozi **38**
Peck, Raoul **32**
Poitier, Sidney **11, 36**
Prince-Bythewood, Gina **31**
Riggs, Marlon **5**
Schultz, Michael A. **6**
Sembène, Ousmane **13**
Singleton, John **2, 30**
Smith, Roger Guenveur **12**
St. Jacques, Raymond **8**
Tillman, George, Jr. **20**
Townsend, Robert **4, 23**
Tyler, Aisha N. **36**
Underwood, Blair **7**
Van Peebles, Mario **2**
Van Peebles, Melvin **7**
Ward, Douglas Turner **42**
Wayans, Damon **8, 41**
Wayans, Keenen Ivory **18**

Film production
Daniels, Lee Louis **36**
Gerima, Haile **38**
Greaves, William **38**
Hines, Gregory **1, 42**
Lewis, Emmanuel **36**
Martin, Darnell **43**
Onwurah, Ngozi **38**
Poitier, Sidney **11, 36**
Randall, Alice **38**
Tyler, Aisha N. **36**
Ward, Douglas Turner **42**

Film scores
Blanchard, Terence **43**
Crouch, Andraé **27**
Hancock, Herbie **20**
Jean-Baptiste, Marianne **17**
Jones, Quincy **8, 30**
Prince **18**

Finance
Adams, Eula L. **39**
Banks, Jeffrey **17**
Boston, Kelvin E. **25**
Bryant, John **26**
Chapman, Nathan A. Jr. **21**
Doley, Harold, Jr. **26**
Ferguson, Roger W. **25**
Fletcher, Alphonse, Jr. **16**
Funderburg, I. Owen **38**
Gaines, Brenda **41**
Griffith, Mark Winston **8**
Hobson, Mellody **40**
Jones, Thomas W. **41**
Lawless, Theodore K. **8**
Lewis, William M., Jr. **40**
Louis, Errol T. **8**
Marshall, Bella **22**
Rogers, John W., Jr. **5**
Ross, Charles **27**
Thompson, William C. **35**

Firefighters
Bell, Michael **40**

First Data Corporation
Adams, Eula L. **39**

Fisk University
Harvey, William R. **42**
Imes, Elmer Samuel **39**
Johnson, Charles S. **12**
Phillips, Teresa L. **42**
Smith, John L. **22**

Fitness
Richardson, Donna **39**

FlipMode Entertainment
Rhymes, Busta **31**

Florida A & M University
Gaither, Alonzo Smith (Jake) **14**
Humphries, Frederick **20**
Meek, Kendrick **41**

Florida International baseball league
Kaiser, Cecil **42**

Florida Marlins baseball team
Mariner, Jonathan **41**
Sheffield, Gary **16**

Florida state government
Brown, Corrine **24**
Meek, Carrie **6**
Meek, Kendrick **41**
Tribble, Isreal, Jr. **8**

Flouride chemistry
Quarterman, Lloyd Albert **4**

Focus Detroit Electronic Music Festival
May, Derrick **41**

Folk music
Bailey, DeFord **33**
Chapman, Tracy **26**
Charlemagne, Manno **11**
Davis, Gary **41**
Dawson, William Levi **39**
Harper, Ben **34**
Jenkins, Ella **15**
Odetta **37**
Williams, Denise **40**
Wilson, Cassandra **16**

Football
Allen, Marcus **20**
Amos, John **8**
Anderson, Jamal **22**
Barber, Ronde **41**
Barney, Lem **26**
Briscoe, Marlin **37**
Brooks, Aaron **33**
Brooks, Derrick **43**
Brown, James **22**
Brown, Jim **11**
Bruce, Isaac **26**
Buchanan, Ray **32**
Butler, LeRoy III **17**
Carter, Cris **21**
Cherry, Deron **40**
Culpepper, Daunte **32**
Cunningham, Randall **23**

Davis, Terrell **20**
Dickerson, Eric **27**
Dungy, Tony **17, 42**
Edwards, Harry **2**
Farr, Mel Sr. **24**
Faulk, Marshall **35**
Gaither, Alonzo Smith (Jake) **14**
Gilliam, Frank **23**
Gilliam, Joe **31**
Green, Darrell **39**
Green, Dennis **5**
Greene, Joe **10**
Grier, Roosevelt **13**
Hill, Calvin **19**
Lanier, Willie **33**
Lofton, James **42**
Lott, Ronnie **9**
McNair, Steve **22**
McNabb, Donovan **29**
Monk, Art **38**
Moon, Warren **8**
Moss, Randy **23**
Motley, Marion **26**
Newsome, Ozzie **26**
Pace, Orlando **21**
Page, Alan **7**
Payton, Walter **11, 25**
Perry, Lowell **30**
Rashad, Ahmad **18**
Rice, Jerry **5**
Robinson, Eddie G. **10**
Sanders, Barry **1**
Sanders, Deion **4, 31**
Sapp, Warren **38**
Sayers, Gale **28**
Sharper, Darren **32**
Shell, Art **1**
Simmons, Bob **29**
Simpson, O. J. **15**
Singletary, Mike **4**
Smith, Emmitt **7**
Stewart, Kordell **21**
Strahan, Michael **35**
Stringer, Korey **35**
Swann, Lynn **28**
Taylor, Lawrence **25**
Thomas, Derrick **25**
Thrower, Willie **35**
Upshaw, Gene **18**
Vick, Michael **39**
Walker, Herschel **1**
Ware, Andre **37**
Watts, J. C., Jr. **14, 38**
Weathers, Carl **10**
White, Reggie **6**
Williams, Doug **22**
Willingham, Tyrone **43**

FOR
See Fellowship of Reconciliation

Forces Armées du Nord (Chad; FAN)
Déby, Idriss **30**
Habré, Hissène **6**

Ford Foundation
Thomas, Franklin A. **5**
Franklin, Robert M. **13**

New York Nets basketball team
Erving, Julius **18**

New York Philharmonic
DePriest, James **37**

New York Public Library
Baker, Augusta **38**
Dodson, Howard, Jr. **7**
Schomburg, Arthur Alfonso **9**

New York Shakespeare Festival
Gunn, Moses **10**
Wolfe, George C. **6, 43**

New York state government
McCall, H. Carl **27**

New York State Senate
McCall, H. Carl **27**
Motley, Constance Baker **10**
Owens, Major **6**

New York State Supreme Court
Wright, Bruce McMarion **3**

New York Stock Exchange
Doley, Harold, Jr. **26**

New York Sun
Fortune, T. Thomas **6**

New York Times
Boyd, Gerald M. **32**
Davis, George **36**
Hunter-Gault, Charlayne **6, 31**
Ifill, Gwen **28**
Price, Hugh B. **9**
Wilkins, Roger **2**

New York University
Brathwaite, Kamau **36**
Campbell, Mary Schmidt **43**

New York Yankees baseball team
Baylor, Don **6**
Bonds, Bobby **43**
Jackson, Reggie **15**
Jeter, Derek **27**
Strawberry, Darryl **22**
Watson, Bob **25**
Winfield, Dave **5**

Newark city government
Gibson, Kenneth Allen **6**
James, Sharpe **23**

Newark Dodgers baseball team
Dandridge, Ray **36**

Newark Eagles baseball team
Dandridge, Ray **36**
Doby, Lawrence Eugene Sr. **16, 41**

Newark Housing Authority
Gibson, Kenneth Allen **6**

***The News Hour with Jim Lehrer* TV series**
Ifill, Gwen **28**

NFL
See National Football League

Nguzo Saba
Karenga, Maulana **10**

NHL
See National Hockey League

Niagara movement
Du Bois, W. E. B. **3**
Hope, John **8**
Trotter, Monroe **9**

Nigerian Armed Forces
Abacha, Sani **11**
Babangida, Ibrahim **4**
Obasanjo, Olusegun **5, 22**

Nigerian Association of Patriotic Writers and Artists
Barrett, Lindsay **43**

Nigerian literature
Achebe, Chinua **6**
Amadi, Elechi **40**
Barrett, Lindsay **43**
Ekwensi, Cyprian **37**
Onwueme, Tess Osonye **23**
Rotimi, Ola **1**
Saro-Wiwa, Kenule **39**
Soyinka, Wole **4**

NIH
See National Institute of Health

NII
See National Information Infrastructure

1960 Masks
Soyinka, Wole **4**

Nobel Peace Prize
Bunche, Ralph J. **5**
King, Martin Luther, Jr. **1**
Luthuli, Albert **13**
Tutu, Desmond **6**

Nobel Prize for literature
Soyinka, Wole **4**
Morrison, Toni **2, 15**
Walcott, Derek **5**

Noma Award for Publishing in African
Ba, Mariama **30**

Nonfiction
Abrahams, Peter **39**
Adams-Ender, Clara **40**
Allen, Debbie **13, 42**
Allen, Robert L. **38**
Atkins, Cholly **40**
Ballard, Allen Butler, Jr. **40**
Blassingame, John Wesley **40**
Blockson, Charles L. **42**
Bogle, Donald **34**
Brown, Llyod Louis **42**
Buckley, Gail Lumet **39**
Carby, Hazel **27**
Carter, Joye Maureen **41**
Cole, Johnnetta B. **5, 43**
Cook, Mercer **40**
Davis, Arthur P. **41**

Dunnigan, Alice Allison **41**
Edelman, Marian Wright **5, 42**
Elliott, Lorris **37**
Fisher, Antwone **40**
Fletcher, Bill, Jr. **41**
Ford, Clyde W. **40**
Foster, Cecil **32**
Gayle, Addison, Jr. **41**
Gibson, Donald Bernard **40**
Greenwood, Monique **38**
Harrison, Alvin **28**
Harrison, Calvin **28**
Henriques, Julian **37**
Hill, Errol **40**
Jakes, Thomas "T.D." **17, 43**
Jolley, Willie **28**
Jordan, Vernon E. **7, 35**
Kayira, Legson **40**
Kennedy, Randall **40**
Knight, Etheridge **37**
Kobia, Rev. Dr. Samuel **43**
Ladner, Joyce A. **42**
Lampley, Oni Faida **43**
Lincoln, C. Eric **38**
Long, Eddie L. **29**
Mabuza-Suttle, Felicia **43**
Malveaux, Julianne **32**
Manley, Ruth **34**
McBride, James **35**
McKenzie, Vashti M. **29**
McWhorter, John **35**
Mossell, Gertrude Bustill **40**
Murray, Pauli **38**
Naylor, Gloria **10, 42**
Nissel, Angela **42**
Parks, Rosa **1, 35**
Smith, Jessie Carney **35**
Tillis, Frederick **40**
Wade-Gayles, Gloria Jean **41**
Wambugu, Florence **42**
Wilkins, J. Ernest, Jr. **43**
Williams, Terrie **35**

Nonviolent Action Group (NAG)
Al-Amin, Jamil Abdullah **6**

North Carolina Mutual Life Insurance
Spaulding, Charles Clinton **9**

North Carolina state government
Ballance, Frank W. **41**

North Pole
Henson, Matthew **2**
McLeod, Gus **27**
Delany, Martin R. **27**

Notre Dame Univeristy
Willingham, Tyrone **43**

NOW
See National Organization for Women

NPR
See National Public Radio

NRA
See National Resistance Army (Uganda)

NRA
See National Rifle Association

NRL
See Naval Research Laboratory

Cumulative Name Index

Volume numbers appear in **bold**

Brand, Dionne 1953— **32**
Brand, Elton 1979— **31**
Brandon, Barbara 1960(?)— **3**
Brandon, Thomas Terrell 1970— **16**
Brandy 1979— **14**, **34**
Brashear, Carl Maxie 1931— **29**
Brashear, Donald 1972— **39**
Brathwaite, Fred 1972— **35**
Brathwaite, Kamau 1930— **36**
Brathwaite, Lawson Edward
　See Kamau Brathwaite
Braugher, Andre 1962(?)— **13**
Braun, Carol (Elizabeth) Moseley
　1947— **4**, **42**
Braxton, Toni 1968(?)— **15**
Brazile, Donna 1959— **25**
Breedlove, Sarah
　See Walker, Madame C. J.
Breeze, Jean "Binta" 1956— **37**
Bridges, Christopher
　See Ludacris
Bridges, Sheila 1964— **36**
Bridges, Todd 1965— **37**
Bridgewater, Dee Dee 1950— **32**
Bridgforth, Glinda 1952— **36**
Brimmer, Andrew F(elton) 1926— **2**
Briscoe, Connie 1952— **15**
Briscoe, Marlin 1946(?)— **37**
Britt, Donna 1954(?)— **28**
Broadbent, Hydeia 1984— **36**
Brock, Louis Clark 1939— **18**
Bronner, Nathaniel H., Sr. 1914-1993
　32
Brooke, Edward (William, III) 1919— **8**
Brooks, Aaron 1976— **33**
Brooks, Avery 1949— **9**
Brooks, Derrick 1973— **43**
Brooks, Gwendolyn 1917-2000 **1**, **28**
Brooks, Hadda 1916-2002 **40**
Brown, Andre
　See Dr. Dre
Brown Bomber, The
　See Louis, Joe
Brown, Charles 1922-1999 **23**
Brown, Claude 1937-2002 **38**
Brown, Cora 1914-1972 **33**
Brown, Corrine 1946— **24**
Brown, Donald 1963— **19**
Brown, Eddie C. 1940— **35**
Brown, Elaine 1943— **8**
Brown, Erroll M. 1950(?)— **23**
Brown, Foxy 1979— **25**
Brown, H. Rap
　See Al-Amin, Jamil Abdullah
Brown, Hubert Gerold
　See Al-Amin, Jamil Abdullah
Brown, James Willie, Jr.
　See Komunyakaa, Yusef
Brown, James 1951— **22**
Brown, James 1933— **15**
Brown, James Nathaniel
　See Brown, Jim
Brown, Janice Rogers 1949— **43**
Brown, Jesse 1944-2003 **6**, **41**
Brown, Jesse Leroy 1926-1950 **31**
Brown, Jim 1936— **11**
Brown, Joe 19(?)(?)— **29**
Brown, Joyce F. 1946— **25**
Brown, Lee P(atrick) 1937— **1**, **24**
Brown, Les(lie Calvin) 1945— **5**
Brown, Lloyd Louis 1913-2003 **42**
Brown, Ron(ald Harmon) 1941— **5**
Brown, Sterling (Allen) 1901— **10**
Brown, Tony 1933— **3**
Brown, Uzee 1950— **42**

Brown, Vivian 1964— **27**
Brown, Wesley 1945— **23**
Brown, Willa Beatrice 1906-1992 **40**
Brown, Willard 1911(?)-1996 **36**
Brown, William Anthony
　See Brown, Tony
Brown, Willie L., Jr. 1934— **7**
Brown, Zora Kramer 1949— **12**
Bruce, Blanche Kelso 1849-1898 **33**
Bruce, Isaac 1972— **26**
Brunson, Dorothy 1938— **1**
Brutus, Dennis 1924— **38**
Bryan, Ashley F. 1923— **41**
Bryant, John 1966— **26**
Bryant, Kobe 1978— **15**, **31**
Bryant, Wayne R(ichard) 1947— **6**
Buchanan, Ray 1971— **32**
Buckley, Gail Lumet 1937— **39**
Buckley, Victoria (Vikki) 1947-1999 **24**
Bullard, Eugene Jacques 1894-1961 **12**
Bullins, Ed 1935— **25**
Bullock, Anna Mae
　See Turner, Tina
Bullock, Steve 1936— **22**
Bumbry, Grace (Ann) 1937— **5**
Bunche, Ralph J(ohnson) 1904-1971 **5**
Bunkley, Anita Richmond 19(?)(?)— **39**
Burke, Selma Hortense 1900-1995 **16**
Burke, Solomon 1936— **31**
Burke, Yvonne Braithwaite 1932— **42**
Burks, Mary Fair 1920-1991 **40**
Burley, Mary Lou
　See Williams, Mary Lou
Burnett, Charles 1944— **16**
Burnett, Chester Arthur
　See Howlin' Wolf
Burnett, Dorothy 1905-1995 **19**
Burrell, Orville Richard
　See Shaggy
Burrell, Stanley Kirk
　See Hammer, M. C.
Burrell, Thomas J. 1939— **21**
Burris, Chuck 1951— **21**
Burris, Roland W. 1937— **25**
Burroughs, Margaret Taylor 1917— **9**
Burrows, Stephen 1943— **31**
Burton, LeVar(dis Robert Martyn)
　1957— **8**
Busby, Jheryl 1949(?)— **3**
Buthelezi, Mangosuthu Gatsha 1928—
　9
Butler, Jerry 1939— **26**
Butler, Jonathan 1961— **28**
Butler, Leroy, III 1968— **17**
Butler, Octavia (Estelle) 1947— **8**, **43**
Butler, Paul D. 1961— **17**
Butts, Calvin O(tis), III 1950— **9**
Bynoe, Peter C.B. 1951— **40**
Bynum, Juanita 1959— **31**
Byrd, Donald 1949— **10**
Byrd, Michelle 1965— **19**
Byrd, Robert (Oliver Daniel, III) 1952—
　11
Byron, JoAnne Deborah
　See Shakur, Assata
Cade, Toni
　See Bambara, Toni Cade
Cadoria, Sherian Grace 1940— **14**
Caesar, Shirley 1938— **19**
Cain, Herman 1945— **15**
Calhoun, Cora
　See Austin, Lovie
Callender, Clive O(rville) 1936— **3**
Calloway, Cabell, III 1907-1994 **14**
Camp, Georgia Blanche Douglas

　See Johnson, Georgia Douglas
Camp, Kimberly 1956— **19**
Campanella, Roy 1921-1993 **25**
Campbell, Bebe Moore 1950— **6**, **24**
Campbell, Bill 1954— **9**
Campbell, Charleszetta Lena
　See Waddles, Charleszetta (Mother)
Campbell, E(lmer) Simms 1906-1971 **13**
Campbell, Mary Schmidt 1947— **43**
Campbell, Milton
　Little Milton
Campbell, Naomi 1970— **1**, **31**
Campbell, Tisha
　See Campbell-Martin, Tisha
Campbell-Martin, Tisha 1969— **8**, **42**
Canada, Geoffrey 1954— **23**
Canady, Alexa 1950— **28**
Canegata, Leonard Lionel Cornelius
　See Lee, Canada
Cannon, Katie 1950— **10**
Carby, Hazel 1948— **27**
Cardozo, Francis L. 1837-1903 **33**
Carew, Rod 1945— **20**
Carey, Mariah 1970— **32**
Cargill, Victoria A. 19(?)(?)— **43**
Carmichael, Stokely 1941-1998 **5**, **26**
Carnegie, Herbert 1919— **25**
Carroll, Diahann 1935— **9**
Carruthers, George R. 1939— **40**
Carroll, Vinnette 1922— **29**
Carson, Benjamin 1951— **1**, **35**
Carson, Josephine
　See Baker, Josephine
Carson, Julia 1938— **23**
Carson, Lisa Nicole 1969— **21**
Carter, Anson 1974— **24**
Carter, Ben
　See Ben-Israel, Ben Ami
Carter, Betty 1930— **19**
Carter, Butch 1958— **27**
Carter, Cris 1965— **21**
Carter, Joe 1960— **30**
Carter, Joye Maureen 1957— **41**
Carter, Mandy 1946— **11**
Carter, Nell 1948-2003 **39**
Carter, Regina 1966(?)— **23**
Carter, Rubin 1937— **26**
Carter, Shawn
　See Jay-Z
Carter, Stephen L(isle) 1954— **4**
Carter, Vince 1977— **26**
Carter, Warrick L. 1942— **27**
Cartiér, Xam Wilson 1949— **41**
Carver, George Washington 1861(?)-
　1943 **4**
Cary, Lorene 1956— **3**
Cary, Mary Ann Shadd 1823-1893 **30**
Cash, Rosalind 1938-1995 **28**
CasSelle, Malcolm 1970— **11**
Catchings, Tamika 1979— **43**
Catlett, Elizabeth 1919— **2**
Cayton, Horace 1903-1970 **26**
Cedric the Entertainer 1964(?)— **29**
Chamberlain, Wilton Norman 1936—
　18
Chambers, James
　See Cliff, Jimmy
Chambers, Julius (LeVonne) 1936— **3**
Channer, Colin 1963— **36**
Chapman, Nathan A. Jr. 1957— **21**
Chapman, Tracy 1964— **26**
Chappell, Emma C. 1941— **18**
Charlemagne, Emmanuel
　See Charlemagne, Manno
Charlemagne, Manno 1948— **11**

Dawes, Dominique (Margaux) 1976—
11
Dawkins, Wayne 1955— **20**
Dawson, Matel "Mat," Jr. 1921-2002 **39**
Dawson, William Levi 1899-1900 **39**
Day, Leon 1916-1995 **39**
Days, Drew S(aunders, III) 1941— **10**
de Carvalho, Barcelo
See Bonga, Kuenda
de Passe, Suzanne 1948(?)— **25**
"Deadwood Dick"
See Love, Nat
Dean, Mark E. 1957— **35**
DeBaptiste, George 1814(?)-1875 **32**
DeCarava, Roy 1919— **42**
Déby, Idriss 1952— **30**
Dee, Ruby 1924— **8**
DeFrantz, Anita 1952— **37**
Delaney, Beauford 1901-1979 **19**
Delaney, Joseph 1904-1991 **30**
Delany, Annie Elizabeth 1891-1995 **12**
Delany, Martin R. 1812-1885 **27**
Delany, Samuel R(ay), Jr. 1942— **9**
Delany, Sarah (Sadie) 1889— **12**
Delco, Wilhemina R. 1929— **33**
DeLille, Henriette 1813-1862 **30**
Dellums, Ronald (Vernie) 1935— **2**
DeLoach, Nora 1940-2001 **30**
Delsarte, Louis 1944— **34**
Dennard, Brazeal 1929— **37**
DePriest, James 1936— **37**
Devers, (Yolanda) Gail 1966— **7**
Devine, Loretta 1953— **24**
Devine, Major J.
See Divine, Father
DeWese, Mohandas
See Kool Moe Dee
Diallo, Amadou 1976-1999 **27**
Dickens, Helen Octavia 1909— **14**
Dickenson, Vic 1906-1984 **38**
Dickerson, Eric 1960— **27**
Dickerson, Ernest 1952(?)— **6, 17**
Dickey, Eric Jerome 19(?)(?)— **21**
Diddley, Bo 1928— **39**
Diesel, Vin 1967(?)— **29**
Diggs, Charles C. 1922-1998 **21**
Diggs, Taye 1972— **25**
Diggs-Taylor, Anna 1932— **20**
Dinkins, David (Norman) 1927— **4**
Diop, Cheikh Anta 1923-1986 **4**
Diouf, Abdou 1935— **3**
Divine, Father 1877(?)-1965 **7**
Dixon, Julian C. 1934— **24**
Dixon, Margaret 192(?)— **14**
Dixon, Rodrick 19(?)(?)—
See Three Mo' Tenors
Dixon, Sharon Pratt 1944— **1**
Dixon, Willie (James) 1915-1992 **4**
DJ Jazzy Jeff 1965— **32**
DJ Red Alert
See Alert, Kool DJ Red
DMC 1964— **31**
DMX 1970— **28**
do Nascimento, Edson Arantes
See Pelé
Dobbs, Mattiwilda 1925— **34**
Doby, Larry
See Doby, Lawrence Eugene, Sr.
Doby, Lawrence Eugene, Sr. 1924-2003
16, 41
Dodson, Howard, Jr. 1939— **7**
Dodson, Owen 1914-1983 **38**
Doley, Harold, Jr. 1947— **26**
Domini, Rey
See Lorde, Audre (Geraldine)

Donald, Arnold Wayne 1954— **36**
Donegan, Dorothy 1922-1998 **19**
Donovan, Kevin
See Bambaataa, Afrika
Dorsey, Thomas Andrew 1899-1993 **15**
dos Santos, José Eduardo 1942— **43**
Douglas, Aaron 1899-1979 **7**
Douglas, Ashanti
See Ashanti
Douglas, Lizzie
See Memphis Minnie
Dourdan, Gary 1966— **37**
Dove, Rita (Frances) 1952— **6**
Dove, Ulysses 1947— **5**
Downing, Will 19(?)(?)— **19**
Dozier, Lamont
See Holland-Dozier-Holland
Dr. Dre 1965(?)— **10, 14, 30**
Dr. J
See Erving, Julius Winfield, II
Draper, Sharon Mills 1952— **16, 43**
Drew, Charles Richard 1904-1950 **7**
Drexler, Clyde 1962— **4**
Driskell, David C(lyde) 1931— **7**
Driver, David E. 1955— **11**
Drummond, William J. 1944— **40**
Du Bois, W(illiam) E(dward) B(urghardt)
1868-1963 **3**
DuBois, Shirley Graham 1907-1977 **21**
Ducksworth, Marilyn 1957— **12**
Due, Tananarive 1966— **30**
Duke, Bill 1943— **3**
Duke, George 1946— **21**
Dumars, Joe 1963— **16**
Dumas, Henry 1934-1968 **41**
Dunbar, Paul Laurence 1872-1906 **8**
Dunbar, Sly 1952—
See Sly & Robbie
Duncan, Michael Clarke 1957— **26**
Duncan, Tim 1976— **20**
Dungy, Tony 1955— **17, 42**
Dunham, Katherine (Mary) 1910(?)— **4**
Dunn, Jerry 1953— **27**
Dunnigan, Alice Allison 1906-1983 **41**
Dupri, Jermaine 1972— **13**
Dutton, Charles S. 1951— **4, 22**
Dutton, Marie Elizabeth 1940— **12**
Dymally, Mervyn 1926— **42**
Dyson, Michael Eric 1958— **11, 40**
Early, Deloreese Patricia
See Reese, Della
Early, Gerald (Lyn) 1952— **15**
Eckstein, William Clarence
See Eckstine, Billy
Eckstine, Billy 1914-1993 **28**
Edelin, Ramona Hoage 1945— **19**
Edelman, Marian Wright 1939— **5, 42**
Edley, Christopher (Fairfield, Sr.) 1928—
2
Edmonds, Kenneth "Babyface"
1958(?)— **10, 31**
Edmonds, Terry 1950(?)— **17**
Edmonds, Tracey 1967(?)— **16**
Edwards, Eli
See McKay, Claude
Edwards, Esther Gordy 1920(?)— **43**
Edwards, Harry 1942— **2**
Edwards, Melvin 1937— **22**
Edwards, Teresa 1964— **14**
Ekwensi, Cyprian 1921— **37**
El Wilson, Barbara 1959— **35**
El-Hajj Malik El-Shabazz
See X, Malcolm
El-Shabazz, El-Hajj Malik
See X, Malcolm

Elder, (Robert) Lee 1934— **6**
Elder, Larry 1952— **25**
Elder, Lonne III 1931-1996 **38**
Elders, Joycelyn (Minnie) 1933— **6**
Eldridge, Roy 1911-1989 **37**
Elise, Kimberly 1967— **32**
Ellerbe, Brian 1963— **22**
Ellington, Duke 1899-1974 **5**
Ellington, E. David 1960— **11**
Ellington, Mercedes 1939— **34**
Ellington, Edward Kennedy
See Ellington, Duke
Elliott, Lorris 1931-1999 **37**
Elliott, Missy "Misdemeanor" 1971—
31
Elliott, Sean 1968— **26**
Ellis, Clarence A. 1943— **38**
Ellison, Ralph (Waldo) 1914-1994 **7**
Elmore, Ronn 1957— **21**
Emeagwali, Dale 1954— **31**
Emeagwali, Philip 1954— **30**
Emecheta, Buchi 1944— **30**
Emmanuel, Alphonsia 1956— **38**
Ephriam, Mablean 1949(?)— **29**
Epps, Omar 1973— **23**
Erving, Julius Winfield, II 1950— **18**
Ericsson-Jackson, Aprille 19(?)(?)— **28**
Esposito, Giancarlo (Giusseppi Alessan-
dro) 1958— **9**
Espy, Alphonso Michael
See Espy, Mike
Espy, Mike 1953— **6**
Estes, Rufus 1857-19(?)(?) **29**
Estes, Simon 1938— **28**
Estes, Sleepy John 1899-1977 **33**
Eubanks, Kevin 1957— **15**
Europe, (William) James Reese 1880-
1919 **10**
Evans, Darryl 1961— **22**
Evans, Ernest
See Checker, Chubby
Evans, Faith 1973(?)— **22**
Evans, Harry 1956(?)— **25**
Evans, Mari 1923— **26**
Eve 1979— **29**
Everett, Francine 1917-1999 **23**
Everett, Ronald McKinley
See Karenga, Maulana
Evers, Medgar (Riley) 1925-1963 **3**
Evers, Myrlie 1933— **8**
Evora, Cesaria 1941— **12**
Ewing, Patrick Aloysius 1962— **17**
Eyadéma, (Étienne) Gnassingbé 1937—
7
Fagan, Garth 1940— **18**
Faison, George William 1946— **16**
Falana, Lola 1942— **42**
Farah, Nuruddin 1945— **27**
Farmer, Art(hur Stewart) 1928-1999 **38**
Farmer, Forest J(ackson) 1941— **1**
Farmer, James 1920— **2**
Farmer-Paellmann, Deadria 1966— **43**
Farr, Mel 1944— **24**
Farrakhan, Louis 1933— **2, 15**
Fats Domino 1928— **20**
Fattah, Chaka 1956— **11**
Faulk, Marshall 1973— **35**
Fauntroy, Walter E(dward) 1933— **11**
Fauset, Jessie (Redmon) 1882-1961 **7**
Favors, Steve 1948— **23**
Feelings, T(h)om(a)s 1933— **11**
Fela 1938-1997 **1, 42**
Ferguson, Roger W. 1951— **25**
Ferrell, Rachelle 1961— **29**

Gumbel, Greg 1946— **8**
Gunn, Moses 1929-1993 **10**
Guy, (George) Buddy 1936— **31**
Guy, Jasmine 1964(?)— **2**
Guy, Rosa 1925(?)— **5**
Guy-Sheftall, Beverly 1946— **13**
Guyton, Tyree 1955— **9**
Gwynn, Anthony Keith 1960— **18**
Habré, Hissène 1942— **6**
Habyarimana, Juvenal 1937-1994 **8**
Hageman, Hans 19(?)(?)— **36**
Hageman, Ivan 19(?)(?)— **36**
Haile Selassie 1892-1975 **7**
Hailey, JoJo 1971— **22**
Hailey, K-Ci 1969— **22**
Hale, Clara 1902-1992 **16**
Hale, Lorraine 1926(?)— **8**
Haley, Alex (Palmer) 1921-1992 **4**
Haley, George Williford Boyce 1925—
  21
Hall, Arthur 1943-2000 **39**
Hall, Elliott S. 1938(?)— **24**
Hall, Lloyd A(ugustus) 1894-1971 **8**
Hamblin, Ken 1940— **10**
Hamer, Fannie Lou (Townsend) 1917-
  1977 **6**
Hamilton, Virginia 1936— **10**
Hammer
  See Hammer, M. C.
Hammer, M. C. 1963— **20**
Hammond, Fred 1960— **23**
Hammond, Lenn 1970(?)— **34**
Hampton, Fred 1948-1969 **18**
Hampton, Henry (Eugene, Jr.) 1940— **6**
Hampton, Lionel 1908(?)-2002 **17, 41**
Hancock, Herbie Jeffrey 1940— **20**
Handy, W(illiam) C(hristopher) 1873-
  1937 **8**
Hani, Chris 1942-1993 **6**
Hani, Martin Thembisile
  See Hani, Chris
Hannah, Marc (Regis) 1956— **10**
Hansberry, Lorraine (Vivian) 1930-1965
  6
Hansberry, William Leo 1894-1965 **11**
Hardaway, Anfernee (Deon)
  See Hardaway, Anfernee (Penny)
Hardaway, Anfernee (Penny) 1971— **13**
Hardaway, Penny
  See Hardaway, Anfernee (Penny)
Hardaway, Tim 1966— **35**
Hardin, Lillian Beatrice
  See Hardin Armstrong, Lil
Hardin Armstrong, Lil 1898-1971 **39**
Hardison, Bethann 19(?)(?)— **12**
Hardison, Kadeem 1966— **22**
Hardy, Nell
  See Carter, Nell
Harkless, Necia Desiree 1920— **19**
Harmon, Clarence 1940(?)— **26**
Harper, Ben 1969— **34**
Harper, Frances E(llen) W(atkins) 1825-
  1911 **11**
Harper, Frank
  See Harper, Hill
Harper, Hill 1973— **32**
Harper, Michael S. 1938— **34**
Harrell, Andre (O'Neal) 1962(?)— **9, 30**
Harrington, Oliver W(endell) 1912— **9**
Harris, "Sweet" Alice
  See Harris, Alice
Harris, Alice 1934— **7**
Harris, Barbara 1930— **12**
Harris, Claire 1937— **34**
Harris, Corey 1969— **39**

Harris, E. Lynn 1957— **12, 33**
Harris, Eddy L. 1956— **18**
Harris, James, III
  See Jimmy Jam
Harris, Jay **19**
Harris, Leslie 1961— **6**
Harris, Marcelite Jordon 1943— **16**
Harris, Mary Styles 1949— **31**
Harris, Monica 1968— **18**
Harris, Patricia Roberts 1924-1985 **2**
Harris, Robin 1953-1990 **7**
Harrison, Alvin 1974— **28**
Harrison, Calvin 1974— **28**
Harrison, Mya
  See Mya
Harsh, Vivian Gordon 1890-1960 **14**
Harvard, Beverly (Joyce Bailey) 1950—
  11
Harvey, Steve 1957— **18**
Harvey, William R. 1941— **42**
Haskins, Clem 1943— **23**
Haskins, James 1941— **36**
Hassell, Leroy Rountree, Sr. 1955— **41**
Hastie, William H(enry) 1904-1976 **8**
Hastings, Alcee Lamar 1936— **16**
Hatchett, Glenda 1951(?)— **32**
Hathaway, Donny 1945-1979 **18**
Hathaway, Isaac Scott 1874-1967 **33**
Haughton, Aaliyah
  See Aaliyah
Hawkins, Adrienne Lita
  See Kennedy, Adrienne
Hawkins, Coleman 1904-1969 **9**
Hawkins, Erskine Ramsey 1914-1993
  14
Hawkins, Jamesetta
  See James, Etta
Hawkins, La-Van 1960(?)— **17**
Hawkins, "Screamin'" Jay 1929-2000
  30
Hawkins, Steven Wayne 1962— **14**
Hawkins, Tramaine Aunzola 1951— **16**
Hayden, Palmer 1890-1973 **13**
Hayden, Robert Earl 1913-1980 **12**
Hayes, Isaac 1942— **20**
Hayes, James C. 1946— **10**
Hayes, Roland 1887-1977 **4**
Hayes, Teddy 1951— **40**
Haynes, George Edmund 1880-1960 **8**
Haynes, Cornell, Jr.
  See Nelly
Haynes, Marques 1926— **22**
Haysbert, Dennis 1955— **42**
Haywood, Gar Anthony 1954— **43**
Haywood, Margaret A. 1912— **24**
Head, Bessie 1937-1986 **28**
Healy, James Augustine 1830-1900 **30**
Heard, Gar 1948— **25**
Hearns, Thomas 1958— **29**
Hedgeman, Anna Arnold 1899-1990 **22**
Hedgeman, Peyton Cole
  See Hayden, Palmer
Height, Dorothy I(rene) 1912— **2, 23**
Hemphill, Essex 1957— **10**
Hemphill, Jessie Mae 1937— **33**
Hemsley, Sherman 1938-— **19**
Henderson, Cornelius Langston 1888(?)-
  1976 **26**
Henderson, Fletcher 1897-1952 **32**
Henderson, Gordon 1957— **5**
Henderson, Natalie Leota
  See Hinderas, Natalie
Henderson, Rickey 1958— **28**
Henderson, Wade 1944(?)— **14**
Hendricks, Barbara 1948— **3**

Hendrix, James Marshall
  See Hendrix, Jimi
Hendrix, Jimi 1942-1970 **10**
Hendrix, Johnny Allen
  See Hendrix, Jimi
Henriques, Julian 1955(?)— **37**
Henry, Aaron Edd 1922-1997 **19**
Henry, Lenny 1958— **9**
Henson, Darrin 1970(?)— **33**
Henson, Matthew (Alexander) 1866-
  1955 **2**
Herenton, Willie W. 1940— **24**
Herman, Alexis Margaret 1947— **15**
Hernandez, Aileen Clarke 1926— **13**
Hickman, Fred(erick Douglass) 1951—
  11
Higginbotham, A(loyisus) Leon, Jr.
  1928-1998 **13, 25**
Higginbotham, Jack
  See Higginbotham, Jay C.
Higginbotham, Jay C. 1906-1973 **37**
Hightower, Dennis F(owler) 1941— **13**
Hill, Anita (Faye) 1956— **5**
Hill, Beatrice
  See Moore, Melba
Hill, Bonnie Guiton 1941— **20**
Hill, Calvin 1947— **19**
Hill, Donna 1955— **32**
Hill, Dulé 1975(?)— **29**
Hill, Errol 1921— **40**
Hill, Grant (Henry) 1972— **13**
Hill, Janet 1947— **19**
Hill, Jesse, Jr. 1927— **13**
Hill, Lauryn 1975(?)— **20**
Hill, Oliver W. 1907— **24**
Hill, Tamia
  See Tamia
Hillard, Terry 1954— **25**
Hilliard, David 1942— **7**
Hilliard, Earl F. 1942— **24**
Himes, Chester 1909-1984 **8**
Hinderas, Natalie 1927-1987 **5**
Hine, Darlene Clark 1947— **24**
Hines, Earl "Fatha" 1905-1983 **39**
Hines, Garrett 1969— **35**
Hines, Gregory (Oliver) 1946-2003 **1,
  42**
Hinton, Milt 1910-2000 **30**
Hinton, William Augustus 1883-1959 **8**
Hobson, Mellody 1969— **40**
Holder, Eric H., Jr. 1951(?)— **9**
Holder, Laurence 1939— **34**
Holdsclaw, Chamique 1977— **24**
Holiday, Billie 1915-1959 **1**
Holland-Dozier-Holland **36**
Holland, Brian
  See Holland-Dozier-Holland
Holland, Eddie
  See Holland-Dozier-Holland
Holland, Endesha Ida Mae 1944— **3**
Holland, Robert, Jr. 1940— **11**
Holmes, Larry 1949— **20**
Holt, Nora 1885(?)-1974 **38**
Holte, Patricia Louise
  See LaBelle, Patti
Holton, Hugh, Jr. 1947-2001 **39**
Holyfield, Evander 1962— **6**
Hooker, John Lee 1917-2000 **30**
hooks, bell 1952— **5**
Hooks, Benjamin L(awson) 1925— **2**
Hope, John 1868-1936 **8**
Hopgood, Hadda
  See Brooks, Hadda
Hopkins, Bernard 1965— **35**
Horn, Shirley 1934— **32**